AMERICA
IN MIDPASSAGE

THE MACMILLAN COMPANY
NEW YORK · BOSTON · CHICAGO · DALLAS
ATLANTA · SAN FRANCISCO

MACMILLAN AND CO., Limited
LONDON · BOMBAY · CALCUTTA · MADRAS
MELBOURNE

THE MACMILLAN COMPANY
OF CANADA, Limited
TORONTO

AMERICA IN MIDPASSAGE

By

CHARLES A. BEARD
& MARY R. BEARD

Drawings by
WILFRED JONES

VOLUME II

1939

THE MACMILLAN COMPANY · NEW YORK

PRINTED IN THE UNITED STATES OF AMERICA
BY THE HADDON CRAFTSMEN, INC., CAMDEN, N. J.

Nel mezzo del cammin di nostra vita. . . .

Contents

AMERICA
IN MIDPASSAGE

CHAPTER XI

Urban and Rural Labor in Evolving Economy

UNDERNEATH the stage on which the giant pageant of
politics and business swirled and marched amid the
pomp and circumstance of great affairs, labor kept
on at tasks in town and country, as always in the long history
of mankind. Nothing did or could change that necessity.
Neither the delights that gleamed under the evanescence
of the golden glow nor the detonations of the depression nor
inquiries into the operations carried on by the Lords of Creation nor the tumults of popular elections nor the vicissitudes
in the fortunes of leaders called statesmen nor the contests
of court, executive, and legislature, nor all the bluster of
war chieftains and pronouncements of diplomats across the
borders of nations did or could alter that basis of industry,
statecraft, and war. Whatever editors, columnists, elucida-
tors, commentators, radio announcers, apologists, retainers,
publicists, professors, and all the chorus of condemners and
praisers felt moved to say, exclaim, or print, labor continued
in town and country, supplying the goods and services upon
which participants in the giant pageant depended daily for

their very existence, without which they themselves would have been sent to field or shop to scrabble for their livelihood.

In every age, pagan and Christian alike, master minds had recognized the truth of the axiom that civilization, however low or high its superstructure of magnificence, rests upon labor and that its mutability turns upon the forms and processes of labor. More than three hundred years before the birth of Christ, Aristotle had said: "If every instrument could accomplish its own work, obeying or anticipating the will of others, like the statues of Daedalus or the tripods of Hephaestus, which, says the poet, 'of their own accord entered the assembly of the Gods'; if, in like manner, the shuttle would weave and the plectrum touch the lyre without a hand to guide them, chief workmen would not want servants nor masters slaves." But instruments did not produce articles of use without minds and hands to guide them; hence slaves and workmen were necessary to operate them and merchants to exchange commodities of use. "In the state which is best governed, citizens . . . must not lead the lives of mechanics or tradesmen, for such a life is ignoble and inimical to virtue. Neither must they be husbandmen, since leisure is necessary for the development of virtue and the performance of political duties." As to slaves, Aristotle thought that they were human and deserved some consideration and yet were mere servants of culture for others — for the strong and virtuous.

More than twenty centuries after the death of Aristotle, an American statesman, John C. Calhoun, strongly confirmed the judgment of the Ancient: "There never has yet existed a wealthy and civilized society in which one portion of the community did not, in point of fact, live on the labor of the other. Broad and general as is this assertion, it is fully borne out by history. This is not the proper occasion but, if it were, it would not be difficult to trace the various devices by which the wealth of all civilized communities has been so unequally divided. . . . The devices are almost innumerable, from the brute force and gross superstition of ancient times, to the subtle and artful fiscal contrivances of modern times. . . . It is useless to disguise the fact." The rule had ever applied, Calhoun maintained, and would ever apply to societies enjoying the benefits and blessings of civilization; and neither soft phrases nor words less shocking to beneficiaries than the old term "slave" could fundamentally alter the constitution of things human.

After the advent of Christianity, those idealists known as utopians had also made labor the center of their dreams and speculations but had sought to give to it both dignity and freedom. The Utopia of Sir Thomas More was based on labor in agriculture and the crafts; all men and women were instructed and exercised in agriculture; and besides every man had a trade to which he applied himself. "In a great city and in all the territory that lies around it, you can scarce find 500, either men or women, who, by their age and strength, are capable of labor, that are not engaged in it. . . . The slaves among them are only such as are condemned to that state of life for the commission of some crime, or, which is more common, such as their merchants find condemned to die in those parts to which they trade, whom they sometimes redeem at low rates; and in other places have them for nothing." This was labor in a dreamland and yet Sir Thomas More's utopians were the most highly civilized people that imagination had yet envisaged. Another famous utopian, of the nineteenth century, Karl Marx, saw in labor the source of the thought and energy which were to sweep all humanity into everlasting freedom and build a civilization shared by all. After Marx, William Morris, the princely esthete, whose works of mind and hand gave intense pleasure to idealists, in his News from Nowhere made labor an agreeable and beautiful manifestation of the noblest purposes in the human spirit. Perhaps in origin this utopianism was an expression of Christian ethics which deemed of one blood all mankind, exalted labor, and emphasized the eternal brotherhood of the great and the humble.

§

During the tensions of the midpassage, labor remained in town and country, at the tasks permissible or allotted, in the status which it had achieved, in its thought of its role in the social processes, and in the position of thought to which it was assigned by others; and it was both an active and a passive element in all that occurred. By measures public and private, designed to cope with the depression, labor was, of course, vitally affected. In their efforts to cut costs of production and make profits in spite of contracting markets, capitalists and managers scrapped old tools and methods, introduced new machines and processes devised by inventors and scientists, and stepped up industrial operations, thereby displacing industrial workers and often throwing additional strains on laborers engaged in mass production enterprises. In agriculture, the most conservative of the arts, as well as in machine industry, this subversive movement went forward with terrific speed. Illustrations of the havoc thus wrought were provided for public consideration by Paul Taylor in his Power Farming and Labor Displacement in the Cotton Belt. Theorists might argue whether this ruthless dynamism was the logic of technology, the drive of capitalism, or the outcome of human perversity; anyway, the rushing facts were realities in their span of time.

While private enterprise, doing as it liked with its own within the social constrictions, kept blasting at surviving features of the inherited "order," the Federal Government was helping to bolster up banks, railway companies, shipping concerns, farmers, and industrial corporations by loans, subsidies, and heavy purchases for public works, armaments, and other uses of State; that is, helping to underwrite enterprises which were constantly striving to cut costs and reap profits by the displacement of labor. With shifts in fact went modification in theory. The old conception of the automatic market, maintaining a just and efficient distribution of wealth through rents, profits, and wages, was disintegrating. The fundamental assumption of that theory was peppered with citations from reality — the crack of 1929, continuous unemployment on a large scale, government intervention, inflexible prices, contracting investments, and increasing concentration of corporate control. With these citations went a countervailing theory that an enlarged buying power for labor in town and country was absolutely indispensable to the high-level functioning of dynamic mass production. Since employers rarely increased wages on their own motion the color of economic justification was given, even by participants in the giant pageant, to legislation strengthening the bargaining power of labor for the purpose of enlarging buying power.

Into the dynamism of internal economy were injected ideas and forces emanating from revolutionary events abroad which impinged steadily and immediately upon the fortunes of American labor as well as upon the foreign policies of the United States. In Italy and Germany the free organizations of industrial and rural workers were suppressed by the apparatus of the State, supported by the middle classes. In Italy and Germany democracy was officially derided and the capacity of labor for self-government of any kind was officially denied. In Russia, where government was nominally carried on in the name of labor, assassinations, purges, and executions provoked more than suspicion that proletarian control in the Soviet Republic was growing weaker. News of these events filled columns of journals and magazines in the United States. American capitalists, politicians, and labor leaders were compelled to think again about the monitory experiences of the Old World in labor relations, as they had been made to think about them in the days of the French Revolution of 1848 and the Commune. Even the republic of letters and arts, despite many attempts, conscious or automatic, to provide insulation against the rude jars of practice, resounded with the searchings and arguments of the debate over labor relations beyond the seas, on its borders, and in its midst.

In all ages, indeed, the course of civilization had been marked by labor disturbances — the slave insurrections of antiquity, the peasants' revolts of the middle ages, the populist outbreak of Daniel Shays in the eighteenth century, and in the nineteenth century widespread revolts of industrial workers everywhere in western civilization. Could the history of labor be closed in the twentieth century by dictatorships of any kind, in the name of the middle classes or of the proletariat? Was the American ideal of free farmers and free mechanics, men and women endowed with equal suffrage, merely a transitory illusion? With the inherited system of economy running at a tempo far below its potential efficiency, with millions of men and women unemployed in town and country, with old crafts constantly disrupted by technological changes, could organized labor in the United States continue to function on traditional lines, merely, or at all? Were its responsibilities limited to bargaining with industrial employers over hours and wages? In these issues the mission or fate of the American labor movement was now defined. What was more, so all-embracing were the fortunes impending for the workers in factory, in mine, in office, and on the land, that all the apparatus of wealth, culture, and State resting upon labor became entangled in its destiny. Thus the labor problem stood at the center of American civilization in this latest age.

From the foundation of the American republic, acute thinkers had recognized the basic relation of labor on the land and in the shop to the forms and functions of government, and indeed to the very course of civilization. They had believed that the security of popular institutions depended upon the existence of free land. Jefferson had declared that when Americans were piled upon one another in cities they would go to eating one another as in the Old World, but he had no solution for the problem to be raised in coming years. His close friend, Madison, who also served as President of the republic, forecast a time when the great mass of people in America would have no property of any kind and prophesied that statesmanship would then be really tested. How and with what outcome, Madison did not venture to say. Later, the humanistic wing of American democracy — led by Horace Greeley, Elizabeth Cady Stanton, and Wendell Phillips, for example — clearly understood the tendency to separate labor from property, suspected that a crisis was creeping over the country, and sought ways out of the dilemma. Acquainted with ancient and contemporary political thought, including American speculations on that immemorial theme, Karl Marx, long a European correspondent of Greeley's Tribune, declared the conflict thus comprehended to be inevitable. In the Communist Manifesto published in 1848, he maintained that such struggles had ended in the reconstruction of society *or* in the destruction of both contending parties. Nevertheless in his social philosophy, he formulated a solution : With the spread of mechanical manufacturing, the class of industrial workers will be enlarged, members of the middle classes will be driven down into the proletarian ranks, and in the end the overwhelming majority will take possession of and socialize private instruments of production.

§

In the earlier analyses of the economic course a number of tendencies were missed or at best dimly discerned. Nor did the materialistic view of things always take into sufficient reckoning the psychological forces of culture, taste, and prestige influencing class inclinations. It was generally thought in the nineteenth century that, with the expansion of industry through machine processes, an ever-larger proportion of all industrial societies would be composed of industrial workers living in cities. As a matter of fact, however, after a long period of rapid growth, the number of industrial workers in relation to the total population of the United States began to decline. Automatic machinery and the rounding out of giant construction projects contributed to the downward tendency. Contrary to prophecy there was a relative increase in the size of the middle class, defined as including merchants, lawyers, doctors, teachers, government employees of the upper range, service workers, writers, architects, painters, and other white-collar attendants upon economic processes. It was by the disintegration of freehold agriculture, rather than by the weakening of the middle class, that the proportion of landless, toolless, and homeless laborers was augmented. In the same agrarian shift the landlord class was enlarged and united by "natural" sympathies with the urban middle class rather than with workers in industry and propertyless laborers on the land.

The changing scene had been affected by the reduction of immigration. During the nineteenth century the flow of immigrants had contributed heavily to the ranks of industrial workers. And yet, curiously reversing the theory that capitalists could dictate all public policies, American trade unionists demanded limitations on immigration and, before the twentieth century had advanced far, were able, with collateral aids, to force restrictive legislation through the Congress of the United States. Bars were erected against foreign laborers willing to work in mill and factory for any wage or content to slave from sun to sun on the soil if they could only own a little patch of land however small or barren. When the laws were tightened by administrative measures after the economic crash of 1929, the stream of immigration from Europe dwindled to a trickle. Thus, largely through the efforts of American labor leaders, bans were placed on any proportionate increase in the number of industrial workers as compared with the size of the middle class. Whatever the causes, wherever the responsibilities lay, the fact was of deep significance to the course of American civilization. Dialectics reckoned with it. Realistic thought took note of it.

Within the ranks of the industrial workers so declining in relative strength of numbers, unemployment counteracted the natural trend toward unity and organization. In other words, the labor movement was weakened by the idleness of its members and of its potential recruits. With from seven to eleven million urban workers more or less unemployed — permanently, it was feared — and kept alive only by doles or mere makeshifts of one kind or another, the economic and political power of labor organization was reduced. In explanation of this situation the phrase "technological unemployment" attained a wide circulation, although the dictum rested on no investigation of facts both comprehensive and precise. Unquestionably machines had displaced multitudes of men and women from time to time. On the other hand new machine processes, with their almost infinite subdivisions, had given employment to workers in manufacturing plants, and increasingly to deft-fingered women.

But no system of accountancy offered a balance sheet. If there was no such thing as technological unemployment, as often alleged, there was indisputably a large amount of technology unemployed and millions of industrial workers were positively idle. Moreover the problem for labor organizers was complicated by the increasing use of women, mostly young, and children in the lighter machine industries. Labor officials could cut the competition of children by securing drastic child labor legislation in the progressive states, although the ratification of the national child labor amendment seemed to be impossible. They could attack the competition of women through minimum wage laws after the Supreme Court had sustained this type of enactment. And they could take women into their regular unions; women organizers had long struggled to bring this about in the interest of better living standards. But the swarms of adult men seeking a wage adequate for family care, of young women often burdened themselves with dependents, and of children helpless to exert effective pressure anywhere — all facing the terror of permanent unemployment — presented problems of organization which the most skillful union leaders were unable to solve. As members lost their jobs, they tended to drift out of the unions, whether dues were charged or not. When the contracting economy had no place for them, straight and simple unionism offered no immediate and evident advantages.

The process of organizing industrial workers and holding them in unions was further hampered by seasonal fluctua-

tions in employment, intimately associated with many phases
of the machine process. Since fluctuations were due in part
to methods of advertising and marketing, their worst ravages
could be prevented in some industries by longer-range planning, by deliberate coöperation between management and
labor. Demonstrations to this effect were made in several
industries, notably in the men's garment trade where the
Amalgamated Clothing Workers and the heads of the industry clipped off the peaks and raised the valleys of unemployment by concerted efforts. Yet such arrangements were frequently offset by the spread of general unemployment, the
introduction of displacing machines, and the turbulence of
strikes. That control over seasonal fluctuations was possible
on a larger scale could not be denied. That, if accomplished,
it would diminish the adverse fortunes of many industrial
workers was clear enough. But labor leaders could see in such
control no material increase in the total volume of hour or
day employment by the year; nor could they hope by that
method to stem the trend toward the spread of labor-elim-
inating machinery.

In some respects the plight of workers ousted by the contraction of the market and the introduction of new machines
recalled scenes in the early years of the industrial revolution,
such as George Eliot described so vividly in Silas Marner.
Plant after plant installed amazing inventions. As workers
with hand tools and crude implements had been displaced in
former times, so now even skilled technicians, experienced in
operating complicated machines, were turned into the streets
by the introduction of apparatus still more complicated or
automatic. Often the discharged workers were so old that
mastery of an unfamiliar trade was beyond their opportunity
or capacity. Despite all the treatises on the economics of
industry, despite the experiences of previous times, American
labor leaders in 1938 were almost as much at sea over policies
as were their forerunners a hundred years before. A dismissal wage might be secured to tide them over hunger for a
while, but such concessions added no strength or assurance to

a labor movement essentially concerned with a decent living standard and continuity of employment for the working class as a whole.

Nor did efforts to "stabilize" industry by "spreading" work among selected groups of employees add strength to labor organization. At the beginning of the depression, many employers tried to keep their labor forces together, sometimes at a material sacrifice, in expectation of a quick recovery and recurring need. In response to the desperate call to "spread the work," men and women still earning a livelihood undertook to share their wages with others. Although a larger proportion of workers won continuous wages by this process, in smaller amounts by the month or year, such earnings were below the standard of full employment and the operation afforded no aid to workers for whom even this limited assistance could not be provided. "The living wage" was frequently broken down, even for the employed. Wage earners lowered their own standard and shared their plight with their companions in the downward drift. Despite the fine spirit of sacrifice made manifest, "dividing work" generally meant extending disillusionment and diminishing the strength of labor.

Still another feature of the disintegration lay in multitudes of workers regarded as "unemployable" according to the rigorous requirements of new machine processes. High tension industry fed upon the strength of youth and shoved older men and women out into the streets to fend for themselves if they could. Minds and hands that might have been busy in handicrafts until near the close of life were often unable to keep up with the drive and speed of assembly lines or the stretched-out tasks at looms.

The number of such "unemployables" had been large in times of prosperity. The number grew with the collapse of prosperity. When the business curtailment of the depression came, the older workers were generally the first to be dropped by the wayside. Prolonged idleness diminished their powers. With no work to do for months or years, possessors of skills could easily forget their cunning, lose interest in work, and fall into a deep and shiftless discouragement. Men and women, even boys and girls, slid down the scale of stamina and ingenuity into or toward the abyss of unemployability. How many hit bottom was not officially reported. With all the statistical searching of the time, this mass of phenomena escaped a national survey. Undoubtedly the army of "economic derelicts" was large. Furthermore: it furnished the materials for demagogy, not for rational and effective labor organization. It might respond to romantic nostrums in the absence of sane remedies.

In some measure, usually overstated, the amount of unemployability, especially in the skilled trades, was due to craft-union policies. The strength of craft unionism had always depended to a large extent on the limitation of training and apprenticeship. Between sponsors of technical and vocational education, generally affiliated with employer interests, on the one side, and leaders in craft unions, on the other, there had always been friction if not violent antagonism. In their efforts to save something for their membership amid the devastating disruptions of the depression, craft leaders battled hard against the infiltration of new and cheaper workers by way of vocational schools and apprenticeship. Consequently, as industry rose slowly out of the trough, it sometimes found difficulty in discovering enough highly skilled workers to fill the new openings, among the six or eight million unemployed men and women who hung around on the outside. Compelled to consider the instant need of things, heads of craft unions placed limitations upon the rapid expansion of their own organizations and thus unwittingly enlarged unemployability — that menace to an all-embracing labor movement.

§

With the proportion of straight industrial workers declining, with widespread unemployment continuous, with efforts to stabilize seasonal fluctuations and spread work relatively ineffective in stemming the depression, with the army of un-employables large and perhaps increasing, the outlook for organized labor, compared with times called "normal," was gloomy in the extreme. As the years passed, it became increasingly evident that there was to be no steady march of industrial workers to the position of an overwhelming majority in the population. Within the ranks of labor, the strength of skilled craftsmen, relatively well-paid, fairly secure, and reasonably content with the shape of things present and to come, was clearly diminished. As long as private enterprise had earnings to share, the organizing of labor for bargaining purposes had been a task of relative ease. However, when in large areas earnings became non-existent, when whole sectors of economy depended for survival on money from the Federal Treasury, when the army of the unemployed and the unskilled swelled in size to mammoth proportions, the call to collective bargaining on old lines sounded more or less futile to the masses of the poor. At this conjuncture of realities, a crisis was reached in the labor movement; leaves were turned in the book of labor history; new methods were evolved. Those leaders accustomed to using their minds looked beyond the bargaining technique of the craft unions into complexities that could not be pierced by analysis according to any of their historic formulas.

To some extent, impossible to estimate and often exaggerated, the crisis in the labor movement was accelerated by practices which had grown up in unions long affiliated with the American Federation of Labor. Deriving their strength in part from their monopoly over employment within their respective crafts and from policies deemed advantageous to the crafts, labor leaders in certain fields had often found it possible to apply coercive measures to employers, members of their unions, and independent workers, even to enrich themselves in the process. In fact labor "rackets" appeared in nearly all the large cities and ranged from mere decrees imposed on employers and workers to brutality and murder.

Under the dictation of labor "czars," employers were compelled to hire more men than they needed or adopt operating
methods for which there was not the slightest justification in
economy or even in the welfare of employees. Heavy dues
and special assessments were levied on members of unions
and blackmail on employers. Destruction of life and property accompanied collections and terror reigned in whole
trades. Workers were promised jobs in return for high initiation fees, given positions for a week or two, and then cast
into the streets. A cafeteria "racket" in New York City
brought $2,000,000 a year into the treasury of the labor
bosses. Every now and then when gangsters shot things out
among themselves or the Federal Government caught labor
dictators who had failed to report their true "earnings,"
labor cases were aired in the courts and the broad ramifications of racketeering were revealed to the public at large.

On the basis of documentary evidence, Harold Seidman
described the types and methods of such rackets under the
heading, Labor Czars: a History of Labor Racketeering —
a worthy companion of Max Lowenthal's important volume,
The Investor Pays, both memorials of the age. According to
Mr. Seidman, "miners, sailors, musicians, cloth shrinkers,
furriers, shoe workers, waiters, cooks, barbers, janitors,
window cleaners, milliners, laundrymen, and bakers have at
one time or another come into the toils of the greedy labor
leeches." In the building trades, the electrical trades, public
markets, the restaurant business, and the motion picture
business, such "czars" arose again and again in various parts
of the country, spreading terror, and levying tribute. Sometimes they held power for years. At other times they were
quickly discovered and prosecuted. Many were sent to
prison. Many seemed to enjoy legal and political immunity
despite the fact that their operations were well known. So
far did the disturbances extend that legitimate unions suffered from the disreputable and criminal activities of the
racketeers, unions were disrupted, and revolts broke out in
the rank and file against domineering and dictatorial labor

bosses, augmenting the industrial unrest that accompanied the course of the depression.

§

Immediately after the crack of 1929, William Green, speaking for the American Federation of Labor, expressed anxiety over the diminishing strength of his organization as its dues-paying members fell into the abyss of unemployment. Called into counsel with business leaders by President Hoover, he urged the maintenance of union wage scales to uphold buying power and keep the wheels of mass production turning. As such precepts failed to work and unemployment widened, Mr. Green warned President Hoover that he could not vouch for the passivity of labor if the strain was not relieved by some process. Representatives of the Railway Brotherhoods also protested against the wholesale dismissals made by managers in frantic efforts to pay dividends or to avoid bankruptcy.

Warnings and protests did not stay the course of economic disruption. On the other hand the tightening depression did not raise at once the volume of warnings and protests to unmanageable proportions. The Marxian prediction that a progressive impoverishment of labor would produce revolutionary action, rather than reform, failed to materialize. As a matter of fact, that calculation was not on the program of labor officials at all. Organized labor made no official break with the established rules for carrying on either political or economic transactions. It did not swing wholesale to socialism or independent action in 1932. Although Democratic, on the whole, in its sympathies, it was divided politically, and when the Roosevelt administration was first installed, the American Federation of Labor had no large program of action ready, despite its resolutions on the need for "planning" adopted at previous conventions. Like the Roosevelt administration, the Federation entered upon a career of improvisation.

In the various attacks upon the depression, the Federation

assumed no separate leadership but was satisfied with collaboration. When the demand was made for a federal, state, and local program of public works to set industry in motion and provide jobs for the unemployed, it attended conferences of business men and politicians and merely insisted upon its historic maxim — the eight hour day and the prevailing rate of wages on public enterprises. To secure the formal adoption of this prescription was generally a simple thing. Yet the victory was a minor gain for labor. The public works undertaken by government action consisted mainly of roads, bridges, dykes, dams, and similar types of construction in which machinery and unskilled labor were extensively used. The number of craft unionists set to work by such activities was small in comparison with the total volume of unemployment. When federal efforts to increase employment took the form of "work projects," other than heavy construction, organized labor was again able to force the adoption of a limited prevailing-rate-of-wages clause — for the meager number of hours allotted to men and women on the projects. Granting that it was carried against the protests of men bent on holding relief expenditures to the minimum, still the second victory for organized labor scarcely touched the fringe of the economic dislocation.

If public spending stimulated industry, perhaps kept it from a more general collapse, it left large bodies of industrial workers still bogged in the tragedy of unemployment. The appropriation of millions, even billions, for military and naval purposes, culminating in the super-navy program of 1938, did offer more opportunities to workers in the heavy industries, especially to skilled machinists, although the employment aspect of that bill was not impressive. Here also labor welcomed wages, without inquiring very thoroughly into the foreign policies or the war potentials involved. Labor might be given employment in using the war machines as well as in making them.

At best the armament business was limited and perilous. Carried forward at an increasing ratio, it might in time break the backs of taxpayers, culminate in war, and lead to the supremacy of the military over all labor as promised by the mobilization bill, reported to the House of Representatives by its military affairs committee in 1938. That prospect in the relations of labor to government and employment was not a happy one to contemplate. If, on the other hand, the armament program reached an end, a huge industry would be disrupted and labor would feel the consequences. That prospect was not encouraging either. While Marxists of the Stalinite direction supported the enlarged armament expenditures, with eyes on direct aid to Russia, some American labor leaders regarded the business with anxiety concerning the long outcome. John L. Lewis, for example, foresaw that labor might be buried under the ruins of the war monster. Whatever the secret wishes of individual labor leaders respecting foreign policies, there were no grounds here for jubilation by a labor movement.

When the Federal Government turned from "public works," as a means of moving industry, to direct efforts in stimulating private business through the National Recovery Act of 1933, organized labor received a kind of left-handed recognition. As originally drafted, the Act had been a pure business proposition conceived by the United States Chamber of Commerce; but in some curious maneuvering a labor clause was inserted in the bill — the now famous Section 7 *a*. How it got there was never fully explained to the public. When the recovery proposal came on the carpet, Congress had before it a bill prescribing a national thirty-hour week, designed to increase employment and enlarge buying power. The very sight of that measure, however, was alarming to business and to the Roosevelt administration. So the bill was scotched. Sponsors of the recovery measure then added to the original bill a section assuring to labor the right of collective bargaining under the new codes to be drawn up by industries. Just what was meant by the language of Section 7 *a* no one seemed to know, not even the President of the United States, though a placation of labor was presumably needed. Whether this was the true history of labor's appearance in the Recovery Act or not, efforts to enforce the Section in question brought labor into a somewhat novel relation to government, to industry, and to the vast body of hitherto unorganized workers in private enterprises large and small.

. While industries were engaged in drawing up their codes of fair practices under the Recovery Act, representatives of organized labor participated, on a national scale, in the processes that involved wages, hours, and collective bargaining. As soon as steps were taken to put the codes, including labor provisions, into effect, in factories, stores, offices, and other establishments, leaders in unionism had to reckon with millions of workers who did not fit the old craft categories. Stirred by the drum beating that accompanied the concerted effort to bring about national recovery and invited to share in collective negotiations, industrial "misfits" by the hundreds of thousands acquired an interest in labor unionism which astounded most of all the American Federation accustomed to slow and tedious methods of organization. Thousands of the workers flocked to the unions long affiliated with the Federation. For others, perhaps the larger share, special organizations had to be provided.

Owing to the fact that miscellaneous workers were involved, the new organizations took on the tone, if not always the form, of industrial unions; that is, they were based as to membership on the nature of the commodity produced, such as rubber, cement, or automobiles, and included all the workers in each plant who helped in its making, as distinguished from unions based on special operations, or crafts, and split up in each plant along craft lines. Whatever the intention of the Federation when it sponsored Section 7 *a*, its decision helped to stimulate a flood of activities and agitations destined to shake the American labor world from center to circumference.

If the words "collective bargaining" seemed lucid as printed in the lines of the Recovery Act, practice under them was intricate and full of turmoil. At least five parties were drawn into the processes of enforcement throughout the country. Of labor organizations to carry on bargaining there were now in existence four distinct types: craft unions, which might number many separate bodies in a single plant; company unions, comprising all the workers in a plant, organized and controlled, more or less, by the management; industrial or vertical unions including workers of every type, independent of management, enjoying some degree of self-government, within the American Federation or outside; and the bodies of hitherto unorganized workers called upon by the law to bargain collectively. On the other side of the bargaining table were the employers, acting individually or collectively, who formulated their proposed wage and hour agreements. Framed in vague language, Section 7 a established no one stereotype of labor association for bargaining purposes and, in the circumstances, neither the federal agencies in charge nor the employers nor the labor organizers had any precise guidance. Perhaps an attempt to provide specifications would have defeated the adoption of the Section by Congress.

In the absence of clear guidance, labor actions under the law were chaotic, with federal officials, courts, and even President Roosevelt playing irregular parts in its application. Some employers, especially in the steel industry, resisted the enforcement of Section 7 a in their plants, in the courts, and in the forum of public opinion. Among the steel industries in general, company unions under the control of management practically monopolized labor relations and similar unions were organized in plants that hitherto had possessed no collective bargaining apparatus whatever. To meet the formalities of the Recovery Act, such corporate devices for keeping labor well in hand were altered in minor respects and declared to be in accord with "the new spirit."

Against independent unionism of any kind, the steel industry offered an almost solid front. Efforts by the Federation of Labor to organize the rubber industry also encountered resistance and collapsed. Attempts to introduce independent collective bargaining in the automobile industry precipitated sharp conflicts, involving management, the American Federation of Labor, independent industrial unions, and the Government. The upshot under Section 7 a was agitation and confusion. From its inception the automobile industry had been marked by seasonal and cyclical fluctuations, insecurity of employment, low annual earnings despite high daily wages in certain divisions, speed-up, espionage, and the rapid displacement of workers at an early age; but experiments in unionization under the auspices of the Recovery Act effected few material changes in the employment policies of the industry.

To some extent, certainly, the ineffectiveness of projects for the mass organization of industrial unions under Section 7 a was due to the policy pursued by the American Federation of Labor. The executive council of the Federation announced in 1934 that it would "encourage whatever form of organization seemed best suited to meet the situation and requirements of the mass production workers." Yet in practice the chief officer, William Green, insisted that organizers in the field must respect the rights and claims of craft unions already affiliated with the Federation. Strictly interpreted, his decree meant that when the workers in a plant were organized, they must be divided into as many separate unions as there were crafts represented in the concern, with the non-craft members as an appendix or the main body, according to the nature of the industry. Such was the theory. In practice, as organization proceeded under federal supervision, leaders of craft unions, in their struggle for increased membership, repeatedly clashed with leaders of industrial unionism. For the anticipated unity was thus substituted internal divisions among the workers themselves.

Collective bargaining under Section 7 a did not always mean, therefore, that a representative of labor sat down at the table with management and in conciliation arranged a schedule of hours and wages for all the grades and types of workers employed "in and around" the plant. On the contrary, it was frequently a multiple operation in which the heads of all the crafts represented in the industry participated; and if any one of the crafts was dissatisfied with the settlement, it might refuse to accept the proffered terms. Although a small minority, a single craft might order a strike after all the other labor bargainers had accepted the proposed contract. In fact jurisdictional warfare among unions themselves was a large part of the labor strife of the time.

Frequently managers of good-will, prepared to arrive at a general peace, were baffled by divisions within the ranks of labor. At the same time managers opposed to independent unions welcomed the opportunity to divide and rule and to represent all independent unionism as "utterly irresponsible." Nor could the most faithful supporters of organized labor deny the occasional truth of such charges. In the confusion so engendered, augmented by the use of espionage and intimidation on the part of many large employers, the public and the politicians found it hard to take their bearings. Nevertheless, under the National Industrial Recovery Act, the organization of labor was definitely stimulated, the membership of the American Federation rose from approximately 2,126,000 in 1933 to more than three million in 1935 — and then the Act was declared unconstitutional by the Supreme Court.

§

Notwithstanding the difficulties encountered under the federal intervention provided by Section 7 *a*, labor leaders were generally agreed that they must demand new legislation of a similar nature after the Supreme Court had invalidated the Recovery Act. They believed that it would strengthen their position as against company unions formed, guided, and dominated by employers, against managerial espionage, against the intervention of company and local police forces sometimes armed with machine guns and tear gas. In response to their arguments and to other considerations, partly political, Congress passed the Labor Relations Act, in 1935, to which was given the name of its leading champion, Senator Robert Wagner. The Wagner Act reasserted the principle of collective bargaining in industry, assured to labor the right to be represented by agents of its own choosing, and forbade employers to interfere with the freedom of organizing and holding elections in industry. The general task of supervising the enforcement of the law was entrusted to the National Labor Relations Board, endowed with power to hear complaints against violations of the Act, to investigate, to scrutinize elections within industries, to issue orders, and to defend cases appealed to the federal courts of proper jurisdiction. Immediately contested by employers, the Wagner Act was carried before the Supreme Court of the United States; and, shortly after Roosevelt had launched his campaign for the reorganization of the judiciary, it was sustained, in the spring of 1937. At last industrial workers had something that really looked like a "Magna Carta," offering federal intervention to guarantee their right to organize and hold elections for the determination of leadership and policy.

Although called by its foes "a radical departure" and "revolutionary," the Wagner Labor Act was, in fact, an extension of principles incorporated in older legislation, state and federal. The right of collective bargaining had long been recognized both by state and federal law and by practice. Again and again, disputes within unions over elections and control had been submitted to courts for adjudication. The Norris-La Guardia Anti-injunction Act of 1932, expanding the terms of the Clayton Act of 1916, had sought to protect organized labor against the free use of injunctions in labor disputes, against "yellow dog" contracts penalizing union members, and against other employer practices interfering with the formation and conduct of independent trade unions. These doctrines the Wagner Act elaborated by specifications. Reliance upon the courts for enforcement was now supplemented by the creation of a lay agency for administrative supervision — the National Labor Relations Board, appointed by the President by and with the advice and consent of the Senate.

While federal legislation in support of collective bargaining was by no means a novel feature of the depression, taken in connection with the circumstances of the depression it gave impetus to the labor movement. Workers in regions that had once been the scenes of union outlawry now had a larger sense of freedom — even in the coal and iron districts of Pennsylvania black with soot, livid with the memories of Homestead and 1892. "A man can talk in Homestead," wrote John A. Fitch, a close student of labor history, in February, 1936. The very managers who had been accustomed for twenty-five years to discharging men for joining a union now began to use a new labor language. The mood of the country seemed altered. "Times have changed," explained Mr. Fitch. "New laws are on the statute books, many of them of a character that could never have been anticipated. We've had a 7 *a* and now we have the Wagner law both of which in effect prohibit discharging men for joining unions. We are not lawbreakers. We go along with the government. . . . These laws and other things have created a great nation-wide sentiment about the right to collective bargaining and the idea that a working man has a right to join a union has gained widespread currency." With exuberance, some labor organizers inscribed on banners the words : "President Roosevelt wants you to join a union." Such was the spirit of the new day.

A "changed" attitude also seemed to characterize many great business executives. They, too, expressed a desire "to go along with the government." In the spring of 1933 they had hurried to Washington and urged the President to assume large powers in guiding the country out of the economic morass into which they had helped to lead it. If to many of them the "going along" meant clamping company unions upon their employees, while secretly resorting to industrial espionage, business leaders in general did not openly defy

the government's officials as they had often defied labor
organizers in times past. Some of them turned to the federal
courts, to be sure, in the hope and expectation that the collective bargaining statutes would be declared unconstitutional; but they did not hire "finks" and "undercover men"
for the express purpose of beating up and driving out of
town representatives of the Department of Labor or agents
of the various labor relations boards created under the Recovery Act and the Wagner Act. Usually the most anti-
union manager, devoid of all respect for a labor delegate,
had some respect for that part of the law which was represented by government officials and enforced in some measure
at least. Even the hatred of vigilantes for labor leaders was
not fierce enough to inspire the lynching of men and women
who came as public representatives in the name of federal
authority, to make inquiries, hold hearings, and supervise
labor elections sanctioned by law.

Under the chairmanship of Joseph Warren Madden, the
National Relations Board assumed one of the most difficult
tasks ever undertaken by any agency of American government and, if the actions of federal courts in upholding its
decisions formed criteria of judgment, it discharged its obligations with a judicial temper scarcely to be expected in the
circumstances. It had not gone far, however, when it ran
into a tempest of criticism. Of necessity, the Board was
plunged into the controversy between craft unions and industrial unions and had to make rulings one way or the other on
the basis of votes cast by the rank and file. Very soon the
directors of the American Federation of Labor began to
insist that their type of unionism was receiving "unfair"
treatment from the Board and, besides assailing it in strong
language, they demanded a revision of the Wagner Labor
Relations Act. The Board was also attacked by employers;
and conservative members of Congress, after demanding an
investigation of its proceedings in vain, called for a drastic
modification of the law under which it operated. Apparently
disturbed by this conflict, Roosevelt ordered careful studies

made of labor relations in England and Sweden, while defending the general course pursued by the Board in the enforcement of the law. As the time drew near for the convening of Congress in 1939, signs multiplied to the effect that an effort would be made to amend the Act.

In anticipation of the coming contest, the editors of the Fortune magazine, in the autumn of 1938, made a survey of the operations under the law and reached the conclusion that most of the proposed changes lay against collective bargaining itself. Usually the alterations suggested were not based on a temperate study of the law and the actual proceedings of the Board. Fortune's analysis of the controverted interunion cases dispelled the contention that the Committee for Industrial Organization had been favored over the American Federation of Labor. Warning the public against a rush to tear open the Wagner Labor Relations Act, the editors said: "The balance is a critical one. And nothing can so easily upset the balance as confusion concerning the motives and purposes involved."

§

Whether as a consequence of the new federal legislation or as another incident in a long stream of economic and intellectual tendencies, a terrific clash among labor leaders and within the ranks of industrial workers tore into the labor system and intensified the conflict of other interests in America. Labor leaders had not always seen eye to eye on organization and its objectives. There had been in times past many insurgent outbursts within the American labor movement and to one manifestation the newest upheaval was intimately related. After the Knights of Labor had been undermined and supplanted by the Federation of Labor, disputes had continued between the advocates of organization by crafts and the advocates of organization by specific industries — between craft unionism and industrial unionism. Owing to the very nature of certain industries where the output was the product of many hands, skilled and unskilled, such as mining and automobile manufacturing, the idea of one all-embracing union seemed to be fitting and was attractive to organizers and workers. But from the beginning industrial unionists experienced opposition when they sought to penetrate the entire labor movement, carrying into practice their ideal of the One Big Union.

Despite many historic reverses, they attempted it again on a large scale in the throes of the depression; and over this issue, in part, the labor movement was now ripped wide open. Craft unionists appealed to history in defense of their position and listed the failures of industrial unionism as contrasted with the successes of craft unionism. But the industrial unionists could not be silenced by history already made; they appealed to contemporary "facts," such as the non-craft character of mass production industries, the failure of craft unionists to organize more than a ninth or tenth of the industrial workers, and the inability of such limited unions to deal effectively with what John L. Lewis, head of the United Mine Workers, called "giant combinations of capital." Again political and industrial events were sharpening the struggle within the sphere of labor organization and giving it the quality of a life-and-death combat.

Between the rise of the American Federation of Labor near the close of the nineteenth century and the great depression, marked by the rush of labor to unionism after 1933, the two types of organizations had managed to adjust their disputes. For years, a large proportion of the Federation's members had belonged to unions primarily industrial in character, such as the United Mine Workers, composed of "all men employed in and around the coal mines, regardless of their skill or calling." Meanwhile mass production industries, such as the steel, rubber, automobile, and cement industries, had been occupying an ever larger share of national economy. Responding to new tendencies, the upswing of the Federation's membership after 1933 came in the industrial unions rather than in the craft organizations. Figures were confused but careful estimates gave the crafts a thirteen per cent increase in membership and the industrial unions a rise of more than one hundred per cent. At all events the balance of power within the Federation was moving from the old center.

Unmistakable evidences of the shift appeared at the San Francisco convention of the Federation in 1934. In response to a vociferous demand, the convention adopted a resolution approving "vertical," or industrial, unionism in basic industries and directing the executive council to charter unions among the automobile, aluminum, and cement workers, "and other mass production and miscellaneous industries." As a result of this decision industrial unionists expected a more active campaign on the part of Federation officials to organize the mass production workers. Their expectations were not fulfilled.

When the Federation's convention assembled at Atlantic City in the following year, 1935, its industrial-union bloc presented a series of resolutions calling for the establishment of more industrial unions in specified industries and for modifications in the constitution of national unions already in existence. In support of these propositions, John L. Lewis pointed out that, after twenty-five years of effort, the craft unionists had failed to organize the thirty-six million unorganized workers in the country and could not present a solid front to organized industry. On the other side, industrial unionism was decried as "an exotic importation of groups who do not believe in the American Federation of Labor." Many interests and personalities were involved and the debate was ferocious. The proposals of the industrial unionists were forcefully presented but, in the end, were rejected by a majority of about three to two.

Yet the victory for craft unionism at Atlantic City was not unmitigated. The opposition minority was large — and apparently growing. Uncompromising words were spoken. The executive committee of the Federation was charged with making "raids" on industrial unions and disrupting them by pulling out craftsmen for separate organizations; with blocking effective organizations in great industries, such as radio, rubber, steel, tin, and iron; and with gross neglect of organization work in the aluminum, cement, gas, coke, and other industries. It was accused of sabotaging the resolutions adopted at San Francisco and deliberately opposing the only type of unionism calculated to reach the huge body of unorganized workers. To the indictment equally curt replies were made; sponsors of craft unionism accused the leaders of industrial unionism of being agents of an alien and disruptive communism.

On its face the minority report presented at the Atlantic City Convention by Charles Howard of the Typographical Union seemed reasonable enough. It read: "We declare the time has arrived when common sense demands that the organization policies of the American Federation of Labor must be moulded to meet present day demands. In the great mass production industries and in those in which the workers are composite mechanics, specialized and engaged upon classes of work which do not fully qualify them for craft union membership, industrial organization is the only solution." But, mild as it was, the proposal warmed the memories of old conflicts over "one big union" and "revolutionary unionism." It defied the leadership of the craft executives well entrenched in official positions — the "bureaucrats" of the labor movement as they were called by the opposition. Thus a contest over organizing principles became an irrepressible contest for power — in the labor world and in the larger sphere of politics and culture where labor exerted decisive influences. This was no mere quarrel among kites and crows. It was a clash of powerful personalities, and, owing to the magnitude of the interests now at stake, the outcome of the struggle might well condition or determine fundamental phases of American civilization.

Outvoted at the Atlantic City convention, leaders of the industrial-union bloc held a meeting in Washington November 9, 1935, and there formed a Committee for Industrial Organization under the direction of John L. Lewis. The purpose of the Committee was "to encourage and promote the organization of workers in the mass production and unorganized industries of the nation and affiliation with the American Federation of Labor." In this declaration of purpose there was no revolutionary fire, no communism; there was not even a breach with the Federation. In effect it merely said that, since the Federation already embraced industrial unions and endorsed the formation of more industrial unions, the Committee proposed to perform the function which the executive committee of the Federation had failed to discharge.

Alarmed none the less by this aggressive organizing force, William Green warned the members of the Committee against factionalism in the labor ranks. In reply the Committee cited precedents for its action in the history of the Federation itself, denied any intention of raiding craft unions, and declared its desire to bring new unions into the Federation. At the same time it reaffirmed its resolve. John L. Lewis crisply informed William Green that rather than abandon the rights of thirty million workers his organization would leave the Federation if necessary to achieve this essential object of all organized labor. Claiming to be within the constitution and laws of the Federation to which its members belonged, the Committee took up the work of organization with an energy unexampled in the history of the American labor movement.

Fearing that the growth of industrial unions within the Federation might soon overwhelm by numerical strength the historic dominance enjoyed by the crafts, the executive council, in 1936, called upon the industrial unions of the Committee for Industrial Organization to defend themselves against a proposed order for their dissolution. Failing to receive a satisfactory answer the council "suspended" those unions — ten in all, with a membership of approximately a million workers. On the argument that only a convention of the Federation, not an executive body, could suspend unions, the council turned its back. It could see its fate without a

diagram : if the rate of growth among industrial unions within
the Federation continued, the craft unions would shortly be
outvoted in the convention and on that day leaders of the
industrial type would supplant the existing official hierarchy.
Such seemed to be the tendency of events. At any rate the
executive council decided to expel nearly one-third of the
unionists from the Federation rather than countenance the
struggle within the general organization. A wide cleavage
was made in the American labor movement.

Hitherto when unions and labor leaders had been expelled
from the Federation, the deed had been done rather quietly
and the general public had paid little attention. In 1936,
however, the heat engendered produced an explosion and,
owing to the stresses and strains of the depression, the reverberations were felt throughout American economy. There
was, in other words, a conjuncture of circumstance and personalities that could not be blotted out by an executive decree
from the council of the Federation. Against the Federation-
ists, such as William Green, Matthew Woll, John Frey, and
William Hutchinson, seasoned and experienced, were now
pitted John L. Lewis, David Dubinsky, Sidney Hillman,
Philip Murray, Homer Martin, and other organizers, also
strong in character and ingenious in negotiation. These
opponents were not theoreticians or dialecticians of the type
that had often been suppressed on the floor of the Federation's conventions. They were not Marxists arguing fine
points up in the air. They were men of formidable strength
with their feet on the ground. They represented unions
already numerically powerful. They were social forces in-
carnate and dynamic. Their collision with the stalwarts of
the Federation was no by-play. It was head on, and efforts
at compromise failed to reduce the battle to a tea party.

§

The chairman of the Committee for Industrial Organization, John Llewellyn Lewis, was a veritable son of the

American industrial conflict. Born in Iowa in 1880, graduated from the public schools into coal mines, where his
ancestors for generations had toiled, early drawn into unionizing efforts, rising rapidly as an organizer, Lewis became the
head of the United Mine Workers in 1919. In that official
position he wound his way through internecine strife, played
the game of politics in the fold of the Republican party, used
his big fists on more than one occasion, suppressed Red theorists, learned and practiced both the fierce and the subtle
arts of negotiation and domination. Yet in the process he
received an education in the higher learning of the most
realistic sort. No one in a professor's chair or in any lofty
position of government or business was able to give a calmer
or more penetrating analysis of the structure and course
of American economy — its manufacturing and mining industry, the transportation business, and the financing of
corporate enterprise. Few, if any, among his contemporaries,
had a keener appreciation of the perils in the way of labor
organization or a wider comprehension of its role in civilization. While he could deliver orations on the platform and
pound the table at conferences, he could keep his temper in
the presence of a tumult when that was the better part of
valor, or sit with the repose of a philosopher at a private
discussion of things high and wide, asking questions quietly,
venturing conjectures, suggesting qualifications, exploring
probabilities, looking at all the angles of vision. Certainly
with any Lord of Creation, Lewis could hold his own, when
holding his own was an affair of knowledge, skill in argument,
and tenacity of will.

That Lewis was more than a mere bargainer over hours and
wages, that he had a broader view of politics and economics
and culture, was demonstrated in a broadcast which he made
on March 15, 1938. After summarizing the achievements of
the Committee for Industrial Organization in respect of
hours, wages, and civil rights, he discussed the state of the
nation to whose fate that of labor was linked. He drew attention to the millions unemployed. "Their numbers," he said,

"are steadily increasing, as the nation drifts with terrifying and deadly sureness to the never, never realm of financial bankruptcy, economic collapse, and human tragedy." He spoke of agriculture, banks, and business enterprises leaning upon the Government, subsidized by it. And what of intelligence and leadership in politics and economics? "In the months that have ensued neither industry nor government has come forth with constructive proposals designed to meet the problems of the depression. The federal Congress, lacking adequate or competent leadership, in continuous session for months past, has failed to devise or enact a single statute that would cause a glimmer of hope to penetrate the minds of millions of despairing Americans."

While Congress floundered around, the Politicos and the Lords of Creation fled from reason. "Meantime, cavilling and confusion prevail, and our statesmen and those carrying the responsibilities of the nation's manifold enterprises are reviling each other with an anger and bitterness that defiles, sears, and destroys. Meantime, the population suffers, and a creeping paralysis progressively impairs its functions. What is to be done? Reason calls for a change. More rational policies are indicated. America is menaced, not by a foreign foe that would storm its battlements, but by the more fearful enemy of domestic strife and savagery. It is time for Americans to coöperate. It is time for Americans to recognize each other's right of individual existence. It is time for capital to recognize labor's right to live and participate in the increased efficiency of industry and the bounties of our national resources. It is time for labor to recognize the right of capital to have a reasonable return upon its investment. It is time for statesmen to recognize their nation's peril and to decide to coöperate with labor and industry, to rationalize the nation's processes, and alleviate a nation's distress. Labor is willing to coöperate — now. Let the leaders of the nation's business step forward. Let the statesmen of the nation do the same. Let the council of reason and mutual toleration be convened. American leadership can accomplish this task, and in so doing will preserve its governmental structure and its democratic institutions." While he did not give a bill of specifications in that speech, Lewis made it plain that, in his judgment, an immense, rational, and coöperative effort was necessary to halt the creeping paralysis and set productive industry on its feet. That failing, trade unionism pure and simple could merely share the impending calamities.

Behind the force of his personality Lewis had the force of the United Mine Workers. He was the head of half a million men already organized and operating as a mass union, not as a congeries of craft unions. Its jurisdiction covered all workers laboring "in and around the mine." Its growth had been associated with one of the stormiest industries in the United States, beset by crises, cut-throat competition, price fluctuations, unemployment, and resistance to unionism. In his miner's post of observation, Lewis had seen his organization expand with the demands of the world war and contract in the post-war depression. He had witnessed the slight recovery and then the burst of 1929. But in good times and evil, he had fought to maintain miners' wages, to gain an inch here or a yard there for the mining population, and had gone through many a prolonged strike with that end in view. In attempts to effect unionization in "captive mines" owned by steel companies, he had secured contracts from those giants, while other organizers had tried in vain to unite steel workers. Rebellions against Lewis had broken out in the miners' ranks. Yet he had managed to ride every wave and he commanded greater loyalty and affection in 1936 than at any time in his tempestuous career. As head of the Mine Workers as well as the Committee for Industrial Organization, Lewis was no petty disturber of Federation peace.

In other respects and in his own right, Sidney Hillman, who was associated with Lewis in the Committee for Industrial Organization, was also a labor statesman. In his thinking he too had gone beyond trade unionism "pure and simple," and was both analytical and philosophical in his grasp of the social forces conditioning the labor movement. At the same time he was a positive genius as an organizer and an executive. In 1911 he had carried the United Garment Workers forward along the line of mass unionism and had effected with the management of great manufacturers, Hart, Schaffner, and Marx, an arrangement providing for an industrial board composed of employer and employee representatives authorized to make continuing adjustments under general terms. Three years later, Hillman became the head of the union which took the name of the Amalgamated Clothing Workers, and assumed direction of its fortunes — fortunes marked by an expansion of membership, a peculiar responsibility for industrial output, and a growth in social activities.

Throughout his career, Sidney Hillman had studied the men's clothing industry in which his union operated and had conceived unionism as a way of life, not merely as a pecuniary enterprise. The slogan "bread and roses," associated with the Amalgamated, if it sounded peculiar to business circles and garden clubs, expressed the union's desire for the good life. The son of a Lithuanian wool merchant, Hillman had come to the United States at the age of twenty and started work in a Chicago clothing factory at $7 a week. But he had lived at the Hull House and had taken advantage of its rare opportunities for training in languages, the arts, and social democracy.

When he entered upon unionizing activities, Hillman "shattered union precedents" and continued in that path. He insisted that unions should understand the state of industry, consider its problems of production and marketing, and seek to promote efficiency in its operations. Under his leadership the Amalgamated also assumed responsibility for the welfare of its members, even to the length of embarking upon housing projects. It undertook economic research, employed statisticians, often showed managers how to cut costs and maintain wage scales, and managed a bank of its own. Stranger still, it frequently came to the aid of embarrassed employers and lent them money from the union's treasury to form a bridge over hard times and keep up the rate of employment. By sheer force of intellect and moral courage, Hillman could accomplish results where others merely raged. He was a formidable member of the Committee for Industrial Organization, and the men's clothing workers formed a heavy supporting arch.

More akin to Hillman than to Lewis in social background, David Dubinsky represented still a third type of philosophy and energy. Polish in origin, with a childhood spent in the Ghetto of Brest-Litovsk behind him, Dubinsky had migrated to America at the age of nineteen and started on his American way as a low-paid worker in a clothing shop on the east side of New York. His career synchronized with the rise of sweatshop workers to a position of decency and self-respect through the organization of the International Ladies Garment Workers Union. As low-paid laborers, Jews had not found the doors of craft unions wide open for them. They had been compelled to develop their own organization and gain negotiating strength through their own solidarity. Although associated with the American Federation of Labor, the Garment Workers, in their struggle for a share in the benefits of civilization, had gone beyond mere wage and hour bargaining. Under the leadership of such indefatigable workers as Fannia Cohn, they had established an educational program, built summer camps, founded institutions for recreation, health, and mutual aid, and experimented with dramatics and art. Economic democracy they were seeking to enrich by social democracy. Trained in this school, a leader of this association, Dubinsky combined with hardheadedness in organizing activities an appreciation of the social and political implications connected with labor activities.

§

Men of such calibre as Lewis, Hillman, and Dubinsky were commanding forces. When they set out to organize, organ-

ization moved, backed by the miners and garment workers
nearly a million strong. With unprecedented swiftness, the
campaign swept into its train, through the strategy of the
Committee for Industrial Organization, casual laborers,
transport workers, white-collar employees ranging from
clerks and stenographers to engineers, college professors, and
journalists, and every type of worker in the mass production
industries. Entering plants where company unions seemed
entrenched, where in some cases independent unions had
been crushed again and again, organizers carried stronghold after stronghold.   In February, 1937, the Committee
"breached the united front of the basic industries in winning
a contract with the General Motors Corporation," hitherto
an adroit and indomitable foe. Checkmated by Henry Ford,
the Committee made encircling movements by applying
propaganda and by invoking federal aid under the National
Labor Relations Board which compelled him to present his
claims for exemption to the agencies of the law.

   In the course of its advance the Committee moved on
"Big Steel," with Homestead, the old battleground, as a
center of activity. There, more than forty years before, the
secretary of the Carnegie Company had issued the employers'
declaration of independence; now the new labor leaders proclaimed theirs. "The lords of steel. . . ." ran their manifesto, " have set up company unions. They have sent among
us swarms of stool-pigeons. They have kept among us
armies of company gunmen. Today we do solemnly declare
our independence. We shall exercise our inalienable rights
to organize into a great industrial union, banded together
with all our fellow steel workers. In support of this declaration, we mutually pledge to each other our steadfast purposes
as union men, our honor, and our very lives." The conflict
had been revived. Seven men in it had just lost their lives.

   When the reading of the declaration was finished, the
crowd of auditors marched to the graves of the dead and there
pledged themselves to the cause of labor. All through the
steel districts flew the news and then it produced a national

sensation. While the country was watching the outcome with anxiety, "Big Steel" came to terms with industrial unionism in March, 1937; but "Little Steel," personified in its spokesman, Tom Girdler of the Republic Steel Company, refused to sign on the dotted line and presented a solid front of resistance. For the moment the tide stood still, as the economic recession gave caution to the leaders on both sides of the line. Even so, at the close of that year the Committee for Industrial Organization boasted a membership of more than four million workers.

The rapid rush to industrial unionism was accompanied by new tactics, provoking and reflecting dissensions within the movement itself as well as outside. Included in the novel methods was the "sit-down" strike, evolved perhaps in imitation of contemporary labor innovations in France. Whatever the source of inspiration, the sit-down became epidemic for a time in the United States, spreading alarm and anger through middle class circles from coast to coast. It was especially virulent among industries in which company unions prevailed or where employers had refused to negotiate with independent organized labor. In industrial plants, hospitals, chain-stores, and other centers of work, men and women, boys and girls, stopped machines or other transactions and camped on the premises for the duration of the struggle. Instead of marching out and leaving their places to be filled by strike-breakers, they stood where they were, sat down, ate, and slept in the quarters of their employers. In many establishments strikers prepared for a siege by forming broom and dusting brigades to keep the rooms clean; they organized classes for instruction in various branches of learning, conducted by their better educated associates. In one store, religious services were held on a Sunday and prayers offered. Food and other supplies were passed through the lines by relatives and sympathizers and efforts of the police to dispossess the occupants jeopardized limbs or lives for everybody concerned.

To owners of property, their legal advisers, and guardians

of law and order, sit-down operations presented knotty
problems. As the result of a long historic struggle, finding
expression in legislation and judicial reasoning, certain rights
in connection with labor organization and collective bargaining had been won, such as the right to form trade unions for
the purpose of raising wages, to strike in relation to that
purpose, and to picket, subject to specific and general limitations. None of these rights, however, had been exercised
within the premises of employers. Nor was there any overt
threat to property relations in the "vacation," occasionally
used as a bargaining device, that is, in the sudden stoppage of
work by remaining away from the place of employment.
Sabotage in the form of breaking machines or putting sand
in gear-boxes had been clearly an attack on property, unlaw-
ful from the beginning and later stigmatized as criminal.
But the sit-down did not fit into established legal categories
of any kind. Under the existing interpretation of law it was
an illegal occupation of premises in defiance of the owners
and in many places the police used tear gas and force to eject
the occupants. In other places, where it was endured by
owners and proved effective, its legality was not conceded.
Since the sit-down strike was frequently a spontaneous com-
bustion, even labor leaders shrank from assuming official
responsibility for it, at least in such cases, although they
sometimes took advantage of it to press for negotiations and
terms. Some attempts were being made to formulate legal
rights for workers who held "their places" when the epidemic
died away almost as quickly as it had flared up.

§

Had it proceeded alone as a manifestation of labor unrest,
the industrial-union movement might have immediately
provoked a counter movement tightly solidified and able to
use force against it without the formal restraints of law. But
it did not proceed alone. Exponents of the "normal"
countervailing opinion were shaken by doubts of their own

virtue as a result of disclosures at congressional hearings paralleling this labor advance — disclosures which enlightened the public with respect to munitioneering, the manipulations of railways by banking cliques, and the employment of spies, private gunmen, fomenters of false labor troubles, and the assemblage of arsenals at plants by corporations high and low in the scale of Respectability. As these sordid features were unfolded at the congressional hearings, great metropolitan dailies carried vivid accounts for those who ran to read. Reporters began to fret over their diverse obligations to owners, publishers, editors, and the people at large, and to divulge secrets of their trade. Disputes between editors and publishers on the one side and the makers of so-called "objective news" on the other, the organization of the Newspaper Guild among journalists, and a strike against the Hearst press in Seattle with its anti-labor policy, contributed to the unsettling and churning of public opinion.

Into this ferment of facts and opinions, professional propagandists, known as public relations counselors, and, more openly, radio announcers flung their agitations. Seeing an opportunity to fish in troubled waters, many communists thrust their activities into industrial unionism. Their number was small in relation to the total membership of unions under the Committee for Industrial Organization; their doctrinal creed was disavowed by its leadership — to which communist proclivities could not be justly charged. But since communists were interested in promoting class conflicts or taking advantage of them, they pushed into the limelight and made disturbances incommensurate with their numerical strength. Their very presence in industrial unionism, however, furnished the pretext for opponents of that movement to brand it as "Red." Once more leaders in the work of labor organization were compelled, as they had been again and again in American history, to meet charges of revolutionary, alien radicalism while they pressed forward to improve labor conditions against hostile interests on the side of ownership and management.

Yet the communists themselves did not in truth present a united front toward the labor movement in America. Though capitalist ideologues and conservative craftsmen, lumping the communists all together, did their best to discredit the Committee for Industrial Organization as communist in intention and leadership, really the communists were as divided on principle and tactics as the labor movement itself. The division revolved around the issue of Stalin against Trotzky — communism within Russia, for the time being at least, as against world revolution and world communism in one vast conflagration and reconstruction.

This controversy added inflammatory elements to the strife between capital and labor in the United States. Despising the Stalinite wing of communism with the intensity of disillusionment following utter confidence in utopia, Trotzkyites took delight in pointing out and exaggerating the communistic element in the industrial unions. A small fraction themselves, they would have wielded slight influence had it not been for the energy of the general opposition riding full tilt against the Committee. Riding with it, they obtained for their testimony and for their "revelations" a degree of publicity that could not have been won otherwise. In this state of affairs their writings and agitations gave the press an opportunity to whip up resentment against the only form of unionism that, in the nature of mass production, could offer any method of accomplishing the wholesale organization of labor in the United States.

§

From one point of view, of course, the ebullition of labor unrest seemed to the worried upper classes like a volcanic eruption, without much rhyme or reason, offering no advantages even to labor. Strikers clashed with the police and state troopers. Heads were cracked and bodies broken. Men and women marching toward the industrial plants were shot down in their tracks. Sit-downers were ousted by gusts of poison gas. While dual unionism was splitting the workers into warring camps, stevedores, cooks, waiters, clerical workers, teachers, government employees, nurses, and doctors were making common cause with miners, automobile workers, actors, and reporters. On labor days, instead of the former united front on parade, there were now sometimes two fronts and two parades in many cities, with hooting and jeering on the side lines. Irresponsible strikers, not amenable to any union discipline, broke contracts signed by their representatives and business management. In their haste to avoid the impacts of industrial unionism, employers raced to make terms with the American Federation of Labor and praised where they had once damned. Leaders in the two divisions of labor sniped at one another amid the applause of their respective supporters and their common enemies. Then as a climax to all the uproar came the business recession of 1937. Men and women who had recently sat down in plants now sat down outside — in idleness — or marched on relief agencies and Works Progress officials with demands for "work or bread." With an impatience fanned by the conflict between the Committee for Industrial Organization and the management of "Little Steel," President Roosevelt exclaimed: "A plague on both your houses!"

If, in the circumstances, employers could view with pleasure the wide-open split of the American labor movement, politicians as the brokers and mediators in government were denied the privileges of such a complacent attitude. In 1936 organized labor had penetrated politics with unusual force. While the Lords of Creation were pouring hundreds of thousands of dollars into the Republican war chest, the Committee for Industrial Organization tossed more than half a million into the Democratic fund. Under the auspices of labor's Non-partisan League, sponsored for a time by both wings of the labor movement, Republicans and Democrats were pitted in a rivalry for "the labor vote." In the state of New York an independent organization calling itself the American Labor Party entered the field and threw its support to the Democratic side in national affairs, while insisting on separate representation in local affairs. The size of its vote was surprising, even a source of anxiety, to "the old-line politicos." In the autumn of 1937 the American Labor Party spurned the Democratic machine in New York City, backed Mayor Fiorello La Guardia, a nominal Republican, for re-election, and helped to rout Tammany Hall, blessed against such a fate by Postmaster General Farley. Repercussions were felt in all the industrial states already rent by labor agitations. John L. Lewis supported a labor candidate for governor in the Democratic primaries of Pennsylvania and, when this move was unsuccessful, cast about for another way to make the force of labor felt in the politics of that key state. As Democrats and Republicans girded themselves for coming congressional elections, the hopes of labor rose. Although the substantial gains made by the Republicans were interpreted by such outstanding friends of labor as Senator Burton K. Wheeler to mean a set-back, the future was still open.

Dependent in a considerable measure upon the labor vote in his struggle against the conservatives in his own party and against the possible revival of the Republican organization, President Roosevelt found himself in a dilemma. In an effort to hold things in balance, he sought to keep on good terms with both wings of the labor movement — the officials of the craftsmen and the officials of the industrial unionists. An offense to either side might swing it into the Republican camp. While he kept his channels of communication free, his Secretary of Labor, Frances Perkins, whose branch of government could be called in the circumstances a Department of Domestic Warfare, tried to confine the conflict within the bounds of negotiation. A representative of the Department attended the national labor conventions in 1938 to urge a compromise in the interests of unity, and Secretary Perkins continued to pursue the policy of conciliation.

All in vain, apparently. Committees appointed by the two labor organizations could not arrive at an agreement and politicians were equally helpless. It seemed as if no formula could permanently resolve the contradiction between craft unionism and industrial unionism. Craft unionism, embracing "the aristocracy" of high-paid labor and depending for existence upon a certain supremacy over skilled trades, was necessarily limited in its range and its possible membership. Reaching out for the whole body of workers, some thirty-six million strong, industrial unionism claimed to be "the democracy of labor." Asserting its claim to permanence, the Committee for Industrial Organization — without the coöperation of Dubinsky and the Ladies Garment Workers Union — changed itself into the Congress of Industrial Organizations at a convention held late in 1938, and adopted a regular constitution for the new association of industrial unions.

§

In keeping with the urbanization of economy which accompanied the apparently illimitable expansion of machine industry, the swift advance of industrial unionism, with its strikes, sit-downs, and social turmoil, almost monopolized the attention of that portion of society given to imagining itself the whole of society. Yet events no less crucial for that society were taking place in another division of labor — labor on the land. Tilling the soil had continued through all the ages of human history to bring forth some kind of livelihood whatever the varying fortunes of politics, industry, and commerce. As Miriam Beard pointed out, near the conclusion of her History of the Business Man, dealing with his role in more than forty centuries, "men suffered on the land but survived; while in the cities, they flourished — and faded." Craftsmen in the metropolis of Rome lost their occupations in the dying city; slaves once flogged to labor on the latifundia kept on tilling the earth as it slipped from the hands of their masters who were sinking into dissolution and death. Until the great modern illusion of urbanism, for its brief span, conquered thought, statesmen, poets, and agronomists had

regarded the condition of agriculture — the distribution of
the land among yeomen and the rewards of labor on the soil
— as an indubitable barometer of social security and stability.

Once more, after the severe contraction of capitalism became indisputable even to its economists, and especially after
the great débâcle of 1929 enfeebled the centers of industry
and commerce, concern about agriculture, or rather about
the buying power of those that labored in the earth, rose in
the consideration of all who had capacity for consideration.
This revival of concern found expression in the Agricultural
Adjustment Act of 1933 and kindred legislation. But on the
frank confession of the Secretary of Agriculture, federal
activity affected primarily "the top third of the farmers in
the country," that is, principally landowners great and small,
in the upper ranges of well-being. If it saved a multitude
from foreclosure and ruin, it conferred few benefits, often
personal losses, on tenants, share-croppers, migratory workers, and field laborers, in the much-advertised effort to
establish "parity between agriculture and industry."

In the midst of their deprivations the disinherited made
their woes heard. They held meetings and protested. They
organized unions and struck against the conditions of tenure
and labor. At that point their activities were countered by
acts of vigilante terrorism in rural regions, raising a noise that
reached the White House. Late in 1936 President Roosevelt
responded by creating a Committee on Tenancy authorized
to inquire into the facts of the case and report remedial
measures. With the caution of understatement he remarked: "The rapid increase of tenant farmers during the
past half century is significant evidence that we have fallen
far short of achieving the traditional American ideal of
owner operated farms."

The findings of the President's Committee, expressed in
mathematical language, described an economic tendency of
sinister import not only for working families on the land but
also for the upper circles of the American system. Compre-

hended in human terms, the naked facts depicted a widening area of servitude and misery. "For the past forty-five years," the Committee stated, "the entire period for which we have statistics on land tenure, there has been a continuous and marked decrease in the proportion of operating owners and an accompanying increase in the proportion of tenants. Tenancy has increased from twenty-five per cent of all farmers in 1880 to forty-two per cent in 1935." In the decade from 1920 to 1930 the number of tenant farms rose while the total number of operated farms actually fell. Estimated in terms of monetary value, forty-seven per cent of the land was tilled by tenants or wage laborers. In some of the states four-fifths of the equity in the land was in the hands of landlords and mortgage holders, and only one-fifth in the possession of operating farmers.

In this record of increasing economic degradation on the soil, there was just one little countervailing fact: the proportion of tenancy declined slightly between 1930 and 1935. Farm owning seemed to be on a rise, if a trivial rise. But Rupert Vance entertained doubts. It was true, he admitted, that in the sixteen states of the South a twelve per cent rise in owners had occurred in the period, to offset the growth of tenancy, but "the increase was entirely among white owners with small farms, and most of the gains were in rough upland areas of poor soil. Over one-fourth of the new owners' farms were located in the Appalachian counties of West Virginia, Kentucky, and Tennessee where between 1930 and 1935 many unemployed miners had returned to their submarginal farms. This development can scarcely be regarded as advancing the course of farm ownership. The loss of tenant farms occurred largely among the Negroes in the South." Degradation in the mining industry had driven workers back to soil from which they had fled in despair. The slight downward turn in the rising line of tenancy, on its face indicative of better things, in truth carried evidences of additional worse things.

Nor was the whole story told in the figures of tenancy.

In value, forty-seven per cent of the land of America was tilled by non-owners. Bad as it was, that did not complete the story. Nominal owners were saddled with mortgages, amounting to eleven per cent of the total value of their property. "The true ownership by farmers in the land they till," Vance went on to say, "has reached its lowest point in the Midwestern states of South Dakota, Iowa, and Illinois where it falls below thirty per cent. Next comes the Cotton Belt where the farm operators' equity ranges between thirty and forty per cent." Land, buildings, machinery, stock, and tools were mortgaged. On top of this pyramid stood short-term debts usually representing money borrowed to pay current expenses. In some states more than fifty per cent of the farmers — freeholders and tenants combined — had such outstanding obligations, often secured by liens on coming crops. The past, the present, and the future were bound by debt servitudes.

By statistical studies another cheerful American dream was shown to be deceptive. Armchair philosophers had fancied that tenancy marked a rung in the "ladder of progress" up which the stout young farm laborer climbed to ownership. In many cases he had no doubt made that climb. But the President's Committee on Tenancy dispelled the illusion as a general proposition. Its examination of the facts "indicated that in recent years movement from rung to rung has been predominantly in the direction of descent rather than ascent. It has also indicated an increasing tendency for the rungs of the ladder to become bars — forcing imprisonment in a fixed social status from which it is increasingly difficult to escape."

While the motion upward slowed down, collateral motion extended. Tenants wandered from farm to farm, from land-lord to landlord, from region to region, on foot, in battered wagons, or in dilapidated automobiles, commonly dragging families with them, usually to conditions lower in the scale of living than those from which they had fled. In the spring of 1935 more than one-third of all the tenant farmers in the United States had occupied their present land merely for one year and in many areas the proportion exceeded fifty per cent. White tenants moved more frequently than colored tenants. Had it not been for laws binding debtors to their landlords, the amount of nomadism would have been still larger and the disintegration of communities and steady habits by locomotion would have been intensified; for settlement on the land did not always signify a poignant desire to be there — to pursue life, liberty, and happiness on the soil under any and all circumstances.

Between the growth of farm tenancy and the restless migration of tenants, on the one side, and the depletion of the soil, on the other, immediate relations were evident. Tenant occupancy of land did not last more than two years on the average. Having no long-term interest in the soil he tilled, and little or no capital, the tenant applied only those fertilizers calculated to yield a quick cash crop. "The shorter the operators' time on the farm, the higher the percentage of crop-land in corn tends to be, and consequently the higher the degree of erosion," reported the Iowa Experiment Station. At the same time the transient tenant had slight if any interest in improving the drainage system, the house, barns, or other structures on his temporary holding. From start to finish the tenant process worked for the wastage of the soil and the degradation of human life in all its aspects. Reciprocally, in its turn, soil depletion "contributed materially to the expansion of tenancy and the further impoverishment of tenants and croppers." In the domain of legal relations, state laws respecting the rights and obligations of landlords and tenants provided terms and conditions that made for an acceleration of the degradation. Considering for a moment merely the material features of the situation, the President's Committee reported that the proper use and conservation of the soil "require modification of our present system of land tenure." The bottom was sliding out from under the American dream, with "the degradation of the democratic dogma."

Correlated with increasing tenancy and ceaseless migration were unsanitary dwellings, ill health, biological deterioration, meager education, and the disruption of community ties. As the top soil washed out to sea, the physical and moral resources of human beings were also depleted. Stark in the figures, photographs, and reports stood this brutal reality. When to migratory tenants in this plight were added farm laborers and field "hands," the situation appeared even more tragic. In 1930 more than one-fourth of all persons "gainfully" employed in agriculture were casual farm wage-laborers; "hired men" who shared the life of the farm families were a diminishing group. Having no permanent abode, few comforts, deriving no immediate advantage from the conservation of anything, deprived of all benefits arising from insurance and unemployment legislation, farm laborers had even a shorter shrift than farm tenants. "The situation of the hand laborers in intensive agriculture is especially precarious," laconically remarked the President's Committee. That, at least, was not an overstatement. And the Committee concluded: "Approximately one farm family out of four occupies a position in the nation's social and economic structure that is precarious and should not be tolerated." This, also, was a modest deduction from the facts pertaining to tenants, croppers, laborers, families on submarginal land, families on holdings of inadequate size, owner-families hopelessly in debt, and young people stranded at the bottom of "the agricultural ladder."

Here was a field at least ready for agitation and agitation sprang up abundantly. Tenants, croppers, and laborers began to hold meetings and discuss their common problems. They formed local organizations. The Southern Tenant Farmers' Union was established and quickly reached out for membership and contacts with organized industrial workers. Calls went forth for modifications in land tenure, in the rights of tenants and croppers, in the laws of debt and indenture. Then this movement toward agricultural unionism evoked a counter-movement among landlords and the collateral property interests, industrial and agricultural. Families connected with union activities were evicted from their shacks;

the power of the police and county sheriffs was invoked;
vigilante groups fell upon "the agitators," irrespective of
their sex, inflicted violence upon them, shot some, drove
others into neighboring counties or states, called them "Reds"
— that last word of insult. Thus the frailty of the civil
liberties enjoyed by the landless and toolless was again and
again illustrated. Members of farm unions were blacklisted
or subjected to discrimination in the allotment of such opportunities as agriculture offered. Complaints soon reached
Washington. For a time they were little heeded by an administration engaged in subsidizing the "upper third" of agriculture; but eventually they awakened reverberations in the
Department of Agriculture and in the corridors of the
Capitol. The President's Committee on Tenancy took cognizance of the situation and Secretary Wallace went forth to
see with his own eyes the plight of those who cropped and
toiled in Southern fields.

Though tentative and conservative in the presence of
American folklore of property, the Committee on Tenancy
accepted the fact that the unlimited individual tenure provided in the Homestead Act of 1862 had been a complete
failure in large areas. Having made that confession, the Committee advocated the purchase and leasing of land by a
federal corporation, the limitation of re-sale to farmers by
provisions checking speculation, the reservation of certain
rights to the public, and a guarantee of soil conservation
against exploitation.

In other words, traditional freehold tenure under which
degradation had come about was to be restrained in the community and the national interest. Farming predominantly
commercial was to be supplemented by production for home
use, by coöperative enterprises, by the construction of camps
for migratory workers, by health services and education;
that is, public ownership, limited and conditional tenures,
and coöperative undertakings were called for — on an experimental footing.

Changes in state legislation affecting tenures and landlord-

tenant relationships were also recommended. Restraints
were to be placed on land speculation — a favorite outdoor
sport in America for several centuries. More adequate safeguards for civil liberty were to be maintained. All in all, the
report of the President's Committee, cautious as were all its
terms, was a revolutionary document when placed beside the
myth of the upstanding and independent American farmer
and his family. A. R. Mann, provost of Cornell University,
felt compelled to announce "strong reservations concerning
the proposal for federal landlordism contained in the report."

§

At this point in time, in the midpassage, all comprehending
thought, whether sophisticated or rude, took into account
the obtrusive fact that the future of American society, including the form and process of government, was being conditioned by the vicissitudes, activities, and ideas of urban and
rural labor; that the forms of culture to come turned upon
the lot to be won by or assigned to labor. How profound was
the antagonism or affinity between farmers as owners, debtors, tenants, or field hands on the one side, and labor in towns
and mining communities on the other? How solid or fragile
was the unity of that sector of society called "the middle
class" which sought to be self-contained and so often came
into conflict with labor, rural or urban? Was there anything
more than the demagogue's machinations in the monotonous
clashes between big business and little business, the "trust-
busting" furor based upon the real or alleged opposition between the petty bourgeoisie and the plutocracy? Amid the
swish and swash of contending groups, interests, and ideas,
where lay the center of gravity, if there was one? Where was
the controlling gyroscope for dominating and giving stability
to the course of civilization?

To none of these questions were positive answers provided
by the tumult of events. Efforts to unite farmers of various types with industrial workers continued unabated, but

immediate results were limited and future outcomes were obscure. A party called "farmer-labor" surged to the top in the government of a great state — Minnesota. Across the border in Wisconsin the Progressives, under La Follette leadership, got possession of the government, mainly on appeals to farming and laboring groups, without assuming the Minnesota label. In the House of Representatives in 1938, five of the nine members from Minnesota were enrolled under the Farmer-Labor banner, with Paul J. Kvale and John T. Bernard capably leading. Of the Wisconsin representation, seven of the ten members were listed as Progressives and two of them certainly, Thomas Amlie and Harry Sautoff, were essentially farmer-labor in sympathies. In the Senate both members from Minnesota, Henrik Shipstead and Ernest Lundeen, belonged to the Farmer-Labor affiliation. In the main, however, Senators and Representatives from industrial constituencies, who manifested strong interest in labor, belonged to the Democratic party. In the chamber with the Progressive Senator from Wisconsin, Robert M. La Follette, for example, sat a Democratic Senator from that state, F. Ryan Duffy. In the Solid South, where conflicts were almost entirely confined to the Democratic party, Senators and Representatives of conservative bent were occasionally replaced by members more keenly alive to the agitations of tenants, croppers, field laborers, and industrial workers. From time to time blocs were formed in Congress to promote or oppose certain types of legislation, and bargains were driven between representatives from farming and industrial districts to create majorities for particular bills. But in these shifting configurations were few signs of permanence and unequivocal direction, and in the elections of 1938 labor and progressive forces suffered severe losses in many sections of the country.

Through the history of labor in town and country in the United States since the early years of the nineteenth century, its spokesmen and philosophers had vainly sought unity in some acceptable conception of economy. For a time near the middle of that century they thought they had found it in the homestead movement, which brought agrarians and even socialists into a common cause, and culminated in the enactment of the Homestead Act of 1862. By this process they hoped to guarantee holdings to farmers and permit industrial workers, suffering from low wages and unemployment, to escape from city tenements to free acres in the country. In fact, however, the Homestead law, viewed in the light of the buoyant hopes which inspired its original framers, proved to be almost a fraud upon farmers and industrial workers, as Fred A. Shannon and Paul W. Gates conclusively demonstrated on the basis of extended researches, the conclusions of which were published in The American Historical Review for July, 1936. Vast areas of land went to railway companies and speculators, sadly diminishing the areas of "free homesteads." And, whatever may have been the effect of free land on the lot of industrial workers in the East, it provided no "safety valve" for any huge number of them; nor did it overcome the evils of low wages and unemployment. This much was also established on the foundation of researches by Carter Goodrich and Sol Davison and incorporated in articles appearing in the Political Science Quarterly for June, 1935, and March, 1936. Allowing for divergencies of opinion on details of history, it was to be reported factually that the first immense effort to unite agrarians and industrial workers had attained an elusive success culminating in a default if not a complete failure.

Since the circumstances of 1850 could not be repeated in 1929 or 1938, what were the signs of a new unity? Psychological, as well as economic, differences were evident in thought and action. The memories, skills, and propensities of the handicrafts, which had kept artisans for countless centuries close to the life and ways of agriculture, had been diminished by the machine process. That was known to every one, but neither the philosophers of the labor movement nor the leaders in organization gave much thought to the agricultural end of the economic process. This was especially true of modern communistic thinkers. Marxism was essentially urban in origin and nature. Its heroes, Karl Marx and Friederich Engels, lived long in England and brought their ideological system to its perfection in a society highly industrialized, where agriculture had already lost its grip; and they both felt scorn for old-fashioned tillers of the land. Their disciples in the United States, likewise having little or no contact with the earth, conceived labor mainly in industrial terms, as they pored over Marxian texts in city tenements, apartments, and libraries. When they thought of labor in the country they thought principally of tenants, field hands, and casual workers — the weakest elements on the land; thus pity for the tillers of the soil exceeded interest in agriculture as the basis of all society.

On the other hand, workers in the earth, whether they were owners, tenants, or casual laborers, had, either from inheritance or experience, few affiliations with industrial workers, and were likewise mentally isolated. They often formed associations among themselves. They conducted milk strikes in the urban fashion. They blocked sheriffs trying to sell farms under foreclosure. They knew what it was to labor with bent backs and bruised hands. But the scheme of capitalism and its labor forms had unfamiliar, almost alien, features. Struggling along with a meager cash income or working for twenty-five or thirty dollars a month — and often less — farmers could not instinctively sympathize with industrial workers carrying on strikes to raise wages which seemed magnificent in comparison. Though with the cost of living in cities taken into account, urban wage-earners might still be about on the same economic level as the farmers, differences in ways of life naturally checked unanimity of understanding and hindered coöperation on any scale.

Even so, as conferences, agitations, pamphlets, and debates indicated, a growing consciousness of common interests marked the course of leadership among farmers and industrial workers. If the soil continued to erode and wash out to sea, if the standard of life on the land fell, if the buying

power of farmers sank, how would things fare with industrial workers engaged in producing goods and machinery for
use on farms? The question was asked, again and again with
impressive repetition, by public officials, students of society,
and publicists. If, on the other hand, the wages of urban
workers declined, if unemployment for millions meant no
wages at all, where could labor on the land find markets for
its produce? Farmers with the narrowest outlook could see,
when their attention was directed to the matter, how their
fate, to that extent at least, hung upon the state of industry,
on labor organization, on outcomes of collective bargaining.
As industry and agriculture contracted, as the web of a
mutual fate drew tighter around urban and rural workers,
thought followed, if haltingly and at a distance.

§

The renewal of agrarian unrest broke in upon the beati-
tudes while the golden glow was still shimmering. During
the dissolutions and detonations of the depression, its intrusion widened and its effects deepened; and then amid the
crashes in industry the agitations of urban labor were added
to the agitations of the agrarians. If not united by bonds of
immediate and palpable interest, labor in town and labor in
country were engaged in a common quest for a livelihood and
both disturbed the course of politics conducted in the traditional manner. Their quest for a living on modern levels also
brought discomfort to specific economic interests. For years
the possessors of great fortunes and the members of the
"middle class," so-called, had largely dominated, while they
directed, the transactions of politics and the currents of
thought; but they had often been in antagonism themselves, concealed or above board. Indeed no small part of the
political and social agitations culminating in party demonstrations had sprung from the struggle between "big business" and "little business," between "big men" and "little
men." In this contest the former had been denounced as

"economic royalists," and "trust-busting" campaigns had been waged against the masters of corporations, with agrarian and labor leaders often cheering on the side lines. Then as farm tenancy increased and industrial workers formed huge independent unions, fresh agitations jostled the classic politics of big business and little business and hinted at the desirability or necessity of unity against a common disturbance. With efforts to get American economy on a high production level baffled over a long stretch of years, these agitations assumed more serious aspects. Whether the struggle between the plutocracy and the middle class could be narrowly delimited and carried on indefinitely with the weapons and arguments evolved during the past fifty years became a question of social philosophy, historical interpretation, and time. If it could not be so delimited and continued endlessly without resolution, what forms were the future relations of the two groups to assume, especially in the presence of labor pressures in town and country? And in a showdown what position would labor take?

A mere analysis of the two groups from the standpoint of income yielded no categorical answer. The boundaries of neither were sharply defined, but one striking feature of the period consisted of efforts to disclose the composition and propensities of the respective interests. Though it is true that William J. Ghent and Thorstein Veblen had made such attempts earlier, their findings were only dimly remembered, if at all. So fresh inquiries were "timely." Lewis Corey's analyses, The Crisis of the Middle Class and The Decline of American Capitalism, for instance, applied the Marxian hypothesis and lent countenance to the idea that the country was headed toward a proletarian dictatorship. Alfred Bingham's statistical study in Insurgent America yielded contradictory evidence: the middle class, not that of the industrial workers, was increasing in relative proportions. Franklin Charles Palm's The Middle Classes Then and Now, while tending to confirm Bingham's conclusion, ended with no upshot in respect of policy or proximate tendency. Nor did

Ferdinand Lundberg's Sixty Families, an indictment of the plutocracy, throw much light on the problem of the coming relations between the middle class and the possessors of great wealth. Still, the fervid controversies aroused by such inquiries betrayed a public interest in the subject and the existence of a tension in popular psychology that might conceivably snap if no general economic relief came in sight.

The fact that the boundaries of the plutocracy and the middle class could not be precisely drawn did not mean that their centers of economic gravity and their general characteristics were beyond the grasp of understanding. Whether sixty or six hundred families constituted the dominant element in the plutocracy — a question much debated — was irrelevant. Researches substantiated the general proposition that less than one and one-half per cent of the nation's families at the top of the economic ladder in 1935–36 received a total income which equalled the combined income of forty-seven per cent of the families at the bottom. A high concentration of wealth was a reality, if not strictly measurable.

Nor could the exact number of families in the middle class be statistically determined. In composition it included lawyers, doctors, nurses, engineers, teachers, government employees running into the millions, army and navy officers, business men and women, small employers by the thousands, the police — local, state, and federal — members and officers of the national guard, editors, publishers, actors, artists, nearly all the professional entertainers, clerks, stenographers, and the white-collar careerists in general. According to an analysis by Donald S. Bridgman, published in The Yale Review in the autumn of 1938, the census returns of 1930 showed that "of all the men in gainful occupations 26% were in white-collar positions, professional, managerial, or clerical; 16% were in the skilled crafts; 15% were farm owners or tenants; 33% were semi-skilled or unskilled laborers, very largely in industry, and 10% were farm laborers. Of the gainfully employed women, 43% were in white-collar positions; 22% were household servants; 25% were semi-skilled and unskilled laborers in industry, and 8% were in agriculture, mainly as farm laborers. In the twenty years before 1930, the most rapidly increasing occupations had been in the white-collar group, principally those of the teacher, engineer, and clerk; the major decline had been in agriculture." If to the white-collar occupational groups were added the huge leisure class, women not gainfully employed, the total student body above the grade school level, and the millions of farming families enjoying a certain degree of prosperity, the combination doubtless outnumbered the strictly industrial workers, farm hands, and other blue, brown, and no-collar workers.

There was another consideration of prime importance. The division between members of the middle class and the handworkers in town and country was by no means completely economic. Indeed the income of skilled craftsmen was often far above that of many teachers, lawyers, or stenographers. Furthermore, in the struggle over the distribution of national income, thousands of white-collar employees flocked to trade unions, at least temporarily. In the characteristics of the middle class and its tendencies were psychological elements which did not perfectly correspond to the statistics of income or property; and these psychological features seemed to become more conspicuous as the depression deepened, the unionization of industrial workers advanced, and the unemployed showed some inclination to organize.

Hitherto native oracles had indignantly scoffed at the idea of "class" in the United States as "un-American." The absence of a fixed nobility at the top of the social ladder presumably made the term "middle class" inapplicable to a central grouping in the economic scene. A remarkable degree of mobility — from rail-splitter to President, from farm girl to candy queen — had given the signs of fluidity to American society that obscured the permanence of the gradations behind the screen of rising and falling particles or individuals. When, however, the organization of mass production workers by the millions got under way, evidences of a growing consciousness of identical interests appeared among elements of the middle class, tending to effect a closer solidarity within their own ranks.

An outward sign of this consciousness was to be seen in the changed usage of the term "middle class." For more than a century the British nobility and industrial workers had employed it freely as a phrase fairly exact or invidious. The French had long distinguished the bourgeoisie, as they called the middle class, from the remnants of the old aristocracy on the one side and the peasants and industrial workers on the other. In France the bourgeoisie had been regarded as "that portion of the community to which money is the primary condition and the primary instrument of life." Late in the nineteenth century Veblen had described pecuniary Americans as the "leisure class," dedicated to conspicuous waste and demonstrative thimblerig. Still later Sinclair Lewis had characterized its members as "Babbits," at first with a tone of ridicule and afterward with a positive affection, which helped to make them conscious of their position in society and then proud of their merits. The outburst of stories about life in "the raw" and the flood of proletarian novels accentuated the idea of opposites. In terms of sober scholarship, the publication of such frank treatises as Arthur Holcombe's The New Party Politics, in 1933, served as an index of tendency and a measure of advance toward unification. Fifty years earlier, Holcombe's book would have been as offensive to the American intelligentsia of the Hamilton Wright Mabie school as Marx's Communist Manifesto actually was to the Victorians of 1848. With time a psychological alteration had been effected.

This development in psychological imagery arrested the attention of Franklin Charles Palm who published his opinions on the subject in 1936. While declining to formulate any rigid definition of the term "middle class," he gave a certain approval to an older definition as the "not-so-rich and not-so-poor individuals between the proletariat-labor group and the wealthy capitalists and social aristocracy."

Yet Palm warned his readers against ascribing too much importance to the theory of income or the theory of derivation. He insisted that the members of the middle class must be thought of as possessing "subjective impulses." For instance, the true middle-class person "prizes education because he firmly believes that education is power and because he thinks it essential to democracy. He boasts of impartiality in politics and often observes a suicidal neutrality; but he is easily swayed by demagogues, for deep within him are biases and prejudices. He wishes to be known as a self-made man, capable, independent, self-reliant. . . . Profit has become the center of his thought and every action is in terms of that one purpose — to make money." In the past, money-making had been deemed an occupation on the way to a comfortable retirement; in the present, it had become a kind of continuous steeplechase, monopolizing energies, directing activities, and creating the values of culture.

While Lewis Corey, applying the Marxian theory, thought he saw the middle class diminished in numbers and force by the course of economy and furnishing some potential materials for the labor movement, other observers agreed with Palm in emphasizing the permanence of subjective consciousness and the growth of class awareness among the middle group. Unemployed industrial workers may have regarded themselves as covered by Franklin D. Roosevelt's phrase, "the forgotten man," but Herbert Hoover, pleading for a return of the Republicans to power, placed the forgotten man in the "great economic middle class." Noting the preponderance of cities in public affairs, Arthur Holcombe declared that "our new urbane politics will be middle-class politics" — less selfishly conceived than in previous times. Using income as his measurement, he claimed that, if one-half of the white-collar workers and one-fourth of the skilled workers stayed in the fold, the middle class "would surpass the proletariat in the adult population as a whole." Hewing to the median line of the Greek thinkers in antiquity, Holcombe concluded that "a State which is governed by the middle class is not only safer than proletarian and bourgeois class States, but the best State practically obtainable." This was no surrender to the theory of middle-class defeat; it was a declaration of faith and a call to liberal action.

Moreover, a study of small enterprises, conducted by the Twentieth Century Fund and published in 1936, reported an enormous area of economic activities still occupied by small enterprisers, despite the concentration of wealth, demonstrating the tenacity with which members of the middle class clung to their way of life and subjective purposes. Taking up this line, Robert L. Duffus contended nearly ten years after the crack of 1929 that there were no signs that the middle class was being crushed. "We are still overwhelmingly a middle-class nation," he maintained. "It is harder today to conceive of a solid proletarian lump in the United States than it was a generation ago. We can, of course, conceive a proletariat — in fact President Roosevelt defined one when he referred to the 'one third' which is ill-nourished, ill-clothed, and ill-housed. This one-third would include the worst-off portion of farm renters, share croppers, and laborers, the unskilled worker in every field, and no doubt many clerical workers. The Negro, largely for historical reasons, would contribute heavily to it. But it is doubtful if the Mississippi field hand, the tenant farmer in Arkansas, the migratory fruit picker in California, the 'mucker' on an excavation job, the young clerk in Houston or New York, the country school teacher whose rewards certainly place her in the lowest third of the income groups, the textile operative, the Maine fisherman, have a sense of unity among themselves merely because their incomes are low. The routine of their lives, the geographical conditions which surround them, and the local cultures in which they are embedded, forbid."

If the Wagner Labor Relations Act, the National Wages and Hours Act, the heavy taxes on incomes in support of social legislation, and the growth of organization among the industrial workers all indicated that by some process labor in town and country was exerting pressure on members of the middle class, despite its disunity, the middle class was still motivated by the old subjective forces. "The upper-bracket owning classes can take care of themselves," exclaimed the editor of a small newspaper. "The unorganized middle class has no lobby, no special pleaders. It is largely the middle classes who pay the taxes, take out insurance, own their own homes, support the charities, and form the consuming public. When taxes go up they are the first to suffer. When prices go up their more inelastic incomes feel the hardest pinch. When monopolies expand their stores, shops, and little factories are gobbled up. And if inflation comes their savings are wiped out." Having put forward this thesis, by no means perfect in its economics, the same editor warned his readers that the middle class would not be trampled upon, that it would revolt before it succumbed to the tendency of things.

Other features in the drift of human relations fortified rather than uprooted the subjective interests that characterized the middle class. Although thousands from that general order affiliated with industrial unions, other thousands, forced downward in the wage scale or into unemployment, developed resentments against the more fortunate laborers and skilled workers. Even within the working class in the strict sense were cultural propensities over-reaching the limitations of the class line. The ability to buy furniture, radios, rugs, musical instruments, automobiles, and other signs of the middle standard on the installment plan, often with no payment down, awakened ambitions among rural and urban workers, which countered the acceptance of proletarian ways.

Still more significant, in this relation, was the curtailment of child labor state by state as the depression dragged on, the raising of the working age by legislation, and the enlargement of the school population. Boys and girls in the high schools were not taught merely the crafts of their parents, if any; they studied languages, literature, science, and the other branches of learning once deemed the peculiar possession of the middle and upper classes. The chances of satisfying the tastes thus awakened might be relatively declining; the subjective valuations were not thereby eradicated. Girls, hoping to leap the economic gulf by marriage, asserted the appropriate airs and manners. Wives of industrial workers, though often standing stanchly by their husbands in economic conflicts, naturally felt the pull of the middle-class ambitions exerted by their children.

Amusements, no less than education and refinements, flowed in the middle-class direction, especially the most popular: radio entertainments and the moving pictures. The sales "talks" that accompanied music, the news, jokes, and crooning over the radio stimulated wants not to be satisfied by the meager earnings of the ordinary worker. By the hour and day, wives listened to appeals to vanities and aspirations beyond the reach of the low wage level.

In endless profusion, the moving pictures portrayed the lives of the rich, the luxurious, the idle — their palaces, yachts, sports, manners, and morals. The delineation of plain labor on the screen offered no glamourous escape from the humdrum and appeared seldom in the repertoires of the blocked picture houses, seeking the patronage of the workers. To be sure, the portrayal of crime and racketeering did suggest outlets for sons and daughters of the proletariat into the world of high living, and moving-picture producers took advantage of the "appeal" — an appeal scarcely diminished by the hackneyed retribution that now and then sicklied over the primordial drive of the main argument. But as against the steady and remorseless flicker of middle-class valuations in script, costumes, and actions, the representation of crimes of crude passion seemed merely collateral or incidental. While millions might belong to industrial unions, the pressure of education and amusement worked against belief in the nobility of plain labor — against reliance upon the organization of labor as more than a negotiating convenience — and in favor of other valuations essentially middle class in origin and development.

For the fortification of their interests, deliberately or incidentally, members of the middle class were closely knit in innumerable organizations peculiarly their own : chambers of commerce, local, state, and national women's clubs, the Sons and Daughters of the American Revolution and other patriotic societies, trade associations, fraternal orders, teachers', lawyers', and doctors' associations, and kindred groups, with branches in every community and head offices in great cities. Whenever by direct action or through political pressure, industrial workers achieved some gain irritating to the middle class or rejected the middle-class idea of American values, reverberations followed in the form of resolutions, protests, and counter-measures. Despite the best occasional efforts to be "objective" in reporting, the metropolitan press by headline, position, selection, and emphasis in news presentation, was primarily middle class in attitudes.

That conspicuous organization in the domain of politics and police, the American Legion, together with its feminine auxiliaries, was likewise primarily middle class in official direction, notwithstanding the number of industrial workers among its members and among the veterans as a whole. Although it early berated war profiteers and plutocrats, the Legion grew more circumspect in statements, especially after securing the outright payment of the bonus in 1936; and its weight was, on the whole, against the independent organization of industrial workers, against sit-down strikes, and against all similar manifestations of labor power. While it sometimes frowned upon members who wore soldiers' uniforms in making anti-labor demonstrations, its code of public and private morals was middle class in materiality.

With mechanical regularity until 1938 the National Association of Manufacturers, at its annual conventions, repeated stereotyped doctrines. The manufacturers' economic science long consisted of formulas taken from the body of true faith evolved by classical or middle-class economics.

None of its committees investigated the actions of employers in hiring industrial spies, planting provocative agents in the midst of trade unions, setting working men against one another, importing thugs and ex-criminals as strike breakers. Not unnaturally, it was more concerned with racketeers in the labor movement, with making labor organizations responsible before the law, with preventing the growth of powerful bargaining organizations among industrial workers.

"The closed shop," ran its manifesto in 1937, "limits and prevents the free and full exercise by both employees and employers of their bargaining rights. . . . The practical problems of employment relations — the handling of complaints and grievances, and questions of wages, hours, and working conditions — can best be met by management dealing with its own employees in the light of the local plant and community conditions." Corporations might be national in scope and power; labor relations must be controlled by local management. In other words, at the end of eight years of depression, organized manufacturing in the United States had little more affection for independent trade unionism or its tactics than had the National Socialistic dictatorship in Germany. It was lack of power rather than of will that prevented it from laying down the national law on the subject.

But at its convention of 1938 the National Association of Manufacturers modified its former program in many respects. The faction that demanded forthright denunciations and assertions of doctrine in the historic style was overborne by the more liberal wing. The customary attacks on the New Deal were omitted, the usual criticisms of recent federal legislation were toned down, and an olive branch was offered to organized labor. In a program adopted without dissent, the Association called for a "united effort of industry, commerce, agriculture, and labor in coöperation with the Government." Instead of condemning the Labor Relations Act wholesale, it recognized that "employees who wish to bargain collectively are entitled to do so, in whatever form they determine, through their own freely chosen representatives and without intimidation or restraint from any source." Through many lines of the program gleamed the old animus of intransigence, but it was significant that the Association felt it necessary in deference to facts and opinions to move a little "leftward" toward the center of the line.

That section of the middle class represented by little business men and women was, on the whole, as rigid in its hostility to industrial or any other kind of unionism as the business men of larger affairs in the Manufacturers' Association. Perhaps more so. When the National Recovery Administration was launched in 1933, little business men did, it is true, coöperate with government agents in the drafting and enforcement of fair practices codes. They were as eager as their larger brethren to take advantage of the opportunity to raise prices by collective action. In the process they also accepted the collective bargaining Section of the Recovery Act but that Section, loosely drawn, did not outlaw the company or shop unions organized under the auspices of the employers. Nor, in enforcement, did it compel employers to deal with independent unions wherever they appeared. After the dissolution of the Recovery Administration under judicial decree, little business men in general joined their colleagues in welcoming a return to the "imperfect competition" that had prevailed before the advent of the experiment in collective recovery. A resurgence of economic activity the following year brought a temporary release of the tension.

After the recession of 1937 set in, little business men and women were on pins and needles again, all the more on account of the rapid advance of industrial unionism and its strike tactics in many centers. At a national conference called by the Department of Commerce early the next year, they freely expressed their sentiments and resentments in resolutions which were later modified by their executive committee for presentation to President Roosevelt. In the original resolutions they declared that "unwarranted and malicious attacks on business by administration representatives should be permanently stopped," and that "all forms of federal wage and hour regulation and legislation" should be resisted. Coming directly to the point of labor organization, the little conference demanded nothing less than a total repeal of the Wagner Labor Relations Act, and an investigation of the National Labor Relations Board, then under fire as unduly sympathetic to labor. It called for more curbs on monopolies and on government enterprises, and it went even beyond big business in demanding a total repeal of the undistributed profits tax and a curtailment of public expenditures. Having urged the Government to stay out of the labor relations field, the conference called on it to create an agency for the purpose of making loans "where financial institutions failed to function," that is, where little men and women failed to get credits at the banks. These expressions of middle-class valuations seemed illuminating for the hour and the tendencies.

Into the effervescence of subjective valuations were thrust the "lessons" of Italy and Germany. On the pretext of a communist danger, Mussolini had completely liquidated all independent trade unions and had penalized all independent labor politics. At the same time he had, beyond doubt, laid restraints on small private business and showed a special tenderness for great corporations. Would such "regimentation" be regarded in the United States as a small price to pay for the suppression or execution of labor leaders and the liquidation of "trade union domination"?

Still more instructive had been the "lesson" from industrialized Germany. There also the communist danger had been highly capitalized by Hitler and his party. Nevertheless it was obvious that, while putting down the communists with a strong hand, Hitler had been equally stringent in abolishing independent trade unions, in confiscating their funds, and in imprisoning or shooting labor leaders. The trade-union movement in Germany had been far stronger than in Italy. It embraced a larger proportion of the industrial and casual workers. It was powerfully organized and had large sums of money in its central and local treasuries. Yet independent unionism had been completely destroyed by the police and by the National Socialist storm troops, with only a little more shedding of blood than had accompanied some of the major strikes in the United States. Had this object lesson not been associated with the cruel treatment of Jews in Germany, it would doubtless have been more impressive as indicating the ultima ratio.

The simplicity of the formula was startling: Brand all labor unions, especially of the industrial type, as communist and, while making a social war on communists, suppress all labor organizations. It had been done. It could be done. Although such suggestions were probably depressing to tender minds in the middle class, the employment of spies and provocative agents by great corporations, the speed with which the business forces of any industrial center could be mobilized against "labor agitators," and the tenacity of the vigilante and Ku Klux tradition indicated the existence of volcanic forces beneath the white surface of law and order and the smooth flow of "democratic processes." "If Fascism ever menaces America," wrote an editor, "it will be because we have allowed the big pressure groups of society to squeeze the middle classes into revolt."

That the editor's middle class and the Lords of Creation, with whose fortunes, instincts, and methods it was so intimately affiliated, were possessed by no spirit of genial tolerance in the presence of labor agitations, urban or rural, became manifest in endless declarations and actions. In his volume, You Can't Do That, George Seldes gave a multitude of illustrations well authenticated, and added, for the benefit of those who cared to know more, a list of books, pamphlets, and documents occupying more than forty pages of fine print. Stark and staring before such intelligence as the nation commanded were the pages of testimony presented by informed witnesses to the Senate committee on education and labor, headed by Robert M. La Follette, instructed to investigate "violations of the rights of free speech and assembly and undue interference with the right of labor to organize and bargain collectively."

Indelible in the record were reports of third-degree tortures employed by police in violation of the law; arrests on trumped-up charges and no charges; police beatings in all parts of the country ending often in deaths that went unavenged; parties engaged in tarring and feathering economic dissidents; lynchings in North and South; the expulsion of critical professors and teachers; the Chicago "memorial day incident" at the Republic Steel Works; the use of spies, finks, gas, and bombs by reputable employers of labor; espionage and murder in the Harlan, Kentucky, mining regions; Mayor Hague's "little dictatorship" in Jersey City; the insistence of the Daughters of the American Revolution, members of the American Legion, the Liberty League, the National Civic Federation, chambers of commerce, shipping interests, Crusaders, Sentinels, Vigilantes, Paul Reveres, and other associations wearing the mantle of patriotism, on branding as dangerous citizens well-known persons of independent minds, ranging from Nicholas Murray Butler to Jane Addams, from Eleanor Roosevelt to William Allen White — all denoting violent reactions to labor agitations, to the advocacy of peace, or to the defense of the civil liberties offered in constitutional guaranties — advocacy or defense even when it expressed the most timid liberalism. What anything really challenging would produce could be easily imagined, by the imaginative.

The spirit of the times which prevailed in the military establishment of the United States Government, at least from 1928 to 1932, was given official form in its Army Training Manual No. 2000–25, issued for the instruction of officers and soldiers. Not content with its own function, the War Department entered the domain of civic education and among other things gave its verdict on democracy, for which presumably

soldiers had fought and died, and in the name of which, perhaps, a quarantine war was in preparation. In a single
paragraph it described democracy for the benefit of its men
in training: "Democracy: A government of the masses.
Authority derived through mass meeting or any other form
of 'direct' expression. Results in mobocracy. Attitude
toward property is communistic — negating property rights.
Attitude toward law is that the will of the majority shall
regulate, whether it be based upon deliberation or governed
by passion, prejudice, and impulse, without restraint or
regard to consequences. Results in demagogism, license,
agitation, discontent, anarchy." For five years this manual
of "instruction" was used officially by the War Department
— until protests from outraged citizens and members of
Congress led to its withdrawal. After that action a request
for a copy brought a reply that the Department had no copy
available; a three-hour search in the Congressional Library
unearthed none; everywhere in official circles, silence on the
subject reigned, when inquiries were made. Was the spirit
that animated military opinion on democracy dead?

Two years after the Manual was formally withdrawn,
doubts on that subject were allayed by Harry H. Woodring,
Assistant Secretary of War under Franklin D. Roosevelt.
In the Liberty Magazine, of January 6, 1934, Mr. Woodring
published an article on the Army, opening with the words:
"People who believe that the United States Army is not
ready and able to take charge of this nation in an emergency
simply do not know the facts. Our Army happens to be the
only branch of the Government which is *already organized
and available not only to defend our territory, but also to cope
with social and economic problems in an emergency.* [Mr.
Woodring's italics.] It is our secret insurance against chaos.
It is our 'ace in the hole' for peace as well as war." In this
vein he continued, to prove the point. The execution of the
Army's plans for industrial mobilization, he said, will "*accomplish in a large measure the purpose of those who have advocated
a 'universal draft' of property, money, and civilian labor*"

[Mr. Woodring's italics]. He went on: "It is my opinion that the Army *should* take over immediately some of the activities which are now being handled by some of the new executive agencies. Whether or not it is true, as many hold, that the C.C.C. camps are the forerunners of the great civilian labor armies of the future, I believe that this activity should be expanded and put under the control of the Army. . . . If the Army were so directed, it could organize the veterans of the world war, the C.C.C. men, and through them the administration of the emergency relief, into a system of economic storm troops that could support the Government's efforts to smash the depression. If the Army is not so directed, it will, as always, stand by and await orders."

"Let's speak frankly!" Mr. Woodring declared in large italic type; "*If this country should be threatened with foreign war, economic chaos, or social revolution, the Army has the training, the experience, the organization, and the men to support the Government and direct the country in the national interest.*"

Up until 1934 both law and innocence had supposed that it was the duty of the Army, when officially ordered, to wage foreign war or suppress domestic insurrection. They had not supposed that its obligation included a responsibility in case of "economic chaos" to "direct the country in the national interest." Evidently the War Department, under the New Deal, had made progress — of some kind — in a direction straight as a bullet's course.

When a deluge of telegrams and letters deprecating Mr. Woodring's manifesto in the Liberty magazine flowed into the White House, accompanied by demands for a removal or resignation, President Roosevelt called the author on the carpet. Shortly after the conference, Mr. Woodring gave out a statement to the effect that his words did not mean what they meant to anybody acquainted with the English language. The President did not ask him to retire. He did not resign. The oblivion common to a people that lived on the day's sensations passed over the episode. On the death of Secretary Dern, President Roosevelt made Assistant Secretary Woodring head of the War Department.

Against all such tendencies, protests were made continuously in press, pamphlets, books, meetings, and the courts of law. The American Civil Liberties Union, directed by Roger Baldwin and a group of determined colleagues, innumerable associations concerned with the preservation of rights guaranteed by the Constitution of the United States and the constitutions of the several states, innumerable individuals, and members of Congress kept close watch on activities, organizations, and officials connected with "red baiting," the suppression of legal rights, and propaganda intended to prepare the way for the day prophesied by Harry H. Woodring, President Roosevelt's Secretary of War.

Another sign of determined resistance to the arbitrary spirit was the Southern Conference for Human Welfare held at Birmingham, Alabama, in November, 1938, representing agriculture, industry, labor, and social work. Every form of effort designed to raise the standard of living in that region and to assert the human values of society was discussed with freedom and comprehensively. Tenant farmers, representatives of labor defense organizations, Negroes from various divisions of economy, employers, and specialists in housing, relief, and taxation presented their cases without let or hindrance. And at the close, provisions were made for a permanent pooling of interests and for moving in a solid phalanx upon the menaces to liberty and welfare everywhere in the South.

If a crisis was to come, victory for tyranny would not be easy or be won in a default. Many lawyers, including Frank Walsh, Morris Ernst, and Arthur Garfield Hays, offered their services to defend men and women in celebrated cases involving freedom of press and speech; and even the American Bar Association, spurred on perhaps by the formation of an independent legal society, the Lawyers' Guild, announced in 1938 that it would give special attention to civil liberty. From term to term the Supreme Court of the

United States handed down ringing decisions sustaining civil liberties, North, South, East, and West, in opinions worthy of a place beside the memorable arguments of Mansfield, Burke, Erskine, and Brougham, which featured the slow and toilsome advance of human rights in times past. It might so turn out that those who had been most severe in criticizing that tribunal's judgments in other causes would find it the last refuge against sheer force — if Secretary Woodring's "economic chaos" and "emergency" came, and dust gathered in the silent chamber of the United States Senate.

§

Given the numerical supremacy of the middle class, as the term was casually defined, over urban workers and rural laborers, given its subjective valuations and the lessons of Italy and Germany, limitations on the power of industrial unionism were apparent to all informed observers in the labor movement and outside. The tensibility of those circumscriptions could not be discovered by any method of scientific inquiry at hand. Efforts to test them by practice, if pushed too far, might produce the explosion faintly suggested by "A plague on both your houses." Anything like an exact prognosis was, therefore, out of the question. The amount of elasticity or good-will on both sides remained indeterminate if not indeterminable in both economics and politics. That astute, persistent, and viable statesmanship in the two domains might mitigate conflicts and keep them within the confines of debate and adjustment, apart from sporadic disorders, was probable. As Edmund Burke had said in the eighteenth century, greater changes may be effected gradually over a long period of time than by even the violence of revolution. But how much of this statesmanship was available?

Only one feature of the situation seemed fairly plain. If the prevailing system of economy could be kept running at a certain tempo, a major crisis could be avoided for the time;

that is, if production could be maintained on a level of output that would furnish employment for a large part of the industrial workers, provide revenues for supporting the unemployed on some scale of existence, and sustain the main body of the middle class, a disruptive tension could be indefinitely postponed. The size of the social and State apparatus at the command of the middle class seemed to demonstrate that proposition.

Could production be held on the requisite level and for how long? No one could settle that question. Only one aspect of the problem presented deterministic marks. For three hundred years the high productivity of American economy had been accompanied by the steady exhaustion of land and other natural resources either irreplaceable or replaceable at a high cost. A continuation of that process for another fifty or hundred years, as the engineers of a Mississippi Valley survey had reported, would lead to a wholesale impoverishment of the resources on which American economy had thrived. Only costly collective action coupled with incalculable inventive genius could prevent that impasse in the years immediately ahead. Was the collective action possible, the genius available? Not even the highest competence in the middle class could answer that question.

If domestic tension grew perilous and the productive economy slowed down too far, the explosion into a foreign war was always possible. There had been international frictions ever since the establishment of national States in Europe at the end of the middle ages. Such frictions had been somewhat mitigated in the nineteenth century while the resources of virgin continents were being exploited to feed Europe's pullulating millions, but with the closing of such economic frontiers everywhere the tensions seemed to be increasing. At all events, the statesmen of the leading powers of the world were lecturing and threatening one another, either in earnest or "for domestic consumption." "International" incidents were matters of almost daily occurrence.

War and costly preparations for war were at command. War would speed up industrial economy and once more provide employment. It would enable the Federal Government to put through its "mobilization bill," impose the discipline of martial law upon all recalcitrant persons, and, by "constitutional methods," suppress strikes and labor disturbances as effectively as Hitler or Mussolini had done under a different ideology. But what would a war do to American civilization as historically understood, even if victoriously waged? Or if it ended in defeat for the United States — a possibility, given the shifts and clashes among the great powers — what then? Neither event could be precisely prophesied, but both questions were vibrating in the minds of all Americans who employed intelligence in exploring the relations of urban and rural labor to grand policy.

In terms of civilization, the fortunes, the future, of America, what then did the activities, agitations, and organization of labor in town and country actually mean? To that quandary many solutions, more or less relevant, were proposed. Anthropologists and measurers of intelligence responded that a large proportion of Americans consisted of "morons" and little or nothing could be done about that "fact." In a similar vein practitioners replied that, on the whole, tenants, croppers, and field laborers were "lazy and shiftless"; that they had received their "just deserts"; that the plight of agriculture as mirrored in the report of the President's Committee was simply the outcome of human nature operating on the land; and that restless industrial workers possessing no craft or special skill got all or more than they deserved in the natural, that is, the current, run of things. A multitude of "misfits" had always existed in industry and agriculture and always would. On the basis of such interpretations, the upper third or fourth, or whatever it was, in industry and agriculture could and should proceed as in the past, relying upon the agencies of government for the protection of the fortunate position accorded to them by their merits. If not completely reassuring, this was comforting to the beneficiaries in the upper ranges.

Yet when it was conceded that the situation was due to the moronic, shiftless, and casual nature of labor in town and country, other quandaries remained. Were the white misfits to be deprived of the vote, as Negroes had been in large areas of the country? A strong movement in this direction took form in the North, with a nervous woman as its instigator. If not, how could the upper third or fourth, or whatever its size was, be indefinitely protected against the inroads of politicians and "demagogues" upon their apparently impregnable position? If not, how could prolonged agitation of the business be avoided? Assuming that the "misfit" men and women could be deprived of the suffrage extended to them during the early fevers of democracy in the United States or that the use of the ballot could be rather effectively nullified by a temporary or prolonged use of military power, what of the democratic ideals to which fervent appeals were made, for diplomatic and other purposes, against dictatorships in Europe and the Orient? If these vaunted ideals could be rendered harmless, or supplanted by other devices, there remained a final enigma not to be solved in terms of "just deserts for morons": Is mankind a maker or a victim of history?

§

Underneath the course of the great argument and the emotions that attended it was the drift of economic activities and physical facts upon which even the upper ranges depended for their rewards and security — against which the rhetoric of satisfaction or criticism could avail little. These facts were recorded in the reports of corporations and business concerns — industries and railways — and in the findings of engineers who surveyed the state and utilization of natural resources. Instead of the swift expansion in construction and capital goods industries, which had long furnished the élan of advancing capitalism, had come a definite contraction; in that sense, the real capital of the United States was declining, not rising. The mileage of railways was shrinking; no huge demand for steel rails and locomotives in the old style was anywhere in sight. Nor did the "backward places" of the earth — Latin America, the Orient, and Africa — to which imperialism had looked for such expansion, present the familiar aspects of the nineteenth century. Unemployment on a large scale continued persistently, with no substantial relief in sight. As capitalism contracted, the depletion of crude natural resources upon which industries had flourished and still depended went on, if abated somewhat by the depression.

Both tenancy and freehold agriculture as historically practiced had led and were still leading to a depletion of vast regions, the erosion of the soil, the destruction of fertility, and the impoverishment of the land. If nothing effective could be done in respect of rising tenancy, then physical exhaustion would persist, perhaps at an accelerating speed. If the standard of life on the land, the buying power of farmers, sank, what of the industry, commerce, and professions upon which hung the fate of the upper ranges in cities and towns, all the more now that the promises of imperialism had been exploded by history as actuality?

CHAPTER XII

Sources and Forces of Entertainment

HEAVILY as the pall of the depression rested upon the country — perhaps partly on account of it — entertainment assumed functions of increasing significance for the tendencies of culture. Springing from biological and psychological characteristics common to humanity in all times, it perdured in this time and was adjusted to alterations in the economic conditions in which politics, business, and labor operated, by which they were nourished. Originally, and still in some measure, what Veblen called "a non-mechanical factor of culture," entertainment, was imbedded in the social heritage acquired from the pre-machine age. Primal in emotional sources, apparently as necessary to life as labor itself, entertainment was among the powerful forces that held society together, afforded diversion in the midst of its difficulties and burdens, and yet expressed its tensions and values too, contributing withal to the shaping of its evolution in gross and detail. When commercialized, entertainment could cut two ways: it could thrive like business enterprise on the social heritage; and, like business enterprise with which it

577

became increasingly associated, it could work disintegrations in the social heritage. Its twofold nature was not overlooked in the drift of events.

§

Throughout the ages of civilization the amusements, spectacles, and ceremonies of the people had borne an intimate relation to politics, economy, poverty, riches, labor, leisure, the arts, tools, and intelligence of mankind. Among primitive and rural peoples they were, in origins at least, more or less spontaneous expressions of usages, ecstasies, and motor propensities connected with life and labor processes, such as planting, sowing, harvesting, and with religious interpretations and rituals. Among such peoples diversions were communal, non-pecuniary, little affected if at all by importations, and not devised for export or sale abroad. Processions in propitiation of harvest gods and goddesses, for example, were connected with economic activities indispensable to life, but they were not designed to propitiate the god of the box office or to serve the purposes of the State.

After the State had risen upon the foundations of communal life, its masters seized upon and used, for their purposes, amusements, spectacles, and entertainments, employing and adding to ancient rituals. State diversions were connected with both domestic and outward relations. In Sparta, for example, wrestling and horse racing served a double purpose: they kept the ruling class and its animals physically fit to maintain supremacy over helots and slaves at home and to wage war abroad. In the days of Spartan power, young people of the ruling families, boys and girls alike, took part in athletic displays and pageants and the laurel wreath was deemed a sufficient reward for demonstrations of strength and endurance. When a king's daughter, Cynisca, who kept racing horses, won a victory at a spectacle, she received no purse of gold; the feat and the acclaim were sufficient in themselves. Spartan youths were trained in legends and music and dancing, intrinsically delightful. And yet, like such gymnastics as ball playing, dancing was directed toward the cultivation of martial vigor.

Likewise in the development of the Roman State from kingdom through the republic into empire, the character of amusements and entertainments followed the course of its civilization, until it reached a climax in the deadly gladiatorial contests. As Rome expanded, city mobs were spurred to militaristic hysteria by pageants of conquerors coming home with kings and queens chained to their chariots. Whether really essential to a militaristic polity or not, savage spectacles certainly accompanied the rise and flowering of that system. Generally associated with the fighting passion was sex sadism and this was fed by the tossing of Christian maidens to hungry lions in the circus.

Originating, it seems, in the ancient Etruscan custom of sacrificing slaves and prisoners on the tombs of great warriors, the gladiatorial spectacle became a favorite device of emperors, employed to illustrate their prowess and satisfy the growing mania of multitudes inured to cruel sights and sounds. Titus, it was said, ordered a continuous combat extending over one hundred days, and Trajan celebrated a triumph by the exhibition of ten thousand gladiators. The victims thrown into the arena were taken from prisoners of war, criminals, and slaves — men and women alike being driven into death grapples for the amusement of cheering and jeering throngs. Black lusts were drained to the dregs when human beings and wild beasts were pitted against each other for the pleasure of the Roman proletariat and the lords and ladies of the upper classes. A Marcus Aurelius might turn away from such spectacles to write state papers or to meditate upon the nature and sorrows of mankind, but the crowds that applauded and sustained the empire gloated over such displays of violence and judged successive rulers by the number and magnitude of the brutal shows which they staged for "the people." Such were the diversions of despotism at home while imperialistic wars were waged on the frontier — until the twin monstrosities perished and owls cried from out the palace of the Caesars.

Also intimately associated with the State were the amusements, spectacles, and entertainments of Japan under the Tokugawa shogunate. Athletic exercises for men and women, designed to keep bodies lithe for military purposes continued; but the supreme design of the Tokugawas was to subdue belligerent feudal lords to the discipline of the State and hold Japan insulated from conflicts with the outside world. To this polity diversions were subordinated, even when ancient rituals were retained or modified. The State desired concord at home and refrained from aggression abroad. Hence the fighting class had to be entertained in the interests of peace. Gladiatorial contests would have been out of line. It was rhapsodies over cherry blossoms and plum trees, over moon and mushroom, over fans and the holy mountain, Fujiyama, that were lifted to the height of cults. The ritual of the tea ceremony in an esthetic setting, made still more exquisite by poems, music, and specific apparel, was devised to soothe the nerves of feudal lords; while pilgrimages to view scenes of beauty and holy places supplied pleasure for peasants, serfs, and artisans. For the ends of State, under Tokugawa management, diversions took on pacific forms and lusty fighting men were restrained by the bonds of ceremony and esthetics. Though these bonds quickly gave way after the imperialist powers of the West blew open the gates of Japan and the Japanese State in its turn embarked on conquest, the diversions themselves did not immediately disappear. The tea ceremony became more and more the prerogative of women, but all the ceremonies lingered to give a "quaint" flavor to a civilization grown imperialist in ambition and taste.

If to Americans with little interest in history the records of entertainment in the past and of current practices inherited from distant times and countries seemed mere musty documents in the days of the golden glow, the development of fascism and communism and the rise in western civilization of the Nazi cult of "Blood" gave to the unhistoric-minded immediate and astounding examples of the relations which could exist between the State and diversions. Playing upon the instincts of wanton cruelty, Hitler turned his men loose on the Jews in a manner reminiscent of Roman holidays when Christians were the victims, without organizing this operation into a State pageant. He laid his heavy hands on every form of amusement. Mussolini and Stalin did the same. Giant parades and rituals, the tramp, tramp, tramp of men and women drilled in military manners, with modern lighting casting its exotic appeal, furnished spectacles that might have made a Claudius or a Nero green with envy. The theater, the film, athletics, and even ancient folkways were bent and twisted and subdued to the designs of a military State — a dictatorship — whatever avowed social and economic ends were associated with it. Down to the kindergarten in Germany and Italy were forced the militaristic rituals of amusement. Almost as soon as they could toddle, little boys were supplied with implements of war and their supple limbs and minds were trained to the configurations of war games. Huge masses of people, young and old, were goaded along the path to political and military aggression by the very diversions arranged for them, with the privilege of dying for the dictator as the crown and perfection of hysterical entertainment.

§

In the United States, with its democratic traditions and practices, with the historic subordination of the military arm of the Government to civilian leadership, with the State regarded as an instrument not an end, with the prevalence of pecuniary over political considerations, amusements, spectacles, and entertainments presented aspects appropriate to the milieu and the trend of affairs. Here too were survivals of diversions associated with ancient folkways, kept alive by aborigines, by white natives in farming regions, and by immigrants from rural communities abroad. But in the main, since the rise of cities, other forms of diversion had occupied the principal interest — that is, commercialized amusements, whatever their sources, substance, and appearances. Artificial entertainment, shaped with reference to the financial returns of managers and participants, occupied an ever-larger area of diversion, ranging from prize fights, with huge receipts for directors and fighters, to the gigantic spectacles manufactured by the moving-picture industry. Being essentially pecuniary in motive and thus depending directly upon the state of economy — prosperity or depression — the fortunes of commercial entertainment varied with the fortunes of the middle class, industrial workers, and farmers who supplied box office receipts. For the moment, at all events, the people of the United States showed few signs of devotion to drill-sergeant pleasures. Although standardized products spread, the regionalisms and polyglot population of the country still afforded variations. In the Far West, Indians could indulge in their ceremonies and go so far as to ridicule the white man's tin cans, archaeologists, and social workers. Throughout the nation Jews, Irish, Yankees, Italians, and Negroes could figure in the moving pictures, have theaters of their own, and be amused by themselves and one another. The subjection of them all to a Nordic, Roman, or Muscovite diagram would have been a difficult undertaking, notwithstanding susceptibilities to nostrums during the economic distress.

For a long time, the democratic manners, the comparative freedom, and the relative ease of life in the United States had found expression in corresponding diversions — often called trivial and vulgar by European commentators on American civilization. Though Europeans also had prize fights and music halls, critics of America were inclined to remember only the amusements provided for the upper classes at home, such as fox hunting and cricket, royal garden parties and pageants, and coronation shows. In the United States "everybody" took part in shows of some kind, if only in rollicking laughter over representations of human follies.

Americans were fond of parades, but they did not want parades all the time. They displayed marked propensities for violence in widely scattered, though numerous, cases, but they were neither attuned to the mass shock of the totalitarian violence, deliberately organized and buttressed by fear, nor to the inelastic class distinctions of England and continental countries.

More than once in their history Americans had been subdued to the imperialistic or militaristic psychosis, but they had always displayed resilient powers of release. A nation that had been almost one hundred per cent for war in 1917 could, twenty years later, cast a majority vote in a popular poll for the proposition that it had been a big mistake. When veterans of the world war held annual reunions, they listened, more or less dutifully, to speeches on preparedness and military virtues; but they were more interested in pranks than in anything else. After a week of reunion, they would disband amiably and ride home with their wives in their "old busses" to take up again their customary entertainments — poker playing, bridge, moving-picture shows, baseball games, back slapping, and joke cracking in barrooms and clubs. All this was in keeping with the physical ease corresponding to democratic liberties — a safety valve for distempers and, what is more, a certain pledge against the wholesale fanaticism required for the totalitarian State. If argument could not overcome a Caesar nourishing personal ambitions, people who preferred laughing at slap-stick comedies on the screen to goose-stepping for anybody or anything might conceivably be unable to take a dictator seriously enough to underwrite his schemes.

The old democratic practice of applauding, hissing, and talking back, so foreign to life in Power States, helped to keep alive the looseness and diversity of amusements that in turn nourished democratic sentiments. Since he was not watched by the police, a radio owner could simply turn off the boresome propagandist, crooner, story teller, politician, or announcer, without the risk of a police summons to answer for his conduct. When the people did not like an advertised moving picture they could stay at home or walk out of the theater. Though much given to bathos themselves upon occasion, they also had a flair for the absurd and were restless under any harping on one string. If they approved a film, they sent in "fan" letters voluntarily. If they disapproved, they could and often did deluge producers with protests, criticisms, and denunciations, write letters to the newspapers, and form organizations to strengthen their opposition. And the efforts of commercialized entertainers to catch pennies from every direction kept them alert to the endless turbulence of dissidence.

"To give the people what they want" was to swell box-office receipts; and evidently the people wanted, not one pattern of life, but many. Buying their pleasures in an open market, crowded with competitive offerings, they insisted on exercising the powers of choice vouchsafed to them by their impulses and the opportunities before them. Whether amid this swirling, buzzing diversity, definite and irreversible tendencies were leading toward social forms, higher or lower, or fundamentally different from prevailing customs, was a subject of unwearied speculation, culminating in no settled conclusions.

Nevertheless the very clarity with which the relation of the State to entertainment was brought out in imported films and plays, coupled perhaps with the contraction of American economy and the attendant agitations, excited a finer sensitiveness to the relations between so-called diversions on the one side and government and society on the other. The problem, well known to the historians of morals, came under wider discussion, both popular and philosophical; for even the most casual seeker after release in the United States was subjected to the impacts of scenes depicting armies, red, green, brown, blue, or black, with flags waving and bands leading them on the march. The goose-step of the mind might be vague and shadowy. The pictured goose-step on pavements and roads was visible and definitive.

If such was the upshot of entertainment dominated by a totalitarian State, where was the increasing commercialization of entertainment in the United States headed and what would be its forms and influences in the proximate future? So far the offerings were certainly varied. People were still free to choose and to buy. If the commercial entertainers were giving them "what they wanted," what did the purchases mean in terms of social tendencies? In searching for the lowest common denominators effective at the box offices, would entertainers more and more arouse "the beast that is within us," play upon fears and passions, resort to war propaganda, and portray women in approving attitudes? Or would they, by visual education, offer the people knowledge respecting the good life, the values of creative labor, and the issues of American economy, thus forwarding the quest for the maintenance at least of such civilization as had been developed out of ideals and practices? Since entertainment was now highly commercialized and concentrated, would it follow the practices of centralization so common in capitalist economy and induce regimentation under private auspices? Obviously such questions were far more fundamental than the thought of ordinary dramatic and theatrical criticism.

§

Cultural interests were given new forms of expression by the general introduction, in 1928, of the talking picture which, by rapid inroads upon the industry, soon captured the business. Talking-picture entertainers had to supplement acting by speech and the necessity of employing speech involved the use of words, that is, ideas of some kind. As a result the whole structure of the motion-picture play could be and indeed had to be reorganized. For the vast spectacles of the silent picture, costly to film, could be substituted in the talking pictures the simpler and more compact drama of life in home, club, resort, field, or office, in which mere conversations, orders, and repartee helped to carry the story.

Gesture and facial play had been the reliances of the silent picture — the pantomime. Now sound was geared to ideas, to emotions, and to their visible expressions. But ideas could be conventional, trivial, and commonplace — or creative, provocative, and powerful, whether on high planes or low. Suddenly, therefore, a pantomime industry faced new intellectual problems of some sort. At the same time audiences were brought into a changed relation to the cinema: they now had to use ears as well as eyes and were incited to talk back or at least think back. Thus the psychological aspects of the screen entertainment became more complicated.

As the talking-picture industry made strides in production and projection, the mechanical features were refined. Diction was watched. There were improvements in photography, in the manipulation of light, and in other technical matters, all of which enriched the flexibility, phantasy, power, and artistry of motion-picture entertainment. Color was even introduced though its cost hampered its general use. Taken in combination with various original and supplementary devices, the talking film transformed the motion-picture industry as the country groped its way from one depression to another.

Meanwhile the economic basis of the motion-picture industry underwent a revolution. As the devices employed in production and projection increased in number, intricacy, and cost, many sorts of industries engaged in manufacturing and processing were brought into close relations with the business. This was especially true of the electrical industries. Scenting potential profits in a growing enterprise, financiers showed an increasing interest in the cinema and applied to it the methods which had been so successful in railways, steel, and utilities — successful, that is, from the standpoint of bankers. At early stages in their development, production and distribution in the picture industry had taken corporate form; stocks had been issued and sold to the public; and in some cases bonds had been laid under the stocks. In the natural course, the securities of leading picture concerns were listed on the exchanges and the customary devices of Wall Street adopted in "churning" picture stocks in the market. While related industries and financiers were becoming more closely interlinked with the picture industry, producers and distributors, as their undertakings enlarged, often found it necessary to resort to bankers for credits, short-term loans, and other facilities. As a result, when the panic arrived in 1929, the chief producers and distributors were entangled in the corporate structures of general industry and in the banking and stock-exchange practices soon to be ventilated by Senate committees bent on discovering how large-scale business was actually conducted in the United States.

By 1937 the major portion of the commercial production and distribution in the cinema industry was controlled by corporations, usually with complex financial structures. Some were merely producers, neither owning nor operating theaters for projection. Others combined production, distribution, and exhibition, thus maintaining studios, selling agencies, and theaters. One concern was engaged in the processing of films and, if newspaper reports could be believed, its insiders were engaged in manipulating its stocks. The Universal Corporation, organized in Delaware, the home of high finance, was a holding company. Warner Brothers, one of the leading producers, operated a chain of exhibition theaters numbering about 445. In 1938 Loew's, Incorporated, with producing and distributing subsidiaries, had outstanding $13,604,000 in bonds, a subsidiary debt of nearly $17,000,000, subsidiary preferred stocks, preferred stocks, and 1,599,053 common shares of no par value.

Like most other industries, the motion-picture business was "over-expanded." On the basis of paid admissions, it was estimated by Standard Statistics, each available theater seat was occupied less than once daily and, in view of the fact that most houses gave two or more shows daily, the industry was operating at far less than capacity — at from twenty-five to fifty per cent capacity. It was under the terrific strain that marked the conduct of business in general

— a strain to get a larger share of the consumer's dollar by reaching deeper and deeper into primordial urges.

The grip of the interlocking corporate interests on the production of motion pictures was strengthened by their control over chains of theaters for exhibition and by the practice of "block booking." Under this practice independent exhibitors were offered sets of pictures and required to take all of them as a condition of receiving any, or at least were allowed favorable discounts on quantities. In other words, in order to secure films of undoubted quality and fascination, exhibitors were forced to accept a number of mediocre films, "the run of the works."

Against the requirement, loud grumblings went up to Washington from independent exhibitors and thus the "trust-busting" issue was introduced into the motion-picture business. The Federal Trade Commission conducted investigations, members of Congress threatened drastic legislation, and from year to year the controversy continued, with the customary denunciation of corporate control and the customary praise of "the little man." On each side of the quarrel a plausible case was presented, while the practice continued in spite of the orators. Irrespective of its merits or demerits, block booking marked a tendency to centralization and standardization, and it provided outlets for numerous motion pictures of the most mechanical type, characterized by no distinction in acting or themes. The best that could be said for it was that it helped to stabilize the picture business, as a business.

Studies of the film industry showed that the larger corporations were, on the whole, in a more secure position. Profits for all producers depended mainly on success in securing "stars" who caught popular fancy and lured millions of persons to box offices. With huge funds at their disposal, the great concerns could command higher managerial talent and more "stars" than could their smaller competitors. Minor establishments that relied on two or three luminaries for success might be hopelessly crippled by the loss of a single actor or actress, while the chief establishments could weather such a loss. But large or small, motion-picture corporations ran into troubles as the depression deepened throughout the country. Estimated box-office attendance fell from 3,660,000,000 in 1929 to 2,800,000,000 in 1933. A number of companies were pinched. Radio-Keith-Orpheum went into the hands of receivers in January, 1933. The Twentieth Century-Fox Film Corporation passed through "the financial wringer," exhibiting in the process a fantastic maze of inside manipulations that made some of its imaginary screen stories tame in comparison. Even the collapse of the Van Sweringen's railway empire, so extensively underwritten by the Morgan Company at public expense, was scarcely more bizarre than the "reorganization" of the Fox Film concern.

In the end, as far as there was any end to anything in 1938, the motion-picture industry was highly centralized in financial structure, despite the intense competition for stars and box-office receipts. Bankers and Lords of Creation from other industries were vitally concerned in its operations and fate. On the boards of motion-picture companies appeared persons whose primary interest was financial. A few actors and actresses of competence and talent might still organize companies and secure audiences at one or more "legitimate" theaters, but such an operation was out of the question in the motion-picture industry, with its hordes of distributing agents and chains of exhibition houses. However whimsical prima donnas might like to be in the cinema business, corporation directors and managers were in control of the situation, combining dominance in production with the selection of artists, plays, ideas, and features for presentation to the eighty or ninety million occupants of theater seats each week. Of course corporation managers and directors, engrossed in securing large financial returns, had to consider popular interests, tastes, and vagaries, and that was frequently a gamble. What they could be sure of was that nothing distasteful to corporate trustees and managers-in-general flickered constantly, if ever, on the silver screen. Depending upon the emotions of millions, their enterprise was precarious; but, having a certain power of choice, they could assure the supremacy of what Will Hays, the Picture Czar, called "escapist" presentations. The production of such pictures, he declared, was the legitimate function of the motion-picture industry; and the result was innumerable "beautiful bores."

§

Carrying a huge burden of fixed and contingent obligations, the motion-picture industry had to keep its mind on receipts from admissions. No audience, no profits; no profits, no films. Bound by this necessity, producers and playwrights were forced to bend their energies to making pictures acceptable to the populace. In so doing they were by no means blind to the difference between art and "the business that brought home the bacon." Actors, it is true, were permitted occasionally to indulge in "skits" on their trade or profession, or whatever it was, as in Boy Meets Girl and Once in a Lifetime. And in the seclusion of his elegant office near Wall Street, New York, one of the "top-flight" Hollywood executives, while twirling his Phi Beta Kappa key, could "discuss agreeably" with an interviewer "the gaucheries and vulgarities of the cinema, as a worldly bishop might discuss the regrettable but unavoidable flaws of revealed religion." Since success in the cinema, however, like success in preaching, was based upon the magnetism of appeals to the senses of the multitudes, the educated executive was as quick as a worldly bishop to recognize the role of the "unavoidable."

Of course popular films cost a great deal of money and bankers who advanced short-term credits on the basis of hopes were mindful of the risks. Hence there could be little room for bold experimentation. In the opinion of producers what the people most wanted to see was the sex appeal. Films on that theme, devoid of any social ideology, presumably could be sold in Nazi Germany, Fascist Italy, perhaps in Communist Russia, and in Japan, the land of the Sun Goddess; and Hollywood, like Secretary Hull in the State Department, gave prayerful attention to the foreign market. So "colossal" picture producers made the most of the sex theme. And to meet the universal demand of the sexes, men and women physically attractive were given fabulous salaries for film performances — some running into hundreds of thousands of dollars a year.

An unusual feature of the latest appeal was the flaunting of sex before little boys and girls who crowded the moving-picture houses day and night. Though in countries accustomed to sex slavery, nautch girls, sing-song girls, and geisha girls learned to participate in sex entertainment in their early years, never before in America had boys and girls ranging from six to ten years of age been permitted by the millions to witness daily displays of sex enticements approaching, as near as censorship would permit, to the climax itself. Just what effect "a century of progress" in that kind of education would have upon the morale of human relations and upon the institution of the family no one could say with knowledge but, given the lust for motion-picture profits, joined to the passions of sex, that form of "progress" was certainly rapid.

It was accelerated by the fact that the young persons who paid daily or weekly attendance upon their favorites in the picture theaters were also among the avid readers of the film magazines and tabloid papers in which the divorces, escapades, and scandals of the stars were explained in words as plain as the gestures, postures, and scripts of the cinema. On the screen, the stars lived and played in romantic settings. In Hollywood they lived, played, quarrelled, and made ready for divorces, remarriages, and redivorces, in mansions no less pretentious and gaudy — all befitting their incomes and the morality of the motion-picture industry, of which they were a part.

But the cinematic adults and "the universal infantiles" who everywhere streamed past the box offices, seemed to like magic and fun as well as biology, especially weird stories about the animal kingdom. Walt Disney's Mickey Mouse, for instance, swept through the country and around the world. Only when a Disney picture imputed some disrespect for royal authority did it meet a setback abroad. After the dictator of Yugoslavia banned one such break from the strictly neutral line, the producers of Mickey Mouse had a lesson to take to heart. Untold millions had laughed when Charlie Chaplin in City Lights swallowed a policeman's whistle and then "hiccoughed a high wheeze." Untold millions laughed also at animated cartoons, such as the Silly Symphonies with their dance motifs, at illusions created by painstaking drawing and photography. In the winter of 1937–1938 Snow White and the Seven Dwarfs, a modified version of the famous fairy tale, drew throngs to ticket booths.

Apparently, the perfect entertainment, apart from sex, was the perfect illusion snatched from a world of fantasy occupied by gnomes, talking animals, and dancing quadrupeds. When George Pal arrived from Europe in 1938 with "animated puppets," speculators in the domain of profits foretold new money-making triumphs. Puppets operated by strings had been popular for more than a thousand years. Puppets made in "movie animation studios" might last longer and awaken the glee of peoples for centuries to come. At least the success of Edgar Bergen's talking automaton, Charlie McCarthy, seemed to promise huge laughs and gate receipts for interminable years. Being permitted to say what human beings wanted to say but suppressed, Charlie McCarthy became everybody's prize scapegoat.

Judging by sales returns, historical romances were apparently third in the popular appeal. Like the puppets, they offered a retreat to the land of make-believe, by using exotic scenery and costume, by placing action in remote circumstances. According to estimates of film experts, Disraeli was the favorite picture in 1929 — a story of the Jew who long promoted Tory imperialism in Britain. In the following years, while the agonies of the world war were still in memory and before preparation for another world war had approached ecstasy, Erich Maria Remarque's All Quiet on the Western Front, an importation from Germany, was enthusiastically acclaimed; so was a picture about Abraham Lincoln, who led a great war to its conclusion. In 1931 a story of pioneering in Oklahoma, Edna Ferber's Cimarron, found high favor. Then came the full force of the financial crash, interrupting somewhat the flow of historical pictures since films of that type were expensive to produce. But as business took an upward turn, the historical romance rebounded. American democrats were entertained by kings and queens in a succession of historical pictures and still more historical plays were promised during an upturn in the recession of 1938.

Sex dramas, animated fantasies, and historical romances led in a bewildering variety of pictures but the total range was wide — from news reels depicting events and personalities in the four corners of the globe, to travel reels portraying labor, economy, topography, flora, and fauna in every part of the world. Industries, laboratories, operations in hospitals, eroding fields, slashed forests, flooding rivers, growing crops, wild life, functions of government, airplane flights, battleship launchings, and social work were filmed and exhibited in large theaters for the masses or to selected audiences. Only one note was lacking in the wholesale production and distribution of moving pictures: the note struck by the authors of the dissident fiction which bulked so large in the literature of the time. In the general motion-picture output, bare portrayals of labor conflicts or films showing the plight of a third of the nation were conspicuous by their absence.

Why was this so? Those given to an economic interpretation of events had one answer: the bankers, financiers, corporation trustees, stockholders, and managers for the huge and complicated motion-picture industry, with hundreds of millions at stake, for their own reasons, did not want the conflicts of labor and the misery of a third of the nation to be advertised to their millions of customers. Possibly, however, even participants in labor struggles and sharers of the misery did not themselves wish to see their hard and drab existence represented on the screen when they were seeking forgetfulness. Louis Adamic discovered that the proletariat did not read proletarian literature. Probably it did not want to work in factories and mines in the daytime and behold factories and mines at night in the theatre. It might be that the proletariat itself preferred the realm of fantasy and romance. One film showing a labor war between the Chicago police and strikers at the Republic Steel works could arouse national excitement, but a daily stream of such graphics might have cut down the sustaining box-office receipts.

Struck by the dearth of the labor note in the mass production of the moving-picture industry, a reporter sought an explanation from Rouben Mamoulian, a foreign-born artist, who had caught glimpses of American potentialities beyond the range of most natives inured to daily use and wont. The inquirer received an expert's answer. In High, Wide, and Handsome, Mr. Mamoulian had presented a saga of oil speculation. In Porgy and Bess, based on DuBose Heyward's novel, he had given a picture of servant life in the South, enlivened by the music of Gershwin. Knowing this record, the reporter suggested that the full-length saga of American labor awaited Mamoulian's creative energies — the saga covering the insurgency of the old Knights of Labor, the Molly Maguires, the leadership of the American Federation of Labor, the uprising of the I. W. W., the company union, and State intervention under the New Deal.

Mr. Mamoulian, in replying, contrasted the comparative freedom of music, writing, and painting with the limitations of a mass-production industry dependent entirely upon huge audiences for support. "The picture industry," he said, "is no different from the underwear business, for example. It is completely governed by the law of supply and demand." Many workers in the cinema did try to put as much into pictures as they could "get away with," and "imperceptibly the audience is being influenced to look for more and more in the films. Some day the screen public may be ready for

595

your saga of labor." But the time had not come for it in 1929 or in 1938. Evidently it was not to be expected until a huge national audience was ready for it. Whether such an audience would ever be ready depended upon factors outside as well as within the picture industry.

§

Insistently as mass-production and commercialized entertainment penetrated the texture of society upon which government rests, its relation to the State received scant consideration until the vast rearmament program was authorized under the administration of Franklin D. Roosevelt. In other places and times, the State itself had maintained spectacles that regimented its subjects while undermining the morale upon which it depended in the long run. In the United States, on the other hand, the motion-picture entertainment seemed to lie wholly outside the sphere of government.

Yet, in part, the appearance was unreal. The industry was mainly corporate in form and the corporations which conducted it obtained their charters from state governments. In issuing stocks and bonds, picture companies came within the jurisdiction of the Securities and Exchange Commission in Washington. Concerns that stumbled upon evil days and underwent reorganization encountered congressional investigations and had to answer for their conduct before judges in charge of bankrupts. Under state boards of control, exhibitions were reviewed and censored. Campaign-fund collectors for political parties took cognizance of the industry's resources and in this respect the Democratic party, perhaps as the party in power, was especially favored in 1936. Rumors of legislation pertaining to antitrust practices and block-booking were bruited abroad. Far more germane to the course of civilization in America, however, was the relation of this form of mass entertainment and mass "education" to the ultima ratio of government, namely, armed force.

During American participation in the world war, the moving-picture industry had been the willing and abject servant of propaganda from Washington. After a brief season, while the war-sick nations were washing off the blood of the last conflict, the tension was relaxed. Then as politicians and warriors began to gird themselves for "strong foreign policies" and the anticipated consequences, the motion-picture industry came back into line. War pictures streamed from the studios at home and abroad for the American screen, notably The Singing Marine, Submarine D–1, Annapolis Salute, Navy Blue and Gold, Wings over Honolulu, Hold 'Em Navy, 23½ Hours Leave, Sweetheart of the Navy, You're in the Army Now (with none of the humor of the post-war comedy, You're in the Navy Now), The Road to Glory, Suzy, Professional Soldier, and Charge of the Light Brigade. British imperialism furnished two outstanding films: Lloyd's of London and Wee Willie Winkle. If Americans needed any cues in matters of production, they were aided by a British "saga in patriotism," The Big Parade of the British Navy, turned out by the British film industry in coöperation with the British Admiralty for release around the world in 1935.

To these sources of emotional incitement a few offsets were available. The production of Remarque's The Road Back showed the irreducible antithesis between trench habits and civilian habits; and They Gave Him a Gun suggested dangers lurking in the mere private possession of destructive weapons. An import from England, Things to Come, presented a phantasmagoria of awful events, and the French description of Carnival in Flanders ripped the tinsel and gilt from warfare.

Films inclined in the direction of peace were overwhelmed, however, after President Roosevelt's quarantine speech on October 5, 1937, and the launching of his super-navy program in January of the following year. The transition was not difficult, for the military and naval branches of the Government were willing coadjutors. Their position had been clearly revealed in the Army and Navy Register for April 10, 1937, in an article praising Wings over Honolulu, which called it "a story of naval aviation of some future war." Indebtedness for professional aid was acknowledged by the director of the film: "We are very grateful to the friendly and helpful spirit of the officers and crew of the *Ranger* and the air station. We are working hard to make Wings over Honolulu a picture of which the entire Navy can be proud. If this can be achieved, it will be because of the splendid coöperation of the Navy and the Navy people, officers, enlisted men, and some of their wives." Later in that year, when a superintendent of schools in a midwestern city objected to showing certain war films to the children under his care, naval reserve officers carried on a campaign of criticism against him. Such was the passion of the times.

After President Roosevelt announced his naval expansion policy on January 28, 1938, and encountered unexpected opposition in Congress and outside, his administration turned to the motion-picture industry for assistance in propaganda. Besides helping the newsreels in exploiting the Panay incident in the Japanese war on China, as a part of a campaign for new preparedness, the Roosevelt administration strengthened its coöperation with the picture industry. On April 13, 1938, Variety, an authentic voice of entertainment enterprise, was able to report "progress" in a dispatch from Hollywood: "The Government is showing a more friendly attitude toward pictures since the big naval appropriations, and a closer coöperation is pledged to pictures built around the military arms of service. . . . Washington now is trying to win over picture-goers to need of adequate defense and present the U. S. show of strength."

About the same time the syndicated moving-picture column of the International News Service explained this closer connection between Government and the industry in an illuminating sentence: "Perhaps the reason Hal Wallis obtained such ready permission for Warner Brothers is because Wings over the Navy is propaganda tied up with the recent

billion-dollar appropriation for added naval protection."
The President was determined to have his way and was eager
to see aid given to the production of films that would swing
the people over to his line of policy. For all practical purposes, the picture industry had become a servant of the
Roosevelt administration in respect of foreign, naval, and
military designs. The Secretary of War, Harry Woodring,
had said through the columns of the magazine, Liberty, that
the Army was ready to "take over the country" in time of
a domestic crisis. If the people could be convinced that no
military or naval appropriation could be unnecessary, the
way would be prepared for the ideology of things to come,
for any mask to cover the face of war.

Not content with making sure that the right "slant" was
given to moving pictures connected with its armament propaganda, the Roosevelt administration took care to keep out
counter-suggestions of a pacific nature. When Paramount
Pictures, apparently with the sympathetic "coöperation" of
the Government, was preparing Men with Wings, a saga
dramatizing the development of aviation, it arranged for the
heroine to deliver a vigorous denunciation of war; but,
according to reports of high authenticity, the Government
issued a ban against that speech in opposition to war. A
dispatch in The New York Times, May 28, 1938, declared:
"Government pressure on Paramount Pictures to eliminate
all pacifist preachment in Men with Wings has brought a
rewriting of the final twenty pages of dialogue." The following day, The Times' Hollywood correspondent, Douglas
Churchill, in an article, entitled Peace vs. Propaganda,
reported that "Paramount swaps principles for planes," and
described the way in which government pressure had forced
a reconstruction of the play's conclusion with a view to
eliminating the anti-war note. Commenting on the event,
Variety circumspectly remarked that "unofficial suggestions
from officials in Washington" had been responsible for the
redirection of Men with Wings in harmony with President
Roosevelt's armament policies and propaganda.

Although for a long time it was denied by federal authorities and film producers that they were deliberately united in any scheme of armament propaganda, facts belied the denial. It was a fact that film after film had been made with the coöperation of the armed forces of the United States. It was a fact that recognition of this coöperation was given in technical journals. It was a fact that a full page advertisement of Submarine D–1 in motion-picture trade journals paid tribute to the Navy Department, officers, and men in the submarine service "in grateful acknowledgement of inspiration and assistance." It was a fact that a journalist for the motion-picture industry openly boasted that the film, Wings over the Navy, was "propaganda tied up" with Roosevelt's agitation in support of naval expansion. It was a fact that the Government gave official sanction to coöperation with Warner Brothers in the production of this film. Thus, as a commentator on the facts remarked, the citizens who had to pay taxes for wars and shed blood in them also paid for war-propaganda in the form of "entertainment." An Aeschylus could scarcely have done justice to the scene.

Experience had demonstrated that motion-picture producers and directors were masters of the propaganda technique and knew how to condition popular reflexes for any war that politicians might decide upon in Washington. In 1918, while America was making the world safe for democracy, Cecil B. De Mille, an authority on the screen, had bluntly described the art: "I consider the development of the motion picture . . . into a conspicuously vital factor for the dissemination of governmental propaganda . . . to be most important. . . . And so, Pride of Patriotism — Grim Determination to Win the War — Calm Decision to support every measure of the Government unreservedly to that end, is finally — through nightly and daily iteration — instilled with telling force, into the breast of the spectator — a spectator taken from every class of American." Even before the United States entered the world conflict war films had pointed out "the enemy" and intensified the passions to which President Wilson appealed when he decided to take the country into the combat at arms.

In a republic whose Constitution provided for civilian supremacy over armed force, that vigilance which is the price of liberty took into account the trend of events. Every popular poll showed that the overwhelming majority of the American people wanted to stay out of all imperialist adventures and wars on other continents, although ready to defend America itself to the last ditch. Reflecting this positive public opinion, the National Council for the Prevention of War established a motion-picture department, under the direction of Albert Benham, formerly of Hollywood, studied the film offerings that bore on war and peace, kept close watch on the connections between the Government and the picture industry, and issued bulletins on this traffic. If the Naval Intelligence service of the Government, as alleged in the Senate, investigated and shadowed such observers and critics, politics had not yet reached the point in the American scene where either the War Department or the Navy Department could round up and shoot opponents of super-expenditures for the army and navy bureaucracy.

Within the industry itself and among reporters and critics associated with it were also watchers of events. Right on the spot where "the hope of heaven" burned brightest, Welford Beaton wrote in The Hollywood Spectator : "Each morning the newspapers demonstrate afresh that, of all His creations, Man is the one of whom God must be most ashamed. . . . In our own country today are children being reared in luxury on the profits their parents make by selling Japan war material which murders Chinese children. And we call ourselves civilized ! . . . Nations have become the playthings of maniacs their unwise people blindly follow. A great theme for a great motion picture, but we have no producer with brains enough to see it or guts enough to make it." To one of the two or three true artists that the picture industry had produced in the course of its long life, Mr. Beaton turned with the plea : "Shoulder arms, Charlie Chaplin !

The World needs your Little Man now as it never needed him before."

The news had been whispered that Charlie Chaplin was working on an anti-war picture. But it did not appear. From every "practical" angle, the production of such a film seemed impossible. Costs would be enormous. No "hearty coöperation" from the Government of the United States would be forthcoming — twenty years after the end of the war to end war. If produced independently, distribution could scarcely break through the grip of the corporate industry upon chain theaters and block-booking. Sales abroad — to Germany and Italy, Spain and Japan at least — would be out of the question; nor could Soviet Russia, thirsting for American aid against Japan, be expected to import this film. Even its exhibition in the United States might bring about retaliations curtailing the export of other American films. Time and circumstance seemed prohibitive. Anyway government propaganda held this sector of entertainment.

§

It was one of the ironies of American entertainment that the picture industry could produce no film for wide domestic distribution if it was unpleasing to Hitler and Mussolini. Under the economic theory of "the more foreign trade the better for the country," according to which Secretary Hull proceeded with his so-called reciprocity treaties, the great American film producers received a substantial percentage of their total income from other lands. With foreign governments limiting American exports by "quota" legislation and other restraining devices, with the industry materially dependent upon receipts from foreign sources, with censors abroad scrutinizing every inch of film, American producers would lose huge profits, might be thrown into bankruptcy, by offending in the slightest degree any dictator in Europe. The President of the United States could exert a positive force in the production of war films; foreign dictators could exert a telling influence against democratic films and against films of peace. The most frenzied promoters of the armament race throughout the world had access to American armament films to illustrate "the imperious necessity of the case."

The situation was neatly illustrated by the fate of Sinclair Lewis' It Can't Happen Here, a novel dealing with fascist tactics, methods, and spirit and representing the American democratic spirit in strong resistance to the cruelties, lies, and enormities of such despotisms. In all the years of depression and turmoil, no novel written in the United States portrayed more dynamically the ideals of democracy pitted against the tyranny of the demagogic dictator. Moreover the writer's name and fame had already commanded immense audiences — readers and "picture fans" in America and Europe.

Soon after publication came an announcement that a screen version was "in the works" at Hollywood. Months passed. No film emerged. Questions were asked. Gossip said that agents of Hitler and Mussolini had clamped the iron censorship on the picture. Producers denied the allegation. At all events the anti-fascist film was not produced. From the American people was withheld the privilege of seeing a great national ideal in conflict with fascism personified on the screen. Instead they were offered the "entertainment" of naval and military films. No longer could it be said that the State had no relation to the commercialized amusements of America. What that meant for 1950 or 1960 no one could foretell precisely, but guesses could be made — and all realists made them, if the world imagists looked the other way. Mussolini had shouted that democracy was a "farce" and "a mask for capitalism." History yet to come would test the validity of the thesis.

In the present, behind the smooth front of corporate and official control, restlessness existed among the writers, editors, actors, and actresses who were necessary to the profitable conduct of the motion-picture business. This ferment had been manifested in the agitation over the efforts to unionize the industry, especially after the appearance of the Committee for Industrial Organization in Hollywood. It found tumultuous expression in 1937 when the popular slap-stick. comedian, Hal Roach, a member of the Liberty League, attempted a kind of coup d'état among producers by bringing to the seat of the industry Vittorio Mussolini, the son of the dictator, fresh from his bombing exploits in Ethiopia. Expecting a fanfare of favorable publicity, Mr. Roach encountered a revolt.

On receiving advance news of the young Mussolini's coming, the Hollywood Anti-Nazi League released counterpublicity, stirred up local trade unions, won the support of important stars, and held the threat of a general strike over producers. When the conquering Vittorio appeared on the scene with his host, he met stony glares. Parties organized for his entertainment were suddenly called off; he was publicly snubbed by famous stars; beauties did not dance with him. Screaming circulars quoted his statement that bombing natives in Ethiopia had been "exceptionally good fun." Later it was explained that Vittorio's actual words had been "molto divertente" and should have been translated as "highly diverting," not as "exceptionally good fun." But Hollywood was not troubled about philology and it turned "the social heat on him" until he literally fled from the place, slipped back across the continent, and quietly sailed away for his father's land. The "international incident" was symptomatic. It revealed underlying tensions in the entertainment industry itself. Certainly that; perhaps nothing more.

§

Shortly after the successful commercialization of the sound picture, the newsreel entered the market as a standard feature of exhibitions and entertainments and was soon associated, like armament films, with great politics. Unlike motion-picture plays, the newsreel was free from official censorship, resembling the newspapers in that respect. Operating under such general titles as The Talk of the World, The

Eyes and Ears of the World, and The March of Time, it was often called the "educational branch of the theatrical motion picture." But it was, in fact, a medium for supplying sensational news; and newsreel photographers, in the manner of reporters, went into the field in constant search for "hot stuff." In reality, the picture reporters were forced to undertake far more daring adventures, to incur the risk of battle and sudden death, for they had to go into action with their cameras at the very center of scenes to be snapped. They were compelled to keep up a stream of "thrilling novelties" to prevent their goods from becoming a drug on the market. Since they could not be present at every "stirring" episode that occurred, they had to supplement fortunate "catches of hot news" by the deliberate selection of stated occasions that could be known and prepared for in advance. And it happened that a large proportion of such occasions was "official," that is, governmental in nature.

Although on dull days newsreel photographers in the United States had to be satisfied with reporting bathing beauties, carnival queens, and tennis players, they frequently had political events to film: the launching of battleships and cruisers, naval displays, military parades, army maneuvers, new bombing planes taking off, and bigger tanks going into action. When mere instrumentalities of violence paled at home, actual scenes of wars abroad could be employed to "tone up audiences." When pictures of death, destruction, and suffering on the battlefields of China began to arrive after the summer of 1937, at least one newsreel concern employed them to promulgate the doctrine that American "rights" were being endangered after the fashion of 1914–1917, with the implication that another war for the defense of American rights would become the necessary and proper thing.

That some producers of newsreels were fully conscious of just what they were doing was indicated by an arrangement for a private "preview" in Washington of a film dealing with China, attended by the Chinese ambassador, members of his staff, and officers of the United States Government, including cabinet members. To appear as mere reporters of news, "impartially transmitted," the producers invited Secretary Daniel Roper and Senator Bennett Champ Clark to make addresses to the prospective audiences through the sound track. While on the surface the balance was apparently even, in fact it was the jeopardy to American business interests in China that received the emphasis. Even so, when the film was exhibited in Washington, the public listened to Secretary Roper's appeal with stony silence and gave hearty applause to Senator Clark's plea for staying out of war.

After the films showing the bombing of the American gunboat, Panay, by Japanese airmen had reached the United States, official facilities were tendered to expedite the exhibition of the pictures. To use the language of The New York Times' picture expert: "Aroused by the bombing of the Panay and compelled to crystallize quickly the nation's foreign policy under pressure of disputed incidents . . . President Roosevelt asked the motion-picture industry to show the public exactly what happened to the little American gunboat on the Yangtze." The industry eagerly complied with the request and supplied announcers who made flamboyant speeches calculated to lash popular emotions into frenzy. After reviewing newspaper editorials and newsreel narrations, Walter Winchell reached the conclusion that editorial writers "refused to get hysterical," but "the newsreel narrators put on the big jingo act — noticeable to those over soldiering age." And yet, despite the furious efforts of narrators to whip up the war spirit, theater-goers in general looked at this newsreel and heard the announcement without going into hysterics. From the military point of view, the "big scare" was an almost total loss. Had American citizens at large read in the newspapers that the Panay was in a war zone convoying Standard Oil tankers? In any case, the outcome of the exhibition was a disappointment to the Roosevelt administration, especially to the State Department, if its press releases on foreign policies gave the correct version of its attitude.

Whether the newsreel was a device for education, sheer entertainment, whatever that might be, or propaganda, it became the stormy petrel of Czar Hays' quiet sea of escape. When newsreels of Mussolini's swank troops or Hitler's thumping goose-steppers were shown, friends and foes of the dictators sometimes cracked heads and smashed seats. Shouts of anger attended the showing of a newsreel made in Connecticut in which New London boys appeared as German Storm Troopers engaged in persecuting Jews. Foreseeing fights in theaters, Ohio censors banned this film as detrimental to public morals; it was also kept out of the "Aryan" districts of New York City and similar regions in parts of the West. College boys at Princeton and Amherst hooted and boycotted the Hearst Metrotone News. In fact opposition to his exhibitions became so widespread that producers found it expedient to drop the name of Hearst from the title. Minneapolis audiences broke up in factional fury over pictures of an industrial conflict in that city. The fan mail that poured into the managerial and editorial offices of newsreel companies, following hoots and cat-calls at exhibitions, warned them that their patrons would not quietly accept the fiction that newsreels merely gave "the news that's fit to print." In respect of newspapers that illusion had about disappeared and it was too late for newsreel editors to succeed with pretensions to such "objectivity."

Although no comprehensive survey was made of the newsreel contents over a period of time, the accent in reportage was unmistakable. Acts of violence, whether public or private, "made news" for pictures as well as papers and one impression readily gained from the reels was that violence ruled the world. If actual violence was not enough to fill the screen, preparations for violence on a large scale supplied any deficit. Where the pictures themselves lacked an appeal to hysteria, as in the case of the Panay affair, announcers tried to furnish the stimulating force by vehement words and roaring vociferation. Of course no one claimed that newsreels covered all civilization, including acts of kindness, wisdom, and virtue. But with the regular motion pictures concentrating so heavily on crime and the biology of sex and the news films crowded with scenes of crime and war, the emphasis was on the side of destruction, passion, and brutality.

§

What relation did the technics, art, and emphasis of the moving-picture industry bear to the maintenance and development of society, especially a republican and democratic society? That question rose above all minor points of criticism and appreciation and it could only be answered, if at all, with reference to the characteristics of such a society as set forth by men and women competent to speak through experience and knowledge. High on the list was knowledge of the forms and functions of society and government and the issues arising in their time unfolding. "A free, virtuous, and enlightened people," James Monroe had said more than a century before, "must know well the great principles and causes on which their happiness depends." No less fundamental, equally requisite was virtue, above all in the sense of devotion to the public good as distinguished from the overweening pursuit of private gain or the irresponsible enjoyment of personal passions. In the third place, it had long been an axiom of political observers that while a State resting on force, buttressed by a hierarchy of power, lay and ecclesiastical, and fortified by awe-inspiring ceremonials, might, at least for a time, dispense with virtue, this quality of the human spirit was the active, indispensable requirement of a republic. Also embedded in the necessities of such a society was the supremacy of civilian agencies over that immense interest which had helped to lay all the States of antiquity in ruin, namely, the military interest. And underlying all this were habits of moderation, respect for human rights, prudent conduct of private affairs, without which no society could long endure on a civilian basis.

Accepting as valid the axiom that virtue is an absolute as well as a relative value, Will Hays, shortly after he retired from the Harding administration to serve as the czar of morals in the motion-picture industry, issued his declaration of faith: "We must have toward that sacred thing, the mind of a child, toward that clean and virgin thing, that unmarked slate — we must have toward that the same sense of responsibility, the same care about the impressions made upon it, that the best teacher or the best clergyman, the most inspired teacher of youth would have." Without taking this lofty sentiment as an eleventh commandment, it could be said that everyone who thought about the moving-picture industry in relation to society agreed with Mr. Hays that it did and might have a profound influence on the sustaining morale of American habits and institutions.

Whether Mr. Hays intended that teachers should take his dictum as an unequivocal command or not, they did manifest a persistent and continuing interest in the influence of motion pictures on the children whom they were training for life in American society and citizenship in the republic. In efforts to get at the elusive nature of this influence they devoted attention, of necessity, to the content or emphasis of the pictures, as distinguished from the nominal theme. Through the Committee on Educational Research, formed under the auspices of the Payne Fund, with W. W. Charters of Ohio State University as chairman, a group of teachers and specialists made extensive inquiries into the components, or ingredients, of motion pictures for four years, 1929–1932, with a view to arriving at some consensus of opinion respecting their influences upon youth. One survey, made in this connection by Dr. Edgar Dale of Ohio State University, covered fifteen hundred pictures for the years 1920, 1925, and 1930 and the results were incorporated in The Content of Motion Pictures.

During those three years, according to Dr. Dale's classification, the "love theme" led all the others; crime ranked second with a rating only two per cent lower in 1930; sex as biology came third in 1920 and 1925; comedy stood fourth in 1920 and 1925 and third in 1930, showing signs of increase as the economic depression deepened. War was at first sixth in position, but its status showed signs of rising as the world's rearmaments expanded; after 1930, especially under the stimulus of President Roosevelt's naval and military policy, and with the coöperation of the army and navy, the war theme mounted swiftly, events in Spain and China presumably giving it warrant in the factual substance of contemporary history. So low in the statistical scale were pictures of constructive significance for American democracy that they could be easily overlooked. The heroes of the films, in an impressive measure, were "great lovers," portrayers of biological urges, parasites, criminals, gangsters, and warriors engaged, under law, in killing, burning, and destroying.

In respect of background, the big cities, particularly New York and Paris, were utilized for scenes of wealth and power. These were varied by pictures of splendor in the palaces of princes, from Europe to India, with special attention to sleeping quarters. According to reports on forty pictures showing residences, studied in detail, sixty-nine per cent of the accent was upon life among the rich and only four per cent upon the simple annals of the poor. Most of the actors were young men ranging in age from twenty to thirty, while the actresses on the average were still more youthful; for heroes, the age limit was about fifty-six; for heroines, about thirty-five. A villain might be in his sixties and the vixen in the late fifties, but no hero or heroine was that old. Among the economic occupations represented in 115 pictures, commercial business led the list. About half the women and a few of the men had no known lawful occupations. Little girl actors, effusively advertised, were, as a rule, smartly gowned and coiffed in Hollywood vogues, though toward the end of 1938 youngsters were being drilled for tougher roles. According to one student of the pictures, three-fourths of the output of forty pictures examined made a feature of intimate clothing. The pajama fashion originated by Gloria Swanson continued in vogue, with bathing suits of scant proportions sharply competing, and the "strip tease" gaining.

Only lines from Juvenal describing the diversions of decaying Rome were applicable to the facts in the case. Among 1500 pictures examined, Edgar Dale found that only a small percentage treated love as romance, as enduring personal happiness, as possessing deep social importance. The kiss, so profusely and obtrusively exhibited, lost most of its meaning save as a gesture of biology. Some producers seemed to delight in the innuendo of the promiscuous; but whether it was also preferred by audiences only the admissions could indicate. With love so depicted, crime was closely associated. Every gangster had his "Moll" and interest in crime itself was fanned by manifestations of sex. Criminals were rarely caught and punished in the films. Nor were the subtler forms of retribution often graphically or artistically treated; where punishment did follow crime, that was usually the end of the matter.

In studying 115 pictures in detail, the Payne Fund researchers found that the heroes were responsible for 13 murders, the villains and villainesses for 30. In all, 54 murders were committed; there were 59 cases of felonious assault, 17 hold-ups, 21 kidnapings, and numerous other crimes. The total number of deaths by violence was 71. In short, in 115 pictures, 406 crimes were actually committed and 43 additional ones were attempted, making a total of 449 crimes in 115 pictures, or nearly four crimes per picture. Inasmuch as there were about thirty million admissions of boys and girls under twenty-one years of age to the moving-picture houses every week, such detailed specifications, however discounted and interpreted, was certainly pertinent to the maintenance of the American republic and the basic institutions of American society.

The findings and conclusions reported by the surveys under the auspices of the Payne Fund, coupled with criticism from other sources, produced more than a flurry in the motion-picture industry, with its eyes ever on the box office and public relations. Disturbed by the growing revolt, representatives of the industry cast about for some David to destroy Goliath and found in Raymond Moley, former member of President Roosevelt's brain trust, the appropriate person for the mission. His reply was made in a slender volume entitled Are We Movie Made? published in 1938. Although an expert investigator himself, Moley chose to base the burden of his argument upon a book on Art and Jurisprudence by Mortimer Adler, a professor in Chicago University, passionately engaged in teaching the doctrines of Thomas Aquinas to midwestern Protestants. With little difficulty Moley, aided by Adler, tore up the thesis that science could demonstrate a "causal" connection between representations of crime and anti-social acts on the screen and specific instances of crime and anti-social acts in everyday life. Having done this, Moley treated as unimportant the informed judgment of teachers and other investigators actually in daily contact with children subjected to motion-picture influences; and substituted his judgment, tinctured by cautious qualifications, to the effect that on the whole, by and large, in general, the moving pictures were good for the public, that teachers should stick to their last, and "that each should attend to the perfection of his own business."

No doubt, conclusions on the dispute were largely matters of personal opinion in respect of everyday experience and knowledge; and all the controversy about the "science" of the business simmered down to issues of common sense. It required no elaborate statistical calculations and correlations to convince bystanders that the probabilities were on the side of those who maintained that the strong emphasis in the moving pictures on crime, sex, violence, racketeering, and high living was not conducive to the development and preservation of those virtues essential to the health of a democratic republic.

Most pictures that were well patronized had to have a "kick"; in other words, they had to violate the conventions of rational and prudent behavior. In supplying these surprises, demonstrations of delinquency, open passion, and overt cruelty were commonly employed. In an age of bank crashes and defaulting bonds, intrigue and blackmail were more likely to be portrayed on the screen than devotion to fiduciary trust and to the tender consideration of others — perhaps unwittingly a portrayal of democratic culture as its course was then being shaped. No doubt there was creative intelligence in America, coöperation for the common good, and heroism as social action; but such aspects of society necessary to its continuance and vital to its improvement received relatively little attention from directors of the regular motion-picture industry. For Horatius at the bridge was substituted the gangster preying upon society; for morality, a-morality; for the ethics of religion, incalculable mysteries. If "morality" was drawn upon for inspiration, it was generally to reveal the "horrors" of race suicide, labor conflicts, bolshevism, socialism, and all forms of radicalism in contrast with the "heroics" of patriotism depicted as subservience to the valuations of the pecuniary Respectability.

With physical passions and energies so glaringly emphasized, the theory of the motion picture as a release, as an escape into a world of phantasy, as a pleasing antidote to the monotony and hardships of life was clearly defective, at least as applied by a vast number of commercial films. Far from offering sedatives to audiences, such films suggested stimulation to overt action in line with the portrayals of the screen. This aspect of the business was analyzed and set forth by Herbert Blumer in his volume on Movies and Conduct. After a long study of the subject, Blumer came to the conclusion that the moving pictures are not "merely a device for surcease." For many patrons of the business, Blumer decided, they were "authentic portrayals of life" from which were derived patterns of behavior, incitement to conduct, ideas of reality, and "content for a vigorous life of imagination." In other words, day and night, the motion pictures were arousing in millions of boys and girls, men and women, impulses to actions of passion and violence that defied the moralities necessary to the rational conduct of affairs in society. Resting his case on this ground Blumer stated his summary: "Because motion pictures are educational in this sense, they may conflict with other educational institutions. . . . This is likely to be true chiefly among those with least education and sophisticated experience."

Confirmation of this general finding came from the Newspaper Guild, the national organization of reporters and other newspaper workers. Among the various participants in American life, men and women of the press were not especially addicted to sentimentality and petty moralities. On the whole, among the intellectuals of the country, they were the most realistic in experience and thought. But in 1937 even the Newspaper Guild was moved to protest against the films that touched upon the reportorial occupation. It complained that seventeen pictures produced that year vilified reporters and made workers in the business appear indecent; that five pictures treated them as innocuous persons playing no useful role in society; and that only two pictures presented them as having intelligence and character. It called special attention to the film They Won't Forget, in which a columnist was made to be a home wrecker, and to Back in Circulation, which showed a reporter so devoid of humanity that he could whimsically send a woman to execution or as lightly secure her acquittal. Rumors circulated to the effect that Hearst and other employers close to Hollywood were thus secretly waging war upon their reporters and employees in response to the organization work so successfully carried on by the Guild but, entirely apart from this allegation, it was evident that many newspaper workers were as indignant against the films as some intransigent members associated with the Legion of Decency.

§

To indict the whole picture industry was as foolish as to indict a nation, and yet there was so much social dynamite

exploding before millions day and night on the screen that
protests and counter-actions came from every quarter of
responsibility in the United States. If some objections developed from the overwrought imaginations of puritans, Protestant and Catholic, by no means all sprang from that source.
In fact, as early as 1922, leaders in the picture industry had
become so alarmed by the back-fire that they had organized
the Motion Picture Producers and Exhibitors of America,
Incorporated, with Will H. Hays, President Harding's Postmaster General and the former manipulator of Republican
campaign funds at the head, with the official title of czar of
the business and the functions of a water boy. This agency
of the industry continued to analyze complaints, consult
with objectors, arrange for "previews" before religious societies and women's clubs, and form committees of advice and
counsel. Meanwhile the National Board of Review, a private
organization established in 1909, operated directly and
through local committees as a voluntary agency of criticism
and approval. To such private agencies were added official
boards of censorship in a number of the states, which imposed
various restraints upon the scenes, actions, and lines of pictures before exhibition to the public.

Still protests mounted. By 1934 a Catholic association, the
Legion of Decency, had entered the fray with a national campaign that frightened the leaders of the industry and led to
the imposition of limits approved by Catholic authorities.
Inasmuch as the Catholic hierarchy was engaged in the pursuit of its own ideals and interests, had great economic stakes
in all parts of the country, and was connected with a complex
of economic and political interests in all parts of the world,
its control in practice went far beyond mere matters of faith
and morals, into spheres where political contests raged. Nor
was its control merely confined to moral suasion. According
to Elizabeth Yeaman, in The New Republic of October 5,
1938, it induced film executives, "ninety-nine per cent Jewish," to employ at a high salary Joseph I. Breen, a Catholic
of Irish descent, to act as its dictator-censor for the moving-

picture industry. So with the censorship exercised through threats of exclusion and retaliation by Hitler and Mussolini was associated the iron discipline of the greatest authoritarian church on earth. Against this combination, Protestants sometimes fumed and chafed, but they were unable to affect it in any material respect. In the circumstances the prospects of libertarian democracy receiving any consideration at the hands of the moving-picture industry were not flattering; in fact amounted to something near zero.

Within the picture industry itself, individual directors and actors subjected their products to more critical examination and sought to improve the artistic quality and intellectual standards of their films. Within and outside the studios, some playwrights and players displayed a strong sense of integrity and an interest in the currents of lay opinion that ran through the years. Out of pressures from audiences and criticism, out of genuine artistic impulses, and out of a sincere desire to end the tyranny of biology and the rawness of crime, came many productions of undoubted, if limited, quality. Among them was The Story of Pasteur, of the indomitable French scientist dedicated to the idea of serving humanity through the elimination of disease. Another was The Life of Émile Zola, portraying the great French humanist who valiantly challenged class intolerance and racial bigotry at the time of the Dreyfus affair. Pearl Buck's The Good Earth, a picture of fundamental life and economy in China, conformed to canons of universal value and artistry. If these were products of criticism, then the industry was not lacking in sensitiveness. At the same time idealistic and independent playwrights, directors, actors and actresses were passing severe judgments on their own trade — in letters, articles, and books — under the very eyes of producers and reviewers.

From other angles appraisal and criticism fell upon the motion-picture industry. Teachers and leaders in organized education encouraged the production of films that were informative in character — dealing with inventions, nature, travel, manufactures, discoveries, and the useful activities of normal social living. They urged local houses to exhibit pictures that could be approved for children and to enlarge their offerings of pictures appealing to adult intelligence and aspiration. From year to year various associations of teachers carried on studies and issued analyses and lists of pictures deemed appropriate for use in the schools. In 1938, for example, the National Council of Teachers of English issued a Handbook in Moving-Picture Evaluation, prepared by Helen Rand and Richard Lewis, with the "advice and counsel" of Edgar Dale and Sarah McLean Mullen, specialists in the content of film productions. In communities scattered over all the country, parents and teachers, in regular and special associations, brought the picture output under review and swelled the volume of criticism and appraisal that rolled over the directors, actors, producers, and exhibitors. Going beyond criticism to constructive action, two hundred distinguished educators, artists, civic workers, playwrights, and politicians, disturbed by the growth of intolerance and reaction, organized in 1938 Films for Democracy to produce pictures dealing with the pressing issues of the time in the spirit of humanistic democracy.

The Federal Government itself supplied contradictions to its war propaganda by producing for public use a large number of films showing its scientific and humane enterprises, from the work of the Coast Guard saving lives in storms at sea to the labors of the Bureau of Mines rescuing miners from underground disasters. Flood control, for example, was portrayed in The River, fighting fires on the public domain in Forest Fire, and agricultural extension in Helping Negroes to Become Better Farmers and Homemakers. Since government undertakings touched most phases of American life in their physical settings, motion pictures of public officials in the discharge of their duties covered a wide range of economy and culture. To the large store of federal films, teachers and leaders interested in the future of American democracy could turn for concrete information respecting democracy at work and for inspiriting scenes of public service.

§

In the contest for popular interest, enthusiasm, and patronage, the moving-picture industry pressed hard upon the regular theater, affecting the forms of drama offered and the talents of dramatic artists, if in ways difficult to grasp and measure. Conflict was, no doubt, in accord with the line of experience in the past open to comparison. After the art of the theater in ancient Rome had developed to a fine point through a mixture of Greek learning and principles with Roman originalities, it confronted, despite imperial favors, the growing rivalry of spectacles in amphitheaters and "the maddening excitement of the circus." At length, as A. W. Ward, the British dramatist, described the outcome, "the art of acting had sunk into pandering to the lewd or frivolous itch of the eye and ear; its professors had, in the words of a most judicious modern historian, become 'a danger to the peace of householders, as well as to the peace of the streets.' " The majestic lines of the great dramatists were heard no more, the appeal to the mind and to humane sensibilities died away, and finally the theater crumbled with the circus into ruins as Roman society itself dissolved into fragments.

That a deep gulf separated the moving picture from the drama on the stage was universally admitted even after the talking film succeeded the silent film. Actors in the theater could, if they would, give expression to subtler involutions of thought, to complex ideas of life and destiny, to judgments explicable only in terms of tone and gesture immediately conveyed to auditors. The theater brought actors and audience into direct contact, both creating and stimulating psychological relations essential to the supreme illusions of drama. These distinguishing characteristics of the theater were not and could not be duplicated by the moving-picture industry, with its mechanical devices, its commercial restraints, its performances in the glare of freakish lights, in the presence of technicians and roustabouts, all so obtrusively artificial. Nor was the theater absolutely bound through the box office to the lowest common denominators in America, Europe, and Asia; it could appeal to selected groups in cities and sustain on the boards for years a single play which no motion-picture corporations could afford even to produce on account of its limited audience or which, if produced, would have quickly dropped into the oblivion accorded to the greatest of films.

So attractive was the opportunity offered by the theater for the expression of ideas and the subtler skills of artistry that many film actors, despite alluring salaries, chafed at their routine, deadened by performances in mere studios, before mechanical apparatus, piecemeal, to photographers and stage hands. The inspiring essentials of drama — character, personality, and nuances — were difficult, if not impossible, to preserve in such circumstances. From year to year theatrical journals and reviews reported the discontents of writers, actors, craftsmen, and directors in Hollywood who were not satisfied intellectually and emotionally, though bound physically by the charm of their earnings. Some of them actually turned away from mechanics and luxury, real or potential, to assume the obligations and enjoy the compensations of the stage.

But the transition was not always happy or successful for, in returning to the theater, prodigal sons and daughters were likely to carry the tattoo of the cinema; and experienced dramatic critics were quick to discern the signs of the mechanical studio. When, for example, Alfred Lunt and Lynn Fontanne undertook to interpret Greek legends on the stage, J. Brooks Atkinson, critic for The New York Times, remarked that they might as well have stayed in Hollywood. Their performance, he declared, was clearly "show business" — a "suave and crackling performance of a bawdy jest," admittedly, but a mixture of classical brawling, intrigue, and gossip for the sheer purposes of masquerade. Although such was not the outcome of all translations from the screen studio to the stage, even of other adventures by Lunt and Fontanne, the difficulties involved in movement from the one medium to the other served to widen and deepen the gulf that separated them.

While huge financial corporations with expensive mechanical devices at their command, newly invented, used the moving picture to effect a transformation in historic entertainment, the theater kept its roots in the past, though responding to the spirit of changing times. Its wellsprings of inspiration and ideas, its sources of economic support, its wide range of experimentation in the subtler arts of thought and acting remained substantially unaffected by the revolution that overtook entertainment by the cinema, even if its use of light reduced the use of paint. Groups in small towns and in great cities, moved by dramatic urges as in the most ancient days of the human race, could test their impulses behind the footlights, at a financial hazard exceedingly trivial in comparison with the outlays for Hollywood spectacles. An individual producer could employ an unknown playwright, assemble a few players, and assume risks beyond the daring of huge picture corporations. After all, playwrights and actors, with rare exceptions, had been forced from time immemorial to endure the buffets of pecuniary misfortune; neither prosperity under President Coolidge nor the second depression under President Roosevelt made much difference in that respect.

The motion picture moved along a straight path from highly centralized workshops, under corporate trustees, to the multitude of consumers who took what they got, whether they liked it or not. On the other hand, the theater, large and small, professional and amateur, regular and irregular, chose to twist and turn in town and country. Whereas seven or eight great corporations virtually dominated the commercial picture business, innumerable small theater proprietors had a fairly free hand in controlling stage performances. No little group of playwrights and actors could rent a huge Hollywood plant even for a few weeks, but it could engage a vacant theater, or even a barn, for an experiment. Owing to the relatively small pecuniary commitments of the single theater, mere playwrights and foot-loose actors with the dramatic sense and talents could work up from the bottom, from the ranks of the nameless and unknown, to failure or success on the stage. To use a hackneyed phrase, by no means irrelevant for the times, the theater was far more democratic in sources of inspiration and control than the motion picture. It offered more elbow room. It was more hospitable to the expression of popular opinions. It helped to form stereotypes as well as to impose them. Protected by constitutional guarantees of free press and free speech, the theater permitted a freer ventilation of ideas and interests in the discussion of all great and petty themes of the age.

So constituted, the theater in relation to the moving-picture industry stood somewhat in the position of the farmer, artisan, and small business man as against corporate enterprise in the field of economy and of politics. It possessed a certain degree of economic independence. It allowed a high degree of movement, if only from failure to failure, as in the case of grocers, bakers, and vegetable gardeners. Players could set themselves up in business about as easily as a garage mechanic could establish a wayside gasoline station. Indeed all over the country, barns and small auditoriums were converted into theaters in which local groups or strolling players entertained farmers, villagers, and "the summer people." Individually often unimportant, in mass the multitude of independent theaters and playing groups signified the will to a free public expression of taste in drama, as against the centralizing and standardizing tendencies of the film corporation. Beside the commercial theater there could be the art theater. Although remnants of chain theaters survived the competition of the screen, the theatrical business, in the main, was still "a little business." Its unmechanical whimsies, its reliance upon the strange processes that throw up talent in one year or one decade and mediocrity in the next, made it unattractive to most financiers. The moving-picture business was hazardous enough, but the theater defied all hopes of steady mass production and calculable profits. In remaining precarious, however, like life, it permitted more life.

§

Those branches of theatrical enterprise which were essentially, if not predominantly, commercial in control continued in their historic role, with an eye to box-office receipts. Yet they too underwent some changes with the vicissitudes of the time. As the masses were swept into the moving-picture houses, the old ten, twenty, and thirty cent melodrama, for all practical purposes, disappeared and the heyday of pure vaudeville was also ended. When the country was plunged into the depths of the economic depression, theaters, like the banks, were often closed if not thrown into the hands of trustees or receivers. Having lost the ten, twenty, and thirty cent patronage and pinched by the steep decline in employment, strictly commercial theaters became more dependent upon the classes, that is, the middle and moneyed classes. In response to market exactions, the eternal triangle, the bedroom play, and commonplace though sometimes titillating scenes from small lives were endlessly reiterated, with minor fluctuations as the economic depression tightened, relaxed, and intensified.

As a matter of course also the regular theater kept on presenting crime and mystery plays as well as the eternal triangle, often importing them from England, the original home of the redoubtable Sherlock Holmes. In 1932, when the graph of the business indices dipped almost to the bottom, Edgar Wallace's Criminal at Large, a story of frenzied murder, "enjoyed" a long run in New York to crowded houses. Regional and special aspects of American civilization, always a source of dramatic inspiration, received their customary consideration. Taking a series of Negro legends as a basis, Marc Connelly produced Green Pastures, a vision of heaven, with God presiding, in which religion, philosophy, and the comedy of life were treated with gentleness and sincerity in a medley of folk fantasies. Besides commanding an immense popularity, the play won the Pulitzer prize for the year 1930. As to what it signified critics did not agree but they were united in proclaiming it "a work of art." Life in a little midwestern community flared up before the footlights for a brief season in Torch Song, with characters "pleasantly imagined." Business, reporting, crime, and profanity blazed out during the days of the "bull" market of 1928 in two newspaper dramas: The Front Page and Gentlemen of the Press. With representations of mystery, localism, and particular enterprises ran the usual "revivals," ranging from Shakespeare to Molière, from Ibsen to Bernard Shaw, indicating a continuity of interest in history and in the thought of undoubted Old Masters of the dramatic art.

Although women appeared in the triangle as ever, they received a peculiar treatment on the stage in the age when Nazism was denouncing feminism as a phase of "Jewish liberalism" not to be tolerated. In the play written by Clare Booth and captioned The Women, an all-woman caste of forty actors depicted a set of "city slickers" as a futile crowd, futile even in the home; their chatter was the chatter of the "smart set"; they were devoid of friendship for one another and satirical even in references to maternity; if there was a heroine, she was the economically independent woman who might be called a feminist.

Audiences packed the house night after night to see this play in New York — an outstanding "comedy hit" as its manager boasted. Men laughed and laughed. Was the interpretation of women in this drama a mere portrayal of frustrated and quarrelsome creatures belonging to the bourgeoisie, defeated and befuddled in a realm of conspicuous waste? Or was it a symbol of a sex about to be subjected to the function of rearing soldiers under a fascist ideology? These questions were asked — and found no categorical answer — even in the reply made by the playwright to the prohibition ordered by the British censor when her drama was sent to England for review and possible production. The reason put forward by the censor for his action was the speech against maternity in which one of the women had indulged; that much was illuminating. While The Women was still very popular in New York, arrangements were made to send it on the road as "the nearest thing to an old time carnival on a tour of one night stands in which he [the manager] had ever been implicated."

In Susan and God, Rachel Crothers gave woman another interpretation, with Gertrude Lawrence as its spokesman. She challenged the spirit of war and hatred exemplified in violent political movements and in such a drama of despair as Hemingway's Death in the Afternoon. With "death stalking the earth, death in the morning and evening and night, on land, in the sea, and in the air," it seemed to Rachel Crothers that evil rather than good was dominant on the earth through the folly and indolence of people — men and women alike. Her Susan, accepting God as a symbol of the good, was just an average person, observing and taking part in the affairs of the hour and day. "Personally," said Miss Crothers, "I believe all that Susan says, though not quite as she says it, and I'm with her when she declares 'It's the only thing that will stop war,' but I am afraid her 'bright and shining army which can't be stopped and is marching gloriously on' will have to march very fast indeed now and recruit many new soldiers, or it will be overtaken by the hideous one which is on our heels." Besides attracting theater-goers night after night, the drama of Susan and God won the Theater Club's award as the "outstanding play" for the season of 1938.

§

If many theater-goers did not want to see on the stage, night after night, the visible and outward signs of political and economic conflicts daily reported in the headlines of newspapers, playwrights and actors could not entirely evade the spirit of the times, the drum beats of the economic depression, the reverberations of the New Deal, uprisings among debt-burdened farmers and tenants, or the conflicts of labor that produced the Committee for Industrial Organization. The truth is that dramatists and performers were frequently immersed in the surge of opinions and emotions which accompanied the making of history, great and small, in the United States, itself a part of world history. Workers in the dramatic arts, no less than the Lords of Creation, were certainly alert to the detonations, dissolutions, and bewilderments that followed the wild days in Wall Street in the late autumn of 1929. And it was a proof of elasticity and vitality that the American theater could present, in many cases with notable success, convulsive episodes, realistic scenes, and intellectual clashes, illustrating and, in some measure, comprehending the main clusters of events. Perhaps never before in the history of the American theater were so many and such varieties of crucial political, economic, and cultural experiences presented on the stage within so short a span of years. Whatever the verdict of critics, especially concerned with "art for art's own sake," on this profusion of "social dramas," the very profusion itself was indicative of ideas and moods commingling in the central tendencies in American life.

Was it merely a unique flare-up in history for example, the affair of Sacco and Vanzetti, two "social rebels" put to death in Massachusetts on charges of robbery and murder, which provoked outcries and riots from Boston around the world? In a message to the legislature, the governor of Massachusetts urged that body to relieve future governors of the "difficulties which were forced upon him in 1927 by zealous defenders of persons convicted of first-degree murder" and to consider revisions of the law pertaining to appeals, exceptions, and motions for new trials in capital cases — the exact points of law against which many cogent objections had been lodged during the long contest over the trial of the two defendants. The very year following the execution of the accused, Maxwell Anderson and Harold Hickerson seized upon the raw materials of the trial, the agitations, and the outcome, and wrote for the stage their Gods of the Lightning — a play of harsh and powerful realism. J. Brooks Atkinson, a dramatic critic who kept his head in storms, calmly remarked of the play as acted: "The authors had told their story so forcefully and the actors played with such simple fervor that the effect was cruelly disturbing in the theater. As special pleading, Gods of the Lightning was one of the most effective plays ever produced." From the box-office point of view it was not a "smashing success," but at all events there it was in the repertory of the year 1928 as dramatic idea in action. Within a similar category, involving the administration of justice, came John Wexley's They Shall Not Die, a representation of the Scottsboro case, in which a group of Negro boys on trial for their lives were the center of another national agitation.

While banks were bursting in 1933, depositors were holding their breath, and the New Deal was being inaugurated amid party uproar, Maxwell Anderson launched his political play, Both Your Houses, to which the Pulitzer Prize was awarded. Far more penetrating, more understanding in its grasp of politics and business than The Gilded Age, written by Mark Twain and Charles Dudley Warner in the period of "Grantism," Anderson's drama of Washington in the period of New Dealism spared neither business nor politics, while taking account of idealistic forces operating under the mantle of intrigue. In its personnel appeared the hard-headed manager of machine politics and the young "progressive" from the hinterland bent on "serving the people." The tragic conflict between the real and the ideal, which had torn western thought since the dawn of Greek civilization — and beyond — was brought down to cases in the national capital of the United States. The very texture of "practical affairs" was dissected — that everlasting contest between good and evil that had marked the whole course of world history. Playgoers seethed in politics and acquainted with Washington lost the illusion of illusion as they followed the movement of the play, and Both Your Houses was acclaimed as "the most conspicuous success" of the year.

The following year, 1934, Elmer Rice, whose Street Scene had excited both New York and Chicago a short time before, gave theater-goers an acid test of Fascism and Communism, then the sources of physical riots and verbal battles in various parts of the earth. On the burning of the Reichstag in Germany and the trial of the accused as a basis, Rice built, in Judgment Day, a drama of clashing ideologies and fighting ideologists. Witnesses were divided over its ideas and merits, and critics differed in their opinions, with some reference to predilections, of course, but chroniclers of the theater felt compelled to set it down in the records as among the events of the season. Rice's second play, Between Two Worlds, was another attempt to dramatize the conflict of social philosophies — this time on an ocean liner — literally between two worlds. Its lukewarm reception discouraged the author and he withdrew for a time from the theatrical world, but only for a time.

While the mirage of recovery seemed to lie ahead, despite signs of an approaching recession, the authors of You Can't Take It with You put on, in 1937, the good-natured musical farce, I'd Rather Be Right, and won that year's Pulitzer prize. In this skit on national politics, the ideas and actions of President Roosevelt were the target, but the arrows were tipped with humor; the art of balancing the budget was treated jocosely; and the conflicts between the executive and judicial departments of the government were made amusing. In the process the "dignity of government" was reduced to the level of a "romp." Everybody was happy in confusion. Democracy, despite the plight of its economy, had no ground for fearing disaster. The jolly George M. Cohan, who impersonated the President, resolved the budget dilemma in a "skitting, waggling dance." An effort was made to treat unemployment as a matter of fun by having a labor chorus sing:

> We work all day
> For the PWA.
> Let the market crash,
> We collect our cash.

We sing as we work,
And we work as we sing,
Skit-skat Beety-o !
Skit-skat Beety-o !
Labor is the thing, my lads,
Labor is the thing.

Whether the comedy had animus or not, Liberty Leaguers, smarting under the defeat of 1936, found satisfaction in beholding the victor ridiculed. And so sharp indeed were some of the barbs that timid bourgeois, forgetting the thrusts of "Mr. Dooley" at an earlier Roosevelt, wrote letters to the press in protest against this musical "harlequinade," lest it be popularly deemed lese majesty — against the American form of government.

As the lines between advocates of collective security and advocates of abstention from foreign quarrels tightened, the Theater Guild offered to the public Sidney Howard's The Ghost of Yankee Doodle. In this play "liberal" men and women appeared as Yankee Doodle resuscitated and rushing to a new war for democracy in foreign lands. Its time was set "eighteen months after the commencement of the next world war." Its "hero" was an aviator who placed himself at the disposition of France despite the sinking of an American ship by a French submarine. Its upshot seemed to be a commentary on the folly of mankind and on Americans as prize sentimentalists. "You make that one out! I can't," grumbled the critical Jean Nathan, "unless the mumbling and gargling of the actors played havoc with the playwright's intention. . . . One thing is obvious. The play in its entirety indicates anew that the place for playwrights who have been spending most of their time in Hollywood is still Hollywood. . . . Howard evidently believes that a pregnant play of ideas is to be achieved through a painstaking restatement of the platitudes of the late Herbert Croly [Progressive Republican] indignantly crossed with those of young Mr. Corliss Lamont [Communist] and periodically interrupted

with a wistful quotation from Ruskin or Milton." Whether
in this case the critic was "just," whatever justice might
mean, the play itself held up to play-goers' view a number of
ideas that might help to burn the world if European nations
made repetitions in history.

The uncertainty, alarm, horror, and indignation associated
with the very thought of another world war for anything —
democracy, commerce, fascism, communism, or any other
symbol or image — found expression in Robert Emmet
Sherwood's Idiot's Delight, a title that carried the author's
own interpretation. In the course of the play, the thesis was
advanced that intelligent men and women do not want war,
that they abhor war, and that conscience and self-interest
alike spurn this ancient heritage. Why then does war come?
Characters in the play gave their various answers : capitalism,
munitioneers, and nationalism. Neither the agonized cry
nor the ready answer could enclose all history and solve the
problem, and yet so great was the success of the play in the
United States and at the capital that it caught the attention
of England and was taken to London in the spring of 1938,
to be given in a country furiously engaged in rearmament, apparently against its own will, in sheer desperation.

In conception and lines, Idiot's Delight was so effective
that it evoked debates far and wide. Critics who shared the
view that war is madness spared no praise. Adverse commentators employed all the well-known arguments that had
been heard in parliaments and public assemblies since the
eighteenth century, especially the formula that war for
"defense" is supreme heroism. No student of war had ever
been able to draw the exact line between defense and aggression. Professors who had climbed mountains of documents
and memoirs still quarrelled over the "guilt" of the last world
war, without reaching consensus of decision. In fact, the
author of Idiot's Delight and his critics, unable like all
mortals to "explain" history, left the mystery veiled. Only
one thing was certain in the play : the blame for war could
not all be laid upon women.

The theme of war, always thrusting itself up in domestic affairs, as if incompetence, fear, and evasion could not have it otherwise, formed the burden of the argument in Paul Green's Johnny Johnson, a play of 1936, voiced by a veteran of the world war engaged in trying to allay the new war fever. With the aid of modern stage settings, the ex-soldier sought to bring the idea of peace to life. Eschewing the tumult and rattle of What Price Glory and other exhibitions of battle and sudden death, even in his trench scene Paul Green relied upon the subtler arts of bewilderment and inquiry. Does anybody know what this is all about? How do we get in? How do we get out? What is the upshot for plain people scurrying along streets and around corners? No clear answers were forthcoming. Folly was apparent, but perplexity colored the scenes and the lines. Lloyd George had said that the great powers had "stumbled" into the world war in 1914, and perhaps that was the just word. The playwright seemed to suspect as much in reference to war in general. Though far from a major favorite, Johnny Johnson had its special vogue.

Into the lines and tunes of musical shows also crept notes from the conflicts in economics and politics. Among other playwrights George S. Kaufman, Moss Hart, and Morrie Ryskind bent their talents, singly or in combinations, to the art of depicting politics, not too seriously or at least not too blatantly. While President Hoover was wearing himself out with efforts at "recovery," amid the slurs of Democratic criticism, and making little headway, Kaufman and Ryskind, aided by the musical geniuses, the two Gershwins, Ira and George, satirized the political show in a glittering slapstick circus entitled Of Thee I Sing. Friends and foes of the administration alike laughed, and the committee of Columbia University bestowed the Pulitzer prize upon the authors. In the years when wiseacres were suggesting that President Roosevelt was really the Kerensky of the political crisis, Let 'Em Eat Cake was offered as a kind of sequel to Of Thee I Sing. After the New Deal had made great progress — into the depression of 1937, Ed Wynn took the center of the musical comedy stage with Hooray for What, in which four playwrights had collaborated, for which Agnes de Mille had arranged a dance satirizing the hero as warrior. Without any reference at all to music, many citizens were saying off Broadway : For what indeed ? The great referendum of 1936 had not answered the question. Neither did musical jibes at collective security, war, the administrative alphabet, or handing out political jobs. But they lightened the gloom and eased the tension between "economic royalists" and the "dictatorship" in Washington.

For those who thought politics, and probably history, senseless, Kaufman and Hart provided consolation and pleasure in You Can't Take It with You. In lines that must have fascinated persons who attributed the troubles of the times to "lack of confidence," old Grandfather Sycamore suggested to the befuddled world that "life is pretty simple if you just relax." To members of the audience whose heads were still above the financial waters, the prescription doubtless seemed excellent; perhaps no others had passed through the box office to the auditorium. Yet there was something heartless in the suggestion. After seeing the play, a sociologist had the temerity to contend that "when Rome burns, the least a playwright can do is to say that he is sorry." The comment, however, was scarcely pertinent; nor was the play itself to people outside the theater, who had nothing to take away with them when the judgment day came. If the theme was a trifle irreverent to economic royalists, it afforded no comfort to the millions that had not entered the Economy of Abundance. Anyway Hollywood thought it a good gamble for the screen and borrowed it from the regular theater.

As a rule the plays which struck into the main current of American life were concerned with urban ideas and conduct, but the most successful drama, in terms of the long run, touched upon the sickness of agrarian economy. That was Tobacco Road, a dramatization of Erskine Caldwell's novel of life among the Southern lowly — not the dynamic lowly, but people crumbling into dust. Politicians and agitators, Huey Long and union organizers were making the nation conscious of bottom poor and Caldwell thrust the problem, if with no issue, into the face of theater-goers. He made no concessions to melodrama to sustain the interest. Virtue did not conquer vice, nor did the heroic triumph over the villainous. To all appearances the denizens of Tobacco Road were immersed in a tragedy of poverty and ignorance far beyond their control or the possibilities of escape — hungry Americans, hungry. Did their plight strike chords of defeatism in popular consciousness and so attract the large audiences, one after the other, on and on through the years? Was this the explanation of the popular appeal? Did audiences really know why they liked this story? Critics found difficulty in answering the question, as the play ran through the months and the years — from 1934, on and on — far outstripping in success the dramas of urban realism and revolt. In some cities expurgation was demanded, but New York City took the play straight. Long after Gods of the Lightning was forgotten by casual visitors of theaters, Tobacco Road was being played day and night, a kind of mystery, yet maybe a challenge.

Taking up another phase of the tragedy emerging from the agrarian dissolution in America — the life of casual laborers on large ranches, of lonely, wandering men and derelict women — John Steinbeck dramatized his novel Of Mice and Men for the season of 1937. Told in the powerful simplicity that characterized the story of the Prodigal Son, this tale of two men journeying in search of work, finding work, caught in the iron grip of things, tender in their humanness, finally brought to a frightful climax, had held readers of the printed page in its spell. On the stage it translated itself to pit and gallery and wrung response from even old and weary critics. In every scene and nearly every line it portrayed with throbbing life actualities reflected in statistical tables of the Department of Agriculture, in the report of President Roosevelt's Committee on Farm Tenancy, and in Paul Taylor's monumental studies of migratory labor on the land. The grandest dream of one of the men was to have just a little land of his own, a rabbit, some chickens — something to care for and love. For a moment it seemed as if the earth hunger of fifty centuries, the human hunger of all time, was epitomized in living symbols. Did all the defeated hopes merely suggest faults in the law of land tenure? Or something primordial? Was any other upshot to this tragedy possible? Since economists had not answered these questions, the novelist and the actors were within their rights in leaving the issue of labor on the land staring quizzically from the stage.

§

After the economic collapse of 1929, playwrights, actors, and theaters were carried into an unprecedented relation with the Federal Government. Far-seeing leaders among the makers of the American Republic, with William Dunlap in the advance guard, had called for a national theater to serve as an instrument for the inculcation of republican ideas, manners, and morals. But the early republic let this opportunity slip by and with the passing of John Quincy Adams the idea of associating government constructively with the arts was only kept alive by a stray advocate here and there, such as Julia Marlowe and Kenneth Macgowan. After the Jacksonian uprising little was heard of the "elegant arts" as instruments of public policy, and the theater was left to private interests.

Like most private enterprises, the theater had made fortunes for a few and kept the main body of entrepreneurs and actors in a precarious state, with poverty always just around the corner for the lesser lights of the stage. Long before stocks hit bottom in 1932, the theater, like agriculture, was in the throes of a crisis. The industry was "overexpanded"; there were too many theaters for the effective demands of box offices. Like the railways, the stage was suffering from competition — in this case from the moving-picture industry.

Clever playwrights and actors were lured away by the giant corporations at Hollywood, with huge sums of money as the bait; the cinema was draining off theater-goers; the demand was falling; and famous houses were already going dark when the night came in 1929.

For the theater, as for holding companies, railways, and construction industries, the economic débâcle was devastating as it widened through the years. Great producers went into bankruptcy. Theaters were sold at auction. Lights went out in cities all over the country. Thousands of actors, thousands of men and women who had lived by writing and playing, were turned into the streets with the makers of automobiles, cement, and shoes. In the friendly spirit that had always characterized the profession, their colleagues who remained in employment raised funds, gave benefits, and shared their wealth. But in time the burden passed beyond the limits of private philanthropy.

When at length the Roosevelt administration faced the total economic situation squarely, it confronted the theater. By general consent the country was opposed to the dole, for it kept recipients in idleness and tended to degrade the national morale, while producing no wealth whatsoever. This point of view Roosevelt expressed in a message to Congress and in 1935 the Works Progress Administration was established to create and provide projects that would give employment, occupy beneficiaries at tasks for which they had some experience and competence, and tide them over "until private industry could take up the slack." Among the divisions of this Administration was the Federal Theater Project. The undertaking was at best experimental and delicate but it was carried out with skill and circumspection under the supervision of Hallie Flanagan and her associates.

Of necessity under the continuous pressure of politics, the Theater Project steered its course with ingenuity, pleasing in the process neither the extreme Right nor the extreme Left, but allowing a substantial margin of freedom, befitting the variety of interests in America. It attempted and attained a notable success in reinstating poetry in the drama, using T. S. Eliot's poetic narrative, Murder in the Cathedral, as this experiment. It was the patron for a dramatic version of Sinclair Lewis' It Can't Happen Here, after this play had been suppressed or rejected by Hollywood, following a protest from places where it had happened. In harmony with more democratic conceptions, the Federal Theater Project organized a number of companies to present It Can't Happen Here in all sections of the country, and "for the first time in the history of the American theater, the curtain rose simultaneously on twenty-one stages in eighteen cities from the Atlantic to the Pacific, presenting twenty-one different versions of a new play by a distinguished American author." With propriety, it was presented in Washington, the capital of the nation, where decisions significant for the future of democracy were being made from year to year. While irate citizens were flinging charges of dictatorship at President Roosevelt, throngs of theater-goers all over the country were watching in this play a conflict between power and freedom, on the stage, under federal patronage.

By remarkable unanimity of opinion The Living Newspaper — in a strict sense the creation of the Federal Project — was accorded the honor of being a "lasting contribution" to American drama. Under government auspices a number of researchers, reporters, and writers dramatized the leading issues of the time and presented, by means of actors on the stage, events and personalities that made headlines for the daily press. Into this Living Newspaper were introduced, for example, the question of agricultural relief: Triple-A Plowed Under; a résumé of the news: Highlights of 1935; labor disputes and the law: Injunction Granted; and public utilities: Power. These plays were crowned by a more difficult undertaking: One Third of the Nation — the housing issue with its elements of fire hazards, disease, and crime-breeding tenements, against a background of rack-renting. When the Federal Theater Project announced a dramatization of the theme for an opening in February, 1936, the advance sale was so large that bookings were made for the following May. Finally George Bernard Shaw became sufficiently interested in the American federal theater by 1938 to grant it the right to produce his plays; he cut his royalties to the low figure established by the Project, and his dramas were widely performed. Eugene O'Neill consented to a similar arrangement.

The limited funds allocated to the various federal projects helped to restore the primal elements of ideas and character interpretation to the American theater, so long confused and overlaid by the expensive operations of scenic painters, costumers, mechanical inventors, and allied artists and craftsmen. Under the financial limitations of the Federal Project administration, complicated and costly scenery was out of the question, and so was elaborate costuming. Besides, all parts of the country called for the privilege of seeing the plays produced by the Project, and its companies could not carry around with them cars full of scenic properties. To be sure some setting was necessary, and so managers turned to the lighting effects developed by the motion picture. Light was relatively cheap and almost infinite in flexibility and variability. Where special results were required or were appropriate, it was employed, as the director explained, "to emphasize the living bodies of the actors." At the same time, with its limited funds, the Project was able to employ at its peak in 1937 approximately 12,700 workers who had been in or on the edges of poverty and despair.

According to reports for that year, nearly ninety-five per cent of the Government productions were written by American playwrights. The Project operated in twenty-eight states, as well as the District of Columbia. It sought to stimulate interest in the theater in communities, "sixty per cent of whose adults and children have never before seen living comedy and drama." The coöperation of local organizations, clubs, societies, and civic associations was solicited and, it was hoped, the foundations of permanent activities were laid in all regions of the country. Experiments in

Atlanta and Savannah, for instance, were taken over by local organizations as regular civic enterprises. Plays were given in villages that had never seen actors on the stage, in Civilian Conservation Camps, in orphanages, hospitals, prisons, veterans' homes, schools, and colleges, ranging from the Dakotas to the Mississippi delta, from Maine to Seattle. More than twenty-two million people, it was estimated in 1937, had witnessed performances under the auspices of the Federal Project, and thousands of local communities, hitherto beyond the theater belt, had been brought into some acquaintance with playwriting and acting.

About all the activities of the Federal Theater Project, as about all the devices of the New Deal, criticism foamed. Commentators, passing judgments born of their particular frames of experiential and intellectual reference, often scoffed at the federal plays, rating them as deficient in construction and poor in performance. Why waste money on "bum writers" and "ham actors"? it was freely asked. This question could be answered as quickly and easily as the other question: "Why shouldn't the poor and unemployed everywhere be allowed to starve?" Such questions involved, of course, matters of taste and insight by no means as exact as problems in Euclid. If only the plays approved by Jean Nathan, for instance, were admitted to the stage, would there be any reservoir of theatrical resources from which to derive the best? And what in fact would be the best?

When fitted into the larger context of cultural history and cultural resources, the Federal Theater Project's operations suggested a connotation far wider than that of particular theatrical criticism, namely, the obligation of the Government toward the arts as source and force in social life. However considered, the Federal Theater Project was more than a spasmodic event in American history. The organization and administration of the project, notwithstanding the shortcomings, criticisms, and failures, were among the extraordinary upthrows of the economic crisis. Whether for good or ill, whether for the enrichment or impoverishment of the cultural resources upon which society, industry, and government depend for existence, whether permanent or impermanent in influence, judgment would be rendered, as in all cases, by history as actuality yet to come, not merely by the verdicts of contemporary critics, dramatic or social.

§

While full judgment waited on time, the legislature of California took up the idea of public responsibility and coöperation in relation to the drama by designating the Pasadena Playhouse as an official State Theater. For several years The Playhouse had been functioning. Summer after summer it had held a Drama Festival built on some particular theme. In 1937 the subject was the Great Southwest, the historic unfolding of which was enacted gravely and with reference to authentic characters and events. This festival opened with an English version of Gerhart Hauptmann's poetic play of the Spanish conquest, Der Weisse Heiland, under the English title of Montezuma, but critics called the performance "passionless and lifeless" and attributed its pallor largely to the German playwright's lack of clarity in interpreting that series of historic events. Nor did the attempt to portray the rise and fall of the Catholic conquest of California fare better in the criticism; the result was described as a "Chamber of Commerce entertainment, with white velvet charro costumes, bespangled china poblanas, and the singing and dancing which belonged to neither Old California nor Mexico." In short, the effort was dismissed as merely a "civic pageant," not true drama. A third play, however, Night over Taos, by Maxwell Anderson, originally produced by the Group Theater in New York in 1932, was ardently defended as "a production which in poignancy, power, and moving force is worthy to be set alongside some of the most thrilling experiences in the contemporary theater." A second European, Franz Werfel, was drawn upon for a fourth play, Juarez and Maximilian, but the poetic fire of its printed lines burned low

in the spoken lines. In the American play, The Girl of the
Golden West, a natural quality of acting was regained, only
to be lost again in The Rose of the Rancho. Then "significance" returned with the closing bill, Miner's Gold, the
story of quick wealth won in the Southland seeking social
recognition in San Francisco — a tale carrying the theatrical
series to the period of the twentieth century.

That the Federal Theater Project was not limited in influence to its own operations received confirmation from
many quarters. To the International Ladies Garment
Workers Union, for instance, it furnished aid to the Union's
musical skit, Pins and Needles, which became a Broadway
success and then was taken on a national tour. As employment rose with the progress of recovery in 1936, actors from
the Project returned by the hundreds to the regular theater
and many playwrights found outlets for talent in private
fields. Definite borrowings of techniques were made from
federal projects, as in the case of Kaufman and Hart's The
Fabulous Invalid, a defense of the living theater.

Meanwhile, two young "graduates" from the federal
theater, Orson Welles and John Houseman, organized the
Mercury Theater in New York and opened with Julius
Caesar in modern dress, to a highly interested audience in the
theatrical metropolis of the country. Making use of modern
lighting and sound devices, they accented the play itself,
quickened its speed of action, and intensified its passion.
So appealing was the contemporary implication of Julius
Caesar presented in this style that the audience clamored for
other "great plays of the past presented in the modern way,"
for other "classical plays excitingly produced." Once more
the illusion of permanence amid the illusion of change was
conveyed to theater-goers. With dictatorship weighing
heavily on the public mind and bulking large in the daily
press, with refugees from its persecutions daily walking down
the gang planks of steamers docked in this New World, as in
the early days of the republic, Americans again hurried to the
theater to behold "resistance to tyranny," to see the resur-

gence and challenge of Caesarism embodied in personalities and events on the stage.

When The Cradle Will Rock — an operetta by Marc Blitzstein dealing with a steel magnate's war on trade unionism — was banned by the Federal Theater Project, following an indignant outburst among some of the taxpayers, Welles and Houseman took over the production on their own responsibility. In performance as well as theme, it was unquestionably radical. As for technique, it adapted a method developed by Clifford Odets. The actors were at first seated in the audience and the musician remained on the stage to play accompaniments at the piano. From their seats in the audience actors sang their lines, including martial hymns of labor, thus transforming the illusion of "play acting" into the appearances of a militant labor meeting.

A forerunner of the Mercury group was the Theater Union which enjoyed a four-year career, from 1933 to 1937, on the outskirts of Broadway, specializing in the struggles of labor in the modern world, with occasional thrusts at the menace of war. Eight plays were produced during its brief existence. It opened with Peace on Earth, more argumentative than dramatic, in the opinion of austere critics. It followed with Stevedore, Sailors at Cattaro, Black Pit, Mother, Bitter Steam, Let Freedom Ring, and Marching Song, the titles of which proclaimed the themes. With a view to attracting "the mass of the people," otherwise diverted to the moving pictures, admission charges were fixed at low figures. To make possible cheap admissions, costly scenery was eliminated in favor of the irreducible minimum. Although in time an unbalanced budget halted these leftist producers in their mass appeal, the production of John Howard Lawson's Marching Song was so well received that it finally reached the main theatrical district of Manhattan.

Less definitely located in the spectrum of political colors, the Group Theater opened a more successful career with Paul Green's The House of Connelly, in 1931, and managed to win the plaudits of the metropolitan press as well as full houses for a number of its performances. Among other things, the Group pioneered with plays in which actors were placed among the members of the audience and the theater was transformed from stage to gallery into a single meeting. So attractive was the novelty to novelty-loving New Yorkers that middle-aged dowagers of the middle class, who normally supplied a large part of all theater patronage, seemed to enjoy active participation in labor meetings, as drama, with revolutionary fire and action sweeping through to a conclusion. Although, naturally, the Pulitzer prize was bestowed upon the Victorian romance, The Old Maid, enthusiastic audiences, including many maiden ladies, clapped lustily at Clifford Odets' series of labor plays: Awake and Sing, Waiting for Lefty, Till the Day I Die. The politics of the nation might not be going left, or anywhere on its way, but Clifford Odets demonstrated that there was an audience for drama built upon the conflicts of the industrial world, reported in newspapers and uncovered by the Senate committee inquiring into civil liberties under the direction of Robert M. La Follette.

"These young people are succeeding in doing what they set out to do," wrote Winifred Smith in The Survey. "Instead of turning back to sentimental versions of our forefathers' conflicts — whether with a foreign enemy, as in Valley Forge, or with their own traditional inhibitions and conventions, as in The Old Maid . . . these strong, fresh talents are living the life around them, probing its tragic depths, pointing out its inherent contradictions and its painful injustices, and making theater-goers wince with the realization that, for all our boasted high standards of living in America, our day is one of the cruelest eras in human civilization." But she quoted a declaration of Virginia Wolff in another connection to point a moral in this relation: "This force of theirs, this smouldering heat which breaks the crust now and then and licks the surface with a hot and fearless flame, is about to break through and melt us together, so that life will be richer and . . . society will pool its posses-

sions instead of segregating them, and . . . all this is going
to happen inevitably." Having made this positive assertion
relative to the midpassage, the writer concluded her opinion
with the question: "What more can the theater contribute
to our common life?"

In some cases a playwright could get a hearing at the
Group Theater in the byway and a commission from a producer more centrally located at the same time, showing that
the division between art and pecuniary considerations was
not as sharp as cynics sometimes asserted. In a single year
Robert Ardrey's Casey Jones was announced for the Group
Theater, and How to Get Tough about It for the Martin
Beck Theater. According to rumor the latter was really a
propaganda play revolving around a steel strike, cement
workers, and the "socially unassorted." To the gossip the
playwright replied that it was nothing of the kind; that it
refuted, or attempted to refute, the theory that the meek
shall inherit the earth and to raise the issue whether anybody
with ideals can make headway in the tough world. To leave
that query unanswered was possible to meditation, but words
and action, even in drama, did make an answer in fact, if
only provisionally and tentatively.

The vitality of the sociological group was again illustrated in 1938 by the organization of the Playwrights'
Company composed of men with "wisdom and experience,"
not "fledglings." Under its auspices were immediately produced two successful plays: Knickerbocker Holiday and
Abe Lincoln in Illinois. Once more the power of collective
effort was demonstrated. It was on the basis of group experiences that the American Theater Council was formed
in 1937 for the purpose of criticizing manuscripts and inducing a greater flow of high-grade plays for the country.

§

With bold experimentation shaking the traditions of playwrights and productions, what was taking place in that much
acclaimed source of dramatic expression — the world of

schools and colleges? With what themes was it concerned? What creative imagination did it foster or display? It was a poor institution of learning indeed that did not "do something in dramatics." After all, Eugene O'Neill had studied at Harvard and Princeton, Maxwell Anderson at the University of North Dakota and Leland Stanford; and Archibald MacLeish at Yale and Harvard. Turning from inspiration purely academic, Stephens College in Missouri called Maude Adams to give instruction to girls in dramatic expression. Undoubtedly there were relations, if often tenuous, between the schools and the stage. Playwrights and actors did not burst into full power without encountering some educational experiences, somewhere.

But judging by the collegiate plays produced on campuses and frequently outside, the formal world of dramatic education was little affected by either the regular theater or the course of national affairs. In the year 1937 the fifty-year-old Mask and Wig Club of Pennsylvania University presented Fifty-Fifty, a bit of fluff, as light as air, the mimicry of women by an all-man cast attaining the acme of masculine interpretation. At the center of the banter was Mimi, a gypsy, a child-woman of Hawaii, who persuaded her father to modernize the tribe by adopting fifty trailer gadgets tendered by her salesman-lover; and so equipped with modernity, the gypsies glided to a new habitat in the fiftieth state — to the delight of old graduates in the audience. Afterwards the student players slipped away to their dancing. The flight from substance was almost complete. But in 1938 the Club took a sociological turn in All Around the Town, a satire on celebrated features of contemporary civilization, ranging from night clubs to dictators and radio broadcasting.

From the Workshop at Yale, with its superb theatrical equipment, a group of six persons organized as the Eastern Collegiate Players, came forth with two one-act plays, Gift of Gold and The Bride Wore Red Pyjamas, written for motion-picture devotees. The leader of this group lamented that audiences "had been sitting through the same old

Westerns, domestic dramas, and gangster operas for years without a whimper," and concluded: "We know that we were quieter than most of these and perhaps a little shorter." When the Collegiate Players submitted their plays to the judgment of girls at Smith College, they received a verdict that the "little venture would set the American theater back fifty or sixty years" — a judgment that might lack in historicity more than it did in emphasis. Despite the adverse conclusion of the Smith girls, the Players gave 427 performances on tour, conceding at the end that while their show was "nothing to make an audience stand up and cheer, it was one that they would listen to, laugh at a little, and even applaud now and then." Pleased with this achievement, the group planned to adjust its sketches to the average motion-picture patron and ignore any high-hatted minority likely to be present.

To celebrate the forty-ninth anniversary of dramatics at Princeton, the Triangle Club chose to "put on" a musical comedy in 1937, called Fol-de-rol, fashioned on the frivolity of the English Restoration period at the end of the seventeenth century. With this play the Club, carrying twenty-five dancers, toured the East, Middle West, and South during the holiday season. Everywhere it was greeted by Princeton alumni, their families, and friends, with a cordiality which implied that no intellectual interruption had come in the Princeton tradition through the flight of years. While the Princeton boys were going back to the English Restoration for inspiration, girls at Barnard clung to the Greek drama, as they understood it, impersonated horses in chariot races, and tried to be Pan or Dionysus. In such fashions were illustrated the advantages of collegiate training in the classic sources of dramatic inspiration and in the art of histrionic expression.

§

In the strange times of the midpassage, entertainment by radio expanded with the pressures of mass production, as in-

ventions and improvements in devices flowed out of laboratories and workshops; and it responded to those forces, financial, intellectual, and moral, which affected other forms of
diversion and communication. As in the case of the moving-
picture industry, broadcasting on a national scale tended to
come within the control of relatively few corporations possessing large capital and equipment; and these corporations
in turn became entangled with banking on the one side and
with supply interests, especially the electrical industries, on
the other. They borrowed money; their stocks were sold on
the exchange or over the counter; capitalists with funds to
invest could buy into them and exercise the rights of stockholders in determining the policies of management and the
selection of broadcast themes. Like the moving-picture
industry, the radio industry was engaged in mass production.
Dependent almost entirely upon advertisers for their revenues
and profits, national broadcasting concerns had to reach out
for the millions, for the lowest common denominators, ignor-
ing in the main "the select few, the élite, the precious."
Under such pecuniary drives, entertainment over the air
went wider and deeper throughout American society than
any other type of amusement, diversion, or suggestion.

Through the installation of the radio in private homes and
hotels, in offices and shops, in schools and other institutions,
in motor cars and trains, on tractors and plows, the market
for receivers became almost universal in America. Special
devices furnishing "free-wind" power enabled rural homes in
regions not yet electrified to have the radio; farmers' wives in
their kitchens could listen to an all-day program indoors
while their husbands in the fields could get the same out of
doors. As they toured for fares in the cities, taxicab drivers
could divert themselves with their dials. For the leisure class,
radios were designed to fit lounging chairs and coffee tables.

While tonal quality of reception was being improved, the
keyboards for tuning in were being made as "easy to read as
a ruler." In a split-second, the owner of the "refined" radio
could get the station he desired merely by pressing the button

marked with the call letters. And on the basis of sales after January, 1937, business leaders looked forward in August to 9,000,000 buyers of these perfected instruments for that single year. August forecasts ran the figure for radio sets of all kinds in the homes up to 26,000,000 and added 5,000,000 for autos. On that basis radio manufacturing proceeded.

Through radio enterprise, including the radio-phonograph combination, the broadcasting business reached comparable proportions. The number of broadcasting stations mounted to 674 as of October, 1937. Cincinnati acquired a million-dollar station, built according to modern architectural taste and containing an auditorium seating 600 persons, twelve studios, a music library, and twenty-eight offices for the administrators. The Rockefellers provided New York with Radio City, in which the National Broadcasting Company settled permanently, occupying palatial quarters high in the sky.

Seeing that the radio was becoming a powerful competitor for advertising and in the distribution of news, proprietors of newspapers reached out for control and by the end of 1936 at least 168, or about twenty-six per cent of the commercial radio stations, were under the dominance of newspapers or their affiliates. In 1938 promoters were so enthusiastic that a project for a broadcast newspaper — Nation — was actually on their docket. Inventors were trying to perfect a method for producing from the radio news a kind of continuous newspaper automatically printed on receiving machines installed in homes, by the bedside if desired.

As the demand rose for "features" to be broadcast, supply concerns were created to furnish stations with any kind of verbal or tonal commodity on a minute's notice and in wholesale lots. One of the high stakes in this branch of the industry was held by amusement specialists known as Tin Pan Alley, domiciled in New York City. In 1937 it was equipped to turn out daily wares for hundreds of stations about as fast as manufacturers could roll out cars or lipsticks. It also furnished highly-paid song writers to the moving-picture producers of the land. "Constant bustle" kept the offices at white heat. According to a reporter who surveyed an establishment, "a movie outfit wants a specified number of ballads on specified themes before a specified date. A radio band leader needs a new swing tune for a definitely scheduled program. A soprano orders a theme song. The publisher himself must have a dreamy waltz to balance a new catalog. As deadlines approach for melody orders, song teams work straight through lunch and dinner and, if necessary, far into the night." Tin Pan Alley, in short, was as hysterical as the mad market which it served.

Knowing that they had a competitor in the radio, and yet unable to prevent its expansion, adventurous moving-picture producers decided to benefit from the supply business at least. Well acquainted with the fact that "what is given away in millions of homes cannot be sold for an admission price," they formed alliances with commercial sponsors of radio broadcasts in 1937 and sold the talent of their studios in the market of the air. In Your Hollywood Parade a manufacturer of cigarettes brought the stars of the Warner Brothers to the national assembly of radio listeners. But this experiment provoked more questions of a pecuniary nature: Would the people now prefer to "listen in" at home beside their sets instead of going to the movie houses to look? Or would they be incited by what they heard at home to pass through the box offices on their way to see as well as hear?

Perhaps such questions were to be answered by television, bringing more pecuniary dilemmas to the radio and movie industries alike. With intense concentration, inventors worked to make this device technically effective and commercially marketable. Although the date of that achievement could not be fixed, the thought of American entertainment and instruction was energized by faith in the impending event. It was contended by critics of the microphone that its "cold, mute" aloofness could never make a Henry Irving or an Ellen Terry out of any actor or actress, nor a Patrick Henry or a Daniel Webster out of any politician, however magnetic voices might be in themselves. But if television was to be perfected the dynamic personalities of actors, politicians, and other public figures could be made visible to their audiences, and in some measure more alive. While the subtlest forces uniting speaker and auditor in warm relations could not be induced even by television, sight blended with sound promised to raise the temperature of American amusement, diversion, and discussion in the home.

Program by program the interests and passions of the throbbing universe were enlisted in the service of the radio. Lonely women in isolated cottages could be entranced every day, if they wished, by the crooning of the "women's sweetheart" — not as of old a troubadour hymning heroics but a paid hack chanting of You, You, You — or they could pick up items touching the conduct of their households and the management of their children if they so desired. Farmers at their chores in barns or fields could get weather reports, prices of crops, baseball scores, or the joking of Amos 'n' Andy. In country or town, persons to whom good music was an esthetic delight could tune in on symphony concerts put on the air by the leading orchestras of the nation, varied by grand opera distributed from its great center in New York City.

Even into the music programs, however, were injected the rush and roar of a factory-like enterprise. "The idea seems to be," complained one customer, "to give at least eight or nine items, with the result that the performers are breathless, while the condition of the listener is one of complete exhaustion. Instead of cutting programs in half so that everything can move along in an orderly manner, the pace is so feverish that the final chords of one number have hardly faded when the announcer is back again detailing the next item." Time was costly and not a moment was to be lost.

The factory taint attached to symphony concerts and operas was made especially obtrusive by the introduction of advertising. Such music was expensive to broadcast. Only the biggest advertisers, the "financial angels," could afford to sponsor it, and for sponsorship the pound of flesh was taken. Before concerts opened, auditors were put in a frame of mind for musical appreciation by the announcement of the soap, perfume, or gadget that was paying the bill. During pauses, announcers kept audiences aware of the commodity that was serving as patron saint. And at the end, when enchanting strains were sinking into memory, came the renewed tender of the sponsoring soap, perfume, or gadget. So music was charged with the blares of the marketplace. This had definite drawbacks, but radio listeners in America accepted them, though not without complaint. Perhaps they were more willing to take advertising with their music than to pay for it themselves through an annual tax on radio sets.

Carrying music, story telling for young and old, sporting events, comic skits, news reporting, prize fight announcements, and similar diversions, broadcasting programs were pitched to the general level of the vast audience. It seemed that almost everybody who had anything to say and nearly every idea bidding for popular allegiance had a hearing. Minorities protested that they were not accorded their due proportion of space and the necessity of paying for it was a handicap to them. Yet among the items, amounting to more than seven thousand daily in 1937, few interests that attracted any considerable proportion of the population eluded review in one form or another.

And here and there in the democracy of the profusion serious efforts were made to introduce and apply intelligence and artistry. After he had discovered that delicacies of tone as well as stridency could be transmitted, the great conductor, Leopold Stokowski, consented to broadcast symphony concerts. For months he had worked directly with radio engineers on the problem of refining transmission, and after making his first successful demonstration he continued to labor at the task of perfecting the mechanical device. Such efforts in behalf of culture were rewarded by popular appreciation; and quick to make use of anything that "paid its way," owners of broadcasting stations saved "time" for the

best that musicians could produce. Toscanini and Paderew-
ski became as popular in the air as they had been on the
platform.

Yielding to the demand for manifestations of intelligence
amid the great noise, broadcasting companies allotted some
room, often grudgingly, to poetry, drama, book reviewing,
education, information tests, and the discussions of public
questions, apart from the arguments of politicians. Thus
Shakespeare's Twelfth Night eventually competed for
popularity with Mae West's sex appeal. In 1937 Archibald
McLeish's dramatic poem, The Fall of the City, a tragedy of
dictator worship, went over the air in reply to the orations of
contemporary dictators who shouted to democrats in America
through the microphone. Under the auspices of the Town
Hall of the Air in New York City, the chief issues of the days
were debated by speakers of competence, subject to the
criticisms of hecklers.

As to the effect of all this uproar upon the multitude of
listeners, estimates were more difficult to formulate than in
the case of the moving pictures, and the best of calculations
remained little more than guesses. Amid all the din, however, one thing could not be refuted: contemplation, meditation, and quiet reading were made increasingly difficult for
men and women throughout the country. If a father or
mother wished to do a little thinking or to read a book, the
children might insist on having noise. Children had, it is
true, always indulged in clatter of their own making, limited
somewhat by their physical strength, but now canned rumbles,
thumps, and rattles poured out of radio sets, unremittingly
and ceaselessly. Even adults, formerly accustomed to read
in silent rooms, acquired the habit of sitting with books open
on their knees, if open at all, while the radio blared or crooned
its rival attractions. At home or abroad, in hotels and streets,
at bars and on railway trains, and in taxicabs, the everlasting
cacophony went on day and night. It was not surprising,
then, that James Rowland Angell, former president of
Yale University, after serving as an adviser to a national

broadcasting concern, confessed somewhat disconsolately that education, even in the most diluted form, was a kind of waif in the radio storm.

§

Everything considered, attempts to measure, appraise, and evaluate the influence and promise of the radio, especially in relation to democracy, brought few positive results. Unmistakably, in totalitarian countries, where the radio was a censored government monopoly, it was an instrument of sheer authority for enslaving the minds of auditors, crushing opposition, and producing a rigid uniformity of thought and feeling. In the United States on the contrary, where the business was in private hands and to a large extent competitive, broadcasters relied almost entirely upon advertisers for leadership. Only great corporations, with immense resources, could afford to pay for expensive programs. Would business concerns, therefore, enmesh all actors, musicians, orators, producers, announcers, crooners, educators, and commentators in their scheme of values and proprieties? Would such concentration reënforce economic conservatism, strengthen vulgarity, and drive the American mind to an undemocratic Right? If so, and business enterprise could not of its own motion find a way out of the dilemma of unemployment and mass poverty, would the radio merely make more explosive the snap of the tension when it came? Such questions inevitably made the issue of free speech over the radio a prime consideration, and in so doing brought the Federal Government, representing all classes and interests, into the discussion of the radio's future.

Indeed there was no way for owners of broadcasting stations to keep the Government out of the scene. By its very mechanical nature, radio broadcasting could not be left solely to "free enterprise." The number of wave lengths for transmission was limited and too many stations in a given area would lead to mutual interference and destruction. Only a small number could operate successfully in the United States and the radio industry composed of competing interests could not, or did not, police itself. So control by the Federal Government was invoked, the number and location of stations compatible with efficient service was determined, and no station was allowed to proceed without a federal license. Otherwise there would have been utter chaos. To administer the "order" thus established in the air, the Federal Communications Commission was created and given power to license private concerns on the basis of "public convenience and necessity." For a time the Commission left some of the radio spectrum, or series of wave lengths, in individual hands free from licensing and control, but in 1937 it assumed supervision over practically the entire range.

With the adoption and extension of federal supervision, all the old conflicts of economics and politics reached this field of interest. When Frank R. McNinch was appointed chairman of the Communications Commission by President Roosevelt in 1937, he laid the cards frankly on the table. Was the radio industry a public utility, a kind of monopoly subject to specific types of regulation? Or was it a competitive industry, holding down prices while, in the higgling of the market, advertisers paid the bills? Did not the high charges made by some companies and the concentration of control over chains in the hands of relatively few concerns indicate that the radio was following the trend of corporate centralization in general?

Since neither the Government nor the American people could arrive at a conclusion on the merits of trust-busting and regulation in other industries, how was any major decision possible in respect of the radio? If private monopoly was intolerable, what would happen if the radio became a government monopoly? Broadcasting companies, it was alleged, had censored their programs and speakers, or at all events had exerted selective pressures on them. But how could the existing freedom of speech, such as it was, be preserved if the Federal Government assumed direct charge or operated the industry, as in Great Britain, through a government corporation? Around these questions revolved a prolix debate. If the industry was to continue, permanent evasion of such issues was impossible.

A neat question, touching this problem, involved the form and support of radio programs to be transmitted to neighboring Latin America — a matter which seemed to many citizens and officials to become exigent after European dictators, hostile to democracy, began supplying their propaganda, even in the guise of music, to the nations south of the United States. What, then, could be offered by the United States as a democratic offset and as a means of awakening sympathy among peoples who had not experienced democracy? What, precisely, was this democracy to be explained over the air? Were Amos 'n' Andy, bedtime stories, symphony concerts, and kitchen recipes adequate to the occasion, or was something else needed to convince the people beyond the Rio Grande that the democratic way was the best of all ways? In just what terms was American civilization to be described as the grand contrast to the culture of fascism? Since exaggeration comparable to the extravagances of European utterances was demanded as an offset to such propaganda, exactly what kind of exaggeration would most effectively serve that purpose?

CHAPTER XIII

Mainsprings and Ranges of Letters

No less than the makers of entertainment, the makers of letters worked in the substances and styles of the age. The business of America is business. . . . High plateau of permanent prosperity. . . . Another downward slide in agricultural prices. . . . The spectre of poverty vanishing. . . . Foreclosure of farm mortgages. . . . Republican policies. . . . Hawley-Smoot tariff bill. . . . Crash in Wall Street. . . . Reassurances from Washington. . . . Millions of tons of top soil washing out to sea. . . . Stocks. . . . Bonds. . . . Brilliant opening of the opera season. . . . Hollywood Hit. . . . Colossal. . . . Stupendous. . . . Crime. . . . Stocks. . . . Bonds. . . . Unemployment mounts. . . . Hilariously funny. . . . Stocks. . . . Bonds. . . . Bread lines. . . . Sweepstakes. . . . Millions idle. . . . Bankruptcies. . . . Army Maneuvers. . . . Election. . . . . Save rugged individualism. . . . Roosevelt promises an adequate navy. . . . Crop control plan endorsed. . . . More millions idle. . . . Suicide. . . . Save liberty. . . . Bank crashes. . . . Dancing lessons at reduced prices. . . .

Schools close doors. . . . Bank holidays. . . . New Deal inaugurated. . . . N.R.A. . . . A.A.A. . . . C.C.C. . . . P.W.A. . . . C.W.A. . . . Abundant life. . . . Signs of recovery. . . . Supreme Court blocks New Deal. . . . Foul breath of Moscow. . . . Twelve million idle. . . . Roosevelt carries forty-six states. . . . New hit from Hollywood. . . . Ill-fed, ill-nourished, ill-housed. . . . Roosevelt's plan for revamping judiciary. . . . The Constitution in danger. . . . Communism. . . . The Constitution in danger. . . . Learn swing. . . . War rages in Spain. . . . Kidnapers busy. . . . Big Apple. . . . Sit-down strikes. . . . War in China. . . . Recession. . . . Idleness rises. . . . Syphilis must be stamped out. . . . Birth control goes forward. . . . Debts. . . . Deficits. . . . Vigilantes. . . . Business strikes. . . . More railway bankruptcies. . . . Super-navy. . . . Civil liberties. . . . National defense. . . . Depression. . . . Trade agreements. . . . Catholic protests against films deemed favorable to Loyalist Spain. . . . Quarantines. . . . House votes billion for navy. . . . Whither? Why? Whither? Why?

Ears could not muffle the detonations nor could eyes misread the headlines that daily recorded shocks and agonies, diversions and pleasures. The coldest of hearts were not chill enough to congeal the distempers and resentments surging up in the course of personal and social transactions. Where life was, there was the clamorous insistence of personalities and events. To live was to know — at least something of contemporary fears, hopes, appeals, sufferings, frenzies, escapes, evaluations, decisions, and aspirations. To think as well as to know was to employ some wisdom related to the elements of the situation. To feel and to wonder were to join the quest for an interpretation of the ways pursued by fortune.

Mingled in the minds of writers with impressions received from immediate events were memory and knowledge of the literary traditions in America built up in times past by masters and apprentices and kept alive by the elders of the craft still living. For the precious and the genteel, making the best of both worlds, matrices had been left, for example, by such exponents of the reputable as Hamilton Wright Mabie, Richard Watson Gilder, and Josiah Gilbert Holland. For the larger public, Mark Twain had written prose and Walt Whitman and Vachel Lindsay had written poetry, in a distinctly democratic way, sometimes in joyful acceptance of American life, sometimes reiterating plaints against the lawyers and money-lenders as old as the laments of Daniel Shays.

A third tradition, set by unquestioned masters dead and living, was that of positive dissidence, the inability to accept the American scene. Throughout the course of imaginative literature in America, and particularly since the Second Revolution of 1861–1865, the accent of criticism had been acute. One of the chief mainsprings had been dislike of the plutocracy which burst upon the stage in full panoply during the gilded age, a displeasure burnt into the novels of Edith Wharton, Winston Churchill, and to a considerable extent of Henry James, all of whom were ranked by their contemporaries as literary artists of high order. The values upon which their criticisms rested had been fundamentally middle class in imputation and the source of their revolt had been essentially nostalgia for the past, real or romantic. Sharing in a degree the same distaste for the plutocracy, another dissident school of novelists, represented by William Dean Howells, Edward Bellamy, Jack London, and Upton Sinclair, had as its standard of criticism an idealized future rather than a past — a future neither plutocratic nor middle class but socialistic in its theory and practice.

Unable to submit unreservedly to any one of the four fairly definite types of social valuation, another group of writers had given the country a tradition of literary insurgency without permanently fixing the locus of their exasperation or indicating the end of their desires. In 1928 Eugene O'Neill, whose work had awakened great expectancy, still seemed unable to break the bonds that confined his genius within the terms of personal struggles and frustration. Robert Frost and Carl Sandburg in poetry, and Sherwood Anderson in prose, voiced emotions that had turned and veered but had no precise terminus. After leaving the American Mercury, Henry L. Mencken remained in a fine fury against the Philistines, fairly bursting his afflatus in a crusade that finally brought him up short in the political camp of Alfred M. Landon. Memories of Frank Norris, David Graham Phillips, and Robert W. Chambers — the mighty Galahads of the joust against corruptionists and plutocrats — lingered as fuel for more vexations of spirit. Neither The Octopus nor The Deluge nor Cardigan was entirely forgotten by the writers who pondered on theme and appeal. With Sinclair Lewis' Main Street and Babbitt continuing in wide circulation, the petty bourgeois was getting a drubbing as severe as that administered to the plutocrat — when the thunder of 1929 announced the opening of frantic days. Nowhere in this heritage of dissident form, style, and interest was there a sign that sheer optimism might soon gloss over the antipathies of times passed and passing.

According to Lewis Mumford, "everyone who grew up" in the period immediately preceding the crash of 1929 "had a conscious or unconscious debt to Van Wyck Brooks." And what was this debt? It was a bill owed to Brooks for his peculiar brand of biting criticism respecting American society, coupled with his keen appreciation of its potentialities for improvement. "Long before the modern movement had begun in American literature, in 1908," said Mumford, "when David Graham Phillips was a promising writer and Mr. Theodore Dreiser was a neglected 'genius' and Mr. Mencken was exercising his European scholarship and his knowledge of Nietzsche, before Mr. Frost had published 'A Boy's Will' or Vachel Lindsay had preached his Gospels of beauty, in a day when the Woodberrys and Barrett Wendells loftily shuddered at Whitman, and the American past was the sort of thing that nice people didn't mention in public, except in relation to George Washington or the Puritan fathers — in these days Mr. Brooks was the first to announce that we had still to discover the body of our country and had still to use its earth and its sky and the experience that lay between them in the creation of American art and thought. Mr. Brooks, throughout this whole period, was perhaps the only critic who both saw the importance of using our American sources, and the equal necessity . . . of holding our own expression in literature up to the highest standard. The school that was interested in standards and values forgot America and, within their narrow university walls, had no commerce with its life; the school that was interested in American life, and dilated on the esthetics of the comic supplement or the exquisite style of the Advertisement, had no values; but Mr. Brooks was the first of our critics, since Emerson's time, to have both, and to keep both equally in view."

In short, a critical strain had characterized strong currents of literature previous to the economic crisis of 1929 — dissatisfaction with the pecuniary culture produced by the enormous growth and power of the plutocracy and its Philistine imitations. The vulgarisms of conspicuous waste, satirized by Veblen at the turn of the century in The Theory of the Leisure Class, had continued to try the spirit of those who worked in imaginative letters. If, as always, censure had been accompanied by belief in some ideal, clear or vague, attained but lost or not yet attained, attainable or perhaps half inevitable, still the censure was unmistakable, sometimes humorous, often bitter.

Unwilling to endure the stresses and ugliness in the American scene, more than one novelist had fled from the New World to more congenial cultures in the Old World. In his Portrait of the American as Artist, published in 1930, Matthew Josephson dealt sympathetically with American writers who went beyond the sea to their Holy Grail in England, France, or Italy. For a brief moment at that time an iridescent apparition seemed to be suspended over Moscow.

If such had been the state of the literary arts in the years before the great depression, if criticism of American economy and culture had long been the insistent motif, what was to be expected after the deluge that followed the general breakdown of 1929? In the late nineteenth century the plutocrat, his ladies, and his politicians had been a theme of literature. Now investigation after investigation and bankruptcy after bankruptcy were unfolding more evidences of their mutuality in interest and operation — revealing some Lords of Creation as betrayers of fiduciary trust and in a few cases even as plain criminals. Finally a President of the United States, popularly applauded, was threatening to drive the money changers from the temple. Were writers to take account of the typhonic events, the fear of social dissolution, the dreams of a reorganized society? Were novelists and poets to rewarm their tradition, their heritage of realism, censure, humor, irony, hope for a better world? Or was America to close its literature? Writing certainly did not cease. What writers, then, what books, what imagery or symbolism, captured esteem and commanded loyalty?

§

A survey of the Best Books of the Decade from 1926 to 1935, made by A. D. Dickinson, covering the years of the golden glow and the black depression, disclosed the intellectual and moral evaluations of the reading public. The survey was based upon 102 sources of information, including library book lists, review digests, group and "expert" classifications, booksellers' selections for the White House, anthologies, and other compilations. Out of such data, more or less statistical, the surveyor arrived at certain conclusions respecting the "best" books of the period, using the term to mean "selected by a consensus of expert opinion as most worthy the attention of intelligent American readers." On this basis Dickinson compiled lists of "favorite authors" and "best books" of the ten years in the several divisions of intellectual interest, general and special. It could be said, of course, that the expert opinion so registered was principally middle class in source; even so, the appraisals expressed the concerns and dominant ideas of the largest reading and writing class amid the upswing and crash of American economy, revolutions and wars abroad, and overturns in domestic politics. Whoever sought to meditate upon American culture thus possessed a group of impressive materials in books widely distributed and elaborately praised in the current years.

At the top of the list of Dickinson's twenty-five "favorite authors" for the years 1926–1935 stood, in order, James Truslow Adams, Willa Cather, Pearl Buck, and Ellen Glasgow — one historical and political writer and three novelists. Mr. Adams' *New England in the Republic, 1776–1850*, published in 1926, had been acclaimed both for scholarship and for grace of style. His subsequent writings on current questions were marked by devotion to the historic ideal of individualism, the advocacy of mild reforms, criticism of the New Deal, and defense of the general principles espoused by the Republican party. He had by no means accepted all the policies pursued by the Lords of Creation, but in the political division his fundamental allegiance lay on their side. Of the novelists, Willa Cather had avoided the stresses and strains represented by unemployment, bankruptcy, defaults, and growing labor unrest and found refuge in preciosities of language, devotion to beauty in itself, and solace in the mystic reaches of the soul; Pearl Buck up to this point had directed her sympathies toward the primordials of life and culture in far-off China; Ellen Glasgow, while personally sensitive to the pending and impending conflicts in America and keenly receptive to the idea of change as necessity, had skirted around the volcanic center of contemporary events in her fiction. Nor was it without social implications that the zestful poet, Carl Sandburg, who had known toil and sweat as a casual laborer and had written of the world he knew, stood at the bottom of Dickinson's list of the twenty-five "favorites."

In the schedule of "fifty best books," evaluated by the survey, the five standing first were Mark Sullivan's Our Times, Douglas Southall Freeman's Robert E. Lee, Pearl Buck's Good Earth, Willa Cather's Death Comes for the Archbishop, and Thornton Wilder's Bridge of San Luis Rey. There was the cream of the years in the judgment of the market. Parrington's Main Currents in American Thought ranked thirty-seventh and Stuart Chase's Men and Machines, forty-fourth. Heading the eight "best books on philosophy, psychology, ethics, and religion" was Will Durant's chatty Story of Philosophy; ranking fourth in this category was Walter Lippmann's genial Preface to Morals; and a place at the bottom was assigned to Bertrand Russell's erudite Philosophy, with less than half the "points" of evaluation given to the work at the head of the roll. In the field of the "social sciences," the Encyclopaedia of the Social Sciences rated first, Chase's Men and Machines second, and Lewis Corey's Decline of American Capitalism next to the last of twenty-five books. Helen Gardner's Art through the Ages crowned the pyramid of "the ten best books on art and music."

In the three years which followed the decade covered by Dickinson's survey nothing occurred in the literary market to alter the general verdict of his statistical returns. No new "favorite" author burst upon the scene with an interpretation of life and values essentially different from that presented by the established favorites. No new "best" book offered either a revulsion or revolution in feelings. At the top, among the best-sellers, favorites, and bests, were Van Wyck Brooks and Margaret Mitchell. They too wrote of past times and dealt with memories. Departing from the caustic analysis and the social framework that had marked his earlier work, Brooks now described The Flowering of New England as he saw it, looking backward in 1936 — spoke of Hawthorne, Emerson, and their friends, of apple blossoms, of splashing rivulets, of the fragrant honeysuckle. With such exultation was this sweetness and light hailed by reviewers and readers that stray objections were buried in the oblivion which could so easily be accorded to doubters in America. The Brooks triumph was almost Roman in its magnificence: eager buyers grasped at edition after edition and the author was crowned with the laurels of the Academy.

Although likewise historical in time-setting, Margaret Mitchell's Gone with the Wind was more rugged in its rhetoric and more resonant with the clatter of the contemporary palace and plaza. While it dealt with the moldering tragedy of the civil war, it vibrated with mighty passions — blind, confident, greedy, heroic, futile. Through its pages pressed ardent youth seeking adventure under arms, slaves, soldiers at war and afterwards, the women of their circles, politicians, and speculators. Rhett Butler, a star performer, might have been a contemporary Lord of Creation battening on war trade, with the trader's contempt for the country gentleman's heroics. Bright colors were offset by black soot. In the trail of the perfume came stench. Nevertheless the characters and events were of times long passed and, if the thought was of necessity contemporary, it was softened and blurred by the illusion of shadowy perspective. So clothed in the appearances of distance, if intelligible to a society still in conflict, Gone with the Wind made a national sensation and sold more than a million copies in the years of the great economic plague.

§

But such surveys of "the favorites" and "the best" by no means encompassed the vast range of American letters; nor did they cover the incomparable richness and diversity of themes and modulations. As a matter of fact, during the radiance of the golden glow and the tempests of the depression, with rushing vitality imaginative writers reached out further and went deeper for materials than in any previous epoch in American literary development. When the market for material goods narrowed and publishers complained of declining sales, dynamic writing seemed to be stimulated, not quenched. If there ever had been an Augustan age in American letters it certainly had not come to a close in falling energies and decaying intellectual powers. Although stocks were in the doldrums and trade remained dull, publishers' desks were heaped high with manuscripts and, discard as they did by the thousands, the volume of their publication continued to be enormous.

For the several forms of media to which writers resorted all human interests and manifestations of life in all kinds of places and circumstances were utilized as content. Authors turned their microscopes on every nook and cranny of geography — regions, cities, towns, villages, lonely farms, plains, mountains, deserts, bayous, lakes, and seas — North, South, East, and West. This they did with such thoroughness that if all other records were destroyed and novels alone survived, students in some distant age could reconstruct from the pages of fiction alone the human geography of the United States in the age of Coolidge, Hoover, and Roosevelt. Every phase of the family, for instance, and in its varied connections was explored and described — love, the eternal triangle, relations legal and economic, parent and child, conflict of generations, and lines of heredity, in all social settings from the idle rich to the idle poor. Classes and races, their characteristics, their cultures, and their clashes were also themes as immediate materials or as illustrations of broader facets of the everlastingly human. All types of persons were pressed into the service of literary artistry: politicians, economic dynasts, labor leaders, industrial workers, farm laborers, brahmins, puritans, cavaliers, feminine careerists, and all the rest. The focus of inquiry was brought to bear on multitudes of "the plain people"; on the ferments among their several orders. Descending to the ultimate unit, the individual, resourceful writers meticulously dissected and described single persons variously circumstanced, making their way in American society, struggling for a living, seeking compensations for suffering, hunting for some gyroscopic principle that would give steadiness and assurance amid the welter, the hopeless discontent, and despairing hope of the times. And although convenience for thinking about the sum of imaginative literature required classification as to theme and emphasis, any classification was bound to be more or less false, so interwoven were the strands of life which ran through the classes of literature.

While many writers still insisted that their function was to sing into the sky if they wanted to or "describe things as they actually were," some of their fellow travelers were conscious of the philosophic implications raised by their very language and saw something to be gained by considering them, if dimly and without gaining any absolute certainty. Among writers, literary critics, editors, and publishers proceeded a vigorous discussion of controlling philosophies for selection and emphasis in imaginative letters and of the writer's role in society. This interrogation and sifting of opinions brought into letters all the currents of thought that had run through philosophy, theology, politics, economics, and historiography for centuries. On every side the Socratic elenchus was freely applied to cherished convictions and enthusiastic ambitions. As imaginative literature was swept nearer to the vortex of great politics and economics, so it was more interpenetrated by the thought, majestic and mean, that had been generated in other manifestations of culture.

Apart from idea, substance, and philosophy, imaginative letters were characterized by great energies, penetrating and searching interest, indefatigable studies first and second hand, indubitable force and literary skill, and a sensitivity to the action and spirit of the time. No longer regnant were the simple hopes of Horatio Alger or the polished refinements of Hamilton Wright Mabie; none was able to "translate the stubbornness of fortune into so quiet and so sweet a style." What was equally significant for the nature and future of American culture was the wide distribution of skills and powers throughout the country. No metropolis or region monopolized them. The intellectual and moral forces for sustained writing seemed to burst out spontaneously in city, town, village, farmstead, desert, and valley, as if some protean urge had shaken the whole nation.

"Contact with life" — with the vernacular, perduring or ever renewed — was the clue to the new writing. In no corner of the literary world did writers wholly withdraw from this vitalizing relationship to copy old masters, refine, whittle, and polish inherited models, to play with convention and tradition in a spirit of literary affectation. Even when they resorted to what was recklessly and often falsely called "escapist" fiction, they did not shine entirely by reflected light.

After all, human nature underlay and survived the fortunes of States, politics, industries, institutions, and academies — pomp and circumstance of every kind — and continued to exhibit its facets and propensities, however colored and deflected by current events. It never wearied of romantic love, the characteristic that so sharply distinguished the family impulse in Western civilization from the categorical regimen of the Orient. Nor did it ever cease to thirst for adventure, for mystery, for the primitive from which it sprang, for the wit and humor that enlivened the commonplaces of life from the cradle through the bridal chamber to the grave. Despite its narrowness and meanness, human nature never failed to display, upon occasions great and small, qualities of character that gave an elevation and dignity to life, even to its trivialities.

In the face of many warnings from philosophers, annotators, and dust sifters, mankind, with or without benefit of clergy, insisted on conceiving history as tragedy, as divine comedy, as progress toward a golden day, or as melodrama, with heroes, heroines, and villains. And respecting the truth of things as they actually had been or were, such conceptions of life, for all any one knew, might be nearer reality than the most solemn treatise composed for personal satisfaction or the classroom or the parlor table. Graphs could reveal variations in American culture, but the breath of life could not be blown into digits, curves, and cubes. To be sure, no writer of fiction brought the whole of that culture into an artistically composite unity. Nor did anybody else. On the American continent there was no tight frame of aristocracy, middle class, and toiling mass, such as had engaged the genius of Byron, Thackeray, George Eliot, and Dickens in England. "The Great American Novel" was not achieved in this epoch of the midpassage — doubtless lay beyond the powers of any genius — but many important and powerful novels were written as the solemn ways of Mr. Coolidge's age merged into the kinematics of the New Deal.

Responding to the multiformity of human experience, imaginative literature ranged from top to bottom, from bottom to top, from the center to the circumference of things. Carrying little or no baggage of pedantry, it could penetrate more swiftly to the heart of human situations and baldly tell truths too shocking for incorporation in the grave pages of sociology or psychology. Whether considered as entertainment or inspiration, it rose above and far outstripped the motion picture, eternally striving to become the agency of the lowest common denominator. It was more plastic, freer in the choice of emphases, less standardized. For many reasons, its influences also ran far beyond those of the stage, notwithstanding the creative liberty and subtle nuances peculiar to the living play; indeed play after play was dramatized from a successful novel. Nor did the formal history, with few women in its pages and fewer romances, compete with imaginative literature in delineating the many-sided manifestations of human nature in action. Over the greatest of State papers and the most accurate statistical tables hung an air of abstractness. In imaginative literature the meaning of such papers and tables could be made as full-blooded as life.

This is not to say that when the plummet reached the depths in all waters that no dregs were stirred and that no writers took advantage of the occasion to exhibit or commercialize wanton prurience. As in every age when preceding order and precious forms had been rudely dislocated by historical events, the pendulum of anarchy had swung far away. That had been true, for instance, in the literature of the English restoration which followed the stern system of Puritanism. Yet when everything was in flux and history was being made at great cost to what had seemed to be eternal institutions, it was difficult, in fact impossible, to determine in every case just where a novel that attempted to depict life as actually lived by men, women, and children of all classes, at all levels of human nature, fell in any scheme of classification separating the prurient in motive from the truth-telling passion of science and art.

No criteria of judgment conceived in terms of mere literary art enabled critics to obtain an unquestionable consensus of informed opinion on the fifty or five hundred books, poems, stories, or essays to be deemed most worthy of admission to the temple of fame. Despite some evident gradations of force in style and substance, any selections from the profuse literary offering, whether for library lists or for historical records, had to be more or less arbitrary and could only serve the purpose of illustrating the variety of ideas and interests represented by imaginative letters. A pretension to a categorical judgment of pure literary merits was bound to be hollow and to be greeted by a torrent of warrantable protests.

§

To the short story the Americans continued to resort like ducks to water. Wedged in between bizarre announcements of manufacturers' commodities for sale, in the magazines, it often seemed a mere appendage to advertisements. Yet a few magazines managed to supply stories without such accessories. Even loaded with advertising appeals to the upper income groups, the New Yorker encouraged a peculiar approach to this form of literature, characterized by whimsy; it was illustrated in Leane Zugsmith's series of stories, Home Is Where You Hang Your Childhood, eventually issued as a separate collection. Without numerous advertising pages, the magazine, Story, transplanted from Majorca to the

United States during this period, manifested a primary interest in snapshot tales as works of art. In 1934 it discovered one of the most original of short-story writers, William Saroyan, who entered its pages with The Daring Young Man on the Flying Trapeze and was soon well launched on his creative career with the coöperation of Mencken's American Mercury.

Saroyan's first little tale dealt with a poverty-stricken writer sleeping fitfully, rising to seek work for sustenance, suffering the pangs of defeat and hunger, dropping back upon his bed for the long sleep but, in the interval of waking, humming the song about a daring young man on a flying trapeze: "a trapeze to God, or to nothing, a flying trapeze to some sort of eternity; and he prayed objectively for strength to make the flight with grace." That the young man succeeded in doing. Grasped in his hand was a one-cent piece which he had found and as he lapsed into his final slumber, he regretted that he had not given it to a child, for a child could buy so many things with a penny.

For a few cents Americans by the thousands were buying the sheets of music about the daring young man and as this music came over the air through the microphone and out of the phonographs, Americans literally by the millions began to sing and whistle in the wind, on their individual trapezes, to God or to nothing, with the daring young man. Thoroughly established on his own course, Saroyan developed the short story as a deft combination of running commentary on life and parable, sinking toward the depths for his subject matter and attaining heights. When Modern Books issued a collection of his stories in 1937, it maintained that Saroyan possessed "a vision as lucid and honest as Whitman's or Rousseau's and clarity akin to the spirit of the early writer-thinkers of the East."

Among the new manipulators of the miniature tale, none was more adventuresome than Erskine Caldwell of Georgia, a Prometheus unbound, using his fire to scorch mankind with accounts of its cruelty, helplessness, ignorance, poverty, and the general inhumanity of man to man. His stories were about people on the soil principally. With the accuracy of his vignettes in detail, the doughtiest Southern defender of regional virtues did not quarrel à toute outrance; but when Caldwell, after using such titles as Kneel to the Rising Sun and The People's Choice, called a collection of his lurid tales, Southways, he was taken to task for implying that such traits and situations as he described were peculiar to the South. Jonathan Daniels, a leading critic of the section himself, also objected to Caldwell's growing inclination to pity his subjects and declared, in effect, that he was exceeding his function as a literary artist in putting his heart into the plight of the wretches whose stories he told. But Daniels was not running away from truth for he said that growing hunger was the great problem of the South.

All Southern localities were made to talk about themselves through the short story. William Faulkner, of Mississippi, undertook to construct a city in that region, Jefferson, with six novels and three volumes of little tales. Among his short stories was a collection entitled The Unvanquished and readers who expected to find only heroes so honored in fiction were surprised to meet Old Granny, a heroine, indomitable though a slave.

In the center of the agrarian middle west, many short-story writers called attention to their region through this medium. Formerly, as Wallace Stegner said in The Saturday Review in connection with Josephine Herbst's novels, westerners had enjoyed "lampooning the culture clubs which sought sordid realism with bated breath and buzzed with indignation when they found it." Now verities were piling up in western fiction and even the cultured were consenting to know the worst as well as the best about their communities. One of the most granitic among the new writers of the short tale was Wallace Stegner himself whom some exuberant critics ranked with Edith Wharton for his ability to tell a story as unvarnished as Ethan Frome.

Taking politics for a gay ride, Katharine Dayton treated

the subject in comic skits which ran in issue after issue of The
Saturday Evening Post. In one of these tales, Mrs. Republican, a comfortable person who loved her quiet old house,
twitted Mrs. Democrat about the "dirt" which had become
so vexing. She had to keep putting up new tariffs, she said,
because the old ones simply would get covered with smoot.
When the Tiger Cat brushed its tail against her knees, Mrs.
Republican exclaimed genially : "Goodness !" In her quiet
old house she could easily forget the Vare machine in Philadelphia.

Foreign politics was a theme chosen by Thomas Wolfe,
determined for once to subdue his volubility and make his
point emphatic. Ancient wisdom had declared that "nothing
is too small to mirror the Buddha" and putting much into
little was surely a fine art. To accomplish that feat, Thomas
Wolfe had more to compress than any of his writing colleagues. But in 1937 the author of the monumental Look
Homeward Angel, a novel of North Carolinians, confined his
turbulent emotions and brought a terrific surge of political
and social ideas to a focus in a brief story called I Have a
Thing to Tell You — his opinion of the totalitarian State in
Germany.

In respect of domestic problems, the short story was a
vehicle for trenchant statements of positions. For instance
the difficulties which second and third generations of immigrants faced in trying to adapt themselves to a new and a
democratic civilization were discussed in the form of narratives dealing with their situation and their ways of handling
it. Irish adolescents in Chicago stood out in bold relief in the
writings of James T. Farrell ; to seventeen stories about them
he gave the title, Can All This Grandeur Perish ? The painful
efforts of Jewish students in the great cities to master the
intricacies of the English language formed the core of
Leonard Q. Ross' merry tales of Hyman Kaplan. Old and
new Americans disporting at Coney Island, the people's
great playground, were the substance of Robert M. Coates'
short story, The Fury, which won an O. Henry award in 1937.

That many of the short stories were more than fugitive leaflets was evidenced in the numerous collections published by the writers themselves and in collections assembled by watchful editors. For example, among the authors' own collections, sometimes grouped under the caption of a leading story, were Stephen Benét's The Devil and Daniel Webster; Dorothy Canfield Fisher's Fables for Parents; Charles C. Dobie's San Francisco Tales; Vincent Sheean's Pieces of a Fan; and Wallace Stegner's Remembering Laughter. With the assistance of Elinor Clark, Horace Gregory collected and published in 1937 a series of leftist brevities entitled New Letters in America. Annually Edward J. O'Brien issued a volume of The Best Short Stories, selected on his principles of excellence, theoretically formal, practically rightist in upshot. And yet, if nothing was too small to mirror the Buddha, neither the short story nor the museum of vignettes satisfied writers and readers who grasped at the fullness of life.

§

Without diminishing the favor accorded to the short story, the "full-bodied" novel continued in vogue and on its larger canvas appeared the shapes and colors of widely assorted social arrangements among the men, women, and children composing American society. At a time when sociologists and hygienists on college campuses were trying to impress upon youth the meaning of the family as a prime social institution, novelists were basing works on the family as they saw it or understood it during the years when millions of families were going to pieces in the high winds of the panic. Gladys Hasty Carroll kept the dignity of life and the worthiness of labor on the land surviving despite business conditions, As the Earth Turns. Ruth Suckow contributed more pictures of The Folks in Iowa; LeRoy MacLeod invited comparisons with farming families in Indiana, in The Crowded Hill. Trilogies and even longer spans of family chronicles were written as interest in what was happening to lines of

heredity, as time unfolded, supplied stimulus for such in-
quiries. New England clans were the substance of Inez
Haynes Irwin's pleasant Family Circle and Samuel Rogers'
Dusk at the Grove — the latter a tale of degeneration.

A Southern family was followed from The Forge and the
Store to Unfinished Cathedral by T. S. Stribling, to its cul-
mination in an atmosphere of commercialized religion, with
Muscle Shoals, the Ku Klux Klan, and the Scottsboro boys
figuring prominently in its setting. Passing beyond ordinary
secular affairs, in These Bars of Flesh, Stribling ridiculed
higher education so remorselessly that John Erskine, reviewing
the book amid memories of his own professorial days, refused
to take it seriously and preferred merely to enjoy it. It was
in Stribling's neighborhood, not far away, that Edward
Turpin of Mississippi traced four generations of Negroes
rising out of their slave past. Marjorie Kinnan Rawlings put
families from the Florida scrub lands on the literary map with
South Moon Under and The Yearling. In 1938 Laura Krey
described the renewal of a planting family in Texas after its
trials in the civil war, under the title, . . . And Tell of Time.
The struggle of a family to become merely rich in a capitalist
society and the proneness of women to waste their affections
on futilities, in vain at that, was the content of a trilogy proposed by Josephine Herbst and executed in part with Pity
Is Not Enough and The Executioner Waits.

One of the most horrendous family novels was Maria
Sandoz's story of her own group in the sandhills of Nebraska.
Her father, Old Jules, had been born in Switzerland and
studied medicine there in his youth. But he came to the new
world and went west to farm. With the ferocity of a lion, he
persisted in subduing a cattle region to crop bearing and in
the course of his career he struck down everything that stood
in his way. His very wives quailed and died in his company
but he found new women ready to try living with him. Here
was man wrestling with the soil in a terrifying fury, in a
strange spot of the earth where nature had incalculable ways
herself, the contest between human will and nature's course

forming a phase of this cyclopean drama of family life in the High Plains.

Second and third generations of immigrants figured in several of the long chronicles: in Meyer Levin's narrative of The Old Bunch, which pursued the fate of nineteen Jewish boys and girls of Chicago freed from sweatshop servitude to adventure in the professions and in politics, to racketeer, gamble, or succumb to parasitism and inertia; in William Carlos Williams' study of middle-class immigrants in Manhattan, White Mule; and in Daniel Fuchs' Jewish group portraiture, Summer in Williamsburg. Using materials on family life to develop the theme of character in slow maturing, Vardis Fisher produced a tetralogy; after declaring that Passions Spin the Plot, he argued that No Villain Need Be. In Roots in the Sky, Sidney Meller placed in juxtaposition the Jewish elders of a community trying to uphold the Talmudic code and their offspring endeavoring to adjust themselves to the contemporary age and place.

The flow of the love story never faltered. But through the changing experiences of these years, it ran into strange channels as it coursed through the trivial and the tragic, from frustration to the triumph of fulfillment, from the intimately personal to the social implication. After eight years of silence, the boy terror of the post-war years who had once emitted tales of flaming youth, F. Scott Fitzgerald, broke out with a story of disintegrating marriage, Tender Is the Night, a recital that displayed more consciousness of milieux. In this so-called "era of business and professional women," Elizabeth Corbett related the life of one, After Five O'Clock. What they experienced in careering Allis McKay discussed in Woman about Town. Women Live Too Long thought Vina Delmar. But Dorothy Canfield Fisher, in The Deepening Stream, permitted a woman born in the gay nineties to live even through the awful experience of the world war and yet arrive at a sense of personal fulfillment. Rose Feld chose a Young Man of Fifty as a study in emotion. Djuna Barnes, unwilling to think of the love life short of a compound of

French, English, and American impacts, framed a novel on that model, Nightwood, for which T. S. Eliot prepared an introduction.

Whether Ernest Hemingway's To Have and Have Not belonged in the category of love stories or social interpretation was a matter of hot debate among literary critics. At all events, when he interrupted his long silence, Hemingway recounted a story of animal vitality resisting enervation, of a man's passionate devotion to his family driving him into a desperate struggle for their existence and his own, to defeat and death. Although many commentators airily dismissed this novel as "leftist" and others charged it with being "hard-boiled" and "indecent," Elliot Paul gave it eloquent and discriminating praise in The Saturday Review. Wherever it belonged in any scheme of classification, it was no simple exploration of subjective propensities. Disturbed as a novelist and a citizen by the amount and nature of fiction representing human beings sinking beneath a sea of trouble, Ellen Glasgow wrote Vein of Iron, a story of dignity maintained under the stress of genuine hardships. Though it was an offset, it was no apology.

As the Freudian fever ebbed, the novel of introspection became less conspicuous, and "extrovert," socially alert fiction achieved more prominence. After publishing in 1933 his mammoth Anthony Adverse, a treatise in psychoanalysis combined with lush adventure and romance, Hervey Allen took a rest. In 1938 he was less subjective and less ambitious; in his comparatively short novel, Action at Aquila, he simply revived the warrior, the least introspective of mortals, as a hero displaying his prowess in civil war.

Back in 1929, while authors of the problem novel in the newer spirit were merely cleaning their typewriters and preparing to write, Sinclair Lewis brought into bas relief a rich man from the automobile world, Dodsworth, engaged in a quest for culture at the heels of a hectic and imperious wife. The applause that greeted the performance was loud but not prolonged. Within a few months mild lampoons were being submerged in tougher fiction and by 1930 a more clearly directed realism than Lewis had yet commanded was pressing into the novel. In that year Charles Norris in The Seed brought this method to bear on birth control; Cornelia James Cannon, in Heirs, on the assimilation of aliens; Julia Ellsworth Ford, in Consequence, on the opium trade; Mary Heaton Vorse, in Strike, on the labor struggle; Gertrude Shelby and Samuel Stoney in Po' Buckra, and Gilmore Millen, in Sweet Man, on the race conflict; Upton Sinclair, in Mountain City, on the role of money and in Little Steel on the conflict of capital and labor; Edwin Seaver, in The Company, on business organization; John Tunis, in American Girl, on the exploitation of the tennis champion. Choosing a broader plot, Irving Fineman undertook, in This Pure Young Man, a critique on the whole of contemporary civilization. In a highly charged Mothers' Cry, Helen Carlisle fairly shrieked for recognition of basic maternal needs.

Racial affiliations, trials and tribulations, peculiar characteristics and modes of meeting life — the minority issue within a political democracy — furnished substance for long stories as for short. From the perspective of the white race, Oliver LaFarge in Laughing Boy and Florence E. McClinchery in Joe Pete, like several other writers, gave their versions of the American Indian. But steadily the Indians were learning to be articulate about themselves. The same was true of the Negro race; it had other interpreters and its own. Based on her personal experiences in modern plantation management, Julia Peterkin wrote sympathetic character studies of South Carolina Negroes. Katharine Hamill, in Swamp Shadow, a novel of the Mississippi low lands, and Zora Neale Thurston, in Their Eyes Were Watching God, a tale of Floridans, also dealt with the Negro character struggling to make terms with life in America.

The insecurity of the Jews on the world stage had repercussions in American literature, although in practice their persecutors were kept within some bounds of decency by democratic politics in the United States. Before Hitler commenced his "Aryan" purge, as early as 1929 when the skies seemed almost azure for most races in America, Robert Nathan made the Jew in a Gentile world the theme of his novel, There Is Another Heaven. In the year of Hitler's rise to mastery over the Germans, Irving Fineman in Hear Ye, Sons warned his readers of a spreading racial conflict involving the Jews — the conflict so serio-comically treated in Lewis Browne's How Odd of God.

Like families and races, individuals as types had their days in the literary court. Men of untamed temper were the subjects of W. R. Burnet's Iron Man and The Giant Swing. Man tamed to labor interested William Wister Haines, author of Slim, an electric lineman, and Archie Binns, whose Lightship described men willing to guard sea lanes for navigators. Men tamed by inner checks called puritanic served as theme for the philosophic scholar, George Santayana, whose The Last Puritan presented a victim of new times caught in a devouring pool of spiritual ruin. Another type of Puritan, the Boston Brahmin, was genially satirized by John P. Marquand in The Late George Apley. It seemed, therefore, that the Gentile in a nation of Jews, Negroes, Indians, and peoples of many other races and nationalities was also getting his due, more or less.

Occupational characteristics, so superficially listed in census returns, stared out of the pages of fiction. In her own way Willa Cather had brought the musician into fiction. Now James Cain did the same thing but in an entirely different fashion. His Serenade, like The Postman Always Rings Twice, belonged to the "hard-boiled" class. Its singer was swept through American-Mexican relations, politics, and brothels, through commercial battles over music in Hollywood, through controversies over the merits of mechanical reproductions of music, through grand opera in New York and back to Mexico where a tragic fate awaited his beloved Mexican woman and deep sorrow came to her lover. Certainly this was no book to be read and enjoyed by patrons of chamber music. That could also be said of Paul Horgan's

The Fault of Angels, a satire on the musical set in a small western town, which received a Harper prize.

As the search light of imaginative letters swung on its axis, its glare was cast upon the politicians. W. R. Burnett in 1936 personified one as King Cole. The political battles between Yankees and Irish, Republicans and Democrats, corruptionists and purists, all in Boston, were the theme of Joseph Dineen's Ward Eight. Under a title peculiarly apt, What People Said, W. L. White ventilated small-town and small-time politics and crooked finance in the middle west, utilizing first-hand facts and intimate experience in a manner that cut beneath the camouflage of conventions. Persons familiar with American politics could visualize through his word pictures smoke-filled rooms with brass cuspidors shining and "the boys" fixing things up. To the surprise of her wide public accustomed to her simple tales of adventure, Mary Roberts Rinehart mingled politics with the story of a woman in The State vs. Elinor Norton.

In a study of The Liberals, which Granville Hicks, close student of the literary tradition in America, called "one of the most exciting novels of our time," the hopes and difficulties of that tribe were set forth by John Hyde Preston out of knowledge and with penetrating consideration. Going backward in time Janet Ayer Fairbank caught up in Rich Man Poor Man the saga of the Progressive revolt under Theodore Roosevelt and traced its evolution through the fortunes of Hendricks Smith, son of a great capitalist, a Harvard graduate, who snapped off from his family pretensions, cast in his lot with the rebels of his day, and worried his way with a suffragette wife through the world war into the golden glow.

Careening both vertically and horizontally through human society, historical novels brought remote times and places into competition with the here and the now for the diversion of readers. Novels of wars, revolutionary and civil, came from the presses with an insistent regularity which implied that neither Hemingway's Farewell to Arms nor Mary Lee's farewell to martial futility in It's a Great War, had exhausted the interest in death and destruction. If, as often alleged, American democracy was basically pacific, its writers produced no great novel of peace as such to offset blood-curdling stories of war passions.

The historical novel was of course an expression of contemporary ideas and interests read into the past. In two novels of the South the vigor of two points of view was illustrated: the nostalgic, in Stark Young's yearning for a past deemed exquisite, River House, written in 1929, followed by So Red the Rose; and, in 1934, the critical, in William Faulkner's story of the decaying old order, called The Sound and the Fury. Honoré Willsie Morrow ended her Lincoln trilogy with The Last Full Measure. Blair Niles plotted a series of historical novels dealing with Latin America and executed a part of the plan in narratives of Guatemalans and Peruvians with fidelity to source materials and a sympathy nourished by experiences among descendants of the peoples whom she described. Combining meticulous research with flights of fancy, Kenneth Roberts, in Northwest Passage, carried a host of readers through frontier intrigues and wars during years before the American revolution, with Major Robert Rogers, the Indian fighter, as the central figure. Reaching back into the seventeenth century, Esther Forbes related tales of colonial Massachusetts, including in her repertory Indian wars and witches and summing it all up under the name Paradise. Gertrude Atherton enlarged upon her novels of statecraft, which had taken early American republicanism and the age of Pericles as their substance, to cover the time of Caesar Augustus and rendered her own verdict — Peacock.

In an age when everybody and everything furnished grist to the literary mill, it was inevitable no doubt that the makers of polite and imaginative letters themselves should be made to stand forth in their settings. Applying her biting analysis to the writers, Dawn Powell, in Turn, Magic Wheel, held up to ridicule the literary circle in New York, its hub of the universe. But with a gentleness as light as a perfume-laden breeze in springtime, Robert Nathan wafted his humor into

Winter in April — in 1938, at that point in the midpassage.
His central figure, Henry Pennifer, had reached the top rung
of the ladder as a critic, a member of the Academy, a Pulitzer
prize winner, emeritus editor of the University Quarterly.
What more could a man of letters ask in this world? The
days of Pennifer's years were now pleasantly passed writing
on small matters, attending meetings of the Academy where
new candidates were discussed, idling hours away over
domestic details. The man of letters as artist was well-housed,
well-fed, and well-clothed. He lived in an appropriate section
of the city. Any disciple of Richard Watson Gilder would
have been charmed with the delicacy of these features common to the correct literary way.

But Robert Nathan did not forget spring clouds. Into the
thin, mellow light of the literary set, of which Pennifer was
an ornament, fell dark shadows from the outside. Old Stuart
Orrin, who had been a literary editor and a discoverer of
talents in former days, encountered Pennifer at a cocktail
party and complained that "the old boys" were writing the
same kind of books year after year. Aware that something
was actually happening in letters, Pennifer replied, "Not the
new ones," and remarked that the new books seemed different
to him. Enlivened by the rejoinder, Orrin thanked God for
the new books and, warming up, rejoiced that "pretty writing" had gone out of style, that the new books smelled of life.
Also into the pale light another shadow fell — Nadia Bala-
kov, whose father and mother had been murdered in the
Bolshevik revolution, whose prayers went up for old Russia,
the Russia before the revolution. And yet another shadow:
a German youth driven from home by the cruelties and dis-
honors of the Nazi revolution, an accomplished linguist and
musician; aflame with the zeal of a great hope, he cast aside
literary pleasantries to fight for the Loyalist government on
the sodden fields of Spain — in the year of grace, 1938. It
did seem indeed that something was happening to polite
letters and the literary set.

§

Poets likewise ranged the wide realm of fact, ideas, and judgments in a world manifesting signs of degeneration and reconstruction. Never was so much poetry published in America in so short a span as during the midpassage. The year 1933 alone produced sixty impressive titles as testimony to the activity of poets. Willa Cather was still reveling in April Twilight. Ruth St. Denis was still dreaming of her mystic dances in Lotus Light. In Innocent Summer, Frances Frost, a loyal native of Vermont, was claiming peace for the soul far away from troubled cities in singing of nature and tradition. But Cale Young Rice sniffed High Perils and Ezra Pound in The Fifth Decade of Cantos lashed harder at his obsession, economic materialism. If Allen Tate remained in the realm of "super-reality" while composing The Mediterranean, Mark Van Doren confessed deep concern for earthly character and made the affirmations of a town and country gentleman, with respect to values, in The Last Look. Louise Bogan sought to unite the concrete substance of things with concern for the metaphysical in The Sleeping Fury. With his distinctive modernist idiom, Horace Gregory sounded the call for No Retreat. The sharpening conflict put a keener edge on Stephen Vincent Benét's poetry; in the Burning City, a collection of his poems, he expressed his passionate revulsion against tyranny — against war, fascism, madness of all varieties, stupidity, and degeneracy.

Only Robinson Jeffers seemed to be content with complete frustration, seeing no escape from humanity's incapacities and violence even in death; Such Counsels As You Gave Me followed Give Your Heart to the Hawks — both statements of the tortured poetic soul in a world infinitely hideous. If the world would become communist, Muriel Rukeyser, like Isidor Schneider and the older comrades generally, thought she would like it very well; her USI, for instance, using items in the daily press as reportage of abuses to be removed, offered a social revolution as the way to clean the Augean stables. That it might be possible to return to the old

American dream in memory at least, to the great westward movement, Helene Magaret implied in The Great Horse. The disillusioning present was the burden of Josephine W. Johnson's Year's End. But if quotability was the test of poetry, Ogden Nash led all the rest in skill. His verse was freer than Whitman's had been — as free as conversational chaos. His satire was contemporary and catholic in its appreciations; his wide-ranging observations on the little and the big — first families, bankers, consciences clean and foul, ditherers, divorcees, politicians, night club revelers, bounders, simplicities with complexities all under the heading, I'm a Stranger Here Myself — exactly fitted the moods of countless fellow creatures.

The great democracy scattered out over the continent, which travelers prefigured in snapshots general and particular, Carl Sandburg commemorated in a long poem bearing the cryptic heading, The People Yes. High and low, far and wide, over plains, amid factories, farms, dust bowls, across mountain ranges, rivers, and lakes, among all unemployments and occupations, professions, jobs, skills, and no skills, this poet wandered, listening to words spoken in trains, in lobbies, filling stations, streets, barns, offices, and shops. Then he reported — the voices, aphorisms, sayings, hopes, and cynicisms of the multitudes. In line after line of his poem fluttered inanities, without evident meaning, or at least with no more meaning than was put into the rattle, clatter, and clack of kitchen, barn, and parlor chattering, whether at noon or at midnight. But through the texture of the poems gleamed flashes of great and homely wisdom — axioms enduring, wrought of strong life, casual comment revealing unbeatable men and women, penetrating observations far beyond the notice of "big shots" at mahogany desks or lecterns or microphones. Corrosive sublimate dripped, page after page, upon formalities, conventionalities, "stuffed shirt fronts," the high proprieties of the high.

Below figures set down in the ledgers and the words in his book, no balance was struck by Sandburg; perhaps, none

could be struck just then, by any poet, had he wished to do
so. Yet some things were writ very large:

> Stocks are property, yes.
> Bonds are property, yes.
> Machines, land, buildings are property, yes.
> A job is property,
> no, nix, nah, nah.

At the moment one clear command rang out:

> First class passengers, keep your seats.
> Second class passengers, get out and walk.
> Third class passengers, get out and shove.

Even so, the people were reaching out "for lights beyond the
prison of the five senses, for keepsakes lasting beyond any
hunger or death."

> The people know the salt of the sea
> and the strength of the winds
> lashing the corners of the earth.
> The people take the earth
> as a tomb of rest and a cradle of hope.
> Who else speaks for the Family of Man?

> In darkness with a great bundle of grief
> the people march.
> In the night, and overhead a shovel of stars for
> keeps, the people march:
> Where to?   What next?

By any test this was more philosophic than the report of the
learned men who fabricated a history of Everyman in three
words:

> Born,
> troubled,
> died.

Travelers with imaginations, not in Altruria — an imaginary land — but in America as it was, encircled the country,
penetrated the crowded streets of cities and the byways of
rural regions, and made elaborate reports on what they saw
and heard in the language of ordinary discourse. John Spivak

looked for people ready to mount the barricades and discovered people merely eager for jobs or bread. Out of impressions gathered on prolonged journeys, out of interviews
with "folks" of all sorts and conditions, and out of correspondence, serious, gay, and distempered, Louis Adamic
assembled in 1938 a mountainous mass of materials in a
rambling fashion, though with some method in madness,
and crowned it with the title, My America — a document
of prime importance for watchers of underlying surges and
tendencies, especially in the North. In an Odyssey all his
own, Jonathan Daniels took in the South as far west as the
Mississippi, with little excursions beyond, talked with the
very best people and the very worst people, discussed matters
economical, political, and sociological with writers, philosophers, planters, tenant union leaders, lawyers, and seem-
ingly everybody else. At the end of his wanderings, he
summed up his discoveries, snapshots, and verdicts in a
single volume, A Southerner Discovers the South, causing
his readers to wonder in just what realm lay the "solid
South" so celebrated in the legends of politics. Compared
with a Don Quixote on an odyssey was Bradford Smith's
American Quest published in 1938 — an attempt in a trans-
continental journey to find the American soul.

§

Framed in the democratic tradition and flavored with dissidence were numerous biographies recounting the personal
experiences of individuals. Distinguished by great labor and
supported by scholarly paraphernalia, they differed from the
stout volumes produced by family gardeners and from the
works of professional historians deemed "scientific" by members of that gild. Although Henry Pringle's life of Theodore
Roosevelt passed the standard tests of the historical profession, it presented no wooden image of righteousness, entire
and intact. Harvey O'Connor's tale of Andrew D. Mellon
and his millions, based on documentation and laden with cita-

tions, worked much havoc with the memorials of that titan in finance and politics from Pittsburgh, called by a friend "the greatest Secretary of the Treasury since Hamilton." Criticized as "unfair," nevertheless O'Connor's biography told truth so irrefragable that even Lords of Creation had to give heed much as they might despise it.

In a similar manner O'Connor dealt with The Guggenheims: the Making of an American Dynasty, monarchs of copper who climbed from peddling to great riches, to the patronage of learning and art, sheathing as with a cloth of gold the smudges of the conflicts that had raged around mine and smelter. It was also upon prodigious research in newspapers, letters, and other documents that Ferdinand Lundberg built his volume on the Imperial Hearst, master of a vast journalistic and industrial corpus, crumbling at the borders and rotting at the center; and his broader treatise on the dynasts, Sixty Families — with their riches, their philanthropies, their newspapers and magazines, their universities, and their politics. Giant figures from the muck-raking age ascended from the grave in The Autobiography of Lincoln Steffens.

Turning upon actors in the American scene a mind trained in the subtleties of French letters and hitherto devoted to such great European characters as Rousseau and Zola, Matthew Josephson drew full length portraits in The Robber Barons of the gilded age. Here were knights of the bags, not of the crags, the great American capitalists of 1861–1901, revived in 1934. Josephson later enlarged his gallery by a volume on their political retainers, The Politicos, who served as negotiators between business and government during the years when the lyrical "Give us what we want and let us alone" rang to the sky in the morning of youth. Although heavily documented and written in historical form, these books brightened the pages of current congressional investigations by resurrecting rugged personalities whose works had spanned the continent and erected an economic tradition. This division of literature Oscar Lewis entered in 1938 with the story of The Big Four — Collis P. Huntington, Leland Stanford, Mark Hopkins, and Charles Crocker, all lusty figures among the barons of old America.

§

Although the makers of polite letters were not likely to admit it and critics were often inclined to overlook it, there was meaning for the matters they discussed in the literature of humor. That too was germane to the interpenetration of opposites pointed out by Bernard DeVoto in his appraisal of proletarian fiction. Moreover in both form and flavor it was distinctly American. In Europe, humor was often mordant and, like politics, bore the stamp of antagonisms almost irreducible. This had long been so — in the scarifying wrath of Dean Swift, the sardonic blasts of Maximilian Harden, and the appalling lines of Daumier. In America, however, humor had generally been homely, earthly, gushing, relatively tolerant — "childish and silly," falling short of wit, said critics given to comparisons.

Humor had rippled into every domain of culture, economy, and politics, as a softening and moderating influence. Many a time in the worst days of the civil war, for example, when men before him, all nominally on his side, were quaking with anger and on the edge of using their fists, Abraham Lincoln had relieved their tension merely by "telling a story." His "yarns" were often artless enough, as simple as fables from Aesop, and possibly irritating to men who were "hell-bent" on having things just their way, but the interlude provided an armistice, eased off passions, and made listeners forget their petty differences, like children diverted by a wise and patient mother. "Why so hot, little man?" The question was frequently an antidote useful to both sides of innumerable conflicts — an antidote conducive to rational adjustment.

The question, for instance, controlled the humor of Clarence Day. From his original Crow's Nest, a watch-tower of his own creation, Day surveyed a wide landscape, occupied by human beings given to curious antics resembling those of the animal kingdom. In After All he described a world "peopled with egocentric men, gracious women, and his favorite barnyard and jungle animals which he used in fables outlining the small absurdities of the human species." With a whimsical air of detachment, he viewed little mortals, strutting about cocksure, imagining themselves most sophisticated when they were most naïve. His laughter even played around the solemnity of that major psychological and sociological obsession — family relations — in sketches of his father and mother, showing the trivial bickerings as well as the permanent formalities of life in a circle distinctly middle class in manners and values.

While Clarence Day joked at simian ways among humans, Don Marquis made a very good philosopher out of a cockroach. The conduct of Milt Gross's Feitelbaum family, unlike the Marxian conception of "bourgeois family relations," was as funny as any of the antics in Clarence Day's domestic circle. Seeing the absurd, amazing, and ludicrous at every point, acres of diamonds glistening, Ring Lardner, Robert Benchley, and James Thurber embroidered letters with sparkles of their own witticisms, during the sternness of Calvin Coolidge's administration, the gloom of the Hoover depression, and the fitful variations of the New Deal.

It was with poetic justice, when Ogden Nash, Milt Gross, Robert Benchley, and Wolcott Gibbs were making merry with the human race, that Negroes began to laugh at themselves and the "superior" whites. They were winning headway against heavy odds in politics and economics and through powerful figures, such as Langston Hughes and Walter White, were demonstrating their capacity for survival in the welter of defeat and hope called civilization. Able to see the ridiculous and grotesque within the tragic, Jessie Fauset, in her Comedy American Style, described the wreck and ruin of lives produced by a colored woman, nearly white, who devoted herself with a tigress's energy to the mission of carrying her family over the line into the white camp. Incidentally Miss Fauset drew jewelled pictures of life among middle-class Negroes and, with humor aforethought, foibles and follies among the whites, including the most futile among them, with whom "aspiring" Negroes so passionately desired to associate themselves. Perhaps in a strict sense Miss Fauset's book belonged neither to comedy nor tragedy but to that mysterious realm where amusement and sorrow melt into a supreme unity. In any case its readers who wept over the absurdities of Negroes must have laughed over the antics of Nordics deemed so worthy of imitation.

§

However excellent the "best" and "favorite" books, however meritorious the volumes written in the democratic tradition or in the spirit of regional or personal exploration, they did not entrance all workers in the field of imaginative letters, nor indeed the entire appraising and reading public. In the midpassage came something like a definite break in the flow of the literary tradition. This new dissidence was not directly concerned with vulgarians of the plutocracy, with monopolists and corruptionists who figured in the muck-raking school of Lincoln Steffens' age. No disciple of Edith Wharton dealt so remorselessly with the clashing habits and customs of the "seasoned" and the "new-rich" classes, both suffering from resentments. That old type of writing by masters no longer commanded the spirit of genius. The new rejection was not that of prudent and cultured merchants crushed by the weight and behavior of upstart plutocrats. Nor was the protest exactly that formulated by William Dean Howells and Edward Bellamy. On the contrary, it was largely an outcry in the name of the disinherited, sometimes called by the outlandish name of "the proletariat." It looked in the direction of the working class, sought to voice its tragedies, and in animus, if not positive upshot, to impress upon readers the message that

something drastic should or will be done to redeem the disinherited, by the will of the disinherited if in no other way.

Grinding poverty, it is true, had never been absent from
the American land despite its fabulous resources and growing
democracy. From early times slaves, indentured servants,
casual laborers, and farm hands had lived near or at the
minimum of subsistence. Apart, however, from the slaves
who were mere chattels bought and sold as such, the proportion of the propertyless had once been small in America as
compared with that in Europe and Asia. Moreover the
dream of endless opportunity to acquire comfort and security
had served in America as a check on the drift of spirit toward
the beggary or turbulence of urban "mobs," so familiar to
the eighteenth century that they filled the mind of Americans, such as Thomas Jefferson and Benjamin Franklin,
with horror. Yet the dream of comfort and security in the
historic style was now growing paler. No optimism could
be so innocent as to obscure the fact of a contracting economy, unemployed millions, and expanding degradation.
Even if there had been no connection with European life
and its events, even if Americans had been isolated like the
denizens of the lost Atlantis, some sense of this reality would
no doubt have been awakened in America and it would have
expressed itself in some literary fashion, unless all vitality
had departed from the people.

Of course America was not completely isolated and,
whether so intended or not, many of the volumes that came
from the presses had in fact a "foreign flavor." Often the
authors of such works were more concerned with the thought
and tactics of Marx and Lenin than with the thought and
tactics of Tom Paine and Walt Whitman. Yet, despite the
fragments or the whole frame of Marxism which gleamed
through much of the new literature, the sources of artistic
creation in American letters of the distinctly labor tendency
lay by no means wholly within that rigid and alien scheme
of ideology. Most, if not all, the writers of this direction
were American born and reared, more or less familiar with

the great literary tradition of the United States. It was not known, perhaps the writers themselves did not know or care, whether their themes, their plots, the involutions of their sentences, or the dénouements were true to the political line drawn by Moscow. The mere fact that a literary design was hailed or abused as proletarian or Marxian meant little and settled nothing, save for appraisers who were insensitive to signs of universality within national particularities. All that could safely be said, then, about the underlying animus of "proletarian literature" was that it pictured the life of the underprivileged of America, caught the irony of the discrepancy between noble theory and poor practice, and let the rays of hope play through the mists, openly or by implication. So conceived, this literature, whether imbued with a foreign flavor or not, was at home in the United States, and as much as Cooper's tales, influenced by Scott's, it could be called indigenous.

However widely they differed over form, style, and upshot, radical writers agreed on certain things. First of all, they believed that life in America, as elsewhere, was pinioned to the nature and fate of the politico-economic system and its conflicts — in other words, to great history as distinguished from family squabbles and village commonplaces. They were conscious of the plight of labor in town and country, of its miseries, struggles, and oppressive fortunes. For ethical or esthetic reasons, or both, they could not or did not close their minds and hearts to this situation. Whether they saw redemption for the disinherited in Marxism or American agrarianism or no salvation at all, they undertook to describe, photograph, and give voice to industrial workers, miners, tenants, share croppers, field hands, and the drifting nomads of the dustbowl and seasonal agriculture. An American literary tradition was thus revitalized with social insight and criticism.

The plutocracy might still treasure its town houses, country places, and yachts, the middle class might still cherish its peculiar securities of property and income, precarious as everything seemed in the economic panic, but dissident writers insisted on thrusting into general thought the specific thought of other values. As Huey Long raged about poverty and under-privilege in the Senate until he was shot down, as the La Follette committee calmly investigating violations of civil liberties received publicity on the first pages of the newspapers for its findings about labor spies, poison gas, factory gunmen, and police beating or killing strikers — all in the service of "the best people," as a presidential committee on farm tenancy traced the steady degradation of labor on the land, innumerable men and women writers resolved that some readers of literature must hear about people who never figured in society columns or adventuresome romance, people who merely toiled and plodded, suffered in silence, protested, questioned, struck back, or aroused the interest of politicians in Washington. Many economists knew that in the long run the permanence of the banquet table itself depended upon transactions outside, and creative artists in letters also had an inkling of this truism.

§

The result was that not a year passed without the appearance in the book marts of one or more novels which concentrated on life and labor in field or factory, in shack or tenement, in regular employment or out of luck. Jews without money, on the East Side of New York City, almost in a ghetto, rose to public view in the pages of Michael Gold. Up from the deep South came the wretched figures of Erskine Caldwell's Tobacco Road. Out of the Far West Robert Cantwell brought the desperate war between laborers and middle-class vigilantes at Centralia in The Land of Plenty. Southern workers were seen migrating from the mountains into the mill towns, in Fielding Burke's (Olive Dargan's) Call Home the Heart and A Stone Came Rolling and in Grace Lumpkin's To Make My Bread, only to be caught in the trammels of exploitation and the necessity of taking up the weapon of the strike in efforts to secure a livelihood. Straight communism was prescribed for white and black share croppers in Grace Lumpkin's A Sign for Cain. From the moving belts and human clashes of the automobile industry in Detroit, James Steele, in a story of The Conveyor, carried an American citizen, surprised to discover that he was just a laborer, to the minds of readers who bought fiction. One must go back to Dickens, a reader declared, to get such vivid reports on labor conditions as Albert Halper delivered in The Foundry; but Halper's Union Square gave vent to laborers' emotions, in a fashion unknown in the Dickens' era, as agitators shouted their solutions to a motley crowd of workers, peddlers, artists, and mere strollers of the streets. The irony of Normalcy and the New Deal alike, Catharine Brody portrayed under the heading, Nobody Starves.

Who, among the many writers of the dissident school — the school of a great continuing and reworking literary tradition — most artistically blended distinction of style with precision of material and propriety of philosophy? This was a subject of argument among the partisans and critics who regarded themselves as "disinterested" reviewers. Proletarian writers, so-called, might praise one another or abuse one another, according to their notions of artistry and the correct political line; in that case, they erected standards for their own dissent. But when the great metropolitan reviews, such as The Saturday Review of Literature, Books of the Herald-Tribune, and The Book Review of The New York Times, granted large spreads of space and considerable cordiality of treatment to members of the newest school of revolt, this was proof of a stronger kind that some of the protestants represented a force of theme and a manner of manipulation meaningful in and for America. Granting that the judgments of the journals of opinion were not infallible, nevertheless they were evidences that Americans were facing the bright glare of social documents without wearing heavily smoked glasses.

§

Symptomatic of the newest upheaval was John Chamberlain's Farewell to Reform, published in 1932, while President Hoover was twisting and fretting in the White House. The title was oracular and the subtitle was definitive: "Being a history of the rise, life, and decay of the progressive mind in America." With an inclusory glance, Chamberlain surveyed the teeming years that followed "the nineties" of the preceding century — their vast economic changes, the protests of the old dissenters, trustbusters, and muckrakers, the fiction of this protest, the lower-middle-class character of "progressive" nonconformity, and the failure of the "liberal" technique. Then, with an air of finality, he buried all that. It had not been without insight and merit, the young critic confessed, but its plaints and its efforts to dissolve the battlements of plutocracy had been in vain: the census returns of modern corporations showed the inanity of its hopes and the ineptitude of its methods.

After the funeral speech, what of the future? Chamberlain faced that question and made replies. Russia "with no six per cents to pay investors" will put a clamp on capitalist expansion. The uncovering of new markets in distant places or in new gadgets offers no promise. Fascism? Yes, it may intervene, but not forever, "for Fascism implies the development of the labor-syndicate idea; and it would be only a question of opportunity before the syndicates attempted their own march to power." What of labor on the land, a continent washing out to sea, the physical base of civilization disintegrating beneath the "labor-syndicates"? Into that final question even the daring Chamberlain did not go. Perhaps, in drawing the curtain of oblivion over progressivism and its works he had done enough for one young man. At all events, he had correctly described the intellectual cleavage that separated "the great tradition" of letters from the thought of the current years.

In illustrating the rupture between the old and the new, John Chamberlain contrasted John Dos Passos with Frank Norris and the juxtaposition was effective. Dos Passos was born in 1896, the exciting year of populism, Bryan, and the crown-of-thorns speech; moreover, he was born in Chicago where the "revolutionary" Democrats assembled to challenge Mark Hanna and gold. Graduated from Harvard while the world war was raging, he served in an ambulance corps under the Red Cross in 1917–1919, spent seasons of searching and appraising in Washington, London, Paris, and Madrid, and was apparently fascinated by the mighty upheaval in Russia. In the buzzing years of normalcy he began publishing and kept on writing in the rosy prospects of the golden glow. His play, The Garbage Man, issued while President Coolidge occupied the throne of contentment, was symptomatic of unrest beneath the seats of the mighty.

Beginning in 1930, while the Lords of Creation were caught in their own melée, Dos Passos published three studies of the American scene, the like of which had never before appeared in American print: The 42nd Parallel, Nineteen Nineteen, and The Big Money, all combined, revamped, and published in 1937 under the title U. S. A. Like a Kansas cyclone that gathers up men, women, children, houses, barns, shops, factories, machines, dry goods, and chickens in a swirl of dust and wind, Dos Passos tore through the years from the close of the nineteenth century and across the continent, scooping into his omnibus events, personalities, scenes, conversations, maladies, stews, aspirations, and follies. Whatever verdict sciolists or philologists might render on this feat, it proclaimed an underlying, persistent, and irresistible rejection of complacency — a dynamic, typhonic, devastating rejection. Such satire might perish from the earth. It might not. Juvenal survived even the Empire.

To whatever category of ideology Dos Passos' U. S. A. belonged, it was certainly not fiction to be enfolded by the adjective "genteel." Here was no soft story opening with a stately mansion in a setting of graceful elms or fragrant magnolia blossoms and finishing at the bridal chamber. Its fibre was hard and its range was as wide as the total economy of American society. Starting with the Spanish-American

War, it raced on through the fruition of imperialist expansion. The reader was introduced at the outset to the symbol of foreign adventure — General Miles, dressed in a gaudy uniform, mounted on a spirited charger to head the great military parade in the national capital, at the verge of the closing nineteenth century, during the administration of President McKinley. General Miles was not long erect, however, for the spirited horse threw the rider in the dust of the capital, suggesting an anagoge. Leaving the President and his successors to rustle papers in their office, the narrative then crashed through time to the point where the utility magnate, Samuel Insull, incarnation of great capitalism, at his trial in Chicago for defrauding investors, confessed that he had made a petty error of ten millions in his accounting, was pronounced "not guilty" by a jury of his peers, and went into retirement on a pension, smiling through his tears.

In the involutions and evolutions of U. S. A., the tale of the promised land of youth led on, under the caption of "Mary French," to a group of workers wrestling with they scarcely knew what; on to stranded young people hitchhiking across the continent, uprooted, while Pullman airplanes roared through the skies above them. In bas relief stood out a typical lad who had been indoctrinated at school with the patriotic ideas of U. S. A. as a fairy realm of opportunity, home-owning, survival of the fittest, and the speed indicative of prowess and courage. He had listened to radio crooners, in the excellent age of the machine, whispering of girls, girls, girls, and he had seen platinum blonds coaxing boys from the screens in motion-picture houses. He had read about millions of dollars chalked up on boards at the Exchange and of big executives with three telephones on their desks, always ringing amid the roar of business enterprise. Misfortune had overtaken the lad, however, not fortune, and, in the closing scene of U. S. A., he is the Vagabond waiting beside the speeding traffic, hungry and footsore, hoping only to thumb his way "a hundred miles down the road."

In the interstices of U. S. A. were newsreels, camera shots, fragments from headlines, blinding word pictures of daily scenes, and stories of life, common and uncommon. The eternal man-woman problem gleamed and sputtered through the pages in all the different settings for its never-to-be-attained solution, though not alone — always with its place in the economic scale. In impetuous yet not altogether disorderly array, were crowded politicians, editors, financiers, gamblers, stocks, bonds, "furreners," detective agencies, livery stables, Manila Bay, automobiles, "the Roosevelt boys," cold wind blowing, Andrew Carnegie extolling the advantages of the higher learning, locomotive firemen, large men fond of whiskey, Eugene Debs in Woodrow Wilson's jail, an infidel believing in Darwin and natural selection, the world war with all its blah, blah, boom, boom, munitioneers cutting melons, Dr. Wilson a man of standing who talked correct English, morgues, reek of lime and death, Y. M. C. A., Mr. Harding praying to God, United States Steel, martial law, strikes, mine explosion, Lindbergh the aviator, Russia, Trotsky, Stalin, Hearst in a black frock coat and a ten-gallon hat, big smash in stocks, down, down, down, prosperity near, "real values unharmed," Roosevelt administration, companies, corporations, J. Pierpont Morgan, and Owen D. Young. On and on passed the pageant to its end — youth thumbing its way down the road — somewhere, nowhere.

If to possessors of the orthodox frame of social reference — profits, progress, and prosperity — the brain storm seemed sheer madness or awful effrontery, it had justification in the historical record, with a multitude of things unmentioned. This version of the U. S. A. might not be wholly true and permanent. But what was wholly true and permanent? Who in high places, with the most efficient research secretaries at hand, could answer that question?

Whether to be praised or condemned, Dos Passos' apparently impressionistic, yet closely-knit portrayal of years and scenes had lofty sanction. Long before it was published,

Herbert Hoover had given some warrant to every passage. Speaking before the Federated Engineering Societies in 1920, Mr. Hoover had said:

"Our economic system [despite its accomplishments] . . . presents a series of human and social difficulties to the solution of which we are groping."

(Dos Passos illustrated them.)

"The congestion of population is producing subnormal conditions of life."

(Dos Passos documented them.)

"The vast repetitive operations are dulling the human mind."

(Dos Passos described results.)

"The intermittency of employment due to the bad coordination of industry, the great waves of unemployment in the ebb and flow of economic tides, the ever present industrial conflicts by strike and lockout, produce infinite wastes and great suffering."

(Dos Passos lifted the lid of the seething cauldron covered by this politico-economic generalization.)

"Our business enterprises have become so large and complex that the old pleasant relationship between employer and worker has, to a great extent, disappeared."

(Dos Passos made pointed references to the new, unpleasant relationships.)

"The aggregation of great wealth with its power to economic domination presents social and economic ills which we are constantly struggling to remedy."

(Dos Passos incorporated these ills in battered and torn personalities.)

§

Also in the forms of poetry the scheme of things entire was drawn into the reckonings of the midpassage. Swinging around a wide circle of urbanism and ruralism, Archibald MacLeish sought to wrest from the totality its guarded meaning. Son of Yale University, graduate of the Harvard

Law School, destined by birth and education for the circle of genteel comfort, MacLeish had been plunged into the world war and thrown back from that chaos shocked and pensive. Presumably he might have joined Richard Whitney at the Stock Exchange, but he turned to letters instead. Tentatively, it seems, he groped his way through unfolding experience, recording his adventures in verse and play, growing steadily in strength and precision. New Found Land was published in 1930; Conquistador, which won the Pulitzer poetry prize, in 1932; and Frescoes for Mr. Rockefeller's City, depicting crassness and beauty, in 1933.

Then in 1937, MacLeish's saga, The Fall of the City — a tale of the dictator's coming and of masses prostrating themselves in the presence of the false, if fair, god — was recited to the public over the radio. This theme was "the pitiful, blind, foredefeated, subhuman, yet all-too-human, bowing of a people before an invading Conqueror, whose actual hollowness is disguised by heavy clanking armor." As the Conqueror lifted his visor a Voice cried:

> The Helmet is hollow!
> The metal is empty! The armor is empty! I tell you
> There's no one at all there; there's only the metal;
> The barrel of metal: the bundle of armor. It's empty!
> The push of a stiff pole at the nipple would topple it.
> They don't see! They lie on the paving. They lie in the
> Burnt spears: the ashes of arrows. They lie there. . . .
> They don't see or they won't see. They are silent. . . .

That was a startling literary event: the actor at the microphone, speaking unprinted lines, emphasizing, giving color and compulsion to words and sentences, an unseen audience at night listening, following, awaiting the climax, transported by the author's moving narrative and the spell of the intonations. And perhaps strangest of all was the fact that MacLeish was an associate editor of Fortune, the new magazine sold at a price which only the rich could pay.

The following year, 1938, MacLeish chose still another medium: a combination of photographic pictures and verse, entitled Land of the Free. From the pictures stared, in livid shapes, personalities and situations recorded in the statistics of labor and tenancy: a coal miner's daughter on an old iron cot, wandering fruit pickers, share croppers, the Republic Steel riot, police wielding clubs against unarmed workers, men and women falling in heaps, trade union organizers beaten over the head by agents of law and order, farmers evicted from homes by dust storms, hovels called homes collapsing into tatters, hard-favored heirs and heiresses of ignorance, misfortune, and neglect, children bending their backs over gruelling toil, thin-lipped, squint-eyed, or pop-eyed men and women stranded in the march of progress to success.

Margaret Bourke-White, Dorothea Lange, Arthur Roth-stein, Russell Lee, and others supplied the photographs of life in the land of the free. MacLeish furnished the words — simple, questioning words; inadequate only because human inventiveness had never found a language capable of express-ing such human feeling, human sorrow, human wonder. Although literary experts inquired whether the poet had really captured the mood of dying hopes, bloody tragedy, confusion, and pulsing fear, there could be no doubt that he had conveyed the contrasts between the "ill-housed, ill-clad, ill-nourished" of President Roosevelt's second inaugural and the American dream of freedom, abundance, and victory.

Wondering fathers, mothers, and children found voice in the poet's voice:

Maybe the proposition is self-evident.

Maybe we were endowed by our creator
With certain inalienable rights, including
The right to assemble in peace and petition.

Maybe.

But try it in South Chicago Memorial Day
With the mick police on the prairie in front of the factory
Gunning you down from behind and for what?
　For liberty?

Between photographs of strikers and police at the Republic Steel Company's plant in South Chicago and of a prostrate laborer vainly trying to protect his skull from a rain of blows, MacLeish questioned the promise of nature and nature's God incorporated in the Declaration of Independence:

Maybe God Almighty wrote it out;
We could shoot off our mouths where we pleased
and with what and no Thank-yous.

But try it at River Rouge with the Ford militia.
Try it if Mister Ford's opinions are otherwise.
Try it and see where you land with your back broken.

What answer had the poet for the question that came hurtling through the pictures of people, land, and factories? No smooth and certain spring into freedom. Perhaps the disinherited had some resolution for the dilemma? Probably not. Neither did the poet, who may have double-distilled the quintessence of the hour and occasion better than statisticians and dialectitians:

We wonder if the liberty is done:
The dreaming is finished
We can't say
We aren't sure. . . .
Or if there's something different men can dream . . .
Or if there's something different men can mean by Liberty,
We wonder . . .
We don't know
We're asking. . . .

While MacLeish left his characters wondering and asking, Paul Engle supplied a definite answer to the big question. In one of his earlier poems, The Troubadour of Eze, Engle had avowed implicit faith in the American way:

Here to my town has the world's
    great power come over
The torn, dream-furrowed ocean,
    and now waits
A stronger form that the New
    World alone
Can give to its old and proud
    nobility.

But in 1936, in Break the Heart's Anger, Paul Engle cast off the spell and avowed himself a disciple of Lenin. Having scrutinized America, England, Germany, and Russia, he could find no praise for democracy; nor for fascism. The riddle of the universe, in his opinion, had been solved by Lenin, if not by Russia.

Often the titles of poems themselves betrayed the underlying points of reference: as for instance Maxwell Bodenheim's To a Revolutionary Girl; Kenneth Fearing's No Credit; Robert Gessner's Cross of Flame; Langston Hughes' Ballad of Lenin and Sharecroppers; Joseph Kalar's Worker Uprooted; Alfred Kreymborg's American Jeremiad; Norman MacLeod's Coal Strike; Harry Alan Potamkin's Haymarket; and Muriel Rukeyser's City of Monuments. Coming from a Utah Canyon to the great city of New York, its ways throbbing, its thought shaken by disturbing events, its people in tumult, Phyllis M'Ginley burst into a Carol with Variations:

> Sing hosanna, sing Noël.
> Sing the gunner and the shell.
> Sing the candle, sing the lamp,
> Sing the Concentration Camp.
> Sing the season born anew,
> Sing of exile for the Jew,
> Wreathe the world with evergreen.
> Praise the cunning submarine.
> Sing the barbed and bitter wire,
> Poison gas and liquid fire,
> Bullet, bomb and hand grenade,
> And the heart of man, afraid.
> Christ is come, the Light hath risen,
> All our foes are safe in prison,
> And the Christmastide begets
> Seven million bayonets.

§

Positive as to the frame of social reference were the novels of James T. Farrell: Studs Lonigan, Gas-House McGinty,

and A World I Never Made. Any controversy about that
he himself dismissed in A Note on Literary Criticism, characterized by Edmund Wilson as "One of the few intelligent
discussions of literature from the Marxist point of view which
have yet been written by Americans." In A World I Never
Made, published in 1936, Farrell centered his story in
Chicago during the year 1911, and gave another picture of a
working class family of Irish origins, struggling in the jungle
of economic scarcity and uncertainty.

The hero of the occasion, if a defeated driver of an express
wagon could be called such, was Jim O'Neill, who knew a
little Shakespeare, married a gay lass, and in her company
slid down hill into endless toil, poverty, and wrangling,
relieved by rare bits of good luck. Their home? Peeling wall
paper, drab red bricks, noise of trains, smell, smoke, and dust.
The bedroom? "The worst in the whole place. Jim glanced
around, junk all over, the dresser in the corner piled with
it, rags, clothes, junk, and the table on the left with a slab
of grocery box in place of one leg; it, too, was piled and
littered with every damn thing in the house." Here lay Lizz,
his wife, "smiling weakly at him, her face round, full, un-
washed, her mouth weak, her eyes dark, a soiled rag under her
chin, her hair uncombed" — bringing another child into the
world that already had too many. In the weary round and
round of toiling and moiling came one stroke of dubious
fortune — a thousand dollars in cash as damages for an
injury to their little boy, run over by a wagon!

Woven into the life of a single family were the lives of
relatives — some begirt by the bands of wage-earning, others
mounting to the rim of the middle class — salesmen, hack
lawyers, politicians of large hopes and small accomplish-
ments. Threading his way through the scene was a little
lumber man with the psychology of a Napoleon in business.
"Well, Peg," boasted Lorry Robinson, "things will pick up.
The possibilities in this country are endless. America is going
to be the richest nation in all history. Why, we've got everything here. Peg, you should see some of my lumber lands.

Resources? They are beyond calculation. We are coming into an age that is bound to be the wealthiest the human race has ever known. Times are a little tight now. I know most of my money is tied up, and I've had to put up every cent I could raise as collateral for loans I needed to swing some of my deals out west. But that's only temporary. . . . The business system is catching its wind again now. Don't you worry." In time, said this little king of big business in dreams, he would divorce his wife and marry Peg — a wastrel and bounder, on her way in the great rich America, now burdened with casualties but certain to be the wealthiest country the human race had ever known. In its fashion, that too was an American dream, not true at the moment all around, but prized and nourished.

Seeping into the minds of little men dreaming of great riches through salesmanship was the animus which Farrell treated as "spiritual success." Is there sales resistance on the ground that times are hard and business is poor? "The power of wishing and concentration is a mighty force that no man can beat. Jesus said that faith can move mountains. And it can! Al, if you wish for something and concentrate on it wholly and completely with strong faith in your wish, there is nothing on God's earth that can stop you! Absolutely nothing! The power of the wish is the mightiest of powers. It is the true kernel of wisdom in the teaching of Jesus. That's what he meant by faith."

It was all well and good to believe in God, the Holy Trinity, and the hereafter, but the business man's paradise was to come on earth. The concentrated wish would bring it. No doubt about it. Only the week before, the wishing shoe salesman had sold a big order "to old Guggins of the High Class Shoe Emporium" in Kokomo. "Before I called on him I sent out a thought-wish that would go through the cosmos and connect up with his psyche." When the salesman entered Guggins' store on his errand of wish-fulfillment, he greeted the crusty codger: "And, say, you're looking fine, young and peppy, just like a college boy." Result? "Well, Al, to make a long story short, he bought three cases of shoes off me. And you know, he still doesn't know how he was sold." Faith, confidence, wish-concentration, they would move mountains, break down sales resistance, master the panic, and make everybody rich, except possibly salesmen who did not have the right line of talk and ought to be digging ditches.

In and out through Farrell's narrative, too, ran threads of politics, the real politics of corralling voters with favors, electing the right boys, playing the game with men of money, holding the jobs, democratic and Democratic politics. "Any workingman who votes for the Republicans," exclaimed the express-wagon driver, "is a damn fool!" It was the right thing to hold a trade union card, strike, wreck wagons, "and punch the living Jesus out of every damn scab who tries to drive one." A mild Socialist of the Debs school protested that "sabotage and violence will never get you anywhere. The bosses like that. They can put the cops on you then, and the newspapers say you're anarchists." That may be "but you Socialists will never get anywhere. . . . You Socialists are lunatics."

Times were hard for Jim O'Neill, but "I'll make my kids something better." Jim was not going to crack his brains about socialism. He would depend upon his own fists and do his own fighting — against scabs who tried to cut wages and take his job. There was, however, a small hope in politics: "Maybe if we get the Democrats in Washington next year they'll give the people some things." Well, Farrell might have added, Woodrow Wilson was elected and he gave labor Samuel Gompers' "magna charta" and the eight hour day for trainmen — and a little later war and the sedition act. Debs got somewhere — that is, in the Atlanta penitentiary, where he stayed until President Harding and Attorney General Daugherty let him out. But Farrell was writing of 1911 and at that time Al thought that by 1931 "everybody in America who's worth his salt ought to be rich." In massing his materials Farrell relied on force, not grace but, as Ralph

Thompson said in reviewing for The New York Times his *No Star Is Lost*, "merely graceful writers come by the dozen."

§

While Dos Passos and Farrell centered their thought mainly upon the realm of urban industry, Erskine Caldwell crashed into the world of letters with descriptions of labor on the land. Before President Roosevelt's committee on farm tenancy had made its statistical report, Caldwell had made reports in human terms: *Tobacco Road* and *God's Little Acre*. Life might be hard for industrial workers near the bottom of the industrial jungle in Chicago, but it was degrading even to idiocy at the bottom of the tenant and share-cropping region. Beside the hunger and futility of Caldwell's Jeeter family, the junk and wastage of Farrell's O'Neill family took on the colors of paradise. In driving sentences, telegraphic in brevity, Caldwell described men, women, children, houses, fields, misery, deformity, imbecility, dirt, and turnips in that never, never land where even animal life could scarcely struggle for existence against adversity, starved soil, incapacity, and misfortune. Delicate sensibilities were not spared. No red roses were added for decoration. The strongest of stomachs could hardly bear the sight. The meanest of realists could not believe their eyes. It was a nauseous dose that Caldwell served his readers. But he would be heard and he was heard. Where readers failed, theatergoers saw, for *Tobacco Road*, in its dramatized form, was enacted steadily in New York City for years, while the New Deal of beneficent planning rose, flourished, and declined. How was that to be explained in a land that placed Willa Cather's *Death Comes to the Archbishop* near the top of the best books?

Widening his arc beyond *Tobacco Road*, Caldwell united barren farm land with a mill in *God's Little Acre* — a novel which Jonathan Daniels pronounced "one of the finest studies of the Southern poor white that has ever come into our literature" and certain to "lift the noses of the sensitive." On Tobacco Road, where hope and aspiration had been quenched, just hungers remained; but in God's little acre, joining mill and farm, human life, while still sordid, manifested vigor, a restless searching for better ways, a few aims, humor, touches of heroism, the sanguine expectancy of labor reaching out for something. An old man digging for gold and a direct-action radical simply would not be crushed, though they got nowhere in the going.

While noble males of the species tossed around in futility, the females, in the stress and strain, sought a way to security and happiness in the labor of their hands. "The men who worked in the mill looked tired and worn, but the girls were in love with the looms and the spindles and the flying lint. The wild-eyed girls on the inside of the ivy-walled mill looked like potted plants in bloom. Up and down the Valley lay the company towns and the ivy-walled cotton mills and the firm-bodied girls with eyes like morning glories, and the men stood on the hot streets looking at each other while they spat their lungs into the deep yellow dust of Carolina." For the older women life was hard enough, cruel enough, but the girls ever anew brought to it the surge of young blood and desire. The treadmill was swiftly turning, broken intermittently by industrial conflict, and then ever turning again; the determinism of biology and of work with things was clear in the picture; if there was any wrath, it was God's wrath; if injustice, it lay in the very nature of the drama. At all events Caldwell kept his frame of reference hidden under the procession and struggle of human creatures.

§

Cutting deeper into the pungency of experience in the world of labor than did Dos Passos and making a wider sweep around economy than James T. Farrell, Jack Conroy in 1933 incorporated his impressions in a saga of toil, The Disinherited. The central figure of this saga was the son of a miner; his associates were the husbands, wives, sons, and daughters of laboring families in mines, mills, and shops and on the land — in town and country. The scene opened in a mining camp dominated by a dump, "like an Old World cathedral towering over peasants' huts." Father did his long daily stint in the mines, when there was work or strikes did not intervene. Brother Dan went into the mines when he was only twelve, despite the child labor law.

While Mother was frying salt pork one day, Jimmy Kerns came with shadows on his face to say — but Mother snatched the words from his mouth: "Tell me, Jimmy! Is it Tom? . . . Then it's Dan." They brought the boy home, all broken and crushed, a sickening sight, to writhe in agony and die. Then Tim took his place. Not long afterward Father was carried home, maimed and bruised by a cave-in, also to die; and "The Methodist choir sang 'Jesus, Lover of My Soul'" at his funeral. Mother took on the double burden and slaved at the wash tub and over the ironing board to keep the family together, day by day losing in the struggle as she grew older and feebler.

As soon as Larry, the Ulysses of the saga, was strong enough to work, he became a laborer in a car repair shop and soon was caught in a vortex of events in that fourth dimension called time. Strike — America enters the war — an "agitator" shouts that it is a capitalist war and is beaten into pulp by an angry mob bent on "the war for democracy" — "Five men for a steel mill. Must be husky" — work in a rubber factory steaming with gas and stench — wage cuts, strikes — scabs, fights, defeat — a gassed soldier coughing on a park bench — trek to the great automobile town — hard, driven labor on the assembly line — Hoover prosperity dawns — rush, rush — crash in Wall Street — the conveyor belt slows down and stops — men out of work — men and women in old cars driving, hunting, growing weaker and poorer, children bawling — "No men wanted" — Hoover-towns of tin and old boards rise on the edges of cities — a job here for a day or two — a job there, for a day or two — a "chance" to lay pavements — "Hey, there, you're drinking out of the 'Niggers' cup'" — what of it for Nordics in the same plight? — down and out — home to Mother in a leaky miner's shack, a pot of greens on the stove, seasoned by a bit of lard — "That'll be fine. . . . Been a long time since we've had any good old wild greens" — odd jobs, odd jobs — "the steam shovel does the work of 500 miners" — "Father always wanted me to be a lawyer or doctor" — hungry men and women in St. Louis march on city hall demanding relief, police throw tear bombs, a gigantic Negro catches the bombs and hurls them back, authorities grant demands (moral suasion or force?) — odd jobs, odd jobs, no place fit to live in — children blue with cold — and on and on — Bosses "lookin' for beef today."

Around, everywhere, women — mothers, aunts, cousins, sisters — yes, and Bonny Fern, a farmer's daughter who looks down on miners' "brats." Gleams of life and beauty for a brief season of youth — marriage, children, shacks for homes — more children — strikes — rags, bones, and hanks of hair — bent backs, leathery skins, watery eyes, rheumatism — hungry kids wide-eyed — one room, two rooms, three rooms, with rickety furniture — bawdy houses on the edges of town — American family life, well, there it is — why have romances, marry, and make the grand start, down hill? — Bonny Fern, yes, she's still beautiful and losing her pride while father is sliding lower, to a sheriff's sale — labor agitations — workers arise! — ideologies and agrarian crises, why not talk American? — Sale day comes to the bankrupt father — farmers and workers gather in old man Fern's door yard — a rope with a noose is hung over a limb — auctioneer, sheriff, and state police (all swank, with guns unloosed) — what am I bid? — one low bid — a few cents, for the furniture — none dares to raise it — one low bid — a few cents — for the farm — none dares to raise that — old man Fern, by due process of law and order, repossesses his home — Bonny still appealing — But, no, Larry has seen family life — it's not for him — into the old car with two labor philosophers and organizers, Ulysses rides away to the west. Why West? No answer. There you are, said Jack Conroy, in effect; it's real; take it or leave it.

Taking it, Sinclair Lewis, in It Can't Happen Here, gave a fascist upshot of the class climax, in which a raucous demagogue, Buzz Windrip, assailing the rich and using their money, hacked his way through democratic restraints and suppressed in violence the voices of wonder and protest expressed in the literature of dissidence. And Lewis drew both plot and figures from the actualities of American life. Possessors of good things in the United States, as well as revolutionary workers, had spoken of the need for "a man on horseback." Neither wanted, of course, exactly what was likely to come, but force was the essence of desire. Senator Huey Long was an embodiment of fury; until overcome by an assassin, he spread genuine terror in politics. He could dine with the rich, heap up treasures for himself on earth, and flatter and feed the poor; yet he could be ruthless enough whenever it pleased him to cut either way in the social scale. Steeped in American experience — tingling with the force of vigilantes and lynchers — It Can't Happen Here, if not, as critics claimed, a supreme work of art, had the substance and air of verisimilitude. Too hot for the moving-picture industry catering to the German and Italian trade, Lewis' story was kept off the screen. It eventually reached theater-goers, as we have said, but only through the enterprise of an actors' project under the Works Progress Administration in Washington. That too was minatory.

§

Defying easy classification, yet certainly outside the domain of the "best," the democratically general, and the sharp-cut "proletarian," were writers of grave disposition who concerned themselves with the ironies, wastes, and frauds in American society, without visibly attempting to bring them into any fixed mold of social ideology, unless perchance a conception of chaos could be deemed a mold. Indeed an overpowering sense of futility, enveloping the small as well as the great, had in times past smitten strong minds, versed in old wisdom and deeply experienced. "He that increaseth knowledge," said the preacher in the Bible, "increaseth sorrow." While carrying the burdens of the Roman empire, Marcus Aurelius had fretted over the vanity of vanities. Centuries later in Germany, on the eve of Hitler's rise to sovereignty, Theodor Lessing, gifted with many tongues, western and oriental, and learned in the philosophies and the arts, reached the conclusion that history-writing was merely an exercise of the art of putting sense into the senseless. The idea that man is simply a faux pas had long burdened Old World thought.

In America, land of "liberty and opportunity," however, the conception of life as chaos, as meaningless, had not flowered into the cogency of literature before the collapse of Mr. Coolidge's prosperity. Afterward, as the economic depression dragged its ugly length through the years, writers began to strike bass notes of futility — for labor, for Lords of Creation, and for their emulators lower in the scale of incomes.

Henry James, no doubt, had once believed nearly everything in the United States to be poor, thin, and too "bourgeois" for the delicacy of his nature. Edith Wharton had expressed this view of the plutocracy while finding some solace in the seasoned families of America. The new futility, however, did not stem from their tastes and notions of the good life. It offered no escape, either to the once "mellow culture" of Italy, France, and England or to a classless utopia by the proletarian route of revolution.

Absorbed in the idea of a "lost generation" hiding away in Europe, Elliot Paul, in Concert Pitch, engraved a story about a group of such frustrated persons in musical Paris, representatives of the post-war cults, insecure and overwrought, fluttering about and indecisive "like a tangle of uprooted plants floating pointlessly on a sullen sea." It was not because these feckless persons were expatriates that futility had swamped them; they were doomed by their own resentments, incompetence, malice, and constitutional inability to face life, their discords attaining "concert pitch." And with what hope of redemption? None, visible, apparently, on Paul's horizon.

Shortly after Lords of Creation had tried to explain to the Senate committee on banking and finance just how the formation of holding companies and the issue of watered stocks and bonds had enriched American economy, Kay Boyle, likewise an American living in Europe, "le doute incarné," as George Sand said of Byron, depicted in My Next Bride the stature and psychology of Antony Lister, son of a New York financier, searching for the art of life — in France. This wandering youth, who had no stomach for his father's office, dabbled, played, wondered, and thought, a little hither and yon, scattering his money, toying with women, stumbling through a narrowing alley to his doom. One day he was seen carrying Henry Adams' The Degradation of the Democratic Dogma under his arm. Another day he put a strange question to Victoria John, an American girl scratching for a livelihood among the wastrels of Paris: "Have you ever read a man named MacLeish? I've never read anyone like him. I've a book of his for you if you'll have it tomorrow afternoon." Here and there little plaintive notes were piped: "Le Poète, doit-il reconnaître l'Empire de l'Age Mécanique?" Should he indeed? If so or not, why and what upshot? No answer. Antony was no good for business, inept in everything else, blundering around, uttering hollow sounds with dim meaning, only a wraith of reality.

And how had Antony Lister got that way? Kay Boyle gave her explanation in Antony's own words. "Where I went to school," he said, "the conversation was the most elegant you could find for the price. The boys used to talk about how many cocktails their mothers served at home in the evening and to how many people, and how many bridge tables they had. There weren't any black people being hung in the

South, the Supreme Court was the highest, the supremest. Buddha had never sat quiet, year after year, reflecting. Nothing was sacred enough to kneel to, not even a mountain, nor an element like the wind, or the rain, nor an astral body."

In that emptiness Antony had spent his boyhood. In his young manhood he could lay hold of nothing that satisfied his spirit. He vaguely thought "that the rich and the poor were not the issue; it had to be something better than that or else he might as well be dead. If you had no money at all you were finished, but also if you had money it was possible you were finished too. Rich or poor, everyone was stabbing everyone else with hate, stabbing in envy and in terror." No light in any direction. "The whole universe on a honeymoon of horror, wedded to their daggers, stabbing their way from one betrayal to the next. Even your own family and friends eager to do it to you."

In this torment, the addled youth confessed: "I am weak, too weak to take up a weapon and go into the orgy, unless I turned it upon myself. . . ." To this outburst, Victoria, deeply longing for America, the land of her birth, replied with equal futility: "You don't have to. You can always get on a boat and leave the country. You can always keep on going." So it might seem to a dreaming girl, as it had seemed to the knights of endless industrial progress in the United States — keep on going and going and going. While the going was good, no question need be asked; when it slowed down or stopped, no answers for any questions. At least Antony could find none: "I can't go far enough. Nobody can. Wherever I am, just looking out of the holes in my skull is enough to scare me. I'm scared of what's happening to everyone and I can't do anything to change it."

Nor, indeed, could Victoria herself, despite the apparent optimism of keeping the faith in her own words: "It's no use, Antony, I know how little use it is. There are two kinds of people in the world, there are the rich and the poor, and if you're the poor you're finished from the first, even though you don't see it right away. You can make a little struggle, very brief, and after a while you begin to see. You see they've got you down and they certainly aren't going to let you up again. It wouldn't be clever at all. Once you got up and were still young enough you might tell what you had seen down there." This came from Victoria's heart, for she was poor and just hanging on to the rim of existence. Antony could not see the situation in the simple terms of rich and poor, although he knew riches and beheld poverty, but he agreed with Victoria about the slight possibility of avoiding the envy and terror of things.

In the middle of futility, Antony had to go back to New York where he had a father called Horace. From this center of the business empire in the machine age, he cabled his wife, Fontana, a kind of sensuous shadow into whose toils he had fallen in Paris: "Wall Street narrow as the bier. . . . Horace believes in the future of gold, silver, copper, steel, and other metals. . . . They've put bars on all the windows because so many people committed it this year now it seems more like a prison than last. . . Nijinsky should have stayed sane long enough to create the dance I see myself doing in wreaths, garlands, festoons of stock quotations on white ticker ribbons. . . . I walk all night after parties or when there're not any. . . . I am not gold, silver, or copper, I am something waiting to be set to music. . . . Mozart forgot me in his eighth year . . . hummed me over between Don Juan and the Magic Flute and forgot me going up stairs to bed in Salzburg. . . . Anaconda Copper, Cerro de Pasco, Seaboard Oil are passwords for departure. . . . New York explodes inside me every time I step out the door. . . . I can't do it. . . . I can't do it. . . . I can't do it. . . . Have you seen a girl called Victoria John she's trapped in ancient Greece." A few days later, Fontana and Victoria, while riding through the streets of Paris, opened up the Paris-American newspaper and read: "Prominent Young Club Man Cuts Veins in Father's Office," and a subtitle: "Antony Lister Takes Own Life. Wall Street Losses Rumored." Fontana turned to her companion and said: "Don't cry. Antony said you never cried." Tears themselves were futile.

If the son of a rich man who had been educated in the most elegant conversation that money could buy could find in the end no impulse or reason for going on, the promise of things was different for Emma Troy, a woman who had made money in the manufacture of "triple-whipped mayonnaise" and set out in a rush to break into "the American aristocracy" at home. Her story Hamilton Basso told under the title, In Their Own Image, published right in the middle of the New Deal, during the feverish quest for "recovery" of things past. Emma was no daughter of the rich. She had worked her way into the business of making mayonnaise and on the crest of success had sold out her establishment to a kind of holding company for a huge pile of income-bearing paper. Spangled with gold, she took her son and daughter, Freddie and Virginia, to Aiken, South Carolina, where many possessors of great wealth spent their winter months in the pursuits of the leisured.

Like the courtiers who danced at the balls of Louis XVI, the "winter set" had created a ritual of inutilities, if with no Most Christian Majesty to serve as the center. Around and around this "round of pleasures," Basso carried Emma, Freddie, and Virginia Troy in their effort to "break into the ranks." Unlike Edith Wharton he did not set the newcomers off as mere vulgarians against the culture of seasoned wealth which through long years had sloughed off the barbarism of manual labor and "the odor of trade." No such purpose or illusion shone through his pages. For Basso, these holders of liquid claims to America's wealth were not merely "new people" annoying to the ordered and aromatic world of established families. Nor were they mere grinders of the faces of the poor. They rose to no such zenith of force. In sum and substance, in relation to going concerns, they were simply useless and, incidentally, wasters. While Basso did not say this so baldly, the cold irony of his story — sayings and doings in Aiken — could leave no other impression.

He made no point of tragedy, comedy, farce, or fraud. His characters spoke and acted for themselves, where they were — in Aiken, for a winter round of pleasures.

There were no happy endings for the mayonnaise family or at least no realization of ambitions. Though the son Freddie was married off, the achievement turned out to be a mess. Virginia, the daughter, having inherited, perhaps, some healthy memories from Emma's days in the mayonnaise kitchen, managed to elude the snare her mother set to capture an impecunious Italian count. And Emma found no prince for herself. As fortune went badly with her climbing, she attached herself to the lower rungs of the social ladder by marrying an advertising man who laughed at publicity and public relations as heartily as he did at the ritual of the Aiken set.

While describing its ineptitudes, Basso allowed the set to hear the rumble of an industrial conflict; but that was, to all appearances, an accident of geography and time. It happened that there was a mill town not far away from the scene of the ritual and that a strike occurred during the season. The rich heard of it and were a bit discomfited. Indeed a boy of artistic proclivities was seen prowling around the homes of the rich, carrying an easel and brush, and was shot as a suspicious character. Neither the strike nor the shooting affair, however, had any evident connection with the mayonnaise family or the doings and sayings in the Aiken crowd.

Never before in American fiction had families of great riches been treated in just such a fashion. In Basso's pages they appeared not as mere vulgarians, or exploiters, or ogres of any kind. They were simply purposeless, useless, futile, in respect of the economy that sustained them. Though inwardly hearty and vivacious, they seemed to be turning yellow, like autumn leaves about to fall. They might drop to earth. They might flutter in the breeze a long time. Basso left them hanging there.

With a similar surgery John O'Hara carved at the system in Hollywood, cutting off the celluloid mask and exposing its inner life, tormented and retching. In Hope of Heaven he framed the dream, the romance, and the ravages of reality. An examination of the precious "studio atmosphere" seemed to discover "no more hope in it than there was in Appointment in Samarra, no more heaven there than there was in Butterfield 8." That meant exactly none at all. In the glittering land of fancy, despite Shirley Temple and all the rest, boundless deceit, passion, and intrigue boiled over in one compact spot. Undeniably that was a harsh judgment and it must have been disagreeable for Deacon Will Hays, Czar of the Movies, and his committees of ladies. Yet it had an outside homology in revelations of the methods employed by some financial magnates in the motion-picture industry — financing being an euphonious term that could cover betrayal of trust, inside deals, and the duping of "investors." Besides, Deacon Hays himself, the very chief of the motion-picture captains, had displayed an amazing virtuosity, in matters fiduciary, as he explained to a Senate committee in describing his relations to Harry Sinclair and the oil scandals while he had been arch financier of the Republican campaign fund. O'Hara's literary conception of the Hollywood scene was, therefore, not wholly out of line with the once orthodox conception of the politico-economic scene over which the Czar of the "industry" presided with such aplomb.

In another place — not Paris or Aiken or Hollywood — just Tenth Street in New York — Edna St. Vincent Millay in the medium of verse presented a few mortals from the busy city holding a Conversation at Midnight, that is, setting forth their interests, ideas, hopes, fears, and ambitions, in 1937, while business, recently at the crest, was slithering downward in its course. Among these mortals gathered after dinner around good whiskey and wine were a man of affairs listed as a stockbroker, a communist poet, a painter, a story writer, an advertising expert, a Roman Catholic priest, and a kind of Olympian host who combined amiability with general agnosticism. For hours the conversation splashed, flashed, and bubbled along like a brook, meandering and getting nowhere. Yet in the splashing and flashing, lights illuminated all facets of American culture — ranging from sports, business, sex, music, and the arts, to religion and politics. The kaleidoscope of American civilization was turned over and over, producing fragments of figures, but no figures. Neither art nor letters nor religion could stop and possess the stream of talk. Giving it up as hopeless, the priest went away early; in such a group he could not command. The advertising man spoke of love as the great need of troubled times, without evoking ardent responses. The artist seemed merely wistful.

At one point, however, the conversation at midnight simmered down to a broad and irreducible antithesis. The stockbroker as capitalist and the poet as communist faced each other and spat fire. From his home in Palo Alto, Herbert Hoover had shouted to the man in the White House whole paragraphs and speeches which could be summarized in a few words: "Regimentation, regimentation. Give us freedom." Perhaps the stockbroker had heard them. Perhaps he just felt like Hoover for similar reasons. At all events he cried out:

Oh, God, why live, to breathe a prescribed and rational air!
   — All free
Opinion, all interchange of vigorous thought, suffocated
By the poisonous motor-exhaust of motor minds!
Passion regimented; curiosity regimented; endeavour regi-
   mented;
Culture, and grace, and all the things I cared for
Equally divided among the mob, and sauced to their taste!
This is the time for the proud to take his pride by the hilt
And slit his bowels with it; this is the time for the individual,
   for me,
To lock himself in his room . . . and get it over with.

This was the cue for the communist who answered in a fierce tu quoque:

You, an individual? — you, you regimented mouse?
You Harvard Club, Union Club, white tie for the opera,
   black tie for the theatre,

Trouser legs a little wider this year, sir,
I would suggest dark blue instead of black, sir,
Pumps are no longer worn, sir,
Mah-Johngg, cross-word, anagram, backgammon, whist,
    bridge, auction, contract, regimented mouse!
Why, you're so accustomed to being flanked to right and left
    by people just like yourself
That if they ever *should* step aside you wouldn't stand up!

. . .

You, an individual?
You salad for luncheon, soup for dinner,
Maine for summer, Florida for winter,
Wife-pampering dog-worshipper!

Where was the synthesis, the resolution of the contradiction? The conversation at midnight did not bring it forth.
The priest had not produced it. The advertising man's love
offered no single wonder-working providence. The host
could tender only the uncertainty of liberalism: both fascism
and communism were intolerable to the human spirit; liberalism might play the eclectic role, pick, elide, combine. But
liberalism seemed to get nowhere. Even so, where were
fascism and communism getting, in terms of precious human
values? Uncertainty prevailed:

Let us abdicate now; let us disintegrate quietly here, con-
    vivially imbibing
The pleasanter poisons.

Although Sinclair Lewis probably did not intend to place
his novel of Prodigal Parents in the class of futilitarian literature, he certainly cast the children of a prosperous business
man, Frederick William Cornplow, and his wife, into the pit
of wastrels, while mixing sex vaporings and communist
fumes in a curious concoction. To be sure, Cornplow was
mighty enough, in Lewis' pages, but his offspring were silly
and hopeless and then as ever the future belonged to youth.
In final analysis, Lewis' panegyric on Cornplow in itself
raised a question: Did the boast spring from fear or assur-

ance? "Cornplow," he said, "is the eternal bourgeois, the Middle Class, whom the Bolsheviks hate and imitate, whom the English love and deprecate, and who is most of the population worth considering in France and Germany and these United States; when he changes his mind that crisis is weightier than Waterloo or Thermopylae." Possibly, but the sweeping assertion boomed with the oratory of the advertising agent and was far beyond the reach of demonstration. In the Congress of these United States, where eternal bourgeois were at the time ostensibly busy making laws, they were also digging their own graves apparently in preparation for burial under a mountain of debts, deficits, inflation, and armaments. Perhaps they would change their minds, if they could, and prove that it could happen here, but if that crisis was to be weightier than Waterloo or Thermopylae it might settle just as much as those historic battles settled for the long movement of civilization. It was possible that warriors and priests would outlive the Cornplows.

§

Continuous insistence that the genteel tradition had become a hollow farce, that democracy of the political tradition was not enough, that fundamental changes in economic and social usage must come, were now coming, coupled with the repeated allegations of futility, introduced a heat almost revolutionary into literary reviewing, appraising, and discussing. The sit-down strike, metaphorically speaking, broke into editorial sanctums, publishers' teas, and assemblies for considering the state of beautiful letters.

The bearers of dissident reports devoid of glad tidings had often known at first hand the experiences of which they wrote — long hours at rattling machines, tedious hours digging in mines, strikes, battles with police, the search for work, riding the rods, clashes with "scabs" and "finks." Their novels rang with an authenticity and an assurance that could not be called artificial on any score and this may have been a factor in winning the reception which was accorded to so many of them in the reviews. At all events, though, in the main, literary criticism, as of old, revolved around the pivot of persistent concern with form and symmetry, style and rhythm, finish and grace, with emphasis on pure, rather than practical, artistry, the dissidents were accorded full hearings beside the "favorites" and the "best." No editors in fact clung so tenaciously to the genteel tradition as to reject completely the men and the women who wrote vivid reports and sizzling tales of life and struggle at the lowest levels of economic subsistence. Literary militancy "made" the front pages of reviews and drew serious consideration from the leading critics of the country.

During his tenure of office as editor of the Saturday Review of Literature, Henry Seidel Canby, though by no means captivated by the proletarian appeal as such, greeted the novels of that school with fair appreciation when they demonstrated literary power and skill. Perhaps more comprehensively, his immediate successor, Bernard DeVoto, continued this appreciation with criticism. Indeed the hospitality of literary critics to the new writers of fiction and poetry was itself symptomatic of a catholicity in spirit extending beyond that manifest in the marketplace and the counting house. Despite some intemperate appraisals and violent encounters, the character of the great literary debate was on the whole a tribute to the quality of American culture and meaningful for its future. Americans were not to Laugh and Lie Down, as Robert Cantwell had phrased it, passively.

In volumes, essays, and little magazines, the Marxists kept harping on a problem more easily stated than solved: "Since the writer is perforce a product of time, place, and social milieu and cannot stand entirely outside his own experience, cannot acquire by any means an Olympian detachment from earthly affairs, how can he avoid giving expression to acquired values and, if he can not escape that necessity, what values shall he choose?" That was a tough nut for Marxists to crack as well as for all writers and critics; and nobody cracked it — to universal satisfaction. One thing was patent at least: the time had passed when young persons could set out upon literary careers equipped merely with Samuel Smiles, Matthew Arnold, and a few of the classics as models of substance and style.

In fact no writers even in the era of high American prosperity had done just that. Before Mr. Coolidge left his office as President of the United States, V. F. Calverton had brought to literary criticism the wide pattern of sociological interest, in a treatise called The Newer Spirit. This was followed by a sociological interpretation of American literature since the civil war set forth by Granville Hicks, a close student of the subject, under the caption of The Great Tradition. With full historical warrant, Hicks declared that ours has been a critical literature, critical of greed, cowardice, and meanness. Then he put this question to his countrymen: How can authors refuse to strike at the sources of the evils they have so constantly attacked? When they choose to go to the roots of things, he insisted they must take the communist line: they must give their support to the class that is able to overthrow capitalism. Pondering longer on the American tradition, Hicks declared in 1938 I Like America; he hoped it would improve its ways, however.

If to youth unmindful of long history the application of the sociological method to literature looked like an original achievement, historians of literary criticism found in it confirmation of a common-sense view long held by masters of literature. Voltaire certainly had written on life, manners, thought, and cruelties under the old regime of the eighteenth century, no matter how many hours he had spent on polishing his sentences. At the opening of the nineteenth century, Madame de Staël had lucidly applied the sociological critique in a treatise On Literature Considered in Relation to Social Institutions. In the Victorian age, John Morley had said in his inimitable way: "Poetry, and not only poetry, but every other channel of emotional expression and aesthetic culture, confessedly moves with the general march of the human mind, and art is only the transformation into ideal and imaginative shapes of a predominant system and philosophy of life." Minor writers could be consigned without disrespect to the region of the literature of taste, graces, stray variations of shade and color. But "the loftier masters, though their technical power and originality, their beauty of form, strength of flight, music and variousness of rhythm, are full of interest and instruction, yet, besides these precious gifts, come to us with the size and quality of great historic forces, for they represent the hope and energies, the dreams and the consummation, of the human intelligence in its most enormous movements." This view Edith Wharton sustained out of her own experience and power as a writer — as one of the masters. The patient study of style was no vain literary pursuit; the born-poet could scarcely evolve Alexandrine verse out of his inner consciousness in New York or Kansas; but it was certain, as the New Deal moved toward its finish, that American literature was becoming concerned with "human intelligence in its most enormous movements." Perchance the hour of great politics was drawing nearer.

The discussion of the literary movement took various forms. In part it was an affair of the writers in prose and poetry themselves bent on examining their own intentions and obligations. In 1937 a throng assembled in New York in their second Writers' Congress to talk about the direction of the literary movement and its relation to society, as members of P. E. N. had been doing in national and international assemblies for some time. The discussion revealed a wide diversity of opinion and judgment about the function of the writer, and participants soon found that the direction of the dissident movement was not to be perfectly straight, narrow, and well-lighted for everybody who took part in it. Marxists made speeches characterized by the fixed idea that literature in America as in Russia must exhibit correctness of doctrine and soundness of verbalism but they differed acutely over the nature of that correctness and soundness. Inasmuch as all Marxists had rejected the Pope, inasmuch as the Russian dictator, Stalin, was too distraught with many other matters to settle the quarrels of Grub Street in New York, who among the Marxists was in fact anointed, consecrated, and authorized to approve or excommunicate? While Marxists wrangled over the correct line, other authors at the Writers' Congress asserted the right to describe what they saw and knew of labor, poverty, and disenchantment without reference to prescriptions authoritative in the temple of the orthodox. It was a lively meeting of dissident minds, observed by crowded galleries.

During the sessions Malcolm Cowley, literary editor of the New Republic, author and poet, retaining memories of a youthful expatriation in Paris, laid stress on the power of revolutionary conceptions in kindling and feeding the fire of creative energy. On the other hand, Edwin Seaver, critic and novelist, warned his colleagues against subservience to shibboleths and dogmas. John Crowe Ransom, agrarian, poet, critic, professor at Vanderbilt University, later transferred to Kenyon College, took the floor to scourge the "amateurs" who appeared to dominate the literary field, and contended that critics must be trained — presumably in the seats of learning by professor-philosophers; this left in a haze the familiar problem: Who is to train the trainers? Other speakers kept bringing back into the argument the force of varied experiences, inner fire, and grand conceptions of life whatever they might be. In the end, the Writers' Congress adjourned without agreements defined in thirty-nine articles of faith, or more or less, and without a manifesto, despite the number of members who came with neat prescriptions in their heads or in their pockets. Naturally, therefore, after the congress was over, a spirited controversy took place in the press over the meaning and the upshot of the literary assembly. One aspect seemed positive, namely, emphasis on the substance of letters.

To this sociological analysis of literature, Kenneth Burke of the dissident school and a participant in the Writers' Congress added a critique entitled Attitudes toward History.

By history, Burke meant the substance of economy, life, and labor, actuality, and culture, rather than the fragments of totality carved out by professors of history obsessed merely by warriors and politicians. It was his contention that the writer interprets life, that is, history, according to his experience with it, and assumes an attitude either of acceptance or rejection of the forms which life displays. The essence of life being permanence amid change, the writer will be, with respect to that essence, passive or disturbed, content or malcontent, sentimentally satisfied or maladjusted and overwrought. Applying this dictum to American literature, Burke inquired whether American writers had at last accepted American life or were still fleeing from its issues and conflicts even by making them despicable. Thus the problem of the determinism or indeterminism in "objective relations" was thrust by Burke into the obscure realm of subjective moods. In his discussion of American literature as history and in his analysis of contemporary writing, Burke seemed to call for the recognition of life in America as theme worthy of the highest intelligence, to demand hard work in penetrating to its substance, and to make imperative the literary master's affection for the competent forms and shades of expression.

Over the tempest raised by disputes about pure proletarian literature, as distinguished from dissident literature in general, broke a torrent of discussion among readers of fiction, poetry, and criticism. The escaping steam was sometimes called the vaporing of little minds learned neither in Marxism nor in letters, and indeed there was some justice in the allegation, for much nonsense was written on the subject by little persons who could scarcely write at all.

After carrying on a searching inquiry, Louis Adamic declared that the proletarian authors were either non-proletarian in origin or ceased to be proletarians when they entered the white-collar career of letters. In the second place, he contended, on the authority of Trotsky, that a real proletarian literature was impossible under capitalism, for the actual workers were too busy "making a living, fretting, agonizing, scheming, and struggling to seize power" and, however energetic, could not find the leisure required for writing. Under a well-functioning communist state to follow capitalism, the proletariat would cease to exist and, in that happy order of things, art would simply be human art. Humanity would be emancipated from bondage to things and class. Whether the literature of revolt was written by the proletariat or not, another question remained: Did the workers in town or country read it?

The answer to this query Adamic sought by traveling far and wide over the country and interviewing the kinds of men and women described in the so-called proletarian literature. On the basis of his journeying and inquisition, he reported that the influence of such literature on the working class was negligible; in fact, nil. Workers in factory and field did not care to read about themselves — about the men, women, and children of the disinherited. They read few novels and fewer books of a general character. Now and then industrial workers bought the Liberty magazine, True Stories, Wild West Tales, or Screen Romance, if they ventured beyond the sensational newspapers, tabloids, comic strips, and picture magazines. "Ninety-nine and one-half per cent" of the American workers, Adamic concluded, in 1934, "seem to me to be practically beyond the reach of radical printed propaganda or serious, honest writing of any sort. This, to my deep regret, is the brutal truth of the situation, and anyone who does not realize it . . . is, I think, ipso facto, open to the suspicion that he is not qualified to write about the American proletariat." Exceptions to the rule, remarkable exceptions, Adamic did find here and there, but they merely served to bring out forcefully the main conclusion of his survey. The following year, in America Faces the Barricades, John L. Spivak made a confirming report: "I am convinced that the American worker does not want to overthrow the government. All he wants is food." The plight of the people was

grievous. What are you going to do about it? Spivak set
down as his answer: "I don't know."

To the further confusion of the Marxians, Robert Herrick,
an elder statesman of American letters, contributed a trenchant inquiry. If, as the Marxists believe, all social movements
and class actions are determined in the very nature of things,
why the laudation of proletarian virtues and why the moral
indignation over capitalist "vices"? If Marxism is the science of prediction, as precise as the science of physics, why
all the righteous heat over the way to the predicted end?
One does not quarrel with water running down hill on its inexorable course. If the movement of history is determined,
it is determined for all classes. And yet, Herrick said, he
could not remember "a single instance" in which this logic
was applied by intransigent writers to show that the employer was under the same bondage to the capitalist system
as the workers were. According to the strict logic of Marxism, both should be represented as caught in a mechanical
trap, but Herrick could not detect in proletarian literature a
single case "where the top dog is presented not with sympathy but with a definite awareness that he too is moved by a
terrifying necessity along predetermined lines of least resistance — the bosses, the executives, the impersonal boards of
directors, all without exception bound to the same coil of
necessity through fear, shame, desire, habit." In short,
Herrick held, the proletarian school was lacking in perception
and failing to apply its own dogma of determinism. If some
of its expositors were right, if Marxism was merely a portrayal of mechanical economy and iron prediction, then Herrick could be deemed more Marxist than the writers who suf-
fused description and revolt with sentiment and evaluation.
But could literature be reduced to physics and still be literature?

Going persistently on his own way, Edmund Wilson directed his thought with increasing effectiveness to the issue
that had engaged the hot concern of the writers' congress,
and indeed of all workers in the domain of letters, namely,

the substance of literature amid its forms and accidents. Having graduated from regular services on the New York Evening Sun, Vanity Fair, and The New Republic, Wilson tried to pierce further beneath the surface of volumes, chapters, paragraphs, and sentences in search of the controlling conceptions that accounted for authors' selections, omissions, and emphases. Whether he dealt with single authors, as with Edith Wharton in an appraisal written for The New Republic after her death was announced, or with a group, as in his volume on Triple Thinkers, Wilson never lost sight of the heart of the business: Under what overarching conception of things has this configuration in letters taken shape? It was no accident then when he turned to an examination of the historical development of socialism from the French revolution through the partnership of Marx and Engels, in his unresting exploration of the forces conditioning or determining the substance of "polite" letters.

In this literary tournament, Bernard DeVoto, critic, essayist, and novelist, likewise jousted. What was the meaning for American civilization — for the trajectory of the future — to be found in all the literature called proletarian? DeVoto made an answer: "Class literature, the literature of any class whatever, quite apart from its esthetic function which may in part at least affect all classes, must serve at least one of two functions. First and most important, there is the function of heightening and unifying the sentiments of the class which it represents. It may confirm or increase their group-consciousness, step up their solidarity, make stronger their sense of power and injury and communion, and create, propagate, and enliven those vital myths, beliefs, ideals, aims, dogmas, slogans, personifications, purposes, and sanctions which are at once the bonds that hold the class together and the energy that makes action possible. Second, there is the interclass function. Literature may be an agency of attack on other classes or of conversion among them. It may assist disintegration, weakening the other classes by making them pity or fear the class it represents, giving them a sense of shame or guilt or futility, hammering at their doubts with ridicule or horror or terror. Or it may proselytize among them, converting the essentially religious symbols of its own myths into symbols acceptable among the religions it invades, and carrying the position by outflanking it with visions of the greater glory to come — or the equivalent in the eschatology of the period. These functions are usually quite distinct. Only rarely and only in great literature will they coalesce. A work of genius may well fuse them together, achieving symbols that are both incandescent for its own class and immediately authoritative for other classes."

This terse summary by DeVoto, covering the class substance of literature and artistic appraisal, certainly had direct application to Marxian forms, efforts, and propensities. Whether it applied also to the whole body of letters displaying economic and political awareness was another, and broader, issue. Nor did DeVoto's judgment on this point take into account the measurement of literary influences on secular history — on the makers of that history. If in time to come American history as actuality should be simplified down to an acute conflict between the owners of property on the one side and the non-owners on the other side — as James Madison and Daniel Webster had feared it might be — then the proletarian literature could be described by distant historians as at least foreshadowing, if not in any manner shaping, the course of things to come.

But there was no way, in any "science," Marxian or otherwise, despite much bold asserting, of knowing in the days of the golden glow and the New Deal whether this conflict, in bald and simple forms, would come to pass. Nor, if it was to come to pass, was there any science for predicting the hour, the circumstances, or the immediate outcome. Judging by European experience and by hints and signs in the United States, Sinclair Lewis could have been right in the verdict rendered by It Can't Happen Here. Although the unquenchable hope of Marxists looked far beyond fascism, wars, revolts, and suppressions to the final day of the spring into freedom, an air of remoteness and uncertainty hung over that assurance. If for the long time, or all time, the course of history was to run against the disinherited, the makers of proletarian letters might well have wished that they had stayed within the confused and blurring lines of "the united front." Neither friend nor foe, however, could lift in 1928 or in 1938 the curtain on that realm of possibilities.

The whole philosophic problem thus posed in Europe as in America was analyzed and clarified in Karl Mannheim's Ideology and Utopia, translated into English in 1937. Class interests and ideas, he affirmed, do appear in society, but they do not lie insulated, side by side, like eggs in a basket. In times of peace and relative well-being, transfusions, modifications, disintegrations occur and, even when tension sharpens the insular character of ideas and interests, no absolute cleavages take place. It was so in respect of any literature that touched life at all, especially the literature of economic and political consciousness. Like realistic writings in sociology and politics, realistic literature dealt with actualities of life and labor, gave voice to peoples and interests, thrust upon the first class passengers, who rode, some knowledge of the second class, that walked, and of the third class, that pushed the wagon — to repeat Carl Sandburg's imagery.

However rough and untraveled the road ahead, the literature of dissidence certainly gave suggestions respecting the way. It expressed and echoed the swelling sentiments that swept every state in the Union in 1936 and shook both the powers and the convictions of those Bourbons who spoke of "restoration." The prose and verse of economic and political sensitiveness were not read by the millions, but they were read and discussed by some men and women, boys and girls, who would help to make history in 1950, 1960, 1970.

§

Like the literature of imagination and literary criticism, with which it was inevitably associated, the newspaper press reflected the tendencies of the time — its mechanics, its centralization, its economies, its moralities, and its ironies. While Berle and Means reported the intensifying concentration of corporate control over national wealth, statisticians of newspaper ownership and circulation traced the rise of dailies correctly called "chain" and recorded the death and consolidation of papers. In 1928 the "chains" dominated 280 daily newspapers. In 1933 they held 361 dailies in thrall, with a circulation of "13,244,574 or 37.4 per cent of the total daily issuance and 11,044,646 or 45.9 per cent of the Sunday," to use the figures of Alfred M. Lee, in his volume on The Daily Newspaper in America.

Mergers and suspensions marked the course of this development. In the decade between 1924 and 1934, "a net decline of 136 units" occurred in the daily and Sunday field. Under the expert editorship of Walter Lippmann, the New York Morning World weakened and died. Hearst was compelled to bury his New York American for want of sustenance. Competitors consolidated until cities of the smaller rank were sometimes "served with news" under the auspices of single concerns. Perhaps the climax was reached when Republican and Democratic sheets in one city rolled from presses under common ownership, with malice toward none, charity for all, and counting house receipts augmented. Although country weeklies and small town dailies continued to flourish, the circulation of urban and suburban papers in rural regions expanded rapidly, with improved roads, the perfection of high-speed trucks, and the advancement of rural free delivery by automobile.

In some measure this centralization was the outcome of ambition and avarice. In some measure it responded to mechanics and economics. Efforts to achieve more rapid printing — ordinary, color, and rotogravure — led to the construction of machines more complicated and expensive. A single plant opened by the New York Daily News in 1930 cost ten million dollars. When other equipment, services, and devices were added to mere plant, capital and current out-

lays mounted. According to reports, the Philadelphia Inquirer was sold in 1930 for eighteen million dollars.

Without world news services, the most expensive plant was
worthless and the cost of these services rose with the area and
intensity of coverage. The outlay of the Associated Press
alone nearly tripled between 1917 and 1931. When wire-
photo reporting was added to telegraph, radio, and telephone
reporting, a new element of expense was introduced. Competition for circulation, on which advertising revenues rested,
led to the increasing employment of special writers for sports,
the arts, the sciences, radio, education, the theater, cosmetics,
lingerie, and accessories, the motion-picture kingdom, wars,
foreign affairs, and every other phase of public interest; and
all this raised the cost of newspaper production. To meet
these and similar charges, ever larger receipts were required,
merely to keep alive, apart from making profits.

In such circumstances metropolitan journalism became a
business that could be carried on effectively only by great
capitalists or great corporations. The day when a brilliant
journalist, such as Horace Greeley, could borrow a little
money or buy a cheap machine on credit and set out on a
career of intellectual leadership had passed. Convinced by
tradition that the press was still a power, families that had
made fortunes in industry and commerce put some of their
millions into journalism. They bought up newspapers or
bought into them and, as more or less silent owners or part-
ners, added the weight of industrial capital to that of the
publishing capital invested in presses, plants, and services.
The extent to which newspapers were actually owned by
capitalists outside the "profession" could not be determined
by any available figures, but there seemed to be few great
dailies built up entirely out of their own earnings, without the
aid of stock and bond issues or bank loans. In other words,
journalism became a branch of business enterprise, controlled
by its necessities, penetrated by its spirit, interlocked with
its fortunes. Editors and readers sank into the background.
Subsidized newspapers could be run at a loss. The capitalist

with his immense resources, supported by advertisers, could alone cope with the costs of publication and supply the multitude with the diversified news, special articles, photogravures, comic strips, and cartoons necessary to meet mass demands.

Coupled with the high capitalization of the publishing industry was a tendency toward uniformity of cultural, political, and economic opinion. In the course of this development the open "crusading" journalism of the type launched in the late nineteenth century by Hearst and Pulitzer declined toward the vanishing point. In their early days they had berated the American plutocracy without mercy, campaigned against trusts and monopolies, and demanded heavy taxation on incomes and inheritances. Pulitzer, however, was now dead and his morning New York World had gone with him to its tomb. His St. Louis Post Dispatch went over to Alfred Landon, the Republican candidate in 1936, and to big pottage. As Hearst grew richer and his interests extended, he shed his old radicalism, actually surpassed Tories in his defense of primitive capitalism, and as he aged he turned his lingering energy to Hollywood, art treasures, and efforts to conserve his decaying estate.

In big journalism, crusading now came to an end. Apparently it did not "pay," especially as the picture newspapers carried off readers, or rather "lookers," who could not stand the strain of construing sentences. Even the Scripps-Howard chain of papers, which had flirted with labor and trust-busting, went over to the Right on all major issues, leaving behind merely the faint incense of diluted sentimentality. Nowhere in the land was a great editor left to battle heroically "for the plain people," in the style of the youthful Hearst or Pulitzer. Only cartoonists ingenious at their craft could now say things by insinuation that once could have been put into double-column leaders. And their number and skill were striking features of the age.

Coöperating with artists of the ordinary comic strip in creating totalitarian imagery on a national scale were the columnists whose effusions flowed across the continent in rising volume. Highest among them, with reference to the number of newspapers served or to circulation claimed, were O. O. McIntyre, "Dorothy Dix," and Dale Carnegie. The first, until his death in 1938, supplied the middle class in the small towns and cities of the hinterland with gossip about life in New York City — the land of dreams for fresh-water automobile salesmen, little executives, realtors, morticians, aspiring wives, and restless girls. The second, "Dorothy Dix," touched a universal chord, by giving advice to the love-sick and the love-lorn of both sexes. The third, Dale Carnegie, provided instruction on such matters of business enterprise as how to turn garage mechanics into sales orators or lift harassed insurance agents into company presidents. By these three columnists, the popular hunger for the trivia of metropolitan gossip, for the experiences of sex, and for the acquisition of riches was cleverly served, while the newspapers gathered in pecuniary rewards.

To that other great lust of Americans — politics — a small army of columnists avidly catered. For a long time Arthur Brisbane, the employee of Hearst, led them all in the number of estimated readers and emoluments, but Brisbane died in 1936 and his name dropped quickly into devouring oblivion. Pitching his thought to the level occupied by such persons as the officers of the National Manufacturers Association, executives of Morgan and other banks, aspiring enterprisers of the middle west and beyond to the Golden Gate, and women of the well-to-do clubs in search of moral and economic security, Walter Lippmann, who had previously attained fame as a liberal, reached a lofty peak as the intellectual purist among the columnists. While his star was glittering in the heavens, Dorothy Thompson, specializing in fascism and communism after years spent as a newspaper reporter in Germany where the two systems clashed so savagely, played upon the emotion of fear and the flair for horror and violence as she ostensibly engaged in discussing American public questions and politics. Among their rivals and associates, Drew Pearson and Robert S. Allen, in a joint syndicate, and Boake Carter, acting alone, were alleged to reach more readers and command more minds, though there was no way of proving the claim; nor did this trio seem to enlist as much affection as the others among the intelligentsia of the upper income brackets, for they were not always tenderly faithful to the honorifics of such circles.

Clearly, there was a diversity of talents and audiences in the syndicate field. Yet the most popular columnists, including the sportive Westbrook Pegler, agreed as a rule on one thing: they preached an economic orthodoxy which the highest pontifex in the United States Chamber of Commerce could usually scan with pleasure and approval. Such deviations as they occasionally allowed themselves could readily be taken as that homage which regularity pays to liberty. It was, therefore, strictly fitting that Dorothy Thompson should receive an honorary degree from Columbia University at the June commencement of 1938. Among the columnists of large following only Heywood Broun kept up a running fire on the left and certainly no university made him a Doctor of Humane Letters. Only incidentally could the First Lady, Eleanor Roosevelt, as a columnist, be called a strict defender of the New Deal.

During the turmoil of the panic and persisting business depression, when new social doctrines were advanced in the country, the popular columnists contributed to the maintenance of uniformity in opinion. Nearly all of them came out openly for the Republican candidate in 1936, laying bare the secret wishes of their accredited Olympian impartiality; and their services were even employed by Democratic publishers not too much enamored of the New Deal. Lukewarm editors, unable or unwilling to attack the Democratic machine or to flout the fixed ideas of their readers, were wont to balance such Democratic editorials as they chose to write by one or more "columns" on the opposite side of the political battle. This operation satisfied their covert desires while giving the semblances of catholicity in free journalism.

Whatever the motives, the syndication of columns throughout the country helped to stifle divefsities of opinion, at least in the press, and tended to spread the uniformity of conservatism even among potential dissenters, at least as far as the influence of newspapers extended. In other words, syndicated columns made for a greater degree of standardization or totalitarianism in the materials editors chose to publish and in journalism as an industry; and the uniformity on the whole reflected a belief in the illusion of permanence.

The actual influence of the columnists, students of journalism sought to estimate but all the relevant facts were not available, and the undertaking was impossible. No instruments of precise measurement were at hand. Promoters of columnism claimed enormous circulations for their clients, but how many newspaper buyers and subscribers read the columnists? Only guesses could be made. Sample surveys showed that the readers of one distinguished columnist voted against his creed in the election of 1936. Similar surveys of another gave opposite results. There was some significance, perhaps, to the fact that with a few exceptions the columnists were fiercely opposed to the reëlection of President Roosevelt, and were thus in accord with the bulk of the metropolitan press. Yet what significance? Though speculative fancy might presume to say, science could not. If there had been no political columnists in 1936, President Roosevelt might have polled more votes or, for aught any one really knew, fewer votes. So slight was exact knowledge of the influence exerted by ideas, tempers, and thought upon the minds of the millions. About all that could be said on the basis of precise information was that there were many columnists, that most of them were against the New Deal, that they made money out of their industry.

The suggestion was even broached that the conservatism of the columnists, added to that of editors in general, helped to intensify the criticism of newspapers that came from the Center and the Left. Certainly this criticism heated the dispute over the vague idea phrased as the "freedom of the

press." The debate became especially hot when President
Roosevelt made a drive against child labor in formulating
the newspaper code under the National Industrial Recovery
Act of 1933 and in pressing other measures directed to the
same end. Since newspapers were among the largest employers of children, especially newsboys, their earnings were
immediately affected by efforts to raise the age limits of
employment, and their reaction was generally hostile. In
resisting the elimination of child labor, several newspaper
proprietors and distributors raised the cry that the freedom
of the press was endangered. Some of their colleagues in the
industry, it is true, disagreed. "Alone among the industries,"
the New York Daily News remarked, ". . . the newspapers
insist on the retention of child labor, in the form of newsboys
and carriers working before dawn or after dark." But the
chief force of the press was thrown against President Roosevelt's proposal. Newspaper representatives were able to put
limits on the code provisions touching child labor and even
then complained loudly against what they were pleased to
regard as attacks on their independence and freedom.

The opposition of the press to restrictions on the use of
newsboys before dawn and after dark was not appreciably
diminished by criticisms and arguments advanced by the
opponents of child labor. Editors commented on the sad
plight of boys in search of employment, and were fond of
saying that "some of our finest citizens have made their
start in life through selling newspapers." Against this optimism was placed the evidence of Warden Lewis E. Lawes,
of Sing Sing Prison : "Recently I had a census taken here in
Sing Sing to determine the number of inmates who had sold
newspapers in their youth. The examination showed that
of the 2,300 men, over 69% had done so. Most of our population is drawn from the metropolitan district, and Sing Sing
receives over 70% of all felons sentenced in this state."
Newspaper proprietors and distributors continued to insist,
however, on the right to make use of child labor and to rest
their case on "freedom of the press." A. M. Lee was speaking

by the record when he said : "Not a little of the unpopularity
of the Roosevelt regime with the daily newspaper industry
arose from its stand on child labor."

In some measure the acrimony connected with this argument sprang from popular confusion respecting the meaning
of the phrase "freedom of the press." Judging by criticisms
directed against newspapers, it seemed to be generally taken
for granted that freedom of the press meant impartiality of
the press; and newspaper proprietors were charged with sup-
pressing and distorting news and deliberately maligning personalities and causes. That such complaints were often well
founded could not be gainsaid. George Seldes, in his Freedom
of the Press, gave chapter and verse for a damning indictment. Nevertheless, in the tumult of discussion, misappre-
hension was evident, for it was not true, as critics often
intimated, that the Constitution of the United States guaranteed the impartiality or fairness of the press. The Constitution merely forbade Congress to make any law respecting the
freedom of the press and state constitutions left proprietors
free to print what they pleased subject to the law of libel
and slander. In short, owners of papers could handle their
industry in their own way. They had a constitutional right
to suppress and distort news and even to malign and they
exercised it to a degree that undoubtedly augmented popular
disgust with the press — a disgust exhibited in the election of
1936 when the advice and appeals of the majority of the
great metropolitan newspapers were spurned by millions of
their readers.

For the popular impression that freedom of the press necessarily implied impartiality of the press, newspaper publishers
were partly responsible. While asserting the generally conceded right to pursue a partisan editorial policy, several proprietors of distinction made pretensions to neutrality in their
news reporting. They used such phrases as "objective news
columns" or "all the news that's fit to print," to assure
readers that they did not suppress or distort the news itself,
whatever they did in their editorial columns. In other words,

they themselves seemed to assume that freedom of the press implied impartiality of the press — or at least of the news — and in so doing they called forth from readers and critics innumerable demonstrations of their partiality.

In truth the ideal of a completely "objective" report on any complicated series of events was an impossible ideal. Necessarily, if not at all by intention, the slogan "all the news that's fit to print" was repeatedly violated. At best the maxim was merely a vague aspiration beyond the reach of the finest resolves. Although such ideals and aspirations were noble in conception and efforts to realize them gave distinction to a few newspapers throughout the country, no publisher managed to scale Olympus.

The very circumstances of newsgathering — the immaturity of many reporters, the rush, the confusion, the limitation of space — conspired against the attainment of "objectivity" and all-around "fairness." A comparison of reports on any single series of events, such as a strike or a mass meeting, published by two or more papers dedicated to reporting in the fulness of the truth was sure to disclose the inadequacy and the falsity of the claim to objectivity. The amount of space assigned to the series varied. The different positions given to the report — first page or sixteenth page — represented estimates of news, that is of "importance" — in other words, subjective determinations of values. The attached headlines signified interpretation, if not an obvious animus. Besides, it was a matter of common knowledge among reporters that each paper had its "general policies" and that, in selecting, condensing, and emphasizing news for telegraphic or telephonic dispatch, these general policies acted as a broad psychological control. It was likewise a matter of common knowledge that in the everlasting search for the sensational, headline writers were prone to seize upon pungent phrases or items, tear them from their context, and give to news reports a "turn" or "slant" which was distorting or suppressive in nature, whatever the intention.

An illustration makes concrete the fallacy of the claim to

objectivity or to reporting all the news that's fit to print. On March 6, 1938, an anti-war rally was held in New York City. It was organized by a small group of citizens opposed to the super-navy bill then pending — a group including liberals and a few Socialists. The meeting was addressed by several speakers, among them General William C. Rivers and Norman Thomas. The following day the meeting was reported by The New York Times to the extent of about three-fourths of a column. The report stated that the meeting had been held under the auspices of a new organization of "Socialists and other liberals." It gave extracts from the address by Senator Robert M. La Follette and then added that "among those who spoke were Homer Martin, president of the United Auto Workers of America; Norman Thomas, Socialist leader; Major General W. C. Rivers, retired, and Bertram Wolfe, writer." And the report was published on page ten, while the rumor that President Roosevelt would soon give the country a "lecture" on phosphates was assigned to the front page with appropriate headlines. By what criterion of "objectivity" was all the space given to Senator La Follette and none to General Rivers? Or the tenth page given to an anti-war mass meeting and the first page to a rumored discourse on phosphates so useful for war purposes?

Evidently not all the news "fit" to print was printed in this case; nor, indeed, did the exigencies of space permit that feat. Given the limited space and an effort to report all the speeches, by what process of selecting a few words from each could a perfectly "balanced" and "objective" report of the whole have been achieved? Only by publishing all the speeches in full, exactly as delivered, could any paper give an objective account of the discourses, and that was practically out of the question.

The fallacy of the "objective" theory of news reporting was also illustrated by comparisons of the "stories" printed on the super-navy issue by two papers of high quality. For example, on March 7, 1938, a dissenting minority, led by Congressman Ralph O. Brewster of the naval affairs com-

mittee in the House of Representatives, issued a report
against the huge navy bill approved by the majority of that
committee. The New York Times and The New York
Herald Tribune made first page news of the report, the
former with small headlines, the latter with big headlines.
Both published extracts from the report, but different extracts. Committed by general policy to the principle of collaboration with Great Britain and collective security, The
Times placed its emphasis almost entirely on the foreign
policy statements of the Brewster report and said little about
the technical objections to the navy bill advanced by the
minority. The Herald Tribune, on the other hand, a "big
navy advocate" and an opponent of President Roosevelt,
used as its extracts from the report sections almost entirely
technical, that is, designed to show that the authorizations
of battleships and other craft already on the statute books
made the new bill unnecessary for efficient defence. How
could two "objective accounts" of the same "event" be so
different, if the two great newspapers concerned were actually controlled by the iron law of objectivity and not by
publishing policies?

The conclusions indicated by such illustrations were sustained by Leo C. Rosten's survey of the Washington correspondents made under the auspices of the Social Science Research Council. Eighty-six per cent of those correspondents
believed that comparatively few papers gave significant
accounts of our "basic economic conflicts." Forty-eight per
cent did not believe that newspapers were equally fair to
"big business" and "labor," while forty-three per cent held
the opposite view and the remainder were undecided. Fifty-
five per cent agreed that their reports had sometimes been
played down, cut, or killed for reasons of policy followed by
their publishers. Sixty per cent of the correspondents said
that their orders were "to be objective," but that they knew
how their respective papers wanted their stories "to be
played."

While such evidence destroyed the "objective" myth, it

also indicated a wide-spread desire for "fair" reporting, and the greatest of the newspapers did give to labor and minorities more space than had been customary in the history of the American press. Unfortunately, however, from the standpoint of a "fair" hearing, the omission of single items could offset all the passages that were printed, as every attorney acquainted with the rules and effects of evidence knew very well.

Discussions of newspaper policies in the matter of objectivity served many purposes. They made American newspapers look like the white hope of humanity in comparison with the enslaved and "reptile press" of totalitarian states. At the same time critical analyses put American readers on their guard against the extravagant pretensions of the press to complete fairness and neutrality. Criticism induced skepticism, sometimes great contempt, and acted as a check on the excesses of the press. Even boys and girls in high schools developed keen eyes for "propaganda" in the form of alleged news. Reporters who presided over the auguries of newsgathering and reporting often laughed up their sleeves, sometimes sardonically. The success of the Newspaper Guild in acquiring members and the action of the Guild in joining the Committee for Industrial Organization were straws in the wind. Whatever proprietors, managers, and editors might say or claim, working newspaper men and women evidently knew that the political science of Calvin Coolidge's age, at least, had passed. Warned against making false pretensions and subjected to close scrutiny, proprietors with a sense of public responsibility and private honor seemed to redouble their efforts, year by year, to attain a higher and higher degree of fair and balanced news reporting. In the situation there were elements of encouragement to citizens of a patient and tolerant spirit.

Among the magazines only a few decided tendencies could be observed. Chief among these, perhaps, was the widening reception given to The Readers Digest, in pocket or purse size, by means of which men and women amid the hurry of

things could get synoptic glimpses of the outstanding articles
in the whole array of magazines. More original was the
Coronet. By the range and diversity of its materials and the
size of its reading public, it demonstrated that the cultural
desert was not as large as critics of philistinism had apparently imagined. Another tendency was the unabashed shift
of older magazines to the Right. The Atlantic Monthly
went over resolutely to the creed of the National Manufacturers Association and shortly afterward seemed to be
engaged in distributing the propaganda of oil interests
adversely affected by the policies of the Mexican government. Its former editor crowned a long life of literary endeavor by making a trip to Spain and publishing a laudatory
account of General Franco's beneficent rule, for the edifica-
tion of the American public.

Most striking of all was the quest of magazine editors for
sightseers as distinguished from readers. On the principle
that what the eyes see must be interesting and thought
provoking, a new magazine brazenly called Look, filled with
gripping pictures, often ingeniously selected, was launched
and soon boasted of more than a million lookers as buyers.
The old magazine Life was taken over by the owners of
Time, filled almost entirely with pictures, and floated to
success on a tide of prosperity. Competing with Look and
Life in profusion of pictures and yet slightly, not dangerously,
radical, another newcomer, Ken, set out to jostle minor
conventions and showed some skill in the undertaking. No
longer was it necessary for buyers of magazines to be wholly
literate. Painted tabloids reached parlor tables.

Meanwhile the vogue set by the dazzle of Time, founded
in the age of normalcy, affected nearly all weeklies of large
circulation. To be brisk, curt, concise, telegraphic, and
bright became the verbal mode of the hour. To print nothing that would take more than ten or fifteen minutes to read
became almost a ruling fashion. Even so complicated a
matter as the collapse of American railways could be summarized and disposed of presumably in a few "crystal-

clear" paragraphs for readers who had but ten minutes to spare from their looking.

Yet one event in the great magazine world, apart from the editorial achievements of the Yale Review, the Virginia Quarterly, and the Southern Review, ran clearly counter to the degradation of the democratic dogma. That was the establishment and success of Fortune under the auspices of the men who published Time and Life. Issued as a monthly, with an expensive format, to sell at ten dollars a year, Fortune was designed directly for the rich, and yet it printed solid and bold articles on highly controversial issues, such as housing, munitions profiteering, labor, and other aspects of capitalism. Its articles were packed with information, characterized on the whole by a rare degree of objectivity, and written in a vein of gravity and concern, notable instances being the discussions of housing and the munitions business. Its policy was penetrated by critical thought and marked by courage. Acutely conscious of the various schemes of reference under which selections of fact and types of interpretation could be made, the editors of Fortune sought to avoid the naïve and attain the comprehensive. Though their surveys were shorter and less heavily documented than those of the old North American Review or the British quarterlies, and therefore not so limited to select audiences, they displayed a freedom from neat formulas and a reach of thought that were unusual to the rich who cared to read the fact-burdened pages.

Popular magazines for women seemed to prefer the deadly dominance of the commonplace. Owned and managed almost exclusively by men, as commercial enterprises, the journals "for women" automatically registered men's ideas of the audience to which the appeal was directed, and their enormous circulations implied that the managers correctly gauged the women to whom they supplied month by month fashion plates, fashion articles, society gossip, tepid fiction, bloodless sentimentality, Cinderellas, Fairy Princes, directions for the use of cosmetics, advertisements of the "allure."

Just as Godey's Lady's Book, even while Sarah Hale was editing it, stuck tightly to domestic sweetness through the military struggles and calamities of a civil war, so the popular women's magazines of the great depression largely adhered to beauty hints and baby-tending during the course of economic and moral disintegration.

A survey of the five women's magazines with huge national circulations, made by Elizabeth Bancroft Schlesinger in 1933, inventoried the stock in trade. "During the six-month period, the five periodicals offered no major articles on power control, immigration, farm problems, economic planning, child welfare, education, the labor movement, taxation, or international affairs. Peace and governmental economy were honored with one article each." Of the thirty-two articles featured by The Ladies Home Journal, "four dealt with the political, economic, or international situation. . . . Among the remaining twenty-eight features, women were introduced to the engaging spectacle of Alice Roosevelt Longworth tripping lightly along the flowery path; in four articles Billy Sunday stormed his way along the Sawdust Trail." In view of the fact that these five journals could reasonably claim thirty-six million readers, the index to feminine taste was suggestive, to say the least. Were millions of women really that indifferent to the forces sapping away the sub-structure of their world? Or was journalism so conceived for women no more representative of women's minds than journalism in general was indicative of all minds?

In the winter of 1937–1938, when magazines were losing circulation and questing for security, The Ladies Home Journal, under the editorship of Bruce Gould and Beatrice Blackmer Gould, changed its tactics, on the assumption that women could be "aroused" to take an interest in public affairs if the Journal awakened among them a consciousness of great issues. Leaving out of account, for practical purposes, the customary interest of women in public affairs, like most of women's preceptors in colleges and universities, the Journal, as if about to inaugurate that relation, sought from women over the country replies to questionnaires respecting their opinions on such matters as marriage and divorce, birth control, the war on venereal diseases launched by the federal bureau of public health, and, more cautiously, on economic and political measures. Encouraged by the replies they received, the editors launched their series, but the titles and contexts of the articles under the new policy showed no radical departures from the earlier policies described by Elizabeth Schlesinger. Women had been and still were interested in public affairs and took part in public affairs, but evidently they had to look elsewhere for enlightenment concerning the major issues of State.

§

Surveys of newspapers and magazines engrossed in the current, the immediate, and hence the superficial, argued for the proposition that the country would have been intellectually impoverished and regimented had it not been for the searching inquisitiveness and daring individualism of workers in the field of imaginative letters. Newspapers played up the sensational and transitory for the delectation of the millions in the fashion set by motion pictures and radio broadcasting. With a few noteworthy exceptions, the magazines catered in a similar way to the same audience. On the other hand writers of imaginative literature, appealing to large yet selected groups capable of sustained intellectual effort for at least a few hours at a time, had more freedom in selection and emphasis than editors and publishers had. Perhaps in the long evolution of civilization what mattered was the thinking of those who did some thinking rather than the lucubrations of those who did no thinking at all.

At all events in the wider latitude granted to them, under the American system of liberty, the makers of letters, less controlled by the technique of medium, by mass production, by corporate interests, and by government intervention, explored and covered all phases of culture in the United

States and with an energy and verve of style that betokened, on the whole, a vigorous mental and literary power. Taken collectively, the letters of the period were marked by a penetration and a thrusting force that signified a growth rather than a diminution of insight and creative intelligence. Even the crudeness that characterized many works was the crudeness of a search for life rather than a sign of decaying talents.

The condition of American letters was thus in brilliant contrast with the degeneration which characterized Roman letters, for instance, in the fourth and fifth centuries of the Christian era, after the passage of Augustan grandeur, as traced by Samuel Dill with broad knowledge in his Roman Society in the Last Century of the Western Empire. In the letters of that period betraying the declining culture, Dill found "conventionality and tradition, slowly but surely fading from lack of fresh impulse and inspiration . . . bald and scrappy gossip. . . . The idolatry of mere literary form combined with poverty of ideas, the enthusiastic worship of great models without a breath of the spirit that gave them enduring charm. . . . Vanity and literary affectation. . . . [Incapacity to speak] in a simple, straightforward style. . . . Sterility and failure of original power. . . . The higher intellect of Rome seems to have been overtaken by a paralysis, and incapable of making any further advance. . . . Erudition without critical judgment, finesse of style, without purity of taste, took the place of originality and enthusiasm for ideas. . . . Civilization became everyday more stereotyped and materialized."

No such pallor of death spread over American letters in the days of the midpassage.

CHAPTER XIV

Esthetic Affirmations

WORDS alone did not, could not, suffice for the assertion of values and ideas; in objects of art and in human gestures, the spirit of men and women also proclaimed experiences and judgments on striving and practice. Discussing the difference between the media of words and paint, Thomas Benton, outstanding American painter, laid down this principle in the magazine, Common Sense: "To begin with, I am puzzled about the instruments and materials used in thinking. What bothers me most about thinking is that it has to be done with words. . . . You get to dealing with relations — and not with relations between what is apprehensible to your senses, like a painter with his colors and his shapes, or a chemist with the matter performing in his test tubes, but with linguistic descriptions of things. A thought takes form in a word pattern — another thought in another pattern. They meet. Out of their conjunction can come the most unexpected progeny imaginable, which, if your mind is active, mature like lightning and run all over the place. To keep from going crazy you have the job of gather-

745

ing in all these verbal brats and putting some order in the confusion of their conflicting pretenses to meaning. You have, generally, to kill a lot which are unmanageable. For killing off your hopeless brats and getting the rest of them lined up, you have that tricky instrument, *logic*. . . .

"I am deeply suspicious about this business of logic. I know that in the art of painting what makes an assemblage of represented things coherent, what sets up sequential relations between them, also distorts them. I know that representations of things of the real world cannot be put into any kind of logical design, in which one part follows from and is linked with another, without being modified, without having some of their aspects subordinated to others, without stressing or squelching parts, without finally losing exactitude of representation. This does not bother me with painting, for painting does not aim primarily at accuracy of statement, as Truth, but aims — if I may risk it — at a value called *Beauty*, at an organization of materials and symbols which by their nature and through their associations produce sensuous and emotional satisfactions."

In this "illogical" medium, esthetic affirmations were made which contained their own judgments. If illogical in the verbal sense, they too expressed values and ideas. Indeed the very cult of non-objectivity, pursuing its quest for the formless, for an "irreducible and sometimes inscrutable Absolute" was itself an evaluation — a rejection of "reality" on some basis of values. At the institution in Chicago, for the promotion of abstract and non-objective art, supported by the Solomon R. Guggenheim Foundation, attempts were made to approach the "Upper Reaches to which the Soul aspires" — The Nirvana, the No Thing perhaps of the ancient East — and examples of this retreat from the known and the flight to the unknown were assembled for the inspiration of students. The body of this collection was the work of a Russian, Vassily Kandinsky, and of a German, Rudolph Bauer, both of whom had experienced the collapse of monarchical realities but adhered to absolutism in the form of esthetic affirmation with "playful imaginations."

For non-objectivity as pursued by the cult, the Baroness Hilla Rebay von Ehrenweisen, long an adviser in art for Mr. Guggenheim, was curator and chief spokesman, and the latest Know Nothing movement in America lighted fires from her flambeau. This is not to say that "purely abstract" art had not already been produced in America. In fact by 1937 when this gallery and school were opened in Chicago, there was a considerable amount of non-objective art in important places in America. Augustus Vincent Tack in 1930 had painted a series of panels in this mood for the library of the Phillips Memorial Gallery in Washington, D. C., and his work had been called by an enthusiastic critic one of "the most notable artistic achievements of the present day." It was an expression of emotions, it seemed, "which each individual must interpret according to his own spiritual understanding."

But all the abstractionists, native and foreign, did not go so far toward aloofness from the known and the visible. Some of them maintained that their products did not represent a flight from life but, on the contrary, the great reality itself. These heretical exponents admitted that their art was abstract but they declared that it suggested "joy and esthetic motion" amid the gloom of tragedy and frustration. Their forms, they said, "were not ghostly-pure-spirit-suspended" nor designed to "freeze a sublime non-intellectuality." They recognized that "after all an artist must live some super-worldly existence to create super-worldly art and few did." Explaining their divergence from the pure superworldly view and insisting upon their memory of life, they argued that their output resembled rather the "semi-abstraction of an Einstein and carried generative force."

For its mystical imputations, Sheldon Cheney gave the palm to Oriental art "above that of any other continent," in his review of A World History of Art published in 1938, praising the Far Eastern testimonial to experiences beyond rational analysis and disapproving the humanistic, intellectualized western art of modern times. But however intellectualized the modern western art might be, it had to deal with abstraction as idea if it had the vigor of beauty and meaning. For instance, the most chaotic surrealist picture was built on the abstract idea of chaos in contradistinction to the idea of dynamic symmetry governing the precisely ordered flower arrangement in an Oriental art form. Life as confusion. Life as a divine system. Both abstractions. In non-objective lines, rhythm could be conveyed no less than with the movement of figures. Sculptured human beings with abstract heads, with no faces, were fully capable of expressing personality — the personality of posture and gesture, for the face is not always the measure of distinction in the case of man, woman, or child. Sargent was able to convey it in a hand or an arm.

Enveloped in the controversy over meaning and beauty, the impulse to paint, draw, and carve worked its will in America during these latest years in the time of man. To combat madness in art, as she called it, Mrs. Frank Granger Logan, Chicago art patron, rallied around her a corps of other art patrons and devotees at the shrine of the conventional and agitated for "sanity in art." Censoriousness was thus not confined to the nations ruled by dictators. "The academic painter, even the least inspired," she maintained, "will be found to have constructed his picture on a better pattern than the most exalted modern."

Near to the earth and often of the earth earthy the main body of artists worked to interpret what they felt and saw as life, experience, struggle, and ideal. In their media, in oils and water colors, in bronze, wood, stone, marble, and alabaster, in song, in compositions for musical instruments, with dancing feet and arm gesturing, in steel, glass, and prefabricated materials, they spoke their minds about human nature, human behavior, and human purposes in society. When they had commissions to fill, they often filled them according to specifications deemed desirable by their patrons.

But sometimes they took the matter into their own keeping or deviated from the sketches submitted. Now and then the public grumbled and riots even occurred on occasion, attended at one such an affair by the slashing of a portrait. Often the public knew nothing about the origin of a mural's composition and emphasis, but it learned about one artist's willfulness when his work was ordered removed by his patron, after it had gone upon the wall.

§

In the golden glow and on through its lingering memory as hope of recovery, painters decorated the walls of public and private buildings — of city and state edifices, of banks and private clubs, of railway stations and department stores, of dwellings and colleges — with compositions glorifying commerce and industry or the pleasures they brought in their train. Smooth portraits were painted for the well-to-do who, of course, wanted to look handsome in their pictures. Busts of public officials and leading politicians multiplied at the hands of sculptors and were placed in imposing positions; in the halls of fame effigies of the famous multiplied. Congress appropriated large sums of money to Gutzon Borglum for carving the faces of four Presidents on a mountain cliff.

"The sword on the event" remained a favorite theme in war memorials and equestrian statues, but Harvard University ventured a trifle beyond it by commissioning the American Old Master, John Singer Sargent, to place on the wall of its Widener Library, after the world war and shortly before his death, a mural depicting peace springing from the body of the soldier dead. For the Elks' Memorial in Chicago Eugene Savage in 1930 painted two enormous murals on the same theme: The Armistice and Paths of Peace. With notable fidelity, however, to local military history and heroes, state capitols clung to battle scenes.

Economic institutions entered the stream of mural consciousness with commissions for works of art commemorating commerce and industry. The Merchandise Market of Chicago invited Jules Guerin to produce for it a gleaming portrayal of The Markets of the World; for the Kaufman store in Pittsburgh, Boardman Robinson was invited to paint the movement of commerce from the days of the Persians and Arabs and his product received a gold medal from the Architectural League of New York. The Groos Bank in San Antonio was adorned by Paul R. Cook with events in banking. A new Edison structure in Los Angeles glorified power with the esthetic aid of Hugo Ballin. To lighten the severity of its plant which made grinding wheels and machines, the Norton Manufacturing Company of Worcester, Massachusetts, in 1929, when Tyrian rays were purpling the business heaven, ordered for its administration building a series of murals by Arthur Covey "to bring to the senses of the workman the nobility of his task, and to express, through the high appeal of art, the spirit of the organization which recognizes primarily the human element." That glowing year when news was attractive, John W. Norton was commissioned to depict its dissemination for the building occupied by the Chicago Daily News. That year also the new building in New York acquired by the brokerage firm of Lee, Higginson, and Company, promoters of Krueger's financial adventures, was dressed up in a series of murals by Griffith Bailey Coale, who utilized a "novel and interesting painting process" to represent a Pageantry of the History of Commerce by Sea.

Devotion to habitat governed innumerable selections of artists and themes. In this connection California's self-esteem exceeded any flight of fancy in which her real estate offices could indulge. What was said to be "the largest set of murals ever put on canvas" became the proud possession of the Los Angeles Public Library; for their completion in 1933 the artist, Dean Cornwall, had worked five years recounting the history of the city and the state. Throughout the nation it was generally assumed that history was identical with "Progress of Man" and art affirmations were made in that spirit far and wide, with captions reciting the epic quality of man's struggle through the ages always upward and onward.

While pride in national progress was exultant in painting, rapture soared to the empyrean at the touch of an "inspired" composer of music. In 1928 the Musical America prize was awarded to Ernest Bloch's "America" played simultaneously by the five leading symphony orchestras of the United States, the conductors of which had served as the judges in the contest made up of ninety-two competitors. Six movements formed the elements of this composition, built on a historical conception, the first movement bringing America to the year 1620, the last hymning the future. In the interval the melodies of the civil war were introduced. The conclusion was a swelling anthem to America — the Epic Rhapsody. In this period also, women of the clubs opened their programs for great occasions with a hymn entitled "America the Beautiful."

Strong as was the motif of progress in painting and music, it did not monopolize esthetic interests any more than big business embraced all economic activities. In the midst of what seemed to be firm unity, esthetic affirmations were made in diversities almost as numerous as the kinds of commodities turned out by machine industries. Among the diversities were included thrusts at the confidence of optimism, paralleling the rejections palpable in letters and the fact-finding energies of researchers and investigators.

On the subject and emotion of religion, esthetic affirmation ran the gamut from the most rigid fundamentalism to free questing for the spiritual essence. No writer comprehensively described this artistic movement, but its vitality was displayed throughout the nation. In 1928 Sister Mary Stanisia of Chicago painted Christ among the Doctors for St. Luke's Cathedral in St. Paul. He Hath Sent Me to Heal was the message inscribed in a mural by William De Leftwich Dodge for the Virginia Baptist Hospital at Lynchburg. For a Negro congregation not far from New York City aspiring to the ownership of a mural, Ruth Krylenko, a Russian-American, painted Christ as the workingman and advocate of brotherhood. As for religious music, Ernest Bloch, a loyal Zionist, composed a new musical service for the Reformed Synagogue in New York City, grounded on a laborious study of Jewish history. Under the patronage of the Warner Brothers, Hugo Ballin, in 1929, painted episodes in Jewish history for Temple B'nai B'rith in Los Angeles.

And as the zest for murals spread over the nation, paganism as well as religious conformity was unrolled in classical allegories; for instance, in Arizona, where land and sky are so little broken in their intimacy by intervening forests, the Legend of the Earth and Sun was revived for the Arizona Biltmore Hotel at Phoenix. The vogue for pagan themes was intensified by the popularity of archaeological and geological excavations, and to this stream of influence anthropology and the theory of evolution contributed their incitements. In the Field Museum at Chicago, as an illustration, Charles R. Knight placed in 1928 seven murals dealing with prehistoric life as unfolded by the studies of scientists — the first of a projected series of twenty-eight pictures. At Pomona College in California, according to José Clemente Orozco's own explanation of what he had done, Prometheus was given high place upon a conspicuous wall as the bearer of fire to humanity. Less ambitious, the Country Club at Detroit accepted a Zodiac of Sports by a more conventional painter as a ceiling adornment.

Geared to the idea that opportunity was waiting for artists without number to demonstrate their talents, art schools enlarged in size and expanded their instruction. That faith seemed not to weaken even when Wall Street was dolorous, for 1933 events in the art world included the initiation of mural instruction at the School of the Boston Museum of Fine Arts and the organization of a Guild of Fresco Painters in New York. While the season of expansive luxury was still open, discussion of the possibilities for "a great American art" resounded over tea cups and in academies. Art "activity" flourished, its energies illustrated in countless exhibits of painting and sculpture, in the launching of new magazines devoted to art, in the quantity and character of the books on art which moved in a steady procession to the marketplace, and in huge sections of newspapers assigned to the news and criticism of art events. Certainly there was an art movement in America during the golden glow, and its dominant characteristic was the serenity of assurance rather than the dynamism of a tumultuous creative urge. The nerves of artists, patrons, and critics were not seriously ruffled by any grave presentiment of things to come.

A clue to the nature of this art movement was given by Henry Ladd of Columbia University in his concise volume entitled With Eyes of the Past. Deeply troubled as far back as 1928 by the common habit of forgetting that great art is something perennially fresh and alive, the author discussed the art movement of the hour as a phase of the general spirit of the times. "Appreciation of art today is believed to be a necessary part of culture," he said. "The conviction is so universally held that a large part of our educative machinery has been turned to the production of artistic capacity. Periodicals devoted to art have increased their circulation; museums throughout the country have enlarged their endowments and suffered the indignities of publicity for the glory of the cause. Even department stores have exploited the glamour in modern art or the precarious splendor of the antique with, one sees, tangible profit. There has come upon society an enormous will to believe in art which has encouraged a maximum attitude with a minimum learning to evoke enthusiasm and confound taste.

"The awe which has thus been generated has reached immeasurable proportions; it has thrown about the fine arts a cloud of mystification, a sentimental and false reverence, which tends to isolate them from their normal province of enjoyment. Even our conscienceless and incomprehensible youth have become seduced into a low seriousness about higher things which enjoys none of the sharp observation, the humor, the liberty that characterize the more real aspects of their shocking young lives. The general disintegration of inherited illusions about life has not cracked the shining faith in art. This faith, indeed, has for a good many individuals so confused the direction of their natural inclinations as to have very nearly inhibited the possibility of esthetic pleasure."

That was one kind of faith, though not the only one, however dominant. Another sprang from an intuitive feeling that a material civilization was not in itself sufficient for the human spirit; and thus a quest for more satisfaction continued — a quest, in fact, as old as history. In a civilization filled with machines, smoky with fumes from factory chimneys, so motor with activity that it seemed to be always running away from itself, and yet having a rich cultural heritage, complete peace of spirit was impossible; and discontent with the hard features of this civilization turned increasingly to the thought of tapping esthetic sources. For many years Lewis Mumford had been sounding alarms, expressing objections to mechanization as an end rather than a means of life. Yet annoyed as he was by popular complacency with mechanical activities and products as such, Mumford was himself torn by contradictions in the course of his development; he had a deep appreciation of the handicraft arts while arguing that art must reflect contemporaneity, and he encountered perplexities in his search for a way of combining the art of living with the exigencies of machine production.

§

In truth, American artists had never accepted universally the mechanics and democracy of American life. Many workers in the plastic arts, like workers in imaginative literature, had fled from the worship of the dynamo, declaring that the economy of American life was incompatible with creative art. Shaking the dust of the "plutocratic democracy," as they called it, off their feet, they had pursued and continued to pursue the beautiful in distant lands where, in "seasoned cultures," they assumed, adjustments to the commonplace could be avoided and untrammeled sensitivity could be their happy lot. Near the middle of the nineteenth century the sculptor-poet, W. W. Story — after a trip abroad from the land which his distinguished father, as lawyer and a justice of the United States Supreme Court, had found ample for his great talents in law and government — settled in the Anglo-American colony in Rome, there to be enveloped in the classical tradition and become so saturated with it that he could dedicate his arid ecstasy to immortalizing Cleopatra in marble and verse.

Struck by the flight of young Americans from their own scene and its interpretation in the mid-nineteenth century, an Englishman ejaculated: "Whatever the American men of genius are, they are not young gods making a new world!" Certainly not. With few exceptions they were hovering, like "moon calves" chewing their cuds, around ruins of a time long passed and losing themselves in its legends. They were imitative, not creative. And as late as 1929 the "passionate pilgrims" were still imbued with the idea that older civilizations had the shrines at whose altars the neophyte could find lasting peace. Meeting in Europe an exotic and enchanting variety of customs, sights, and values, they assumed that foreign societies were stable and that as long as they remained expatriates they would not have to endure the changeful progress of American life, the boastful self-assertions of American industrialists, the "vulgarity" of American masses, the noisy machines of a nation dedicated to business, and the general mediocrity of a "frontier folk."

In his Portrait of the Artist as American, written during the reign of Babbittry, if published in 1930, Matthew Josephson, loyal disciple of Jean Jacques Rousseau, defended the retreat of Henry James and other dissident geniuses to an older civilization "where some quantum of individual liberty is still to be enjoyed — or even to regions of a primitive culture where liberty is embraced to the exclusion of all other advantages." In fact, several American artists, including literary artists, so revered the distant past that they could

even "go primitive." "We're the *disinherited* of art!"
Josephson made the "wrecked painter" exclaim like a Henry
James. "We're condemned to be superficial! We're excluded
from the magic circle! The soil of American perception is a
poor little barren artificial deposit. Yes! We're wedded to
imperfection! An American to excel has just ten times as
much to learn as a European! We lack the deeper sense.
We have neither taste nor force. How should we have them?
Our crude and garish climate, our silent past, our deafening
present, the constant pressure about us of unlovely conditions, are as void of all that nourishes and prompts and
inspires the artist as my sad heart is in saying so! We poor
aspirants must live in perpetual exile!"

Democratically inclined American tourists who encountered the émigrés in their dear little dark little corner of Paris
or in the "smart sets" of Rome were astonished at the
degree of hostility the fugitives entertained for everything
American, almost to the point of being dehumanized. Few
expatriates could express good words for democracy in the
United States and with such democracy as existed in Europe
they were little concerned, if at all. On the contrary with
assured complacency they harked back in their minds to "the
finished ages" or eventually joined the deriders of democracy
in the style made so vocal and final in Moscow. If non-
political in mentality, they could easily slip into the habit of
disapproving "everything distasteful to their souls" which
so characterized the post-war years.

This long indulgence in exoticism was made possible for
the expatriates, as it had once been for many of their European masters, by the prosperity of business enterprise, while
it lasted. In the wake of merchants, traders, and concession-
seekers, the artists of Europe had been going to the four
corners of the earth to feast their eyes and gratify their
feelings in experiences with the unknown. Gauguin had
escaped from France to pleasure in the South Seas. "The
little customs officer, Henri Rousseau, spent his life recaptur-
ing in fantasy the memories of his one Mexican trip. Matisse

added the Near East to his domain, and a Persian or an Arab would understand his art and its relation to their culture. But the flight into exoticism met with success only as long as there were new cultures and countries to provide new material. The Futurists of Italy under Marinetti decided to face instead of flee from the machine. They deified it and made it part of their programme. The Cubists had moved in the same direction, deliberately choosing geometric patterns and reducing even the human form to the essential forms of machine parts."

After the upsurge and decline of the Cubists, a younger generation, victims of the war, disillusioned, frightened, confused, rebellious, sometimes brutal, displayed the chaos of their minds and the agony of their nerves in the canvases they painted and in the objects which they carved. For a time young American émigrés basked in that atmosphere. But a day arrived when they had to scurry home for two reasons: the reduction in that "quantum of liberty" which had been attracting non-conformists from the art circles of America and the devaluation of the American dollar or its total disappearance from their pockets.

"Dear old Europe" was ceasing to be a haven for malcontents. After the Russian, Italian, and German dictators achieved totalitarianism in economic and political supremacy, they glorified their power by commanding artists to serve the dictatorships. Writers as well as painters, sculptors, designers, and even craftsmen were compelled to conform beyond any compulsion which their kind had ever experienced in America, from its yeomen and patrician to its industrial years. Elasticity in esthetic pleasure was coming to an end in Europe. If the revolution was possible of acceptance by native artists it was scarcely to be borne by many outlanders.

Up to this revolution European artists in misfortune, economic or spiritual, like the Americans, had been able to wander freely to distant places of patronage. Far back in history, Greeks had followed in the wake of the city-building and city-decorating Alexander the Great; afterwards they had gone to Rome, their next conqueror, if sometimes as slaves bought to celebrate power by their skills. From Italy, artists had gone to Spain, and from Central Europe to France and England, seeking adventure, work, and appreciation. And since the eighteenth century when Benjamin West, the American colonial, reached the proud position of a court painter under George III, wandering artists from America had been entrusted with the portraiture of monarchs, members of the nobility or business magnates, and the very pope himself.

Now, however, most monarchs were tumbled from their thrones and that patronage had almost disappeared. Lords and ladies, instead of seeking the publicity of portraiture, were more inclined to withdraw from the public gaze in a desire for safety first. In Russia even the bourgeois were ruled out as subjects of art unless for purposes of derision. Finally Hitler and his advisers fiercely censored artistic expression, removed at will finished canvases and statues from German galleries, began to demolish synagogues, and set up canons of taste they deemed strictly fitting for the insurgency of brawny men under arms. Even the Orient was, for practical purposes, closed to foreign artists after the outbreak of Japanese fascism in the course of aggression in China. Wandering might be directed to the South Seas still, but not to all of them. The quest for excitement, work, appreciation, and pleasure in distant places seemed to be as a tale which was told. In this situation returning Americans substituted apologies for their former condemnation of the American culture. That prized "quantum of liberty" was mainly in their homeland, they discovered to their great surprise. Moreover, to the newest civilization, from the "seasoned cultures," exiles, voluntary and involuntary, turned for an asylum.

§

Partly through support given by the returned natives and by exiles coming in a new wave from Europe, but more especially through enthusiasms at home, a different art atmosphere was created in America and an approach was made to the making of a finer civilization in the United States. Over the outcome of this quest, pessimists were dubious as ever and optimists hopeful as ever. The music critic, W. J. Henderson, refused to see signs and symbols of genuine esthetic feeling in America upon which to build great art. Music, he said, had its roots in national lyricism, rhythm, martial zest, religious majesty, and a patrician economy — all lacking in the new world and incapable of transplantation. "It is one of the auspicious signs of the times," he admitted, "that efforts in the direction of improvements are numerous. Some are assuredly good; some are at least questionable. Radio broadcasts of artistic music in schools should produce results. The organization of thousands of high school bands may or may not be laudable. Tell me what those high school bands are playing and I can tell you whether they are raising or lowering the standard of taste among the young. Tell me what your children are singing and I can determine even more. If they are discovering their sense of beauty through the daily practice of 'Smoke in Your Eyes,' I do not believe they are journeying toward the stars."

To such doubts, Roy Harris, among others, replied: "Why limit our expectations to the mighty Beethoven?" And in view of the conditions on the trans-Atlantic continent in 1937, he added: "I imagine all the great masters would welcome a vacation from Europe these days." Anyway, he said, "music reflects the spirit of the social environment from which it arises. It passes from one generation, one nation, one century to another, always seeking the social fermentation in which it thrives. . . . Music is no more a dead art today than we ourselves are dead people. And American music is in a particularly provident spot. We have been growing up in just the same cycle of development in which Germany and Russia matured. We have gone through the first period of musical culture: that of importing our musicians and our music. We have gone through the second period: that of developing our own musicians, who are supreme in interpreting the music of other nations (with the possible exception of conductors). We are entering the third period, wherein the quantity and quality of our musicians and our audiences demand a new native music, conceived in the mood and tempo of our time." Coming back to America from a European sojourn in the summer of 1937, Serge Koussevitsky, conductor of the Boston Symphony, announced that "European composers simply have nothing to say. Our American composers are consistently better artists." Presumably this was a contention that art was no longer a monopoly of older civilizations, that new energies were astir on this side of the Atlantic.

In fact they were, and around all the arts now swirled critical inquiries and affirmations respecting their nature and their relation to the society in which they had their being and flourished. As Ruskin had hammered into the heads of the English, art was closely connected with the crafts, with the whole state of society, and the great art of sincerity and genius had sprung from this relationship. Re-emphasized in America by the debate over the arts, Ruskin's axiom was applied in making discoveries in the New World, and "America the beautiful" was given a thorough investigation. Very soon the inquiry got as near to the bottom as Erskine Caldwell's Tobacco Road. The long popularity of this drama in the art center of the country — a drama enacted in sheer dust, without so much as a blade of grass visible in the background of human life — gave notice that emotions were stirred by revelations of degradation in "the land of plenty — by abstractions in the concrete." Against these emotions all artists could not be entirely insulated. Nor could they be kept "pure"; that is, entirely shut off from the other categorical declarations made by artists in imaginative letters and by thinkers and practitioners in economics, politics, and social reconstruction.

As the debate over the arts expanded, penetrating deeper and deeper into the social milieu, objective and subjective, upsurges of esthetic feeling from below enriched the discussion. Though Hull House and Greenwich House, like other social settlements in the major cities, had early explored sources of artistic expression among the industrial workers and given opportunities for explicit demonstrations in settlement studios, men and women who had climbed to the top of the business or artistic ladder had generally supposed that men and women at the bottom were devoid of sensitivity to "the finer things" reserved for the elect. But times were changing, and all over the United States, especially after the coming of the federal art projects, artists from urban quarters and from rural regions helped to correct this point of view.

Another factor contributing to the extension of the debate on esthetics was the wider social use of the camera, which had been steadily improved in the matter of mechanics, especially light controls. Through the skilled manipulation of the camera by Margaret Bourke-White, Russell Lee, and other experts, following the path blazed by Stieglitz and his disciples, photography was turned from depicting unwrinkled faces and the machine to examining life and work among all sorts and conditions of people. Thus the imaginations of the artistically inclined were enlivened by photographic vistas of the polyglot population and the democratic task. To countless Americans who had now "Seen Their Faces," the desire for more beauty in American life became mingled with the desire for a better organization of labor and a wider distribution of its fruits.

The esthetic quest was merging with the social quest. "Aesthetic enjoyment and artistic creation are anticipations in our civilization of what the Good Life would really be," declared Irwin Edman, writing on The World, the Arts and the Artist in 1928, from his chair in Columbia University. "Such happiness as is present among our contemporaries is the happiness of those who are doing work that is itself delightful to them and enjoying things that are themselves a delight. . . . The image of a perfect society is not that of aesthetes in a museum but of artists at their work. The function of the arts in civilization at present is largely that of a dilettante escape for the observer, a truant absorption for the artist. In a rationally ordered society all work would have the quality of art, all enjoyment would have the immediate and glamourous character of aesthetic appreciation." That was not to disown the dynamo and revert to handicrafts. It was to say that democrats, even in the age of machine industry, must enjoy esthetic experiences if their labor and living were to be satisfying. The words "art," "democracy," and "culture" became more commonly associated.

To the members of the American Association of University Women, Lura Beam, director of their newly-planned art education, explained in 1936 the significance of the program in terms of this tendency. "Art is a statement of the interaction of the individual and society," she said in introducing the subject, at the annual convention. Then she proceeded to show that "in seven years the old channels of introspection have opened again in painting and new directions and content appear. The Chinese influences come via painters of the Pacific Northwest and the exposition of the European situation by Russian, German, and Austrian émigrés. Around Fourteenth Street (New York) and partly by way of Mexico an assertive minority paints only three panels — the bankers, the strike, and the breadline. These brushes paint mines, machinery, railroads, science, oppression, propaganda; no madonna unless she upholds a malnourished child, no cross unless it is marked 'opium of the people.' For art is the synthesis of a time. . . . The artist is thus the pioneer in the interpretation of the individual and society. . . . He resists the mold, the mold presses on him, the mold is stronger. Man resists, absorbs, adapts, becomes average. Or, at the two extremes, he wrecks himself in refusal, or he pioneers against environment and makes new patterns. This residue of the struggle between the natural man and the inevitable environment is personality." Logically of course a democratic society should give the freest play to personality.

A similar point of view was elaborated by Philip N. Yountz associated with the popular art movement at The People's Institute and at this moment with the federal art project, in his foreword to the book on art by Ladd. "Books about art," he brusquely asserted, "are a dangerous form of literature because they are apt to be misused by educated but unintelligent Philistines as a substitute for art itself. Just as the pedant comes to look on book knowledge instead of venturing to have thoughts of his own, so many readers fancy they are studying art when they are actually studying about art. . . . The path to independent judgment in the appreciation of painting begins with a knowledge of the best critical thinking of the past, though it does not by any means stop there. With this background and much study of pictures themselves, one may soon begin to hold his head erect, daring to praise what is meritorious though perhaps unpopular and to scorn what is cheap and imitative. Such independents are the real allies of the artist. It is their discrimination and intelligence that inspire him to exert his best efforts and it is from them that he receives his most valued approval."

The doctrine that art must free itself from the dogmas of the schools and refresh itself by contact with life at work was supported by Thomas Craven in his treatise on Modern Art. Though some of the modernists felt that Craven was a renegade, a commentator in The Nation rejoiced: "Craven has anatomized the new man and the new movements with a penetration hitherto unmatched by any historian or critic of our time. He strips their solemn pretentiousness from the abstractionists, the surrealists, the snob artists, the Bohemian cults which make art out of other art in a world where the fresh impulses of life never penetrate. If his ultimate appraisal of the achievements of modernism gives small comfort to the radicals, it gives even less to the traditionalists, whose painting 'has ceased to become work and has become genteel behavior.' . . . One feels that the author has gazed with profound dismay upon the Gallic aping and posturing of American painters these many years. The situation has

called for strong language, and he has mastered all his resources of invective, sarcasm, and contempt in order to sting
his readers into a sharp awareness of a sad, sad spectacle."
In short, an American art form, if it arrived, would come as a
result of absorbing old art forms and transfusing them with
the spirit of indigenous experiences, as great Italian art had
come.

In the gilded age, the public at large had not entered
extensively into the dispute over art values, but now even
the making of everyday commodities for the market involved
heated arguments. As long as prosperity flamed and flared
in industrial economy, designers by the thousands were
employed to render articles of use more attractive, articles ranging from kitchen utensils, tableware and bathtubs
through fabrics to automobiles and trains. From the distant
day when primitive woman had given form to the pots in use
at the hearth to the latest hour, objects of utility had both
expressed and invoked esthetic pleasure. But they had not
done so uniformly. Commercial demands, induced by hectic
hunts for markets, had interrupted theory and practice in
their unified course and relegated designers to the task of promoting the sales of gadgets which constituted larger and
larger areas of industrial output; that is, designers were
required to stylize products in terms of the competitive
market and a quick turn-over of commodities. Necessarily
this practice often ran contrary to the rule — a law of beauty
— that the best of design is that which attains the highest
functional perfection. Since the new mass production was
more closely related to purses than to art, to salesmanship
than to utility, protests arose against the ready acceptance
of the mere glitter and glamour expressed in stream-lined and
polished objects and that form of commercial art was subjected to criticism from various angles.

Facing more responsibility, a great engineering school, the
Massachusetts Institute of Technology, began to fall into
line with the critical trend. In advance of its 1938 Alumni
Day, the chairman of the committee, John E. Burchard,

announced in the press that a leading feature would be a symposium on the "influence of science and engineering on modern art." Two schools of thought, he said, would be considered: "The first and more conventional point of view of the older group of artists is that which holds that science, engineering, and the machine are tools of art, and, so far as esthetics is concerned, exist only to provide new facilities for the arts. The second point of view, the philosophy of the younger school of industrial designers, is that the artist is the prism through which the rays of esthetic potentiality engendered by the machine are focused. Under this conception the artist seeks to use the machine and its products in undistorted form merely to direct the natural workings of the machine into the logical forms which mean beauty." In connection with the symposium, an exhibit of modern industrial arts was projected to "include only those products of science and engineering which, either because of the influence of the industrial designer or as a natural result of thorough-going and sincere application of science and engineering, are in themselves beautiful."

The discussion of beauty and art widened out to the schools of philosophy which now contributed thought about the very nature of the esthetic sense, its sources, and manifestations. Works on esthetic theory, as distinguished from treatises on artistic practice, began to be prominent in publishers' lists, and arguments were heard from all the schools of speculation: the absolutists, the formalists, the empiricists, the universalists, the institutionalists, the pragmatists, and the geneticists, to vary somewhat the broad distinctions sketched by Katherine Gilbert in her Studies of Recent Aesthetics. On behalf of the absolutists, art was defined as a concern with the One Big Reality — a spiritual world, beyond appearances, eternally true and good; and criteria of esthetic judgments as imperative as the ex cathedra pronouncements of the pope were provided for orthodox believers. The phrases of the old and endless debate on art for art's sake were rolled over again, with variations and minor additions.

Voices were also heard, speaking "an American language." It was a characteristic sign of the times that John Dewey, dean of American philosophers, came to regard the issue of art as so important that he brought his profound learning and his sensitive humanism to bear upon it in a volume on Art as Experience. Rejecting absolutism in esthetics as in philosophy, refuting the isolation of the formalists and specialists, Dewey related art to ways of social life, to forms of government and economy, to democracy, thus revitalizing a tradition to which Tolstoi, Ruskin, and William Morris had given force. Art and the artist Dewey placed in their political and social context. That was to say : The artist is a person, with a mind influenced by values and interests arising out of society ; art is a language or form of communication ; it is an endlessly creative function ; it expresses conceptions of life, such as freedom, equality, tyranny, servitude, war, or power. Having a social setting and rooted in universal human values, art finds in the freedom, tolerance, mobility, and respect for labor, which characterize a democratic society, conditions favorable to inspiration and expression. In an argument for years overdue, Dewey contended that great art cannot be brought into being merely by having museums filled with loot gathered by war or money or simply by meticulous study of forms peculiar to old societies ; it must be indigenous, expressing phases of humanity in the strivings of the place and the time. Thus Dewey drew art into the main stream of American history and philosophy, broke through the restraints of class, and gave esthetics an organic connection with the humanistic aspiration of society.

America was sufficiently sophisticated now for important and impressive symposia, one of which was arranged by the Baltimore Museum of Art in the spring of 1938 to discuss the naturalistic movement in art led by Courbet. The participants traced out the ramifications of the naturalistic movement in science, literature, music, and the graphic arts of today. The Johns Hopkins Press published the whole debate.

§

It was during this ferment of taste, experience, and opinion, this contest of emotions, ideas, and interests, that the Federal Government, in common with state and municipal governments, undertook the deliberate and conscious patronage of the arts and in the process encouraged a popular art movement of extraordinary proportions. Artists and the wide public were now united as they had never been before in America. Art was becoming public art in a new sense. In the long history of mankind, art had presented many aspects. Primitive art had expressed communal organization and purpose; for brief periods and in given places the individualism of the bourgeois, with their hostility for State and Church, had expressed itself in art; monumental art had generally been an affair of State or Church, or both, of aristocratic institutions hierarchal in form, evoking passionate loyalties and lifting their devotees in their noblest moments to causes and dreams larger and more enduring than themselves. Now, through the patronage of the arts by the government of the United States, art was again to be a public affair, but emphasizing in form, color, and line the esthetic affirmations of a democratic society wrestling with profound social disturbances, yet dreaming dreams of a greater dignity for man.

By the subject set for treatment and by the master-apprentice relationship which the undertaking required, American democracy was now directed to the production of social art. The subject was the American Scene in all its aspects and this gave free rein to popular experiences as sources and attitudes for art. In employing professional artists who no longer had other patrons, the Federal Government instructed them to commune with the people at large — the fountain-head of democratic government. Literally millions of people were thus invited to see beautiful things for the first time, and what is more, to try their skill at drawing, painting, modelling, and the other forms of artistic expression with no other object in view than expressing themselves

with relation to the American scene. Through such a contact
with popular art, even academic art was energized. Moreover what had hitherto been only a revolt against philistinism and preciosity deepened in the understanding of art as
social meaning.

But this development, in truth, represented continuity
rather than sudden innovation. A long line of precedents lay
behind it in the erection of public buildings, public memorials, and government commissions to sculptors and muralists. An elaborate program of federal construction had in
fact already been started in the national capital in the age
of normalcy. Chief Justice Taft had set his heart upon and
helped to plan a gigantic temple for the Supreme Court.
Herbert Hoover, while Secretary of Commerce, had started
a monument to business enterprise, — an enormous palace
to house the expanding activities of his Department. Authorizations or projects also covered separate buildings for
the Departments of Labor, Justice, Agriculture, Interior, the
Post Office, and the National Archives. And as unemployment rose to the point of national frightfulness, the execution
of these designs was pushed forward to provide work for the
idle. Excitement was added to excavating and erecting by
decisions respecting the location of these buildings, as L'Enfant's grand plan of the nation's capital was now being given
a wider fulfillment. For the architecture of the structures,
as well as their location, congressional approval had to be
secured; and politics, as in all things congressional, played
its part in determining appearances.

The result was far from pleasurable to all the people. The
miles and miles of columns supporting nothing and the tiers
upon tiers of steps leading up to Greek or Egyptian portals
in the age of elevators were condemned as mere "archaeological architecture" by critics who preferred the symbols of
contemporaneity and the conveniences of function. Hostility
was not only vocal but well organized by 1936 when John
Russell Pope, who had designed the shelter for the National
Archives and other Washington buildings, proposed to honor

Thomas Jefferson with a Pantheon. Many citizens had experienced no enchantment as they stood before the pseudo-Greek temple in the dim recesses of which "Honest Abe," the rail-splitter born in a log cabin, had been made to pose in a manner suggesting a Zeus or an Apollo, instead of a man of the people as he truly was. It was more appropriate, they insisted, to have the mortal simplicities, the directness and responsibilities of democratic statecraft in America symbolized in the memorials of the national capital.

Among the severest critics was Joseph Hudnut, Dean of the Harvard Graduate School of Design and formerly associated with the Columbia School of Architecture. Writing on the Twilight of the Gods for Magazine of Art, the journal of the Federation of Arts, Dean Hudnut said in 1937: "I am aware that symbolism and romance are inescapable elements in architecture. They are highly desirable elements also, provided one does not pay too dearly for them. The price of Washington is colossal. To attain a 'perfect harmony' of classical form, to create a stupendous symbol of the power and permanence of the Federal Authority, to satisfy a romantic sensibility towards that quality of form which was established by the Early Republic (as if scale and magnitude had nothing to do with the quality of form!), we deprive the Federal City not only of that sense of a heroic past which is the true source of dignity in cities but also of that organic order (itself a kind of history) which is a condition of power in all the great traditions of architecture."

While the Dean was arguing in the sober terms of his profession that this architectural style did not fit the spirit or function of American government, Robert Littell and Harold Stuermer, in Today, a weekly journal of opinion, were declaring journalistically that the style made "Washington seem like a museum of caution and paralysis." They strenuously objected to the failure of the New Deal to take advantage of its opportunity to "reflect its own beliefs in stone, and affirm in its architecture the determination that government shall not be a cold, impersonal pile of rules and red tape, but

a close friend of the people and a bold leader out of mediocrity and confusion." Names applied to conventional public
speakers, particularly "stuffed shirts," were commandeered
to describe this conventional building. With historical injustice it was also called "Hooverism." But as it continued to
find favor under President Roosevelt, critics said it represented the trade agreements so dear to Cordell Hull, the
Secretary of State: while America was exporting industrial
and apartment architecture, she was importing public architecture. What was the real balance?

To some extent an offset to imports was obtained in the
decorations. When in 1934 the Procurement Division of the
Department of the Treasury, to which the task of securing
murals and statues was assigned, entered upon its responsibility, it was widely agreed that art in America "underwent
its most eventful year of the past two decades." Enthusiasts
called the esthetic affirmations made under this regime the
greatest artistic events in three centuries of American art.
Unquestionably the zest of the Federal Government for
visual interpretations of its role was marking a revolution in
its leadership with respect to design and decoration. In 1937,
for example, Boardman Robinson finished eighteen mural
panels covering 1025 square feet in the Department of
Justice.

Organized in December, 1933, the Public Works of Art
Project was financed by a grant from the Civil Works Administrator to the Treasury Department and over its fortunes
Edward Bruce was called to preside. At the capital and out
over the country where federal buildings were being erected,
embellishments proceeded to take form under this Project.
Artists were employed at craftsmen's wages. At the capital,
they were selected and supervised directly by the Treasury;
in the sixteen regions into which the Project was divided,
regional committees and sub-committees were charged with
this responsibility. In 1935 the Painting and Sculpture
Section of the Procurement Division of the United States
Treasury Department, organized in 1934, consolidated and

extended this national enterprise and announced competitions for mural assignments.

Edward Bruce, who was given such power over art in America, was both a financier and a painter. Among his own productions was a mural executed in 1931 for the San Francisco Stock Exchange and hung over the mantel in its Board room — a picture of the local business district with the Golden Gate just beyond. In 1933 Bruce went to England with Cordell Hull, as a delegate to the London Conference; and during its sessions, on the initiative of the Secretary of State, an exhibit of his art was held in London. Known on both sides of the Atlantic, an experienced painter in sympathy with the New Deal, Edward Bruce pressed not only for results but for creditable results in the art projects under his administration. In some instances he had to yield to sentimentality when he preferred vitality, but on the whole his supervision of painting and sculpture under federal auspices was deemed so competent by professional artists that the Architectural League of New York awarded him its Friedsam Medal in 1937 for his "outstanding achievement" and Harvard gave him an honorary degree.

As for fortunate artists who won important commissions to decorate the capital, on the whole they too deserved medals in that they responded to their opportunity for communicating with the people through visible forms in a spirit of public service such as had actuated great artists in other times and places. "Exactly as it would be absurd to imagine a Giotto or a Piero making his mural illustrations unintelligible to the peasant who came to them with faith, so it would have been absurd for Reginald Marsh to have made his murals in the Post Office Department at Washington unintelligible to the man in the street or for Henry Varnum Poor to make his panels in the Department of Justice meaningless to a clerk in the building."

If such was the theory, practice did not always signify genius in communication. The monstrous figures, male and female, which sat before the portal of the Supreme Court temple were notable mainly for their ponderosity. Nor was communication of other sorts always acceptable to the public for whom it was intended, as Rockwell Kent discovered after impressing his political conceptions upon a mural for the Post Office Department; when some one deciphered an inscription within his composition, his leftist tendency was called to public attention and the matter was ordered corrected. But critical interpretations of Justice by Henry Varnum Poor seemed to provoke no bitter protest against their validity, and among the quantities of paintings and statues completed for Washington in these years a substantial number of the esthetic affirmations were technically competent and alive with social statement, freely expressed.

Out of want, unrest, and fear a general Federal Art Project took form in 1935 as a measure of relief, its periphery extending to work in all the arts and crafts whether utilized for the embellishment of buildings or not. As the construction of private buildings came to a halt, architects were thrown out of a livelihood. As funds for museums shrank and private collectors began to convert their Old Masters into cash and curtail patronage, painters and sculptors lost their means of support. As mills closed, designers of fabrics and other commodities walked the streets with no employment in sight. As magazines lost subscriptions and publishers their market for books, writers and illustrators, editors and critics were checkmated in their careers. How were the numerous orchestras to survive and the musicians generally? By the thousands, artists of all kinds faced destitution and were compelled to ask for public relief.

For the precipitous let-down in art commissions, the nation was no better prepared than it was for the collapse on the Stock Exchange. In respect of art casualties, however, statistics were less satisfactory, since art could not be measured numerically like declining stocks and defaulted bonds. The fact that several thousand artists, in a population of 130,000,000 people, were deprived, in 1933, of ways to earn their living, if set beside the fact that millions of industrial workers were out of jobs, might have been dismissed by mere statisticians as a meager item in the social reckoning. That it became a large item in this accounting was due to the deep-rooted convictions of influential Americans with reference to the role of art in civilization and to a keen recognition of the plight into which artists had fallen.

"During boom years architects, particularly in the larger offices, became imbued with the psychology of their clients," avowed Talbot Faulkner Hamlin, a member of the American Institute of Architects, in August, 1933. "All the Hooverian dogmas of individualism, salesmanship, profit-making, were swallowed unquestionably," he went on to say. "Architectural magazines were full of articles on the money-making side of the profession; the architect was often a promoter and a business man rather than a designer. As he became immersed in financial schemes and details, his professional position weakened; the architect was merely one of several cogs in the machine of corporate and individual profit chasing. Then came the falling off in investment building between 1928 and 1929 and the stock market crash; and one after another the great hotels and office buildings paraded into bankruptcy and foreclosure. The profit chasers sought other fields; the architect was forgotten. He learned bitterly of the gratitude of wealth, and all his grandiose promotion schemes vanished. Out of it all he found he had won only small pay, worry, and a loss of professional prestige."

In 1932 architects were reported as having less than one-seventh of the work they had in 1928. The crumbs that fell from Dives' table grew scantier and scantier and yet graduate recruits from schools of architecture continued every year to enter the scramble for such crumbs as there were. Elaborate corporations employing designers, organizers, and managers of great buildings waited a while for orders that did not arrive and then steadily reduced their forces or drew the curtains and locked the doors. Lesser business establishments engaged in designing small homes fared a little better and hoped for a public housing program to provide them with work; but that program also lagged, leaving minor alterations or repairs in tenements and shops or houses the mainstay of such concerns. Even the smaller firms had to face the competition of architects out of work as the total income from architectural enterprise slumped in 1932 to a fifth of the 1928 figure. If many men and women hitherto employed in architectural labors could make adjustments, many others could not.

"Some have turned artists or interior decorators," Hamlin reported. "One makes decorative maps. One, with a musical avocation, plays the piano for a radio circuit. Another is a taxi driver. And many have gone into commission selling — that last chaotic field which modern finance and industry have developed to absorb those technologically and otherwise unemployed — and hawk over the country everything from pencils to life insurance." But like the scholar who, after his dismissal from a leading university for having opposed America's entrance into the world war, tried unsuccessfully to sell washing machines for his daily bread, architects did not find it possible to transform themselves immediately into high-powered traveling salesmen, handling just any kind of goods.

As helpfully as their own situation permitted, members of the profession aided one another in the crisis, "perhaps the worst that has overtaken a similar body." They opened an Emergency Work Bureau in New York City, for example, and secured some commissions for the applicants, such as traffic surveys for the State Housing Board, participation in the Columbia University Energy Survey for the United States, and model-making and measurement drawings for museums. However, the fees they charged, though far below the architect's customary rewards, were often contested and the workers on relief tasks hurt themselves and the profession by accepting such slight returns for their labor.

The very styles of architecture which did materialize during the general prostration indicated "symptoms, at heart, of exhaustion and despair," in the opinion of Hamlin. Architects "played safe," the "joyless conservatism" of Hoover's Department of Commerce building in Washington illustrating that timidity and ennui. In 1933, at the World's Fair in Chicago, structures "almost without architectural meaning," devoid of the "great architectural problems of plan, material, use and proportion," betrayed, according to Hamlin, a similar feeling of "insecurity and doubt, in the actual terror of destitution which these last years had brought to the architects especially."

By 1935 the number of unemployed musicians, painters, sculptors, architects, writers, playwrights, actors, and dancers had grown to such an extent that the country faced the possibility of an utter collapse in the art movement. With professional artists roaming the streets hunting for work, what prospect could students training for a livelihood in the arts see ahead when they left the "threshold of life"? If America could not support artists, it was surely poverty-stricken in things of the spirit as well as of the purse. To the forefront came a fundamental question of civilization itself: Are the arts to be viewed merely as luxuries to be lopped off when the economic machine is in trouble?

The very hope of "recovery," not to mention "progress," was involved in the question, since industry itself depended upon the preservation and development of skills in the arts of design. For at least fifty years American business men had recognized this dependence, and international competition had made it clearer to them with every passing year. To stimulate the home market, artistic skills were equally imperative and yet the risk of hopeless deterioration in skills was apparently imminent. Deeper down in psychological sources lay the peril of dissolution that threatened aspiration and the creative spirit so intimately associated with the arts, humble and great, and so important as sustaining forces in the growth and preservation of society itself.

For the awakening of public interest in the state of the arts, the Bohemians of the prosperous age were only slightly, if at all, responsible; they had often fled to places more

delightful to their eyes than the American scene or had con-
gregated in the alleys and corners at home for idle "conversation at midnight." The awakening came from two sources,
apart from the obvious income needs which were mainly
responsible : one, the more or less quiet and steady leadership
of men and women who had given privileged segments of
the population the advantages of concert-hearing and choral-
singing, museum-visiting, the enjoyment of and training in
the arts; the other, the folk art which had weathered the
hazards of time and furnished a basis on which to build
public art. The merging of these two streams of interest and
action created a New Horizon in Art, as Holger Cahill expressed it. And toward the challenging illumination of the
new horizon, the American democracy blazed its way, experimentally.

With extreme pleasure Eduard Lindeman, from the van-
tage-point of his long social work, hailed this movement "out
from the alleys of Bohemia and onto the highways." But it
was not merely from the alleys of Bohemia that artists
marched toward the assumption of public obligations. In the
ateliers of established artists still receiving commissions, men
and women caught the vision of a democracy in dire cultural
and economic distress and they moved from their secure
positions along the path to be marked "the American way,"
carrying others with them toward a collective effort to meet
the menace of an artistic collapse. Indeed so many Americans rejected the idea that the arts could be neglected or
lopped off when the economic machine was in trouble that
federal, state, and local governments were induced to assert
leadership in saving and promoting the arts by administrative and financial measures. Had there been no appreciative
public behind them, even Aeschylus, Bach, and Michelangelo
could not have demonstrated their genius, as Maxwell
Anderson averred.

The new measures did not, however, signify the very
beginning in the relation of the American State and the arts,
as many protestants seemed to suppose. For more than a

hundred years in the United States, governments had given commissions to artists in connection with public buildings and memorials; there had been "political" artists and architects since the first days of the republic. Again and again politicians had projected great public works, buildings, parks, and monuments with a view to giving "fat jobs" to political contractors and designers associated with them, as well as to serve interests of utility and esthetics. Often indeed considerations of profit had outweighed public interests of any kind. And in such circumstances artistic beneficiaries had accepted the fruits of politics as "natural" and "proper." When the idea that planned public works should "take up the slack" in employment during slumps in industry came into vogue early in the twentieth century, and was generally approved, few citizens regarded the commissions that went to artists as a form of "contemptible relief."

But no such expedients were adequate to handle the economic dislocations of the arts in 1933 and the following years, any more than the privations of industry and agriculture. Artists, no less than home owners and industrial workers, were human beings, and government actions directed against the economic reverses, unless deliberately partial, also had to take them into account. Were artists and the rest of the unemployed to be given doles and allowed to lose their skills, to sink into lethargy and despair? That question President Roosevelt faced definitely in January, 1935, and in his annual message to Congress he declared that "continued dependence upon relief induces a spiritual and moral disintegration fundamentally destructive to the national fibre." For haphazard relief and scattered public-works undertakings, he proposed to substitute "selected and planned" projects which would provide general employment at such useful undertakings as would afford "permanent improvement in living conditions" or create "future wealth for the nation."

Accepting this program as sound in conception, Congress gave appropriate authorizations; the Works Progress Ad-

ministration was set up under the direction of Harry Hopkins; and in August, 1935, the Federal Art Project was
organized as a division of that Administration. Arrangements were made for the employment of musicians, actors,
writers, painters, sculptors, architects, etchers, frescoists, and
photographers; and at the peak of the load thousands of
persons were engaged in public arts projects. Conceived as
emergency measures for the occupation of the unemployed
and the maintenance of skills and attitudes, these projects
developed into a cultural movement and received such strong
commendation that a permanent federal bureau for the promotion of the arts in America was proposed in Congress in
1938 and widely sponsored in the country.

To Jacob Baker, a believer in experimentation and liberal
in his tastes, Harry Hopkins entrusted the general supervision of all the relief projects for artists, actors, writers, and
musicians. As his aides Baker chose Holger Cahill, an authority on folk art, an outstanding museum technician and
art critic, to direct work in painting, sculpture, and the
crafts; Nikolai Sokoloff, organizer, and for many years director of the Cleveland orchestra, to head music projects; Hallie
Flanagan, in private life Mrs. Philip H. Davis, director of
the Experimental Theater at Vassar College, to manage the
theater project; and Henry Alsberg, an editorial writer for
the New York Evening Post and a foreign correspondent
for liberal magazines, to take care of the writers project.
When Mr. Baker left the government service on his own
motion in 1936, Mr. Hopkins selected for his position Mrs.
Ellen S. Woodward, of Mississippi, who was then in charge
of the women's division of the Emergency Relief Administration. Associated with the federal relief program from the
beginning, Mrs. Woodward had previously been a member
of the state legislature and executive secretary of the Mississippi State Board of Development.

By May, 1937, $46,000,000 had been spent on the arts
through the Works Progress Administration, an amount in
excess of the government subsidy in any other nation for the

maintenance and promotion of art in its various branches. France in 1937, for example, was spending only $6,000,000.

The federal enterprise was not to be appraised, however, solely in terms of expenditure, absolute or comparative. Despite the lavish outlays for art training, museums, and galleries, despite achievements of a high order, Americans had done relatively little, under either private or public auspices, to stimulate universal interest in the arts and deepen esthetic experience among the broad masses of the people in cities and rural regions. Estimates placed the number of men, women, and children in the United States who had never had the pleasure of seeing or studying original works of art, deemed great, at a figure as high as ninety per cent. This calculation included thousands of teachers charged with elevating the tastes of the young.

Though music of a sort was "as indigenous as corn-on-the-cob, jazz, breakfast food, and comic strips," though song rolled from the slate mines of Vermont where Welsh quarrymen were employed and from the coal mines of Pennsylvania where miners of other origins still sang the songs of their ancestors, though Negroes swayed and lilted as in plantation days, though the radio carried grand compositions to more homes over the land, still there were millions of Americans who had heard only chants or hymns and Americans without number who knew only the crudest rhythmic forms or the "canned music" of the radio. Only in the most backward places of the earth were there people who knew as little of esthetic pleasure as multitudes in great areas of the United States — in "the drought lands of the Dakotas, in the Corn Belt of Nebraska, in the hay valleys of New England, in the culturally isolated settlements of the Ozarks and parts of the Carolinas, on the tobacco roads of Georgia, and even in some sections of Greater New York, Chicago, San Francisco, and Los Angeles." But at last the American democracy was to explore this form of its great unknown — to pioneer on new lines.

The spirit guiding the enlargement of artistic expression

was set forth by Holger Cahill in an exposition of working
doctrines. "The organization of the Federal Art Project,"
he said, "has proceeded on the principle that it is not the
solitary genius but a sound general movement which main-
tains art as a vital, functioning part of any cultural scheme.
Art is not a matter of rare, occasional masterpieces. The
emphasis upon masterpieces is a nineteenth-century phenomenon. It is primarily a collector's idea and has little
relation to an art movement. When one goes through the
galleries of Europe which preserve, in spite of war, fire, flood,
and other destructive forces, an amazing quantity of works
from the past, one is struck by the extraordinary amount
of work which was produced in great periods. During the
early part of the twentieth century it is said that some forty
thousand artists were at work in Paris. It is doubtful if
history will remember more than a dozen or two of these,
but it is probable that if the great number of artists had not
been working, very few of these two dozen would have been
stimulated to creative endeavor; in a genuine art movement,
a great reservoir of art is created in many forms, both major
and minor. . . . If American art is to continue, the talents
of the younger generation of artists must not only be encouraged but must be given an opportunity to develop." In that
mood and with that same faith, his colleagues in the Federal
Art Project directed their respective enterprises. Dr. Sokoloff reminded the public that "training for the participation
in music" is as desirable as training for performing music
and "remedies a weakness which has long been recognized
in America's musical life, the decline of the amateur."

To take care of all the artists in need and make a social
return to the supporting nation at the same time was the
combined problem and ideal for the administrators in charge
of this public works program. Of course every person on the
list of projects was not a genius or even technically very
competent. Nevertheless all of them had been identified in
some way with the profession of art. And their tasks were
assigned as far as possible according to their disciplines and

talents. For example, more than half of the artists were directed to photography, to making posters, designing stage-sets for the federal theater projects, and to other activities in applied art. Some were sent out over the country to manage art galleries and art centers, opened in town after town where good pictures and sculpture had never been seen before, even by the teachers in the schools. In fact 600 new art centers were established in churches, settlements, and schools, in many cases with financial aid from cities and private citizens. In these centers local residents were invited to hear lectures given by the government teachers, to see the exhibits, and if they so desired to attend classes in painting, sculpture, etching, photography, music, the drama, writing, and other branches of art. Hitherto relatively little thought had been given in the United States to community expression in artistic forms but within an incredibly short time a million persons, old, middle-aged, and young, were enrolled for the study of art in centers under public auspices.

Especially manageable and appealing to the whole country was the Music Project which found employment for several thousand musicians, set up laboratories for the encourage-ment and training of composers, organized musical programs, stimulated local participation by communities, and carried music into hospitals and other institutions. In the congested quarters of great cities and in far-scattered and isolated com-munities throughout the United States, concerts were given, young and old were invited to participate and try their talents, local groups were formed to assure a continuity of interest and services, and the love of rhythm was enriched by a finer experience. Within a few months 4000 works by 1400 native composers were rendered, many mediocre, some positively bad, others called "distinguished" by competent critics. Scarcely a state was untouched by this novel enter-prise in public leadership and private coöperation. In 1938 more than 6000 musicians participated in the national music week organized by the Music Project; programs were exe-cuted in forty-two states by symphony and concert orches-

tras, bands, opera and choral groups. By that time the
number of attendances recorded at musical events held under
the auspices of the Project had risen to more than 85,000,000
and coöperative arrangements had been perfected with innumerable established musical organizations. Singing societies began to hold inter-community festivals. Indoors and
out-of-doors America was brought within the spell of un-
canned rhythmic sound.

§

Severe critics of the Roosevelt administration decried all
such activity as "boon doggling," as a departure from the
fixed principles of American government. On the merits of
particular performances experts in esthetics could differ radically. But unquestionably federal responsibility for the promotion of science, letters, and the arts had the sanction even
of supreme authorities among the founders of the republic.
In his first annual address to the first Congress of the United
States, President Washington himself had declared that
"there is nothing which can better deserve your patronage
than the promotion of science and literature." Speaking of
the national university which he wished to see founded, he
said : "I have greatly wished to see a plan adopted, by which
the arts, sciences, and belles-lettres could be taught in their
fullest extent, thereby embracing *all* the advantages of European tuition." In commenting on his Farewell Address to
the nation, in after years, Washington expressed regret that
he had omitted references to education and particularly to
the establishment of a national university "where the youth
from all parts of the United States might receive the polish
of erudition in the arts, sciences, and belles-lettres." Such
views he was moved to announce, doubtless, by his concern
about the development of civilization in America and the
attacks directed by Europeans against the "thinness" of
culture in the New World.

In the very convention that drafted the Constitution of
the United States, indeed, the issue of social refinements had

come up for consideration. James Madison proposed that Congress be empowered to establish a university and Charles Pinckney that it be authorized to found seminaries "for the promotion of literature and the arts and sciences." It was not the so-called "practical arts" alone that the statesmen of the eighteenth century had in mind as objects of solicitude. Their intention was correctly re-expressed long afterward by John Quincy Adams when, as President, he recommended to Congress the enactment of laws "promoting the improvement of agriculture, commerce, and manufactures, the cultivation and encouragement of the mechanic and of the elegant arts, the advancement of literature, and the progress of the sciences, ornamental and profound."

It is clear, therefore, that the concern with and appreciation of arts and letters represented by the Federal Art Project had sanction in the most reputable American theory respecting relations between the State and the arts, although amid circumstances far different in nature. Had statecraft undertaken to foster and guide esthetics in the age of Washington, the patrician culture of the eighteenth century might have been reinforced on American soil. Had statecraft assumed that function in the age of John Quincy Adams, commercial culture might have become dominant, almost beyond challenge. Now in the twentieth century with political democracy triumphant, statecraft, in reaching out to esthetics, reflected the democratic spirit engaged in an effort to conquer the crisis in thought and economy, and was in a position to make arts and letters powerful assets in the balance sheet of national wealth.

At all events by 1935 the President, the Congress, and private citizens intensely regardful of culture in America had become cognizant of artistic resources to be conserved and strengthened, of risks inherent in allowing them to waste and decay. Together they assumed the obligation to foster such neglected talent as the nation possessed and give it a chance to develop by use, supplementing, not supplanting, private endeavors. And why should the idea have received so much criticism ? No artist of the highest academic standing had ever been unwilling to accept an attractive government commission in the years of the golden glow, whatever its political origin or utility. Only in the recession was contumely attached to the public patronage of the arts. Perhaps it was not in the arts that the roots of the controversy lay but in conceptions respecting the economy in which the esthetic collapse had occurred.

When once the decision was made by the Roosevelt administration to provide employment for artists as well as for industrialists, contractors, and industrial workers, it soon became explicit that the thought of contemporary democrats and the thought of the early republicans were alike in that both diverged from the thought of old monarchies in one fundamental characteristic. There was no court in the United States to be served and flattered by genius. Talent, unless it still retreated from the American scene, had to work in and with the common life of America. And it was concern with this life that, from the beginning of the republic, had sustained the ideal of an advancing civilization in America, now to be carried forward in part by the encouragement of art.

§

Not until the Federal Art Project collected the materials did Americans begin to appreciate the extent and nature of their esthetic resources. Beneath the imported academic art, most of which "the people" either never saw or did not understand, in American regionalism the art of the people survived. As an editorial in the magazine Fortune rightly declared in June, 1937, "one thing every sophomore knows about the tradition of American art is that there isn't any. . . . It rests on no peasant handicrafts, no popular taste, no anonymous workmanship. It arrived ready-made from Europe. And the best of it arrived on the *Ile de France* within the last decade in a case marked 'Picasso: use no hooks.'"

From the misinformation given by their preceptors and their attitude toward art, sophomores derived their assumptions in part. Nor did popular writers on American culture have a wide and intimate knowledge of folk art upon which to base their treatises. They, too, often imagined that Americans had little or no taste, inherent or inherited. They paid tribute to craft and peasant taste in Europe and Asia but they were inclined to scorn every species of rustic expression in their homeland as "pioneer" and "frontier" bungling, thereby missing the imaginative resources of an American culture and in consequence the conscious and ingrained traditional feeling that America could actually do important things in the arts.

In fact it was not until the Federal Art Project explored underlying tastes and attempts at their expression, from the seventeenth-century furniture of the people, their silver, pewter, textiles, coverlets, toys, glass, ceramics, embroideries, clothes, woodcarvings, ships, houses, drawings, wall decorations, portraiture, and water colors, for example, to things produced in the twentieth century, that Americans got the slightest notion of the continental resources in artistic matters. The Federal Government's Index of American Design was an immense educational enterprise.

Other nations had long been devoted to their own popular art, had collected specimens for their museums, had enjoyed the fructifying force of the inspiration which professional artists had derived from studying achievements of the unprofessional, had acclaimed their sense of beauty as their distinction, and had received the laurels of outlanders in recognition of their cultural greatness. On the other hand, Americans had been inclined to relegate their folk art, when they encountered it inadvertently, to the realm of the merely "quaint." But this infantile esthetic attitude was educated to more sophistication when in twenty-five states the workers on federal projects, in the spirit of sensitive archaeologists and not of simple antiquarians, explored the people's esthetic affirmations on this vast continental mainland. Off the highways, in the byways, these microscopic searchers found that "homespun art" was not a mere anachronism, that handicrafts still flourished, and that skilled manipulators of materials in many "back regions" had means for surviving the depression that industrial and white-collar workers did not possess.

Impressed by the discoveries and interpretations in the Index of American Design, museums grew more hospitable to folk art. And not only that; they saw in it new values. Painters and sculptors likewise were invigorated by the quality of the near at hand; by contact with sincere and unsophisticated work. Constance Rourke, through her experience with the editing of the Index, found, for example, that "painters staring for the first time at seventeenth and eighteenth century New Mexican painting on wood have been humbled by the devotion of these unknown artists who served a discipline as old as Catholic Spain."

With respect to folk art as a whole in America, the discipline, it might be added, ran back through the aborigines to the very beginning of all art when the appreciation of beauty was associated with the most elementary production of commodities for everyday use at the hearth and in the field. It represented an eternally human insistence upon attractions for the eye, a will to express self in meditation and work imaginatively; and when such art was now assembled and re-emphasized, it quickly became recognized as a social asset. Thus the magazine Fortune, reviewing the Index to American Design, made that comprehension articulate. "Men cutting weather vanes out of iron and blowing goblets out of glass and shaping plates from clay," it avowed, "did not cease to exercise their sense of form and color merely because the oil painters had quit or run away to Italy or stopped drinking. Women sewing quilts and stitching samplers continued to use their eyes and their imaginations. Wood carvers and furniture makers went right on concerning themselves with the lines of their figureheads (for their seagoing vessels) and the just proportions of their cabinets. The popular arts, the practical arts, the arts which always must exist in a living society, whether the artists find them or not, survived and were vigorous."

Among the artists who did find them was Charles Sheeler, one of the earliest disciples of modernism to do it. Born in Philadelphia, his own background was urban. His art education had been pursued both in the United States and in Europe but it did not leave him creatively paralyzed. On his return from a third trip to Europe, he drew closer to folk art in America, to a study of form as function, spending much of his time in Bucks County, Pennsylvania, where the fine old barns elicited his enthusiasm. He studied intensively the art of the Shakers too and became steeped in the idea that "every force has its form." Deliberately looking for the real beneath the meretricious, he discovered the American heritage, assimilated it, and gave to his painting of barns, boats, flowers, and human beings not only a high plastic quality but an integrity suggesting the spirit of the original handicraftsmen, the vitality and beauty of flora, and the vigor of healthy life.

What was true of handicrafts as an American art affirmation was also true of music, as the units of the Federal Music Project discovered. These units collected or recorded "the early music of Mexico and Texas — on the plains and the border, Acadian and Creole songs in Louisiana, African melodies sung by the Negroes of the Mississippi bayous, the folk songs of the Southern mountaineers, white and Negro spirituals from the Carolinas, settlers' songs and songs of Indian origin from Oklahoma, early Spanish songs from California, liturgical music from the California missions, songs sung by the Penitentes of New Mexico, music brought into Mexico in the time of the conquistadors." Though federal workers were not the original explorers of this heritage, they widened the investigation. Symphonies based on the songs of the mountain people of North Carolina had been composed in the music department of the university of Chapel Hill. Carl Sandburg had published his American

Songbag. The two Lomaxes, father and son, had wandered among the people and issued volumes of the songs they had heard among cowboys and fieldhands, among Negroes in the cotton fields and Negroes in jail. But the Federal Music Project helped to call the attention of the entire country to the wealth and meaning of the music heritage and to shake academicians out of their routines.

In the merging of the academic and the non-academic, Charles Seeger, teacher, lecturer, assistant to the director of the Federal Music Project, seemed to find enclosed the promise of a creatively significant popular music. Writing for Magazine of Art, he said: "Unquestionably, the musical soul of America is in its folk music, not in its academic music; and only in its popular music to the extent popular music has borrowed, stolen, and manhandled folk music materials. On the other hand, the gestures, the nervous energy, the characteristic flair of America — industrialized, sophisticated, learned America — is in its academic and popular, not in its folk music. It is quite as necessary to have an outside as well as an inside. And quite desirable to have both! But they should not fight with each other; for there is every reason to believe each has something the other needs for its well-being and for the well-being of the country. Great musics in the past have been formed out of just such interplay of diversity and integration as can be seen now in American music. There is some reason to believe it is happening again.

"Both the wide diversity and the rapid integration are desirable factors in American music. Diversity without integration, in so large a unit as America, would mean chaos, and might well fit into a state of social, economic, and political anarchy. Integration without diversity spells standardization and regimentation, and would fit only too well with the totalitarianism of fascism. A balance, or complementary of the two, points to the preservation and further evolution of democratic social organization. Actually, this is, I believe, what is happening in American music today."

Along this exploratory line, the Writers Project likewise

carried on an extensive search for folk lore in tales and legends. It promoted studies of the ethnic groups in the United States, surveyed American archives, explored old buildings, and scanned faded photographs, maps, and charts — with the aim of discovering neglected treasures and presenting comprehensive data relative to deep-lying cultural patterns.

That all the arts projects were not merely antiquarian in aim was demonstrated by the response which men, women, and children made to the Government's invitation to paint, model, carve, etch, dance, act on the stage, tell stories, write, design, and photograph. Their eagerness to take advantage of the opportunities offered them proved that reservoirs of creative energies, hitherto unutilized, existed in all parts of the country. Out of them might flow the esthetic interests necessary to the vigorous nourishment of the arts and, for aught any one knew, an occasional genius might in time again illuminate the heavens.

Summaries, even skillfully made, could give no adequate insight into the strength and depth of this national movement. A single clue may be afforded by a single illustration taken from the Painters Project in Chicago. The regional director of that enterprise under federal auspices was Mrs. Increase Robinson, herself a painter, who had long been helping young artists, mainly from the middle west, to carry on their creative work, and educating Chicago in the process. In various ways she had befriended and encouraged such talented young persons as Aaron Bohred, Grant Wood, Francis Chapin, Davenport Griffin, and David McCosh.

Accordingly, Mrs. Robinson brought to her task both abilities and wide experience when she became a government art official; and under her direction the Chicago project produced in 1936 seventy-five murals, "placed or had in process thirty large sculptures and woodcarvings; put up a 114-foot plaster frieze in the new Kish Hall of the Field Museum of Natural History; prepared dioramas for visual education; and produced 40,000 posters for health and safety campaigns." Comparing its exhibit in 1937 with the current exhibit at the Chicago Art Institute, critics accustomed to reporting the products of the academies pronounced it worthy of more than grudging recognition. It was said that the "best young painting" in the middle west was being done by workers on the Federal Project. The democratic aspect of this federal patronage, as directed by Mrs. Robinson, was reflected in its interracial catholicity. Many nationalities were listed among the painters and sculptors whom critics were watching. Their very names indicated the liberalism of the federal policy, for they included such as these: Viviano, Britton, Breinin, Michalov, Stenvall, Murray, Bennett, Millman, Jacobson, and Siporin. In all the projects, men and women of the Negro race were given access to the working tools of art; their products were exhibited with the rest and were acknowledged in a spirit free from racial antipathies.

In California, a similar development took place. Linked with the Federal Art Project this most-western section of the nation proved its power to create distinguished objects surpassing the preciosities of philistinism. In a combination of "faith, freedom, and discipline," its mosaicists achieved decorations commanding the attention of art lovers and critics of the most defiant types, much credit for which belonged to William Gaskin, the San Francisco government supervisor. In this form of art several women did notable work as in fact they did wherever the opportunity was given them. The hospitality shown by the Berkeley Art Gallery was responsible for California's record, in part.

As for sculpture, its comparative expense gave less leeway on the whole to the encouragement of that art medium. Its dependence on building was another factor holding it back. But as federal and private housing crept forward, little by little, sculpture did the same. In some of the housing projects, innovative work was done in carved murals; symbolic statues were made to typify the life and labor of the older residents; and frolicsome animals were sculptured to amuse the children. Through their opportunity to apply modern conceptions of taste and new techniques, artists were led to subdue freakishness in the interests of sincere workmanship. In some cases the residents were permitted to pass judgments on designs in advance of their execution.

An important phase of federal action lay in the effect of the arts projects upon impressionable childhood during the years ranging from extreme youth to maturing adolescence, in school and outside. Whatever promise American life held was to flower out of the rising generation but millions of that oncoming population were being cast adrift with nothing substantial to employ their active bodies and restless minds. No doubt it seemed foolish to many globe-trotting adults, accustomed to think of art as something completed — the adult product of Old Masters never young, that American children should be given wholesale opportunities at public expense to paint, model, and carve. Having felt awe or weariness in the galleries of other civilizations, many such tourists shouted vociferous condemnation in which they were joined by the weary at home. But other Americans both felt and thought differently. Some of them were disturbed by the social menaces, such as delinquency and crime, which mentally undernourished children, victims in part of the economic casualty, could so easily enlarge. Analytical artists, wise in their knowledge that "eyes on the world" turn there in very infancy and that a peculiar charm of art may represent a childishly direct selection of values, urged that the arts projects be opened wide to youth. Countless children were made happy by this arrangement and an extraordinary demonstration of their power to express themselves resulted from the opportunities provided for them.

Federal projects so extensive, designed to reach all parts of the country and give occupation to old and young by the hundreds of thousands, constituted an art movement that called for an army of competent painters, sculptors, musicians, and craftsmen to inspire and direct. More than technical mastery was needed, of course. Sympathy, insight, and comprehension of the possibilities at stake were likewise imperative. If the movement was to gather great force and acquire the strength of permanence, long and persistent discipline was required.

Yet all the arts projects had an air of improvisation and impermanence. The experiment was an experiment. In part, if not mainly, it had been regarded by the general public at the beginning as a mere makeshift, a form of relief. Skeptics accustomed to concentrate on what they called pure art and to think of esthetics merely in terms of their own tastes jeered at the enterprise, at the paints, daubs, and horrors often — perhaps generally — produced under its auspices. Yet those who studied it closely and in its intimate social setting concluded with remarkable unanimity that immense cultural potentialities might lie in this art movement, might come out of it — and be expressed in some form of permanent patronage of public art. On the other hand, a return of prosperity might lead to the abandonment of the whole Art Project and a restoration of all artists to the private market; or, if American economy continued to deteriorate, artists might be put to digging ditches or marching in military ranks. Nowhere was the nature of the midpassage better exemplified.

After three years of experimentation in the arts under federal auspices, with intense local coöperation, no immediate appraisal could be made on a comprehensive scale; nor could the heavy curtain shutting off the future of American art be lifted. Judgments were numerous; indeed multitudinous. As usual those who knew the least about the vast aggregation of activities were likely to be sternest in scorn and condemnation.

Offsetting the criticism, though by no means fully disposing of it, were citations of indisputable achievements in detail and general verdicts from authorities commanding public respect. For example, it was announced in 1938 that the commission to paint the murals for the New York Public Library, which gossip had once assigned to Whistler or

Sargent, had finally gone to a young worker in the Federal
Art Project, Edward Laning, whose mural for Ellis Island,
The Role of the Immigrant in the Industrial Development
of America, was felt to be worthy of this succession. After
referring to the work submitted to the City of New York by
artists engaged on the Federal Project, I. N. Phelps Stokes,
president of the Municipal Art Commission so long identified
with matters of taste in the metropolis, declared in his report
for that year: "There was a time when many artists, as well
as the Art Commission, feared that the depression would go
down in history as a period characterized by the large production of poor work in painting and sculpture, whereas the
best-informed authorities now agree that it will be remembered rather as a period of renaissance."

§

The arrival of immortal American genius was not assured
beyond a doubt. But since the sources of genius in the arts
lay and had always lain in sensitivity to life and thought
about its meaning, the movement of artists in America
toward that fountain of inspiration and vitality was at least
an encouragement to those who longed for its coming. The
general feeling that "Europe was not a success" revived the
eighteenth-century hope that America might be a success.
The Idea of Progress reverted to its original humanism so
often travestied by recent mechanicians. Now there was
more meditation and discussion of potentialities in the
western hemisphere; more independence of spirit and aim.
Thus the "milk and water" painting of a Puvis de Chavannes,
the pride of Boston when it was placed in her imposing public library, and the swarms of allegorical "lady Justices and
Liberties in classical robes," inherited from the neo-classicists
and widely distributed, were reappraised as "sentimental,"
"lugubrious," and "academic" by a generation disillusioned
with respect to make-believe and yet sturdy in its faith in
life. The vernacular surging up into art was in part protest
and in part fresh esthetic energy.

This tendency was invigorated by Mexican artists so near the border of the United States, affirming their knowledge and taste. In their concern with the indigenous, the Mexicans seemed to be effective exponents of the contemporary revolt against sheer imitation. On their return from a visit to Moscow, whither they had gone to see sights and dream dreams keyed to their own recent revolution, several Mexican artists issued a manifesto declaring: "Our fundamental esthetic goal is to socialize expression and tend to obliterate totally individualism, which is bourgeois. We repudiate the so-called easel painting and all the art of ultra-intellectual circles because it is aristocratic and we glorify the expression of Monumental Art, because it is public expression."

Among the manifestants was Diego Rivera and, though his revolutionary ardor was unmistakable, the spell of his creative art brought him commissions in the United States even from capitalist sources. Catching warmth from warmth, both the San Francisco Chamber of Commerce and Radio City in New York, a Rockefeller enterprise, invited Rivera to paint murals for their walls. For the former, Rivera made concessions in his composition. Apparently he hoped to make none for the latter but when a portrait of Lenin stood forth at the center of his scheme the mural was ordered to be taken down. Even friendly critics in some cases thought this painting was melodramatic.

Another Mexican invited to paint in the United States was David Alfaro Siqueiros, also a signer of the Mexican manifesto. Though he sometimes used the modern blow torch as tool and cement as material for individual experiment, Siqueiros was collectivist in both his ideals and his art practice. While American muralists were to encounter the labor issue as trade unionists demanded the right to do the actual work from designs, Siqueiros and his group of coöperating artists did their own work together, in the style of old Italian frescoists. Siqueiros thought in terms of public art.

In the fervor for emancipation from Europe, Orozco joyfully proclaimed himself a "painter of the new world" and exulted in the very skyscraper as a first step toward Monumental Art in the new world. It was not surprising, then, that Orozco also found patrons above the Rio Grande. For example, he placed a mural on a wall of Pomona College in California and another on a wall at Dartmouth College in New Hampshire. Perhaps few, if any, sightseers or parents of students knew just what the painter was trying to say in his forms and colors, but he declared, as we have indicated, that the Pomona mural depicted Prometheus giving fire to mankind. His Dartmouth mural was not so mythological in theme or so primitive in treatment. It was described as a synthesis of life in America, as life flowing in a fairly straight line from Indian aboriginal sacrifices before the gods of war to modern prostration before machines of war directed by politicos, with education lurking in the environs as something uncannily related to this main purpose of life.

From the Mexican school, while its vitality was strong and its commissions numerous on both sides of the national border, American artists derived a new excitement which affected their own esthetic affirmations, inducing more concentration on the immediate and the known in the social scene. Both in painting and in sculpture this influence was revealed. For instance Boardman Robinson, prepared for the Mexican challenge by his own long concern with the substance of the common life, now revealed his qualified acceptance of Mexican tendencies in a mural painted for a great department store in Pittsburgh; and Leo Katz, working on the theme of Light, moved close to the type of expression evolved among the Mexicans in a mural he executed for the Century of Progress Exposition in Chicago.

A much older Mayan-Mexican bent was to be noted in American sculpture: in its monumental character, however small the figure, in the growing inclination to cut directly into stone instead of modeling through the medium of clay, in the simplification and sturdiness of form, in the architectural quality of the work, in the group compositions, among other signs and symbols. But did sculptors in America merely look to Mayan art for novelties? Or did it invigorate their thought about what they were doing and carry them deeper into consciousness of their affirmations? Doubters even denied this influence but the prominent New York art critic, Emily Genauer, was positive about it. To the skeptics she put these questions: "Have the sculptors incorporated in their own work the monotony of Egyptian figures? Have their sculptures the gravity and stoicism of Chinese things? And are they not more monumental than the little African Negro fetishes from which the sculptors did, doubtless, learn much of the investiture of stiff, angular form with dramatic force?"

§

Decried by the traditionalists and feared by the anti-chauvinists as inconsistent with internationalism, the American Scene was the assignment for all the artists connected with the federal projects. What, then, was the American scene? The Mexicans had been painting their scene as they saw it. What would Americans say through their own techniques? In Magazine of Art, Alfred Frankenstein made his answer: "It is not merely a matter of subject. Thousands of American artists have been painting the American landscape, American architecture, and the American people for generations past, but without remotely approximating this thing called the American scene. What distinguishes the American scene group — Benton, Curry, Wood, Marsh, Hopper, Burchfield, to name only a few — is a highly complex attitude toward the subject, an attitude compounded of romantic emotion and realistic delineation, of a desire to expose the plain, unvarnished facts of American life plus a strong, even sentimental love for the facts that finally emerge. It is primarily, but not exclusively, a phenomenon of the middle west, where the natural landscape is comparatively unspectacular and offers the artist little challenge.

People have been 'exposing' Main Street for lo, these many years, but you can't 'expose' the Yosemite Valley. The American scene thus depicted is basically the human scene. . . . It is an art of people and what they do and the places they live in, not an art of mountains, clouds or the sea." So Breugel, Rembrandt, and Van Gogh, among others, had yielded to their own artistic impulses at other times, in other places, and allied themselves with the fundamental human scene.

For the instruction of directors and directed, Harry Hopkins, relief administrator, laid down just one rule — no indecency. If this curbed the output of nude women, it was no damper on the depiction of "human beings in the dignity of their labor, in the poignancy of their response, the intimation of all they had missed, and that which they have had, their ambitions, contentments, and desires, their full completeness and their lack of completeness," as a defender summed up the work that was being done. All the currents of ideas and interests that worked their way to Letters found articulation in this medium without words.

Just as writers moved from the periphery of life toward its vortex, so artists, for whom the general public was now patron, brought into their thought and its expression the primordials of life and labor. In ancient Egypt, labor had been represented in art as slave toil, which it was in fact. In mediaeval art, labor had often been represented as grotesque with a mingled respect and ridicule. Now in America, labor was made to appear in every style which the American experience had produced — from slave to free, to disinherited. An emancipated Negress in the middle west was painted as if "saying it" with her broom, implying that liberty was not synonymous with paradise.

Bereft of a livelihood in a big city, where could a man go for succor? Several artists in the federal relief project asked that question with oils. The dustbowl — was that the answer? Joseph Vavak's watercolor of a Dust Storm was full argument against it. Pictures in large numbers showed aridity to be no friend of man or beast; the very horses and mules were seen decaying. A Sheeler barn among the comfortable Pennsylvanians was work of art no doubt, in its plastic vitality, but a barn in a dust storm was a barn battling with nature and the elements, giving poor shelter to man and beast, not a pliable thing wholly within the craftsmanship of man. Was not that affirmation also art? Winds and fires, historic enemies of frail mankind, engaged the brushes of many artists, with rain as a variant. In the prints of Japan, gentle rain was one of the characteristic features. But rain in some of the new American painting, notably in Paul Meltsner's, was a cruel thing — a bearer of terror and ruin.

Human life stranded, though temporarily in a Civilian Conservation Camp, was the theme of a young portraitist, David McCosh, himself an artist on relief. What was the lad in transient encampment seeing on his horizon as he gazed off into space? Touching as it did the necessities of life, the work of artists on relief was often drab — as drab as life for the broad masses in America, as pitiable as the little Main Streets of the continent that now stood out in oils still more crudely than they had done in the novel of Sinclair Lewis. Was it then a tragedy for the artist to be an artist of and for the people?

Apparently that "enfant terrible," Paul Cadmus of New York, did not find it so. The sailors in port having a "hot time" with their girls were painted with laughter as wild as nature in her primordial force. Making his affirmations in a concern with the lowly as fierce as that of Caldwell or Hemingway, Cadmus accomplished an overwhelming plasticity of form positively terrifying in its power. Naturally the naval bureaucracy and its patriotic affiliates were appalled by Cadmus' canvases and unwilling to display them prominently, though Cadmus joined in competitive contests.

Joylessness, in vivid contrast, ruled the derelicts who gathered in the All Night Mission, at Bar and Grill, in Siesta, as Eli Jacobi saw them. Though he was called "the

Hogarth of the Bowery," that title seemed more appropriate to Cadmus with respect to a painter's mood. Jacobi made use of the woodcut. Anatole Shulkin of New Jersey was impressed by mob psychology and by the heavy muscles which could come into play when its lawlessness was released; and in the Need for Law, he gave vent to this emotional observation in a mural for the main entrance lobby of the Courthouse in Morristown. Just who were the lawless was an interesting suggestion for New Jersey at this moment in its history.

The need for wise leadership was the affirmation of Mitchell Siporin of Illinois, whose mind was charged with memories of the Haymarket Riot. Leadership he depicted in a series of murals, and his technique was affected by the Mexican artists though he greatly modified their color and forms. Siporin saw "a potential fresco in every poem of Sandburg." The People Yes. And Vachel Lindsay's call to the native genius to complete its soul was like a master's voice:

> Record it for the grandson of your son
> A city is not builded in a day;
> Our little town cannot complete her soul
> Till countless generations pass away.

The young generation on relief, if Siporin had his way, would not wait for more generations to pass away. He called to his own for action, in murals symbolizing the leadership exerted by three western singers of the good life, Lindsay, Sandburg, and Masters; by the political activists, Lincoln and Altgeld; and by Jane Addams, the social democrat.

The utilization of reason was implied. And Jack Levine of Massachusetts was concerned with that theme. Avoiding the wrath of a Daumier at its neglect and the raucous laughter of a Hogarth at human folly, Levine resorted to the devastating wit which only pure reason could command, entitling one of his canvases Feast of Pure Reason and another, Conference.

As the amount of landscape produced by workers on federal projects seemed to affirm the continuity of hunger and love for the land, even where the land was shown to be abused beyond repair, so the amount of portraiture demonstrated the persistence of interest in personality, in spite of the strong emphasis on environment.

All in all, the men and women on relief who were given the chance to state what was on their minds and hearts with respect to the American scene in forms other than words presented remarkable testaments of meditation, criticism, and faith as popular documents offered in return for public patronage. Whatever academicians might think and say with regard to mastery of form, color, rhythm, gesture, and composition, however strictly such affirmations might be relegated to the realm of mere reportage, or sociology, tasteless as many of them were, the broad interpretations of life and scene under the freedom of federal auspices were amazing and vitalizing contributions to a new art movement in America.

§

Moreover the federal encouragement of art affirmations, if only as an experiment in the relief of the hungry, seemed to incite similar and livelier assertions in circles more secure. At any rate, whatever the cause, artistic fervor was not deadened but intensified, and in the intensification new elements of imaginative preferences were evident. Take the matter of portraiture. In discussing this branch of art in connection with a discriminative exhibit of historic illustrations which he had arranged for the Pennsylvania Museum of Art at Philadelphia, E. M. Benson declared: "The lack of fine portraiture in our time is partially the result of a conflict between the artist's social and aesthetic convictions. This accounts for the fact that, with few exceptions, the Lionello d'Estes of the twentieth century have gone unrecorded by our best artists. . . . Although portraiture is not the burning preoccupation of most artists of our day, there is a strong undercurrent of interest in portraiture, mainly among those artists who draw their inspiration from the social scene. . . . The kind of forthright portraiture which this has engendered is a far cry from the commissioned portrait of yesteryear. It is doubtful, therefore, whether the breach between the artist and his erstwhile patrician sitter will ever be healed. What will probably happen — it has been happening since the French Revolution — is that the 'cabinet' or easel portrait will become more and more honest and personal, though not necessarily more subjective; and that this will be accompanied by more formal, although no less sincere, civic portraiture contained in public murals and incorporated into architectural units. Portraiture in photography and the film, because it can be shared by everyone, will, by its concreteness and nearness to life, probably remain the most popular form of portraiture."

Irreverently Peggy Bacon implied that better heads would be acceptable for portraiture. In her rollicking but subtle analyses of available subjects for portraiture, she said "Off with Their Heads," drew specimens to substantiate her decree, and in companionate verses told why this would be wise. In a mood all his own, Peter Blume, young surrealist, growing older, found the face and symbol of Mussolini enough to emphasize at one time. In a picture of the Italian scene, which agitated all the critics, he represented the dictator as a kind of gargoylic Jack-in-the-Box shooting out in front of a sun-colored background painted so skillfully as to make the master of the new Roman Empire, in his foreground of poverty and superstition, all the more sinister.

Few professional artists or critics enjoying private patronage were wholly indifferent to the kind of work done by artists enjoying federal patronage. It is true that some remained irreconcilable in their hostility to "unknown" men and women who dared to affirm their right to speak their minds in the vernacular. But artists of unquestioned standing visited the shabby warehouses and other crude studios, in East Erie Street, Chicago, for instance, shabby because

802 AMERICA IN MIDPASSAGE

the government economized on rent, and attended the public exhibits of this popular art movement to see what was being produced, to observe the skills made manifest, and to meditate on the conditions of esthetic expression and the reactions. When the Design Laboratory in New York, one of the units of the Federal Art Project, which had been developed under the administration of Mrs. Audrey McMahon, regional director, was unable to continue, owing to the dearth of federal funds, it was adopted by the Technical School of the Federation of Architects, Engineers, Chemists, and Technicians, who considered it too valuable to be closed.

In landscape painting even by artists of the academies changes induced by the intense concern with the whole American scene were particularly striking. In the romantic nineteenth century, pretty scenes of peace and plenty on a continent of virgin soil had stirred the esthetic emotion of Americans. In the early years of the twentieth century the forest splendor of America, in spring, summer, autumn and winter, fascinated artists and buyers. But a new mood toward the physical universe in this age of scarcity seemed to take possession of many artists operating under private as well as public auspices. In their portrayal of burnt forest areas, blighted fields, eroded plantations, dust storms, and humanity in retreat from the elements, they appeared to be asking how it came about that man had so mistreated a nature which had offered him friendship in forms of virgin soil, forests, and other resources beyond comparison. While surveys of natural resources were piling up on the desks of engineers and politicians, pictures were multiplying in studios and exhibits as declamations of esthetic thought about the very earth on which American civilization rested. Among these commentaries one of the starkest was offered by Arthur Emptage, national executive secretary of the American Artists Congress — a melancholy scene labeled Work for Scarecrows — displayed in 1938 at his "one-man" show.

Into pictures of still life the more critical affirmations penetrated. A mere basket of potatoes on a bare board was used in one case as a symbol of riches. If the influence of the garden clubs, an outstanding form of women's quest for beauty, was visible in the wealth of floral offerings, the tributes did not always appear now as conventional horns of plenty; the very flowers, at the hands of Charles Sheeler and Georgia O'Keefe, asserted the life principle. Sheeler attained the quality of plastic art in his painting of flowers. In other cases orderly flower arrangements, derived to some extent from Oriental manipulation, stood out against chaotic still-life arrangements, as a re-affirmation of symmetry amid the imbalance prevalent in economy.

Into the style of the age Thomas Benton brought an imagination which Sinclair Lewis described as displaying in paint the humor of a Mark Twain. Benton portrayed frontier scenes on canvas as jocosely as Roughing It did in print and small-town folk amused him enormously. In the temper of the mature Twain, he also fumed over the sufferings and follies of the American people. The Negro share-cropper forced to destroy the cotton which nourished life awakened Benton's infinite pity. To the timeless universal of romantic love he responded with a sensitiveness beyond class or race in a painting sent to Paris in 1938 in connection with an exhibit of American art. The economic calamity, marked by the dissolution of old hopes and faiths and the ferment of ideas as yet chaotic in form, supplied him with materials for endless social representation, as the rush of prosperity had done in earlier days. In murals of indisputable force he depicted the disorder, the confusion, the interplay of optimism and defeat.

Though called a communist by upholders of the genteel tradition, Benton testified in his autobiography published in 1938 that he had no easy solution for the dilemma. "The philosophy that most appeals to me," he confessed, "is that relatively illogical and unsystematic body of comments called Pragmatism. . . . I am convinced that experimentalism is tomorrow's philosophy. I say this because of its flexibility . . . and because it seems to me better attuned to the actualities of emerging scientific invention and of human psychology than any other." Midpassage might well be inscribed as the caption for his thought.

Although for many critics Benton was the one great American painter of these years, he did not accept a sheer nativist creed in art. With a few of his colleagues, he disclaimed fidelity to either national or international dogmas. If through his comparative "objectivity" gleamed an enduring interest in the common ways of labor and life, no artist understood better than he that the distinction between the general and the particular, the universal and the local, could not be drawn in absolute terms.

As in the case of Thomas Benton, so in the case of William Gropper, subtlety and versatility baffled critics bent on stuffing all artists into neat pigeon holes to the left or the right. Like Benton, he too was intensely interested in ordinary life and action, whether he was painting a bar room or a rural landscape for the Schenley Products Company or a town scene in winter time for the Post Office at Freeport, New York, or a water color of "Senators" for the market. With an air of equity, he interwove interpretations with colors. Writing on this quality of Gropper's work, Ernest Brace, an artist appraising another artist's achievements, said with tense brevity: "William Gropper's painting is unequivocally effective. Whether he paints the agile mouth of a senator or the thin, tight lips of a judge, prisoners being marched off to execution or the prostrate victims of an air raid, the briefest glance tells the story. And yet, as with all significant stories, there is much more than plot. It is impossible to turn away without going deeper into the picture, savoring the details of gesture and setting and color and movement which are as closely knit into the picture as a whole as the separate lines of a dramatic climax. Gropper's purpose seems as inseparable from his painting as the pigment."

While men, especially those in charge of purchasing paintings for museums, usually, as Lura Beam phrased it, turned instinctively "toward the male directness, the stout fist, the sword upon the event," constantly renewed in battles, Georgia O'Keefe opposed to that affirmation a feminine point of view. Technically skilled, inclined to symbolism beyond most artists of this day, she had "spent a long time painting lilies, petunias, and those cup-like flowers which have the odd capacity of enlarging to the bowl of the universe. After that she painted heroic sections of flowers which expanded visibly before your eyes. Impossible to tell if they were Jacks-in-the-pulpit or cathedrals or pattern and texture or the tremendous affirmation of male strength. Later, the painting of the little New Mexican churches and of the cross in the desert stood for the sad permanence of religion. The picture of the skull and flowers above the mesas says without words that over and beyond the death wish, life still comes out of death." To the power of her work, museums yielded little by little and in the spring of 1938 the college of William and Mary awarded her the honor of a degree as Doctor of Fine Arts.

Concern with the contemporary age appeared in new contests held by museums and patrons. For a competition set by the Museum of Modern Art in New York, with the Postwar World as the theme, sixty-five artists submitted canvases. Georgia O'Keefe sent in a vision of Manhattan; Henry Varnum Poor expressed himself on the conflict between the arts and the crafts; Hugo Gellert painted capitalism as he saw it on its last line of defense; Benjamin Kopman interpreted militarism metaphysically; and Ben Shan, a pupil of Rivera, recalled the Passion of Sacco and Vanzetti. When the Town Hall Club in Manhattan sought a theme for the bar at the cocktail hour, Luis Mora provided a mural of old New York; for a generation that was celebrating the repeal of the Eighteenth Amendment the affirmation was enlivening.

As artists drew closer to the people and so to life, their fancies were stirred by the potentialities in the print, long known as "the poor man's art." In the days of Jacksonian democracy it had flourished as an effective medium for depicting types, races, and social scenes in America. Stage coaches and pack horses had scattered prints from metropolitan centers to log cabins on the frontier and to miners' shacks in the most distant mountains. After Currier and Ives developed color lithography to a high point, another surge of popular interest almost transformed the print into a national institution. But during the gilded age, with its passion for the ostentatious and the "genteel," and especially with improvements in photography and engraving, this democratic form of art declined in esteem. Importations of prints from Japan accelerated the process; an average American who wanted to decorate a home inexpensively found great pleasure in a Japanese reproduction — pleasure unspoiled by the knowledge that frequently the subject of the picture was prostitution or sex slavery, surrounded in the Far East for the upper classes by the glamour of costume and setting. Only the best of American etchings could meet this competition in the marketplace.

But as technical advances were made in methods of reproduction, as American democracy was again stirred by social conflict, the print, using the term in a generic sense, once more came into its own through a diversity of media : wood cut, linoleum cut, lithography plain and colored, etching, lithotint, and aquatint. Again, as in the uprush of Jacksonian democracy, artists concentrated upon the portrayal, for print purposes, of types, races, industrial, and social scenes. A few titles picked at random illustrate the range of depiction: Early Irrigation Methods in Colorado; New York Harbor, Mine Accident, Machinery, Fish Day, The Flies at Minsky's, Women's House of Detention, In the Park, All Night Mission, Landscape, Dock Scene, Flowers, Unemployed Office, Confusion at 40, Idle Governor. Most of the documents and papers collected by librarians and historians could be illustrated, supplemented, and made living, if not livid, by documentary prints.

To the renewed emphasis on the print, the Federal Art

Project, with its interest in democratic art, gave encouragement and patronage. Reporting on this phase of federal promotion, Holger Cahill unfurled his flag for the print: "As might be expected from its history in this country, the print is extremely sensitive to the contemporary environment, and is an art rich in social content. It would almost be possible to reconstruct a social history of our period from the prints produced on the Federal Art Project. The prints give a fresh and vital interpretation of life as it is lived in America today, and give first evidence of new directions. Every aspect of the American scene is reflected, the cities with their medley of architectural styles, skyscrapers, bridges, interiors, gasoline tanks, factories, subways, railways, airplanes, harbors, farms, cabins, wheat fields, mountains, mines, sports, politics, racial and social types, the whole kaleidoscope of American life." Harry Sternberg's pictures of coal regions were an awful commentary on culture in the American scene.

On the other hand at an American contemporary painting exhibit held at the Whitney Museum and the Museum of Modern Art in New York late in 1937, art, as if accompanying the decline in fervor for the New Deal, seemed to have turned back to conservatism. Discussing this particular collection, Edward Alden Jewell said in his regular column of art criticism in The New York Times: "The Whitney show supplements and reinforces the experience at Carnegie this year, from which one emerged satisfied that the artists of today, considered as an aggregate, have gone in for a wassail of sheer painting, with the world, so to speak, well lost. And again it becomes urgent to add that life has not been betrayed, but rather that a vehement distinction is drawn between the everyday business of living and the holiday transcendence of art."

§

Like the fervor for murals depicting the common life, the ardor for the ballet was a notable feature of these years. Swing had succeeded jazz, it is true; men and women, frantic to jive and shag, were bestowing positive worship upon band and orchestra leaders capable of inciting them to jangling muscular agitation; enormous swing festivals were held in great open spaces such as the beaches near New York; and a language all its own grew up as a means of communion among the itching, shaking, quaking "jitterbugs."

Such an anarchic trend might seem unfriendly to the intellectualized ballet, but in this land of paradoxes the group dance also became a vogue. In essence the ballet was akin to the fresco and the favor granted the one was a favor granted the other form of art. Though solo dancers and rollicking acrobatic musical comediennes still had opportunities for exhibitionism, especially through the patronage of Hollywood, though preciosity, showmanship, and art for art's sake or no art at all, all aloof from social import, still characterized much dancing, five thousand of the ten thousand dance schools in the United States had included the ballet as part of their training by 1937. Ballet groups were organized on college campuses. Museums of art invited the choreographers to dance in their halls amid painting and sculpture. The New School for Social Research in New York added the study of dancing to its economics, psychology, and politics. And the Federal Government gave assistance to ballet groups as a sign of its modernism.

For the ballet, team work was imperative. It was a collectivist undertaking. All its members had important parts to play in interpreting its theme and the monumental character of its art form was claimed to afford the highest creative opportunity to dancers. In the language of a spokesman of the "American Ballet" organized in 1933 by George Balanchine, formerly connected with the Russian ballet, "no slick formulas can be used here. Few, if any, tricks and novelties are of use. Here depth rather than superficiality is sought after; it is a field of research and study rather than one of exploitation and flashy appeal. Here it is the dancer's task to study, sometimes at great personal expense, all that the past has been able to hand down in the way of forms and traditions, and then slowly but bravely to choose, prepare, and build up a personal credo."

For three years the American Ballet functioned under the aegis of the Metropolitan Opera Association, but in the spring of 1938, Balanchine severed official connection on the ground that "the tradition of the ballet at the Metropolitan is bad ballet." Condemning its standards in particulars, he explained that for his first ballet planned for Aïda he had delved into documents in a serious effort to make his troupe's frescoes as lifelike as Egyptian life itself, only to find his audiences, especially the dowagers in them, unappreciative of what he was trying to do. The upshot as far as those audiences were involved was an effort of the Metropolitan to build up its own ballet.

Behind the abrupt change illustrated by Balanchine's action lay a long chain of innovations precursory in nature. Even in Tsarist Russia Michel Fokine, exponent of impressionism in the dance, had recast the decadent ballet of the court system — which Catherine de Medici had fostered centuries ago. By verbal argument and by physical demonstrations he had made the art of the ballet a dramatic play, adjusted to modernism in thought, using action to represent new situations. His fire lighted fires elsewhere as the revolutionary spirit gained momentum. Afterward other imaginative Russians, experimenting with the ballet, tried out the art in the American scene, first at the Metropolitan Opera House. Now Balanchine, an exile from revolutionary Russia, was endeavoring to carry on the ballet in a setting of interests and ideas less devastating than Sovietism to an institution inherited, though with mutations, from the old regime.

By this time the ballet had become domesticated in America in places far beyond the stage of the Opera House, partly under the leadership of Isadora Duncan who had herself revolted against "the dark age" of stage dancing, reverted to the Greek classics for dramatic inspiration, and changed a conventional diversion into an intellectualized medium of interpretation. Drawing inspiration from Pavlowa in part, Ruth St. Denis, Duncan's American successor in the intellectualized dance, acquired a new élan in a spiritual revolt that found satisfaction in the mysteries of the Orient. More quietly but none the less effectively at the Neighborhood Playhouse in New York, Irene and Alice Lewisohn carried on their school of the dance as theater — the essence of the ballet — and to their creative enterprise students and observers had recourse for instruction and inspiration.

For the ballet in Russia music had been a requisite feature; but as this art took firmer root in the United States, it began to separate itself from so much reliance upon accompaniment and to make its form of expression a medium of pure interpretation. Additional impetus was given to the ballet, with or without music, by the visits of Kurt Jooss and his group who performed such vivid compositions as The Green Table, an anti-war ballet, and themes of old Vienna, their home city. From the Orient came other inspirations. Uday Shankar and his Indian mystics with sword dances and other exotic pantomimes suggested methods, if not themes, to Americans. The Japanese dancer, Nimura, in a successful tour, displayed to them feudal patterns, foreign to the American way, and yet suggestive of creative patterns, saying American things.

Under these various influences company after company was organized by Americans to perform the ballet, all breaking with conventions, all attempting to give through the dance impressionistic interpretations of life in action and as idea. Though an old art, old as civilization, group dancing took warmth under the stimulus of the local environment and seized upon its potentialities for commenting on events and civilization. In the golden glow, a comic ballet, directed by Trudi Schoop, made audiences laugh from coast to coast by its composition, Blonde Maris. More sober themes and forms followed, as the economic crisis diminished occasions for laughter, until gravity grew more exigent in the ballet and issues chosen from social and political conflicts became prominent themes for interpretation.

Having departments for the study of the drama, colleges added departments for this branch of drama. Bennington, the newest woman's college in New England, won high distinction for its patronage of the ballet, and festivals were annually held on its campus for the exhibition of the art. Vassar encouraged this dancing as well as experiments in its dramatic workshop, and when the Federal Theater Project had acquired momentum it subsidized the director of the Vassar ballet, Tamiris, whose composition, How Long, Brethren, was a campus sensation carried further afield as part of a program handled under federal patronage. Teachers College at Columbia University and New York University called upon the Bennington dancers for instruction; and on the Pacific coast six or seven colleges in the San Francisco district, not remote from Hollywood, took to this collectivistic dance art really remote from Hollywood's. Under federal auspices a National Youth Administration dance group was organized in San Francisco and its performances were witnessed by large public audiences. In a cycle arranged by Lenore Peters Job, for this group of young persons, a strong democratic motif was chosen, Women Walk Free. A dance unit under the Works Progress Administration was also formed in Chicago to provide expression for artists who had been formerly limited to other art projects.

Women were certainly dancing freely and, as in fiction, they were expressing their intuitive judgments, their comments on life, their criticisms and their dreams without other let and hindrance than the consent of the public to attend their ballets. But this left plenty of room for men in the ballet. Ted Shawn and his companions, all men, devoted themselves to the collective dance form. Mixed groups also worked together to comment on life through the agency of gesture with arms, heads, and feet. Often the touring companies carried no music with them, thus making all attention concentrate on the ideas they were trying to convey. As in the case of the murals, voices of highly irritated people protested at this "arty nonsense," sometimes calling it an "insult to art"; but voices of other people also approved it, as the box offices demonstrated.

Dance theaters invited the public to participate in America's "new art." One was established by the New York Young Men's Hebrew Association and opened with the announcement that "all dancers and groups who feel qualified to give a recital are invited to apply for the use of the recital hall in accordance with conditions which will be sent upon request. The qualifications of each artist will be rigidly scrutinized before the use of the recital hall is granted, since the Dance Theatre considers it almost as important to discourage mediocrity in the dance recital as to encourage first-rate ability."

In keeping with their sensitivity to group rhythm, Negroes searched this medium for an expression of their racial experiences and social views. So the Negro ballet became an interesting feature in the panorama of pantomime in America where the people had a right to say what they wished to say and were permitted to enjoy release. At Hampton Institute, the art was seriously promoted and the Creative Dance Group from that institution gave demonstrations of its talent in New York and other cities, North and South, and at Bryn Mawr. "The itchin' heels" of the race, directed by Negroes familiar with the work at Bennington, now moved together in the ballet to express, through forms technically disciplined, the folk dances and rituals of colored people, their labor themes and spiritual aspirations. Under the guidance of a man from another race, Eugene von Grona, a German, the American Negro Ballet sought to give group dancing a still more theatrical unity. One of its first performances was an interpretation of the story and music from Stravinsky's Fire Bird — a strange undertaking and achievement for artists whose ancestors far from remote had toiled in the cotton fields and rice swamps of the South.

Among the ballet groups which received the highest tributes from watching critics were those for which Hanya Holm, Martha Graham, Tamiris, Doris Humphrey, and Charles Weidman served as choreographers. With remarkable uniformity the themes employed by them were germane to the economic and social vortex. As in the case of artists engaged in public painting and sculpture, they were forced both by their own impulsion and by the exactions of public understanding to identify their work with the experiences of others. Employing modernism in the art form, they also employed modernism in the theme form. Hanya Holm had come from Germany but she developed the ballet at Bennington and in her double experience with life she produced a composition called Trend which ended on the motif of faith in the constructive power of humanity amid decadence and cataclysm. Using music especially scored for this ballet and percussion instruments of contemporary popularity, the ballet leader dealt with the "meaninglessness of forms of living when they are perpetuated as empty shells after their usefulness has been exhausted, and the inevitable resurgence of new forms of vital function out of the inherent powers of re-creation which belong to man by his very nature." In this fashion John Martin, expert on the dance, explained the pantomime to the readers of The New York Times. At Bennington also, Anna Sokolow, trained under the Lewisohns, created a dance, entitled Facade — Esposizione Italiana, an exposition of dictatorial absolutism.

Supported by their own company Doris Humphrey and Charles Weidman traveled far and wide, giving ballet programs to audiences diverse in social composition — in one instance to the annual convention of University Women. Humphrey broke traditions with My Red Fires, among other compositions. Weidman, a humorist in this medium, staged dances for the political skit I'd Rather Be Right and danced The Happy Hypocrite elsewhere. In the summer of 1937, Shawn and his all-men ballet group danced to the accompaniment of the Berkshire Symphony Orchestra at a Massachusetts festival, including in their repertoire a "labor symphony, tribal themes, play, folk and art motifs." As if recognizing the universal in the particular, Agnes de Mille organized an Anglo-American group with interchangeable ballets. As the dance movement reached the ballet stage, the dance film was produced and as a consequence this form of artistry was more widely enjoyed, in fact nationalized in its appeal.

Especially engrossed in the American scene and with leftist sympathies was Martha Graham. Her composition, Primitive Mysteries, had for its basis her reverie about the American aborigines. She also took account of incoming Europeans and of pioneering in Frontier; she was concerned with the current threat of war and its implications in Chronicle; in Theatre Piece she gave her interpretation of the world as it is and in New Dance she offered the world as it might be. Accepting America as her center of thought and action, she proclaimed in American Document her feeling for time, place, perils, and prospects of survival. This is "the most important extended dance created by a living American," said a commentator in The Nation, "and if there has been another in any time more important, there is no record of it."

§

Architecture, like all the other arts, illustrated the conflicts and tendencies of the midpassage. Especially linked to the functional, whatever its vagaries — connected, that is, with industrial processes, office requirements, living, public enterprises, the theater, the museum, the library, and the school — it was associated with the forms and fortunes of all these institutions. In the days of the golden glow, while the boom was on and capitalists were rushing ahead with construction to take up the lag created by the world war, architects were overwhelmed by commissions in private enterprise. Then, after private patronage went into a steep decline and government projects were planned to give employment to technicians, construction companies, and labor, architects were called upon to design structures which were, of necessity, conceived rather in the spirit and terms of the public service.

Projected in the days of brilliant prospects, the mathe-

matical architecture of Radio City, designed by Raymond
Hood, Harvey Corbett, and Associates, swept upward to the
skies amid the detonations and crashes of the economic
depression and worked havoc with real estate interests in all
the neighboring parts of Manhattan. Perhaps it was the last
monumental structure of its kind to be built in America —
an expression of the wealth and power of one man, bent, like
a Pharaoh, upon securing immortality in stone and mass.
To fill its vacant spaces the City of New York was combed
for tenants and special inducements were offered to encourage
them to cancel their existing leases and find shelter in the city
within the city. As the sections were completed, their capa-
cious areas were filled by a multitude of business and social
interests; and the immense pile became more and more the
mechanical center of an urban culture — the center for radio
broadcasting, advertising displays, concerts, moving pictures,
art exhibitions, musical comedies, dancing contests, and
every type of excitement. Its monolithic walls pointing to the
heavens, its gorgeous, if not garish, auditoriums, its gardens,
its open-air pool, its shops, offices, and entertainments all
conspired to draw interests and events within its magic compound.

When the huge thing was nearly completed, indeed while
it was part way up, professional architects engaged in
spirited debates over the merits of its design. Did it have a
"soul"? The question was asked and remained unanswered.
Was it pure mathematics, solid geometry for instance? It
was — almost. As it grew, even its own designers made
changes and were disturbed by uncertainties. One professional architect, commenting in the American Year Book,
called Lee Lawrie's model for the main entrance "noble"
and "beautiful." It fitted, he said, "the ponderous pile
above it, whose very size makes it noble," and it helped
"marvelously to atone for what otherwise might have been
a bit too stark and brutal." In general the words employed
to characterize the pile and its details were "superb,"
"imposing," "startling," "garish," "monstrous," "colossal,"

"enormous project in permanent advertising." No one
seemed to speak of it as "frozen music" or as "Christian."
If anything it was Babylonian in its majesty and pagan in its
spiritual assertions. At all events it was among the wonders
of the world and as symbolic as the removal of Rivera's mural
from its walls.

Two of the world fairs built in this period, in animus at
least, fitted the conception of Radio City. The exposition
called Century of Progress, opened in Chicago in 1933, just as
the economic depression reached its deeps, was an apotheosis
of mechanistic science, machinery, advertising, selling, and
promoting. At first the architectural press spoke of "the
great influence" the exposition would have upon "the art of
the future." Later Harry F. Cunningham, professor in the
University of Nebraska, came to an opposite conclusion in
his annual review for the American Year Book: "The opinion is about unanimous now that the influence will indeed be
great, but it will be a negative influence — a sort of 'Keeley
cure,'" presumably administered to drunkards. If justified,
this prophecy was given little heed, for the enormous exposition, erected for the New York City celebration of 1939, under
the administration of Grover Whalen, the supreme salesman
and advertising agent of the metropolis, displayed in similar,
if more subdued, forms, the fireworks spirit of the great
mechanical show at Chicago. In necessary revolt against the
colossal and obtrusive with which it could not compete, the
administration of the fair for San Francisco in 1939 turned for
designs to the symbolism of old cultures — Spanish-American, Mayan, the exotic, the soft, elusive, pre-machine.

When architects, along with the Lords of Creation, rushed
to Washington in 1933 for financial aid, they encountered
strange pretensions and in some cases a changed spirit. Even
when the real intention of the Government was to invent
"fat contracts" for favorite builders, the ostensible ends and
uses were not private advantage in the form of rents, profits,
and gains by the year but public and collective — official
buildings, housing projects, and resettlement undertakings.

Architects of factories, private office buildings, and apartments had to consider the rental value of every corner, turn, and square foot. Architects employed on public work were not so closely restricted by pecuniary considerations and there acquired, despite red tape, a considerable freedom of imagination and design.

Recognizing at last, if reluctantly, that private enterprise really could not house the bottom third of the nation in habitations worthy of humanity and befitting the resources and skills of the country, politicians and architects set to work on projects for rebuilding large sections of great cities and providing homes for millions of people. So great was the pressure of contractors, building material producers, labor, and social reformers upon governments, federal and local, that a wide area for the exercise of architectural talent in a different mood was now opened out. On public housing projects, to be sure, architects had to watch every detail with a view to cutting costs, but the controlling motive was to give as much light, convenience, and beauty as possible within the limits — not as little as the traffic would bear.

Although with the extension of public functions calling for the coöperation of architects, opportunity was theoretically opened for remarkable patterns of dwellings, postoffices, and other buildings made possible by the new potentialities of materials for supplying light, air, functional utility, and esthetic pleasure, practically the exigencies of politics, the pressures of local customs and building interests, and the demand for speed hampered the spirit of innovation. It was relatively easy for speed of design to match the rush of political pressures, whenever it was a mere matter of collecting stones and mortar, brick and cement, or timbers and nails for the construction of buildings on lines inherited from the centuries; but the problem of expressing beautifully the functional spirit with the wealth of new materials could not be quickly solved at brief conferences among politicians, business men, and architects.

That was a problem calling for great skill and long patience, in combining the sense for comfort, convenience, and beauty with a mastery of the amazing materials which invention and manufacturing enterprise had furnished to the modern market. It was indeed bewildering in its nature. Mere lists of the materials, ranging widely in substance and flexibility, filled bulky volumes, with steel and glass among the simplest and plastics among the most diverse and wonderful. Mastering them and bending them to dreams of use and beauty required time, perseverance, and genius.

Modifying and elaborating the conceptions which Frank Lloyd Wright had worked into architecture, Richard J. Neutra, operating independently and in his own way, emphasized the time element in architectural forms, pointed out the difference between the methods of financing classical building and modern building, and made explicit the consequences of the change from slave to free labor in the construction process — all the while putting up houses, schools, and other buildings as demonstrations of the possibilities of modernism in architecture. In a discussion of the altered psychological attitude in the appreciation of architectural designs, Neutra said: "The most momentous tasks of the architecture of the near future are clearly not individually cherished issues of luxurious waste or extravagant purchasing power of exalted personages, but communal and housing problems. The last 'third of the nation' is being added to the consumers' list. Apart from all considerations of societal morale, the character of industrial production automatically aims in this very direction.

"However, even in the pre-industrial ages down from Swiss lake dwellers to Slovakian and Japanese villagers, building work followed standards, at least regionally accepted as valid. Such standardization was the cause of pleasing and convincing harmonious uniformity in each communal district. In contrast, spasmodic individualism turned our cities into a milling multiform turmoil, where no reliable taste would develop as perhaps it did in classic times, with centuries of frank architectural repetitions and indifference to mere fashion in building.

"Playfulness, biologically legitimate, becomes unbearable license when the Arabian minarets of Hollywood apartment courts rise beside the false shingle roofs of 'English Cottage' real estate offices, and the restaurant structure across the street takes the shape of a brown derby. A responsible new tradition must be built up for the integration of present-day facts and it cannot indulge in the arbitrary picking up of quaint tid-bits. We can follow but one path, that path which true contemporaries of all ages have chosen by necessity: base our creative efforts on the best technical means and standards accessible to us at our historical moment; not live voluntarily below the level of our historical age! Infants appear sweet when they crawl on the floor and use baby talk; adults who rightly adore them look nevertheless awkward and even alarming if they try to imitate them.

"The present stage of technological advance, of informality in living, of growing scarcity of underpaid labor and domestic help, of hygienic cleanliness, of appreciation for natural and open air health factors, of communal responsibility — all this can only be practically and esthetically digested, assimilated, evaluated, integrated, by frank efforts in truly contemporary design, which is witnessed by a growing volume of such building work throughout the world."

How could opportunity be furnished for that kind of architectural designing, provided architects were disposed to shake off tradition and to transform dreams into reality? Evidently alterations would be required in the ideas and methods of productive economy; and the selling pressures behind the amazing new fabrications would have to be channeled into the simpler operations required by the integrated efforts of truly contemporary designing. But this outcome was not altogether fanciful. Colleges and other institutions were beginning to call for competitive designs and permitting the modernists to enter the contests.

So strong became the interest in the functional and the

rational, in the best sense of the terms, that Harvard University made room in its Department of Architecture for Walter Gropius, the former director of the New Bauhaus at Dessau, Germany; and a New Bauhaus was established at Chicago under Laszlo Moholy-Nagly, one of his associates. In these institutions, it was announced, the traditions of the École des Beaux Arts, formerly so dominant in American architectural thought, would be frankly challenged, and the usual professional curriculum supplemented by the study of bio-technics, biology, psychology, philosophy, literature, art, and economics. According to many appearances, collective architecture was to play an increasing role and the profession was to assume heavier responsibilities to the public which it served.

§

Thus within the broad domain of esthetics, amid its orders and confusions, appeared signs of a consolidation in cultural affirmations, as indeed in the social and political world — the signs of a concentration of talents such as had featured the ages called great. Workers in art were reaching for a deeper social rootage. Philosophers and politicians were coming closer to the view that life without art is a poor thing, even impossible, that esthetic forces are among the sustaining energies of every society, large or small.

Nothing save the reconciliation of science and art seemed necessary to complete the tendencies toward such a concentration of talents, and even this inclination was manifest in the land. In his lectures on the fine arts, significantly entitled Scientific Method in Aesthetics, published in 1928, Thomas Munro had made a plea for a philosophy of life embracing both science and art. "Any conception of human behavior," he said, "which omits the writing of poems and systems of philosophy, the playing of violins and the carving of statues, the attempt to appraise these things in logical and intelligible words; or any psychology, which fails to take account of them, is too narrow to deserve the name. It is this narrow-mindedness in some natural scientists which gives continued strength to the mystic and idealist, with their talk of a 'subjective' world, and of realities and values which cannot be reduced to material terms. A philosophy based on such distorted science will rightly appear one-sided and demeaning to those gifted with more sensitive intuitions. While it fails to correct itself, it will be distrusted; it will need supplementing at the hands of religious, metaphysical, and poetic imagination. But a total world-view thus built of maladjusted and conflicting parts can never be fully rational. It remains for science itself to broaden its outlook. Without abandoning its experimental approach, or its conception of the physical basis of things, it can go on to adapt that approach to a more sympathetic study of what Santayana has called their 'ideal fulfillments.' . . .

"That science aims at control of nature, including human nature, does not imply that it must also aim at universal mechanization. For insuring the necessities and comforts of life, large-scale mechanical production is an effective means, and science has therefore developed it. For attaining ideal values, radically different means may be necessary, and intelligent control will then consist in their discovery and application. . . .

"If aesthetics discovers limits beyond which life cannot be made systematic without destroying elements of value within it, then intelligent control will consist in holding system within those limits, and in stimulating variety, surprise, and unanalyzed feeling outside of them. As in government, the attaining of genuine freedom can be the chief aim of scientific planning. Control through applied aesthetics can aim, likewise, not at directing the courses of intuitive impulse, but at freeing it to seek its own paths of adventure and growth, by harmonizing unwanted conflicts, and dissolving the routine mechanical habit."

CHAPTER XV

Science in the Widening Outlook

WORKING in a field of research essentially limitless, taking for their domain all things open to observation and testing, driven by the dynamic of the analytical quest, and claiming liberty of inquiry as an indispensable condition of achievement, scientists, in forging ahead, responded to the impacts and demands of the enveloping world. No more than business enterprise, politics, letters, or art could science operate in a vacuum, be free from the impingement of the forces that buffeted the thought and action of the age. In all times scientists, at least in the course of applications, had sought answers to questions thrust upon them by the given conditions of society, by the state of mankind. At no time had they been born, reared, and sustained in work within the four walls of their research chambers. They had come to their undertakings from various spheres of social life, bringing with them presuppositions and postulates formulated outside or on the periphery of their dominion; and they had lived, while pursuing their investigations, in the lay world with its exigencies, interests, and modes of thinking. The relations of their learning to society were to be called, for want of a more exact word, "organic" in nature, and could not be severed even in theory. Everything that happened, then, during the years of the midpassage, had a bearing, immediate, imminent, or infinitesimal, upon science — upon its substance, its method, and its spirit. Replying to notices of change, while continuing its inquiries, in some measure science itself was transformed.

Proudly but with justification, the Science News Letter could exclaim, with simple, and therefore supreme, eloquence, that the frontier of science "extends from the interior of the atom to the furtherest reaches of astronomical space." Moreover it embraced time, for it took within its view tools of the late ice age unearthed in Colorado, shattered thrones in ancient Guatemala, music and art sixty centuries old in Tepe Gwara, Mesopotamia, "the world's oldest city," and a Babylonian mathematical treatise hitherto ascribed to the Greeks. Beyond human time lay geologic time. In 1937 excavators discovered the fossil bones of a "hippopotamus-sized mammal that lived in Colorado forty-five million years ago when the Rocky Mountains were a flat grassland."

Stirred to practical research by experiences in the economic calamity, scientists sought new substances and contrived new devices for manufacture or for cutting "the costs of labor." When the Government of the United States was wrestling with unemployment, whether technological or not, and seeking the conservation and "wise use" of material resources, scientists were drawn into surveying, planning, and applied action or called upon to consider their relation to all these activities. Finding the potentials of their knowledge and power hampered in application, frontier thinkers among the scientists began to wonder about the forces in civilization that prevented the full fruition of their mastery. As they drove the keen edge of their analysis deeper and deeper into the nature of things, all the while reporting technical findings in a profusion of details, they transformed the "appearance" of "reality" and found themselves plunged into the central problems of philosophy, letters, and art, while making their own contributions to the "understanding" of the issues underlying all thought and conduct.

§

The achievements of the scientific spirit were traceable, in part, in the summaries of events and achievements put forth from year to year by Science Service in Washington. In 1928 it announced the death of Doctor Hideyo Noguchi of the Rockefeller Institute as event, but associated with the occurrence was the memory of the man who had accepted the perils of his exploration into yellow fever — a martyr to research struck down by the disease he was studying. This same year came the report that the Bell Telephone Laboratories had developed a loud speaker with three hundred times the volume of any existing instrument and also the news that photographs had been transmitted by radio across the continent. In 1929 a medley of events hinted at the diversity of scientific interest: the Iowa State College recorded the production of a chemical compound, evolved from corn cobs, three hundred times as sweet as sugar; Yale University broke the ground for a two-million-dollar Institute of Human Relations; Madame Curie subjected herself to gaping crowds in the United States to secure a "gift" of radium; and the success of the new eleven-inch gun "surprise ships" of Germany were proclaimed to the naval world.

In 1930, while President Hoover was confronting the issue of "recovery," scientists went on developing their specialties. Pluto, the ninth planet of the solar system, was discovered. Improved radio beacons promised to make it possible for passenger and bombing planes to land safely in fog or darkness. An "artificial lung" was invented and put immediately into life-saving service. The United States Patent Office issued 49,599 patents and accepted 117,790 applications. Plans were made for the Golden Gate Bridge at San Francisco, with the longest center suspension span in the world.

Astronomers reached the conclusion that interstellar space, instead of being transparent, was filled with diffuse materials absorbing light. A great dispute over the nature of cosmic rays became a sensation; a worker in the California Institute of Technology suggested that possibly the whole universe would in the timeless future fade into a mere nothing save radiation. In 1931 medical research disclosed the fact that a flea could transmit typhus fever, and that new methods had been devised for treating bacteria — an aid in the quest for the causes of diseases. Beside the little was placed the big: the Akron, the largest airship in the world, was commissioned and launched on its fate, to raise new speculations over communications and armaments.

The years immediately following witnessed advances in the conquest of yellow and typhus fevers, the discovery of the neutron, the determination of the properties of "heavy water," record stratosphere flights, the commercial extraction of bromine from sea water, the spanning of the Pacific Ocean by a commercial airline, the unearthing of new evidence confirming the view that human beings lived in America at least ten thousand years before the birth of Christ, the completion of the Boulder Dam, and the shipment of the two-hundred-inch glass disk to Pasadena for polishing, in preparation for the installation of the world's largest telescope. In 1937 "the biggest human skull ever found was unearthed among Indian remains in Virginia. . . . Two new interstellar gases, neutral potassium and calcium, were discovered. . . . Plant cancers, usually caused by germs, were experimentally induced with chemicals. . . . Seventy compounds closely related to life-sustaining chlorophyll were prepared synthetically. . . . The earth's age was checked by studies of radioactive potassium. . . . Scheduled transpacific air travel was established. . . . Two new adrenal gland hormones were discovered. . . . Calcium was successfully used to calm excited patients and banish their hallucinations."

Creative powers within the American civilization were certainly not exhausted. In that judgment of competence represented by Nobel prizes, ten American scientists won first mention amid the golden glow and the shadows: in physics, A. H. Compton, Carl D. Anderson, and Clinton J. Davisson; in chemistry, Irving Langmuir and H. C. Urey; in physiology and medicine, Karl Landsteiner, Thomas H. Morgan, G. R. Minot, W. F. Murphy, and G. H. Whipple. But the list of individuals singled out for honors by no means completed the roll of talents. The truth is that there was an element of injustice in it, as recipients of Nobel prizes were the quickest to concede, for each advance in science rested upon the labors of a multitude and was, in some measure, the next step rendered inevitable by a concentration of efforts on posited problems. Consequently an element of fortuity as well as of genius entered into the "natural selection" of individuals destined to make the culminating experiments and calculations. Nor could it be claimed at the time that the disclosures chosen for decoration were to be the most significant when considered in terms of the morrow. Recognizing the somewhat anonymous nature of the general advance, Science Service discontinued the practice of associating names with specific achievements in its annual summaries.

§

In the main, the advance of invention was along lines of mechanical improvement. No revolutionary device such as the automobile or airplane emerged from laboratory or workshop. Though business men in general hoped that a novel instrument or gadget, to be made by the millions, would lift industry out of the depression, no magician produced it. The opposite occurred: more striking than inventions to occupy labor was the perfection of machines "to save labor." At the end of seven years of depression, it was estimated that the industrial equipment of the country could produce a far larger output than in 1928 with a much smaller force of industrial workers, so rapid was the improvement in the machinery and techniques of production. Incorrigible optimists might continue to say that every new machine "gave employment" and that "technological unemployment" was a fallacy. On the face of things facts did not seem to support the theory. At all events, one effect of the depression was clearly a greater concentration on the cutting of costs by labor-saving devices and an immense display of inventive skills in the creation of automatic machinery.

Although no machine, such as the moving-picture apparatus or the automobile, came out of the laboratory or workshop to furnish employment to millions, many revolutionary devices of the opposite type were in the offing or in process of testing. Month by month the mechanical cotton picker, long an object of inventive inquiry, was improved. If applied to cotton culture along prevailing lines of capitalist enterprise, it would mean the annihilation of the semi-primitive features of that industry, making obsolete the small cotton farm with its mules, plows, and field hands. Efficient application would call for the huge plantation, plowed and tilled by tractors, and cropped by the new machine, producing cotton at a cost so low that American producers could undersell even the drivers of the fellaheen on the banks of the Nile. If this should happen, what would become of the millions of whites and Negroes in the cotton belt already hanging on the weak lifeline of marginal subsistence? Were they to be employed in manufacturing mechanical pickers or to be sustained by a benevolent government? The inventors of the machine themselves trembled at the thought of their Frankenstein monster. And yet to the mechanical picker was added the mechanical "chopper" that might complete the ruin of hand labor on cotton lands, and then a reaper for cutting sugar cane that threatened disaster for more field hands.

Other inventions were less fear-provoking. Devices for the air-conditioning of factories, offices, and houses in summer and winter were brought to a high state of efficiency, with results somewhat incongruous. If members of the privileged class could ride from air-conditioned offices in automobiles to air-conditioned homes, industrial workers and white-collar employees enjoying ideal temperatures in shop and office might find the air of their houses unendurable and even injurious by contrast. Nor did the polar auditoriums of moving-picture palaces in summertime go very well with sweltering streets and stewing slums. Nevertheless, if comfort was one of the marks of civilization, the expansion of air-conditioning devices indicated an upward movement — as had the air-warmed palaces of Roman Britain. Combined with the more efficient placing of machines in plants and the adaptation of lighting facilities to specific processes and operations, they offered ameliorations in the circumstances in which industrial work was carried on. That improvements in the housing of machines might eventually affect the housing of human beings or at least suggest something to industrial managers in search of higher efficiency was among the probabilities of the time.

More relevant than air-conditioning to the problem of human housing was the development of the prefabricated house. Models that seemed to represent the acme of perfection in terms of economy, comfort, and convenience were created by designers. The wide use of special materials, such as rustless steel, chromium, aluminum, and plastics, was forecast by actual demonstrations of potentials. Artistic skill in varying forms and colors within the limits of fixed measurements bourgeoned in laboratory and atelier as functional principles were substituted for loyalty to traditions. Practical tests proved the wastefulness of historic designing, carpentry, and masonry and illustrated the specific economies to be obtained by large-scale production. Yet none of the concerns experimenting in these lines succeeded in the establishment of a vast industry. All were handicapped in their efforts at mass production by vested interests in local real estate, contracting, and building and by encrusted custom. Extraordinary possibilities were certainly embodied in the prefabricated house, but whether private or public enterprise could release them still remained problematical. Did human

powers measure up to undoubted human needs? The answer
to that question did not lie in design or engineering.

Greater success attended the manufacture of a movable
house, known as the automobile trailer. Content at first with
turning out a mere box on wheels to be driven to mountain
or seashore by summer campers, designers and manufacturers
in this field seemed to be catering merely to amusement and
recreation. Indeed this phase of the business remained an
essential interest. But from elementary beginnings, the industry advanced in the direction of technical perfection and
expanding utility. By the use of light metal and plastics, by
the installation in compact form of the latest household devices, manufacturers were able to make trailers that exceeded
at least the comforts of Pullman cars and yet could be sold
at prices within the reach of hundreds of thousands.

Attached to automobiles, these movable homes could be
drawn anywhere and established for any length of time.
Owners with small incomes could spend winters in the South
and summers in the North, perhaps supplementing their resources by local earnings. Municipalities provided trailer
camps and supplied them with water, lighting, and sanitary
facilities. To be sure, problems in health, education, and
social living accompanied the rolling caravans; nevertheless,
within ten years a diversion had developed into a substantial
enterprise, with far-reaching implications. Classical economists had long posited the ideal mobility of capital and labor.
Perhaps one-tenth or more of the population could soon for-
sake landlords and rents, take to wheels and migrate on an
hour's notice.

To that part of the people not moving around in trains,
airplanes, and automobiles, inventors promised to bring motion by the improvement of the television apparatus. From
year to year advances were announced from laboratories at
home and abroad, until by 1938 the main technical problems
had been solved. All that remained was the perfection of
picture reproduction and the design of a machine that could
be sold at a price within the reach of moderate purses. In

1937 a coaxial cable for carrying television messages was put into operation between New York and Philadelphia and television tubes were placed on the market. Already the transmission of photographs and facsimiles had reached a commercial stage and was affecting newspaper reporting and business intercourse. In 1928 photographs were sent successfully from Oakland, California, to Schenectady, New York, by radio. In 1938 such transmissions were everyday affairs.

By that time it was demonstrated that pictures, articles, documents, and even whole pages of newspapers could be sent to all parts of the country, through the air. The hour for a national daily seemed ripe, therefore, since the same general news, features, and advertising could be instantaneously reproduced in every city and the varieties of local news and advertising easily added. Technology had done its work. The adventurous publisher was awaited. Opponents of standardization as an evil in itself seemed on the verge of their last ditch.

Meanwhile the transformation of substances and the creation of new products acquired an accelerated pace. The manufacture of plastics for infinite uses and of artificial fabrics from cellulose released whole industries from dependence on crude raw materials over which economists and diplomats had long been haggling. Cellophane now enveloped almost everything vendible — from plucked chickens to cigars and "boiled shirts"; verily women's dresses were made of it. Synthetic substances hard enough to bore holes in stones or strong enough to resist fire rolled out of laboratories and mills. For innumerable purposes wood and other materials were discarded and bakelite substituted. Synthetic rubber appeared, if in the mirage stage; though the chemical problem was largely solved, costs remained insurmountable for practical purposes. The manufacture of gasoline from coal was demonstrated as a physical fact, but the costs of labor and materials still made it prohibitive as an economic proposition. If silken garments could be devised from "surplus" milk and bath tubs from cornstalks, old channels of world commerce might dry up and the ancient struggle for the ownership of the earth and its resources might be mitigated. When all fantasies were discounted, the theory that there was a natural division of labor among regions and nations according to climate and resources was certainly a distorted view of reality. Another fifty years as revolutionary as the past ten might almost complete the destruction of that picture of the earth and its material determinants on which traditional economies, governments, and national and international policies all rested.

To the drive of universities, special institutes, and commercial laboratories in the industrial sphere was joined a new dynamic — an effort to stimulate agriculture by the scientific use of materials and resources hitherto neglected. Recognizing the difficulties that impeded the flow of agricultural produce to profitable uses, industrial leaders and the managers of experiment stations brought the energies of science to bear on the development of new crops and new commodities to be manufactured from them.

Especially sensational were experiments and achievements in agrobiology, notably "tray agriculture." By successful operations it was established that plants, such as tomato vines, would literally grow like magic in shallow trays of water, if carefully fed exact amounts of balanced chemicals, and would bear so prolifically as to make even "progressive agriculture" look like a primitive art. As usual, claims and counter-claims were filed. O. W. Wilcox, in ABC of Agrobiology, prophesied enormous potentials: perhaps a state no larger than Nebraska could produce all the foodstuffs needed by the 130,000,000 people inhabiting the United States. In the name of practice, farmers called all this forecasting visionary. Nevertheless some of the billions spent on armaments, if directed to agrobiology, might bring ten or fifteen per cent of the dream into execution. Problems were set. Lines of advance were laid down. Even methods for transporting highly perishable milk over long distances and keeping it fresh for weeks were perfected and awaited only the skills of practice to carry them into general use.

§

If proud of their intellectual achievements, many scientists felt humiliated as they observed the various applications of their discoveries and inventions. In the innocent days of the Victorian age, they had shared the impulsive optimism that hailed each device and machine as another sign of "progress." In those times there had been, no doubt, a few critics who scoffed at "cheap and nasty" things made by the machine and bemoaned the huge slums that appeared everywhere in the wake of inventions. Yet in the main, until the disaster of 1929 and the universal preparation for "the next war," scientists could shout down the pessimists. They could point to general gains, setting credits against debits. When such a balance sheet proved ineffective in curbing criticism, they could take refuge in the contention that bigger and better things were really ahead despite "temporary" or "transitional" shortcomings. Or they could lay the blame for the abuse of science and invention on human nature, disclaim their own responsibility, and refuse to debate the merits of progress in bombing planes for war and in poison gas for industrial conflicts. But after ten years of depression and disintegration, in which both the intellectual methods and material achievements of science were heavily involved, the temperature of optimism fell and the delights of willful escape diminished.

In a strict sense, no doubt, scientists had an alibi. The nature of their work called for the spirit of absolute neutrality in the matter of arguments over uses and values. The chemist, for example, as chemist, was not at all concerned during any of his chemical experiments as to whether his discovery was to be employed in healing the sick or blowing bank safes. His business, as chemist, was to find out by analysis the nature, composition, and combinations of substances. To that quest the possible utilization of his findings was irrelevant and preoccupation with human issues would have been disconcerting to his scientific investigation. Moreover there was nothing whatever in the knowledge or methods of science that enabled scientists to speak with any special authority on the subject of uses and values. Nothing in the explorations of chemistry or physics dictated their human applications. In the presence of that issue, scientists, however profound their learning in physics or chemistry, had to rely upon morals, mores, and ethical judgments common to the general mass of the people. The Nobel prize winner might differ from the garage mechanic over the desirability of a war on Japan, let us say, but no laboratory experiments enabled him to prove that his verdict was "better" or more in accord with "truth." A master of physics, engaged in expounding economics, was not necessarily wiser than a labor organizer or a more perspicacious interpreter of history than a poet.

Despite the spirit of neutrality reigning within their circle, scientists did not work in a void. Among the problems that attracted their attention, some carried more unneutral implications than others. In the domain of physiology and medicine, including their physical and chemical aspects, positive problems of human welfare could scarcely be escaped, save in the field of pure research. The state of human beings suffering from typhus or yellow fever, for instance, had to be examined and one evident part of inquiry along such lines was a comparison with, or a creation of, a different state, known as health or well-being. A particular scientist might be interested in extending the ravages of typhus for use in "the coming war," but this was not the main problem suggested in practice by investigations of its nature.

The spirit of scientists was also activist. For the prosecution of researches, funds and laboratories were necessary. Stoppages in income for dwellers in ivory towers arrested interest and certainly awakened some curiosity in respect of causes. Outside the chambers of pure research were the practitioners of science — engineers, industrial chemists, the huge body of technologists. Their possibilities of activism, to say nothing of a living, depended upon the rate and curve of industrial production. When their beautiful machines slowed down or came to a dead stop they were inclined to ask for a reason. The question might not be scientific in form, but it was a "natural" one. Besides facing problems of operation blocked by business recession, technologists faced problems of increasing productivity, of putting new inventions and discoveries into use. Why make them, only to have them perish? In reality, therefore, it was impossible to insulate scientists and their researches completely from life and work in general.

§

How can the magnificent discoveries of science be put to the most efficient and most desirable human uses? The query was not new but the intensity of interest now engendered in the problem gave promise of exploration and action. Among physicians, recognition of the challenge led to searches for answers and for ways and means of practice. After all, doctors from time immemorial had come into the closest contact with humanity and its needs. An engineer making cigarettes in Durham, North Carolina, saw few of his "ultimate consumers" and thought little about them, but all practicing physicians, seeing their patients, had to consider their science in terms of its everpresent human outcomes. Furthermore professional ethics, as theory at least, forbade them to apply purely economic canons to relationships with patients and to turn the helpless out of doors in the manner of the managing technician under the necessities of a business slump. Doctors were bound by a historic oath and a system of moral conduct supposed to control the application of their knowledge. Perhaps, having taken over the healing arts of primitive women and ancient midwives, modern physicians, men as well as women, had inherited some of the sacrificial spirit displayed by mothers from time immemorial.

Whatever the sources of their inspiration, within the science or outside, physicians took leadership in the quest for the utmost beneficial use of discoveries and inventions in their domain. In 1927, when the golden glow was almost at its height, the Committee on the Costs of Medical Care was organized under the direction of Dr. Ray Lyman Wilbur, funds amounting to more than a million dollars were granted by foundations, and an investigation was begun into every nook and cranny of public and private health. The general field was broken down into minute subdivisions and competent specialists were engaged to explore them without fear or favor. At the end of five years the Committee produced the most comprehensive survey of illness and of facilities for coping with it ever made in the United States — indeed a monument in the long history of medicine. Fact statements, painstaking and precise, were supplemented by conclusions with reference to proposed actions in perfecting medical services throughout the country. Although there was some dissent in the Committee, the majority agreed upon recommendations which were called, and rightly, "revolutionary" for the United States, in their demands and implications.

The conclusions so startling to Americans unfamiliar with health insurance in Great Britain and Europe could be summarized under five heads. Medical services should be grouped around hospitals, that is, community institutions. Public and private health services should be made "available to the entire population according to its needs." The costs of medical services should be put on a group-payment basis through insurance, taxation, or both. The function of studying, evaluating, and coördinating medical services belongs to every state and community; for the policy of haphazard drift must be substituted the policy of collective planning and action. After a criticism of medical education so exclusively concentrated on scientific techniques, so neglectful of the social aspects of costs and practice came the fifth conclusion: medical education should be broadened by laying stress upon the prevention of illness and upon the social

obligations of the profession. Sustained by an immense array
of special studies, statistics, and expert testimony, the final
report of the Committee in 1932 shook physicians in general,
and laymen as well, out of their complacency and started a
nation-wide discussion of sickness and healing that seemed
to gather momentum as time passed.

Support for the collective action suggested by the Committee was augmented by subsequent studies. For instance,
a house-to-house inquiry conducted by the Federal Public
Health Service in the winter of 1935–36 brought out the
generalization that, on an average winter day, six million
men, women, and children were unable to work, attend
school, or pursue other usual activities on account of illness,
injury, or gross physical impairment resulting from disease
or accident. Forty-two per cent of these unfortunates were
afflicted with chronic diseases. The amount of illness in the
United States was appalling in its magnitude.

This illness, moreover, bore a relation to economic status.
By a wide sampling study, the Service reached the verdict
that about sixty-five per cent of the sick persons belonged to
families with an annual income of less than $1500, and that
eighty per cent were in families having incomes below $2000.
The duration of illness was longer in the low-income group
and the extent of medical services received by victims of illness varied roughly according to income schedules. The
illusion that "hospitals were open to everyone" was completely dispelled by the realities of the situation: over sixty-
five million people lived in communities of ten thousand or
less, or in rural areas, with no immediate hospital facilities,
and eighteen million lived in counties where there were no
hospitals of any kind. On the one side, millions of people
sick. On the other side, facilities available, doctors and
nurses idle for lack of paying clients.

Such were indubitable facts, and yet they did not dictate
an unequivocal policy of social or public medicine. As in all
debates over policy to be adopted, the outcome depended on
preliminary assumptions or major premises, involving an

interpretation of civilization and its course. Since industry, society, and general welfare depended upon sound bodies and sound minds, from that point of view the United States presented alarming aspects. On this matter doctors agreed. Moreover civilization depended, if to an immeasurable extent, upon individual intelligence and the sense of personal responsibility. On this truth too there was a general agreement. It was likewise established that a certain correlation existed between income and illness.

But at this point opinion broke into factionalism. Critics of social medicine presented itemized expenditures by the very people who lacked appropriate medical and dental aid : millions for patent medicines, millions for radios, millions for movies, millions for lipsticks and other cosmetics, millions for gin that gave drinkers stomach disorders, millions for numbers rackets, millions for prize fight tickets, millions for sweepstakes and race-track gambling. From such facts it was reasoned that people who would rather lose money on numbers rackets than spend it for medical services deserved slight consideration at the hands of government and no consideration at the hands of taxpayers asked to meet the medical bills. Why should radios be bought out of meager incomes and medical service be supplied free or below cost ?

If the conventions of the American Medical Association faithfully represented its membership, doctors were on the whole against any material changes in historic practices. At its assembly in 1934 the Association strongly condemned both voluntary and compulsory health insurance. Physicians who organized or served voluntary associations for the maintenance of medical services on the basis of fixed annual or monthly fees from the members were assailed for "unethical and unprofessional conduct" and occasionally haled into court under statutes put on the law books in the name and interest of the medical profession.

Yet as the agitation proceeded, there appeared to be a decided increase in the number of physicians eager to see the fullest possible use of their science and sympathetic with the collective approach to the solution of the problem. At the convention of the American Medical Association in 1937 the New York delegation presented a set of resolutions indicating that the profession in the Empire state was moving rapidly in the direction of what was loosely called "social medicine." The adoption of the resolutions, materially altered by amendments though they were, betrayed at least some drift in medical thought since the declaration of positive immobility three years before. About the same time the opening of a clinic by the Group Health Association in Washington to a large number of federal employees raised the issue of associational medicine in the very center of government circles and precipitated a legal contest as well as an emotional outburst.

The literature on social medicine produced during the ten years' debate contained all the familiar phrases and assumptions underlying the contemporary discussion of economics: individualism and communism, self-help and community responsibility, American way and progress, greatest country in the world, unfinished business, planning and autonomism. Practice displayed similar contradictions: private hospitals and public hospitals, high charges and charity, public health services in bewildering variety and private practice in the old style, group doctors and individual doctors, doctors concentrating on the main chance and doctors generously giving time and money to social medicine, collectivism emergent in public agencies and associational clinics, and rugged individualism good and bad.

By the year 1938 the drift of discussion and practice had deposited in the thought of the country the idea of compulsory health insurance for the lower income groups, along the lines of British legislation. Bills were drafted and introduced. Debate was started. If precedent in the rise and development of legislative action in other matters still had force, then the United States was on the way to supplementing the old practices by state medicine of some type, added to, rather than completely supplanting, the historic freedom of private practice. A Congress that had hesitated to attack the evils

of quack remedies and their carriers of advertising would
doubtless balk at enacting a national health law, but a powerful movement of thought and energies was headed in the
direction of a social medicine that would give fuller release to
the dammed-up and frustrated forces of medical science,
curative and preventive. At the New York State Constitutional Convention during the summer of 1938 a proposal
authorizing the legislature to establish health insurance was
approved, submitted to the voters, and adopted.

§

Like scientists engaged in medical practice, engineers were
concerned with applications bearing directly on human
interests and conduct. It was true that they did not always
have before them as an immediate end the specific and somewhat determinable welfare of determinate individuals; nevertheless their researches and applications were constantly
directed, more or less, to human uses, constructive or destructive. They were not, however, complete masters in their own
household. If a corporation raised money by selling stock to
the public and ordered an engineer to build and operate a
plant that merely duplicated an existing plant for the output
of which no market could be obtained, it was ostensibly the
engineer's business to build and operate the superfluous
establishment, not to reason why or why not. If a lumber
company ordered whole counties denuded of timber and left
barren as eroding wreckage, it was apparently the engineer's
function to denude and let nature take her course. If politicians decided upon a foreign war, for whatever reason
assigned, engineers were expected to take orders, produce,
and apply engines, chemicals, and gases ever more frightful
and destructive. Neither individual welfare nor social welfare in the large was the controlling conception in the
engineering profession as such. As long as its members found
employment, in the bright days of alleged general prosperity
under the auspices of President Coolidge, repairing ravages of

the world war, overcoming the housing shortage, and building plants to meet demands created in part by copious lending to impecunious foreign borrowers, members of the profession could look upon their work and pronounce it good.

Yet, from older days in the rise of engineering, some engineers, such as Nikola Tesla and Charles P. Steinmetz, often called dreamers, had been impressed by the contrasts between engineering knowledge of matter and force and engineering practice considered in terms of human welfare; between potentials and achievements; between operating postulates and possible postulates. During the closing years of the golden glow, under the leadership of Herbert Hoover as Secretary of Commerce, engineers had piled up mountainous evidence of waste in designs, in production, in the use of materials in private industries; and the existence of even greater wastes had been noted in discreet hints. Out of their inquiries had come proposals and, to some extent, actions coöperative in nature, under the auspices of the Federal Government, with the special aid of the Bureau of Standards in Washington.

By that time the "science of management," associated with the name of Frederick Winslow Taylor, had broadened its interest beyond the immediate relations of industrial workers to materials, beyond the plant itself, and was taking into account various elements of industry, education, and social living that made for the efficiency and, correlatively, for the happiness and welfare of workers outside the shop. Speaking in 1931 at a Senate hearing on the establishment of an economic council, the director of the Taylor Society, H. S. Person, traced the growth of managerial interest and added: "I think I perceive, in the history of the extension of this principle and technique of control in ever wider areas of managerial responsibility, the compulsion, in order to conserve stabilization accomplished in any lesser area, to reach out and stabilize the influencing environment."

Shortly after the publication of a symposium on civilization, Whither Mankind, in 1928, a group of prominent engineers in New York City, taking the volume as a kind of provocation to their profession, issued an answer formulated by leaders in science and technology, entitled Toward Civilization. In their own volume, to use the language of the editor, technicians "recognize their responsibility for the future of humanity, see in the materials at hand the promise of great advances for mankind, and are already seriously considering the drift of things and the nature of the readjustments necessary for a better future." Somewhat later the American Engineering Council created a committee "on the balance of economic forces," with Ralph E. Flanders, former president of the National Machine Tool Builders' Association, as chairman, and the committee went into complex problems of balancing technology in operation against consumer requirements, controlling money and credit in relation to industrial processes, increasing human well-being through progress in industry, and adapting public works to public needs.

While the economic crisis was at its crest in 1933, a committee selected by the Society of Industrial Engineers submitted a report on the Economic Significance of Technological Progress, together with a memorandum on Technocracy which had made such a sensation during preceding months. Among other things, the committee concluded: "The advent of the new mode of production alters the position of labor and management in industry. Productivity of labor is determined more and more by the nature of technological process and equipment employed and less by physical strength and trade skill. Hence, compensation for work stands in no relation to old piece rates and time rates. Failure to recognize this fact has resulted in the increasing intensification of work and in deterioration of earning capacity. . . . We are suffering not from technological unemployment, but from the unemployment of technology. The inadequate purchasing capacity of the majority of the population restricts the market necessary for the full utilization of the existing means of production. Unregulated competition led to the duplication of productive capacities of the past."

Inquiries conducted by engineering committees were supplemented by individual investigations into the reasons for the antithesis between technology half-defeated and technology employed at high power. For meetings of societies and for technical journals, specialists engaged in these investigations, for example, Walter Rautenstrauch, Bassett Jones, David Cushman Coyle, and Walter Polakov, prepared statistics, graphs, and demonstrations bearing on the problem of bringing technical resources into the fullest possible use. By the papers and books on such widening inquiries vigorous controversies were started and strong currents of opinion bearing on the issue were set in motion. When in 1938 the National Economic and Social Planning Association surveyed courses on economic and social planning, economic policy, industrial policy, resources planning, and community planning offered by American institutions of learning, it discovered that a widely scattered, apparently spontaneous, and yet fairly general, concern with the utilization and rationalization of material and technical resources had arisen in these intellectual centers of the nation.

In one field, that of public works and conservation, the engineers of the period made substantial contributions to thought about the underlying purposes of technology and the fuller use of its potentials, though the initiative seldom came from purely engineering circles. The source of inspiration was rather that small group of persons within the Roosevelt administration who were considering the breakdown in economy in terms of national areas and long-time planning. At all events, under the auspices of the National Planning Board, later called the National Resources Board, and other agencies of the Federal Government, numerous special studies were made which increased the public knowledge of natural resources, called attention to the science of efficient use, and proposed the integration of public works on a large scale. The conservation of natural resources was, of course, an established principle, but features of novelty appeared in the efforts to obtain complete pictures of the total situation, to discern the direction of tendencies, and to devise the positive measures of constructive action required by the all-round application of engineering rationality. While it could not be correctly said that perfection was attained in the conclusions based on such surveys, the researches and formulations marked a widening of engineering thought far beyond the borders of planning and operating individual plants — toward the periphery of technical potentials.

Among the documents so prepared were reports on the watershed of the Mississippi River; on maladjustments in the use of land resources in the United States; on forest resources, problems, and policy; on soil erosion, soil conservation, and flood control; on wind erosion areas and control practices; on the use of "little waters" in relation to the land; and on public works planning. Another engineering inquiry was devoted to the study of the influence of inventions on the development of society, the cultural readjustments required by technological change, and the probable effects of new industrial devices already in process of creation. In response to a request from President Roosevelt a group of distinguished scientists, including Karl Compton of the Massachusetts Institute of Technology and Robert A. Millikan of the California Institute, presented to the country an imposing list of technical problems awaiting solution and the collateral issues involved in the human uses of material and scientific resources. Besides presenting an eloquent essay on the contributions of science to civilization, their reports went into specifications respecting latent powers awaiting release and achievements yet to be accomplished.

Both the findings and the recommendations of the federal committees and agencies revealed a broad range of interest. Nothing pertinent to the problems set was too small for examination. No measure of national policy indicated by engineering rationality was too large for exploration and conclusion. Called upon to study soil conservation, for example, the National Resources Committee went into microscopic details. On the basis of minute investigations it estimated that the annual soil loss included approximately sixteen million tons of nitrogen, thirty-six million tons of potash, fifty-three million tons of calcium, sixteen million tons of magnesium, and three hundred twenty-two million tons of organic materials. It found that crops and pastures consumed from one-fourth to one-half of the total amount and that the remainder was lost by erosion. Patient observation at one point in the state of New York showed that the run-off of rain water from a given area of corn land was nearly seven times as much as the run-off from the same area of meadow land. Ingenious calculations of rainfall in different parts of the country over a period of centuries revealed variations from year to year and cycle to cycle, but relatively slight changes in the long trends. On the basis of these and similar studies, federal authorities worked out conservation and flood-control legislation involving nation-wide coöperation among federal, state, and local agencies and individual farmers and concerns. New statutes were placed on the books and hard work was begun without the sound of drums and trumpets, those boisterous instruments deemed indispensable by politicians and warriors.

Another indication of the tendencies in technical thinking was the six-year plan for public works published by the National Resources Committee in 1936. Originally, public works, such as river and harbor improvements, had been generally regarded as the rightful spoils of politics. Engineers had planned and directed the execution of particular projects as ordered by Congress in "pork barrel" legislation. Somewhat later came the idea that public undertakings should be used to provide work for idle contractors and unemployed workmen in times of business depression — "to take up the slack." Through a combination of petty politics, local greed, and the frustrations of crisis, many works of undoubted utility had been constructed. At the same time millions of dollars had been wasted, despite engineering excellence in detail, and the relation of such works to the total economy of land, forests, and water had been neglected.

This dark jungle of engineering performances the Resources Committee illuminated by inquiry and exploratory thought. Besides making recommendations on the construction of dams, irrigation plants, levees, and other control projects, it proposed a coördination of hitherto unrelated policies and projects with reference to "the promotion of public safety, public health, the public convenience and comfort, and the establishment of high living standards." Coming down to blueprints, it worked out precise methods of procedure pertaining to public and private interests and definite calculations respecting the apportionment of costs with relevance to general and local benefits.

The application of the engineering mind to the study and solution of problems involving the beneficial use of technology on a national scale, freed from immediate time and market limitations, was accompanied by an increase in the number of engineers employed on public projects. Although government services had always attracted engineers, especially civil and military engineers, the major portion of technical graduates had gone into private enterprise. The largest pecuniary rewards lay in that division of economy. Only there could an engineer hope to rise, perhaps through the channel of management or promotion, into the exclusive circle of the high income recipients. There, too, was greater freedom from red tape.

Lured by dazzling prizes, engineers became consultants for great corporations and undertook to defend specific economic policies as well as purely engineering projects. So strong had this tendency become that it was often difficult for a federal, state, or municipal agency to find competent technicians who could hold a fair balance between public and private interests. Distinguished professors in engineering schools steadily supplemented their salaries by serving private concerns and were often accounted valuable "educators" in proportion to the magnificence of their clients. Given the material circumstances, this development had the characteristics of inevitability.

But during the years that followed the crash of 1929, graduates of engineering schools tramped city streets and rural roads with the proletariat looking for work. In the overwhelming rush of business enterprise upon the Federal Government for assistance, the "need for public works to give employment" was constantly emphasized by leaders in private enterprise — by contractors, cement makers, and capitalists who found the investment opportunities of business closing rather than opening. On this occasion they were stayed by no goblin of communism or collectivism. So appropriations for public works multiplied. Scientific planning for forestry, land use, water control, highway construction, and power developments eventuated in actions that employed thousands of engineers in the public service. The regulation of utilities and other forms of private enterprise called for engineering competence on the government side as well as the private side.

In this changing scene, engineers skilled in the "public relations" of their profession came into demand. And no scientific mind could be long at work in the middle ground between collectivism and individualism without acquiring characteristics foreign to the consultant of the old type who accepted the formulas of classical economics as akin to, if not identical with, the formulas of physics or mathematics. Into the professional societies now filtered a growing number of engineers employed in the public service or in closer contact with that service and its requirements than the old-style members. Technical institutes took note of emerging educational requirements and courses in social economy edged their way into schedules loaded with physics, chemistry, calculus, and bacteriology. How far the trend would go could not be discovered by consulting a table of logarithms, but the direction was clear enough.

In the long run, the explorations of individual engineers and the great studies of land, water, and other resources in relation to beneficial uses would presumably influence all technical thought. The elements of physics and mathematics

remained the same. Chemical combinations remained unchanged. But the first-hand contacts of engineering minds
with nation-wide efforts to control materials and forces for
humane ends, to make wholesale adjustments to the inexorable ways of nature, to provide employment for capital and
labor, to bring governments, corporations, and individuals
into effective combinations for the general welfare — all
served to push out the borders of scientific thought. Fresh
problems of research and application for physicists, chemists,
biologists, and engineers were formulated, suggesting fruit-
ful projects of inquiry along functional lines. Whether the
mandate of the times and circumstances was considered as a
mere matter of creating employment for members of the
profession or a mighty call for the full use of technological
potentials, germinal ideas exfoliated in scientific thought,
even in the laboratory and the drafting room.

Influences were reciprocal. Engineering surveys and inventions crashed against government, business, and historic
practices. A political economy that was still based upon the
handicraft philosophy of Adam Smith, despite all trimmings,
qualifications, and adaptations, was badly shaken by engineering assertions and achievements. Committed to a respect
for facts and to the use of the rational method in all procedures, the very spirit of technology ran counter to the
myths, symbols, and habitual assumptions so regnant in the
domain of law, politics, and economic speculation. An
engine constructed according to physical theory either
worked or it did not work. If it did not, the theory was
revised or the engine was scrapped as a failure, for flat contradictions between theory and practice were unendurable
in the scientific world. When Harold Loeb and his engineering associates indicated by the calculations summarized in
The Chart of Plenty that the production of wealth, as a
physical fact, could be immensely increased in the United
States by applied engineering rationality, perhaps doubled,
politicians and economists showed signs of cutting loose from
the theory that capitalism was automatically efficient and of

inquiring into the problem of bringing realities more in line with potentials.

Judging by experience it seemed probable that the growing recognition of the fructifying relations between science and culture in general would prove to be correlatively stimulating. For example, it had been forcefully demonstrated that war and preparations for war had called forth new scientific energies in response to different demands and had promoted scientific knowledge and achievements. Again, on the other side, the contrivance of new building materials by engineers had precipitated a reconsideration of acquired architectural theories. Could not national demands in the interests of human welfare as great as those expressed in war also act as a persuasive incitement to scientific exploration on a scale more vast than ever experienced? Inasmuch as science, long confined largely to the study of form or matter and force or energy, was now reaching out more actively into the study of function with the aid of a different logic and mathematics, the probability of an affirmative answer was all the more promising.

§

At all events, facing, like capitalists with idle plants and industrial workers without employment, the undeniable fact of tremendous powers going to waste, enormous resources of nature and skill unapplied, with scarcity and suffering oppressing the nation, scientists and engineers not entirely subdued to laboratory routine saw in the crisis a summons to action akin to that prevailing in the medical profession. That their interest might diminish with another outburst of prosperity was possible; that it would completely disappear was improbable, for economists were giving the antithesis between performance and potential an increasing consideration. For instance, meticulous studies carried out by the Brookings Institution, published in America's Capacity to Produce, indicated to popular surprise that even in the years of alleged prosperity machine industry had been running far below its capacity considered in narrow terms and, despite criticisms directed against it, the essential proposition of the Brookings report was incontrovertible.

Translating its findings into monetary terms, the Brookings Institution estimated that "this increased productivity would have approximated fifteen billion dollars. Such an increase in the national income would have permitted enlarging the budgets of fifteen million families to the extent of $1000 each, adding goods and services to an amount of $765 (on a 1929 price level) to every family having an income of $2500 or less in that year, producing $608 worth of additional well-being for every family up to the $5000 level, raising the incomes of 16.4 million families whose incomes were less than $2000 up to that level, increasing all family incomes below the $3500 level, by forty-two per cent, adding $545 to the income of every family of two or more persons, or giving $125 to every man, woman and child in the country." To this statistical presentation of unrealized powers, the Brookings Institution attached a document on America's Capacity to Consume which indicated the extent of the human needs unfilled by applied science and industry. About one-fifth of the families in 1929, the great season of prosperity, had incomes of less than $1000 a year, while "nearly twenty million families, or seventy-one per cent, had incomes less than $2500."

Such reports on frustration increased the skepticism already entertained by inquiring scientists of high standing in their special fields. In dedicating a new building of the Mellon Institute in 1937, Irving Langmuir could say in the customary language of optimism : "Our greatest hope for future well-being and prosperity lies in further applications of science." But Alexis Carrel, in his book on Man, the Unknown, fairly cried out in the spirit of criticism : "The enormous advance gained by the sciences of inanimate matter over those of living things is one of the greatest catastrophes ever suffered by humanity. The environment born of our intelligence and our inventions is adjusted neither to our stature nor to our shape. . . . The groups and the nations in which industrial civilization has attained its highest development are precisely those which are becoming weaker and whose return to barbarism is the most rapid. But they do not realize it. They are without protection against the hostile surroundings that science has built about them." Nor could Raymond Fosdick, one of the presiding geniuses of the Rockefeller group that had done so much for natural science, enjoy the comfort of an unshakeable faith; so he posed the issue: "Is man to be the master of the civilization he has created or is he to be its victim? . . . Will this intricate machinery which he has built up and this vast body of knowledge which he has appropriated be the servant of the race, or will it be a Frankenstein monster that will slay its own maker?"

While the resounding threats of Fascism were echoing across the ocean, Edwin Grant Conklin, distinguished for his achievements in biology, as president of the American Association for the Advancement of Science in 1937, chose to discuss the theme, Science and Ethics. He conceded that many scientific specialists dismissed ethics as a matter of no concern to them, and then reminded his colleagues that "free thought, free speech and free criticism are the life of science"; that "these freedoms are stifled in certain great nations 'with a cruelty more intense than anything western civilization has known in four hundred years.'" What have scientists done to win and maintain these liberties? "In spite of a few notable exceptions," Conklin answered, "it must be confessed that scientists did not win the freedom which they have generally enjoyed, and they have not been conspicuous in defending this freedom when it has been threatened." Asserting that every program for human welfare of necessity includes both science and ethics, Conklin pleaded for their union in scientific thought and action. And he made an emphatic appeal for the cause of freedom and responsibility. "We, who are the inheritors of the tradition of liberty of thought, speech, and press, and who believe that freedom and responsibility are essential to all progress, should use our utmost influence to see that intellectual freedom shall not perish from the earth." In this spirit the Association established a series of conferences on Science and Society devoted to exploring the relations of scientific knowledge and activities to the problems and interests of humanity.

Looking upon technology from the outside and yet a careful student of its social repercussions, Lewis Mumford explored in many directions the cultural roots and implications of scientific work. After patient and penetrating researches in history and practice, he set forth his conclusions in two large volumes: Technics and Civilization, published in 1934, and The Culture of Cities, in 1938. Running down through long centuries, he traced the conditions of mind and economy favorable to science and technology and then demonstrated the reciprocal influences of the two worlds in a manner that belied the isolation of science and scientists from cultural forces and obligations. As to the future, it offered, Mumford thought, tensions and dilemmas rather than soothing confidence: "In the development of the neutral valueless world of science, and in the advance of the adaptive, instrumental functions of the machine, we have left to the untutored egoisms of mankind the control of the gigantic powers and engines technics has conjured into existence. In advancing too swiftly and heedlessly along the line of mechanical improvement we have failed to assimilate the machine and to co-ordinate it with human capacities and human needs; and by our social backwardness and our blind confidence that problems occasioned by the machine could be solved purely by mechanical means, we have outreached ourselves. When one subtracts from the manifest blessings of the machine the entire amount of energy and mind and time and resources devoted to the preparation for war — to say nothing of the residual burdens of past wars — one realizes the net gain is dismayingly small, and with the advance of still more efficient means of inflicting death is becoming steadily smaller."

Out of his search for answers to the questions in his mind, Mumford came to this conclusion : "We are now entering a phase of dissociation between capitalism and technics; and we begin to see with Thorstein Veblen that their respective interests, so far from being identical, are often at war, and that the human gains of technics have been forfeited by perversion in the interests of pecuniary economy." Instead of ascribing, in the popular style, all the special advances in productivity to capitalism, Mumford insisted that many of those gains were "in reality due to quite different agents — collective thought, coöperative action, and the general habits of order — virtues that have no necessary connection with capitalistic enterprise." Without surrendering to the cheerful dream that Nature or God or the Machine would automatically open paths out of contemporary frustrations, Mumford detected signs that the organic, the ethical, and the esthetic were beginning to dominate the material and forecast a wide reconstruction, rural and urban, which would unite with the efficiency of the mechanical industry the excellence and the delight of wholesome living and working.

§

Notwithstanding the wealth of volumes, journals, reports, and technical papers produced in the course of scientific research, relatively little material was offered pertaining to the nature of scientific methods and thought in relation to other forms of activity and speculation. In accordance with the mandates of their interest, scientists usually concentrated upon a firmer and finer analysis of things called matter and force. If the proceedings of the several scientific societies formed any basis of judgment, the minutiae of specific knowledge increased almost in a geometrical ratio. Nothing organic or inorganic seemed to be left untouched, as instruments for analysis, observation, and measurement were multiplied and refined. "Fields" regarded as highly specialized fifteen or twenty years previously were broken into smaller areas, as

unfolding scientific inquiry marked off realms yet uncon-
quered. Although for a time the economic depression diminished the funds available for research and placed some check
on the flow of new workers into the domain of science, it
placed no discernible impediment in the way of scientific zeal
or the output of reports. For that situation, democratic
liberty was responsible in part.

Here and there, however, in the publications which
emerged from the scientific world were testaments to shifting
interest and suggestions of new affirmations akin to those
appearing in letters, esthetics, and social thought. Among
the signs of the time was the evident decline of concern with
the kind of metaphysical physics which Jeans, Eddington,
and Whitehead had supplied from England and Robert
Millikan had popularized in the United States during the
cheerful days of prosperity. At all events, no scientists
now wrote big books in their vein or captivated popular
fancies with similar assumptions. This is not to say that
their works left no indelible impressions on forms of scientific
and speculative thought; but rather that something had
happened as the edge of analysis was applied to the higher
reports on the nature of nature.

Among scientists as well as laymen developed a suspicion,
if nothing more, that these physicists, masterful in their own
domains, had read their own theological predilections into
the appearances of the realities with which they dealt. The
suspicion was deepened when theologians and even evangel-
ists could seize upon the indeterminism of "the new physics"
and employ it in fervid arguments for freedom of the will,
if not for the whole scheme of innocence, fall, and redemption.
To be sure, Jeans, Eddington, Whitehead, and Millikan were
not responsible for the uses made of their declarations, but
their successors in physics seemed to grow more cautious.
Perhaps psychological inquiries into epistemology, that is,
the relation of the knower to the things presumably described, suggested warnings if not open skepticism.

Apart from metaphysical conceptions applied to it, the

work of physicists exerted a profound and continuing influence on all thought, philosophical and social. "It is, it appears, characteristic of the past thirty years or more," explained Alfred Cohn, in his work cited below, "that, in an unusual degree, a growing knowledge has instilled the belief, founded on deeper insight into natural processes than was possible to Locke and his successors, that there exists a vast difference between appearance and reality. I refer, of course, to the fact that atoms, as we are told, and consequently all matter, which they compose, consists to a small extent only of so-called 'solid' substance; this 'too, too solid flesh' is, in fact, far from being as solid as has been supposed. The appearance of things is indeed vastly different from reality. The realization of this discovery has had, as one can easily be persuaded, far-reaching consequences, both in physical theory and in the philosophy which reviews these theories and their underlying data critically."

Just what picture of nature scientists would finally acclaim, with unanimity, as having appearance corresponding to the reality, however, remained uncertain. At one period in the nineteenth century they had employed the imagery of the mechanical model: the physical world was a mechanism and it could be described in the non-mathematical language employed, for instance, in a simple description of a steam engine. A few among them still clung to this terminology and hoped that, after the new physics had settled down, the simple terms of mechanism would be again sufficient. Others expressed doubts as to its adequacy. In an essay on Modern Concepts in Physics and Their Relation to Chemistry, Irving Langmuir took his place among the skeptics. "We have no guarantee whatever," he concluded, "that nature is so constructed that it can be adequately described in terms of mechanical or electrical models; it is much more probable that our most fundamental relationships can only be expressed mathematically, if at all." The conditional phrase, "if at all," was arresting. That was, indeed, the query which rose on all sides among searchers for the connections between reality and appearance, between the nature of the world and visions of it, whether scientific, artistic, historical, literary, or theological.

Although no scientist now wrote a huge volume in the manner of Jeans and Eddington in mediation between scientific method and thought on the one side and lay method and thought on the other, Alfred Cohn, in a lecture entitled The Difference between Science and Art in Their Relation to Nature, incorporated with other essays, in his Medicine, Science and Art, published in 1931, projected adumbrations of the form which such mediation might assume in coming years. Trained in medicine, a specialist in cardio-vascular diseases, a member of the Rockefeller Institute for Medical Research, equipped with European experience and languages, Cohn was in a strategic position to describe the nature of scientific work and its relations to the rest of life and thought.

Science, he said, in language fairly intelligible to laymen, "is that effort which men keep making to understand deeply events in this world and in the universe and the method of their occurrence," and it proceeds by analysis, observation, classification, meticulous description, and interpretation. The definition was broad: "Not long since, the study of nature was confined to the non-sentient world, the world outside the perceiving mind of man. But times change. . . . A new and vigorous assault is in progress, destined perhaps to illuminate, maybe to annihilate, the old doctrine which separated mind and body. . . . Critical philosophers are again beginning to concern themselves [with] that world of the mind which seems to lie outside of and actually to escape the will but which, nevertheless, is accessible to experience and appears in fact to be that part of the mental apparatus in which experience, often completely forgotten in our waking hours, is stored. . . . This function of the whole human organism is also a phase of nature."

While scientists in general go forward with analysis and description into details, the most powerful intellects among them, Cohn contended, have another object: "To make statements about the world, and as few of them as possible, the proof of their value being that they be genuinely descriptive and permit the deepest possible insight into its processes." This is exactly what Harvey, Newton, Clerk-Maxwell, and Einstein, for example, actually did. Any layman could understand that, even one who saw no connection between the indeterminism of physics and the free will of theology. School children could read in their elementary texts that "every mass tends towards every other mass with a force varying directly as the product of the masses and inversely as the square of their distances apart." That was a majestic generalization about an almost infinite number of particularities in "as few words as possible." It could be grasped by any mind able to comprehend the ancient rule: "The squares of the two containing sides joined together are equal to the square of the hypotenuse."

More significant in adumbrating coming forms of scientific interest were Cohn's conclusions respecting the nature of the scientist and the scientific method. The conception of complete objectivity, of a mind entirely empty of concerns and presumptions, he dismissed without hesitation: "We no longer believe that the eye of any beholder is disinterested. Nor, as a matter of fact, can I learn that this was ever believed to be true." In examining the history of great scientific discoveries, Cohn took cognizance of meditation, inspiration, and intuition, as well as knowledge and experience. Archimedes, according to tradition, observing the water of his bath overflowing as he stepped into it, suddenly solved a long-pondered problem and was so excited by the flash of insight that he ran home without his clothes, shouting "I have found it! I have found it!" Similar incidents illustrating the scientific method Cohn derived from the lives of Harvey, Kepler, and Newton: "Their solutions were, in the present sense, all intuitions — the nucleus of their thought had slowly been maturing, had long been dormant, had been the continuous irritant that left them no peace, until an arrangement in some simple order dawned upon them. Harvey, in describing his discovery that the blood in animals circulates, confessed, 'I frequently and seriously bethought me, and long revolved in my mind'; and in the end declared triumphantly, 'I began to think whether there might not be a motion, as it were, in a circle.'"

This instrument of science, called for convenience intuition for want of a better word, Cohn defined as "the function by which, as the result of experience, usually extensive and often profound, I know with incredible swiftness, within the time of a lightning flash, what inference I must draw in an argument or what action I must take in a difficult situation. I have used the phrase 'experience usually extensive and often profound.' Because I have experience of this sort, though I need not be conscious of its possession, I can in argument or a situation arrive at a conclusion far in advance either of one inexperienced or of one not previously interested in a related problem. I arrive at the result I need quickly; I telescope, as I say, with the speed of lightning, the thought perhaps of years which engrosses ponderously the energy and the time of other men. . . . Of the process itself I can say little. The function is not one of the conscious reason. Indeed, the conscious reason cannot force it into activity. This much can be said: the extra-conscious activity requires the painful preparation which is the function of the mind in its conscious period."

What Cohn actually did in his report on the nature of science, therefore, was to bring scientists into that stream of social and psychological realism so long a force in general thought. Without condemning, he eschewed mysticism, related the scientist to his medium of experience, and sought the roots and nature of that "inspiration" or "intuition" to be found in great science and art. Independently, sociologists had reached the conclusion that the mentality of each normal human person is encircled by "a social frame of memory," is not a tabula rasa, an empty sensitive plate, at any time, in acts of observation, procedure, and thought. The problem of genius or hero or leader in science, Cohn left unsolved, just where sociologists had left it in their domain, after giving positive intimations of its elements. But by stating the problem and by tracing the differences and similarities of science and art, he gave recognition to the steadily accumulating impingements of social environment upon science and to the intimate relations of science and art.

In essence Cohn's testament was an indication of a movement toward the unification of the many divisions of human interest long sundered by petty minds unable to wrestle with it and by generous minds unwilling to face it or paralyzed by its ramifications. If the movement was to continue, there were grounds for the expectation that all the arts and sciences would be enriched by interchanges and brought more intimately into the services of the life and society that nourished them.

From another angle of vision, that of the mathematician, Alfred Cohn's summation of trends in science was confirmed — by Tobias Dantzig in his Aspects of Science, published in 1936. Physical science, he reported, has abandoned "the naïve realism of the classical period. . . . It has recognized the anthropomorphic origin and nature of human knowledge. Be it determinism or rationality, empiricism or the mathematical method, it has recognized that man is the measure of all things, and that there is no other measure." The efforts of scientists to rationalize all nature and all history have failed. Attempts to supplant, to support, or to demonstrate the validity of religion by the scientific method have likewise come to naught. Even the ideas indispensable to scientific thought, such as inductive inference, space, duration, motion, derive their validity from neither logic nor experience; they are rooted in race sublimations and are "tinged with collective predilections." Scientific theories are linked with action; they take meaning from action, and they are revised as action proceeds. Science as such knows no single absolute. Nothing in "these amazing electrons" dictates action. The sources of action lie in mankind and, by collective predilections, the sphere of action is created and enlarged. Therein science works. Only therein can science work. If Dantzig's report was correct, the separation of physical science from the texture of all human thought, interest, and action was not even theoretically possible.

At bottom, then, the experiences classed under the head of science did not differ in any absolute manner from experiences in other so-called domains of human interest. Its votaries were disturbed by "outside" events, shared the hopes and frustrations common to mankind, and responded in some fashion to the insistent demands of practice. The idea that they were a peculiar group working without any assumption or preconceptions respecting the nature of things and thought, on the basis of "demonstrated" and "indefeasible" facts, steadily lost prestige as inquiries into the character and background of scientific methods, activities, and generalizations proceeded. No unbridgeable chasm, for instance, separated the scientist from the artist in methods of work and intellectual operations. The forces of culture penetrated, it was recognized, the laboratory of the physicist as well as the closet of the politician, and conditioned thought and conclusions there prevailing. Nor did scientists, any more than anybody else, escape unscathed the gravamen of the tragic conflict between the ideal and the real that had tormented great spirits for centuries and had inspired momentous actions designed to draw them closer together.

CHAPTER XVI

Frames of Social Thought

As in physical nature the flash of lightning always precedes the roll of thunder, so in human affairs the flame of thought has always gone before a transformation in the social arrangements of mankind. In Machiavelli, it presaged the triumph of the National State over the ruins of feudalism and the disruption of the Church Universal; in Montesquieu and Rousseau, the overthrow of absolutism; in Adam Smith and Ricardo, the flowering of capitalism; in Mary Wollstonecraft, the dissolution of the patriarchal regime; in Marx and Engels, the upswing of the world-wide proletarian movement; in Sorel, Pareto, and Mosca, the uprush of fascism. Was there such a flash in the United States during the tumults of the midpassage, and, if so, what was presaged?

§

As in previous years, the function of writing voluminous and systematic works on government, economy, society, and social destiny was assigned mainly to professors in the academies, or to men and women trained in the academies, although newspapers in expressing contempt for an idea found endless satisfaction in caricaturing it as a professor with a mortarboard on his head and a scholar's gown hanging from his shoulders.

This allocation of erudite thinking to the academies did not mean, however, that the professors had a monopoly on thought or that they excogitated their premises and syllogisms wholly within ivory towers. As in other times thought was expressed in the homely sayings of the people-at-large, in articles, essays, manifestos, editorials, belles lettres, and works of plastic art. If at first glance such classification as to origins seemed to mark a division of thought distinct enough to require wholly separate expositions, more deliberation suggested a pause. In fact great treatises on philosophy couched in language far beyond the reach of peasants and artisans had always rested more or less and continued to rest more or less on the broad base of maxims or axioms representing the common-sense experiences of ordinary humanity. Even natural science, as E. W. Hobson explained in his Domain of Natural Science, sprang from the observations of primitive peoples and, in its development, revolved around common-sense assumptions and "animal faiths," despite flights into the realm of higher physics and metaphysics. Franklin Giddings' sociological axiom, "consciousness of kind," expressed in another form the old saying, "Birds of a feather flock together." Nor could the hardest-headed practitioner in economic affairs, without renown as a thinker, maintain that he had no idea of what he was doing — no idea gathered up in association with his fellows, fellows having their background among the people.

Whenever a great system of thought, called philosophy, got down into the dusty way of life as a dynamic force — and such systems often had — the intrusion and drive were due, certainly in part, to the fact that the system, in essentials, expressed or was translated into current proverbs and maxims sometimes of hoary age. Thus, for instance, in his recondite philosophy of history, Hegel assumed, like farmers and housewives, the existence of God and the manifestations of God's will in human affairs. Farmers and housewives also had known something about conflicts and contradictions in life though they had not formulated a dialectical coverage. In transmuting Hegel's dialectics and applying it to practical politics, Karl Marx reduced it in the Communist Manifesto to terms intelligible to the proletariat of all lands.

Indeed thought in every age had seemed to flow in a kind of cycle, out of current proverbs into erudite coverage and back again into common sayings. The process was illustrated in 1931 when Albert H. Wiggin, head of the Chase National Bank, engaged in instructing a Senate Committee at Washington, based his philosophy of finance on the maxim of "let us alone," therewith merely repeating a "truism" of the marketplace that had formerly got into the heavy pages of Adam Smith and David Ricardo and out again into the marts of trade.

In the effulgence of the golden glow, the most general system of American thought, upon which professors and nearly everybody else drew for inspiration, was that of smooth and ready acceptance of the prevailing order, from which Satan and nearly all evil had been effectively banished. Its central conception was that the United States of America was a pretty good place, just as constituted. Its special interests were comfort, convenience, pecuniary advancement, emulatory display, salesmanship, unbroken progress in the straight utilitarian direction, and efficiency, with education as a preparation for the realization and enjoyment of such interests. Its philosophy was on the whole "matter-of-fact" and pragmatic. Our world will go on very much this way forever; and if disturbances should arise, we can "recover" the past again by doing more of the same thing we had been doing. There will be no more devastating jars to the American social order, no more wars, revolutions, cataclysms, and national tragedies.

Even after the glow had faded, faith in this system continued to be general and was compressed into neat linguistic forms such as: return to prosperity, recovery, restoration, bigger and better, bad luck today, better luck tomorrow, stage a big come-back, and the good old way. So soothing and pervasive was the creed that clergymen, as a whole, seemed inclined to preach fewer fierce sermons on man as a sinful creature, a wicked beast, and to spend more time in denouncing "Reds" than in condemning the "works of the devil." Under the popular system of thought, man had become "a pretty good fellow," and would continue to be as long as he followed his acquisitive nose assiduously enough.

While all went well with the best of systems, neither business men nor politicians nor practitioners of any type paid much attention to the logic-chopping and hair-splitting of professors occupied in refining the maxims of Adam Smith, Ricardo, Boehm-Bawerk, and John Bates Clark. Occasionally the irate alumni of a university rejoiced in the expulsion of a professor who got too far off the beaten track but they bothered their heads little, if at all, about furious disputes over marginal utility or the relation of competition to the survival of the fittest, or fine distinctions between production and consumption. The situation changed, however, after the depression spread desolation all around. Then economic and political practitioners began to search feverishly for explanations of the plight into which they had fallen and to wonder how they could get out of it. Then the keepers of the higher learning were remembered and the function of systematic thinking received more consideration than had been the case in the days of automatic prosperity.

§

While the economic stringency struck at the financial resources of the educational system from the universities to the elementary schools, the influence of the academies on American life increased rather than diminished during the midpassage. There were a number of reasons for this expansion of influence. One was the larger proportion of college graduates in positions of public and private power, partly owing to the lavish support which had been given to the higher learning and the rush of young people to its seats. Presidents Coolidge, Hoover, and Franklin D. Roosevelt were all college graduates: Coolidge from Amherst; Hoover from Leland Stanford; and Roosevelt from Harvard. Not only that. Seven of the ten members of Roosevelt's Cabinet were college graduates: Cordell Hull held a degree from Cumberland University Law School; Homer Cummings from Yale; Claude A. Swanson from Randolph-Macon; Henry A. Wallace from Iowa State College; Daniel Roper from Trinity College, now called Duke University; Harold Ickes from Chicago University; Frances Perkins from Mount Holyoke. Only three members of the Cabinet were outside the category: Henry Morgenthau had spent a brief season at Cornell; James A. Farley and Harry Woodring, according to Who's Who, had come up through the university of hard knocks. Among the Lords of Creation deemed masters in the world of business enterprise, as we have seen, a large majority were college graduates, the New England institutions providing the major portion of the leadership. Evidently the days of log-cabin Presidents and office-boy wizards of finance had come to a close. Even among village bankers, members of town councils, and state legislators, as well as clerks and minor office holders, the proportion of college-trained men and women was phenomenal.

While the thought cultivated in the higher academies percolated through graduates into business and government, the universities and colleges were taking possession of the whole public school system as well as private schools. Prohibitions on child labor had lengthened the school years for more boys and girls, and the curtailment of employment opportunities in the depression had served to stretch out the education of young persons in high schools and colleges. By subsidizing thousands of students through the agency of the Youth Administration, headed by Aubrey Williams, the Federal Government enabled them to advance further in education. The intensified competition in the race for teaching positions, even in elementary schools, gave superiority to men and women who held the higher degrees. No longer was it easily possible for boys and girls just out of elementary schools or high schools to find places within the system as teachers. Thus the influence of the higher learning penetrated the entire process of popular education.

College graduates who did not go into teaching were now more inclined than formerly toward political action as a type of personal career or toward official public service. When opportunities in private business contracted, the once belittled "government job" did not seem so contemptible and, besides, improvements in the personnel administration of government, coupled with a growing interest in public welfare, made the civil service more attractive than ever to ambitious youth. Through one channel or another, therefore, the spirit and learning of the academies were insinuated into all divisions of public administration.

Into business as well as teaching and government, the influences of the academies reached with ever-increasing force. Since most of the Lords of Creation had been college men, in some instances their minds reverted to their old preceptors when the best of all possible worlds about which they had heard so much on campuses was badly damaged by events in the marketplace. To be sure they did not always remember the names of the dons under whom they had been trained; when a graduate of Harvard, class of 1906, was asked to name some professors who had made an impression upon him in his college days, he could recall only the distinguished Professor Taussig as "Professor Towsig." But the memories of others were better. Besides, business men of the larger establishments had long been accustomed to have at beck and call college-trained accountants, engineers, and other specialists to tell them what they wanted to know and hear. A few corporations employed "economic advisers" from the academies and a prominent financial house put upon its staff a teacher of finance to instruct it in the theory of money.

Consequently, when the alarms of the business crisis pierced their air-conditioned rooms, any of them in search of thought could press a button to summon his philosophic and literary consultant. It was in keeping with the state of things, accordingly, for Albert H. Wiggin of the Chase National Bank, to give as a handout, to the press and a Senate committee groping in darkness, a one-page summary of right thinking in the shape of a succinct formulation of classical economics by Benjamin Anderson, once of Missouri, now the "economic adviser" of the Chase Bank.

When the Liberty League was organized to "sell" the philosophy of big business to the voters, it took counsel with a few friendly professors and their disciples in the profession of law, as well as public relations experts. At its successive conventions and in preparing its literature of thought and propaganda, the National Manufacturers Association likewise drew upon text books and academicians whenever necessary to confirm established convictions. In a strict sense, of course, this procedure was not an innovation, for the covering of interest by ideology had been a common custom in ages past. The divine right of kings had its Filmer and Bossuet. In 1852 the theological, economic, anthropological, and sociological demonstration that chattel slavery was the best possible system in the circumstances was perfected in a treatise frankly called the Pro-Slavery Argument, composed by Thomas R. Dew of the University of Virginia, professor of history, metaphysical, natural, and national law, government, and political economy. Whether the elaboration of manufacturing theory in 1935 or 1937 meant that the demonstration of manufacturing practice was insufficiently convincing to the generality of people, or that manufacturers were in a fair way to become philosophers could not be determined on the basis of any data lending themselves to tabulation. It did seem to indicate, however, that business interests were not entirely content with their inherited wrappers of thought.

Even more imperative than in private business was systematic thought when planning and action in government were involved. After all, private business had no legislative and executive unity; it was a congeries of particular interests requiring limited if exact knowledge respecting particular enterprises; and, if one or more great corporations went into bankruptcy, the episode was not necessarily ruinous to the nation. On the other hand, government embraced all interests, economic and cultural; persistent thought about it had to be comprehensive, systematic, and informed by immense knowledge, unless government was to fail and bring other institutions down with it. This fact had been recognized during the eighteenth-century crisis with which the Constitution of the United States was designed to deal; and it was fortunate for the country that the chief architect of that frame of social thought, James Madison, trained at Princeton, was an assiduous student of history and government and a systematic thinker as well. Madison was as indispensable to the convention that framed the Constitution as were the hard-headed men of practice associated with him in the undertaking.

It was more than a coincidence that in the great crisis of 1929 in commerce, economy, banking, and finance, analogous in many respects to the breakdown of 1786, systematic thinkers trained in universities were again drawn upon for counsel and public service. They had, of course, not been entirely neglected in times immediately preceding. For instance, the Industrial Commission, charged with investigating economic conditions in 1898, had made extensive use of college men in the course of its inquiry, especially of Professor Jeremiah Whipple Jenks of Cornell University; and to Professor Jenks was committed the task of writing its report on Industrial Combinations and Prices.

This precedent President Hoover was following when, in September, 1929, he called upon a research committee composed of professors, "to examine and report upon recent social trends in the United States with a view to providing such a review as might supply a basis for the formulation of large national policies looking to the next phase in the nation's development." Through the agency of numerous experts the Committee made exhausting if not exhaustive researches and reported changes in every department of American life during the preceding decade or beyond. One thing it declared indispensable: "Willingness and determination to undertake important integral changes in the reorganization of social life, including the economic and the political orders, rather than the pursuance of a policy of drift." It is true that in his brief foreword to the Committee's report, finished in October, 1932, President Hoover displayed no great enthusiasm over the findings of the Committee, but by that time three years of business casualties had indicated rather conclusively that profound changes were in fact taking place in American economy and society.

When Franklin D. Roosevelt took the reins of government he made wholesale use of professors as counselors and administrators. During his first campaign and after his inauguration, he was surrounded by a group of personal advisers from universities, which included Raymond Moley, Felix Frankfurter, Rexford Tugwell, and Adolf Berle, popularly known as the "Brain Trust." Three of the group, Moley, Tugwell, and Berle, were given official positions in the Roosevelt administration for periods short or long; and many other officials were drawn from university circles, for example, M. L. Wilson in agriculture; O. M. Sprague and Jacob Viner in finance; Thurman W. Arnold in enforcement of antitrust laws; and James Landis in the securities and exchange commission. Indeed the use of professors became so general that it was made a target for ridicule and attack by political and business critics, and so contemptuous became the derision of the "brain trust" by the opposition that a member of the Cabinet shot back: "With what part of his anatomy should a man think?"

Nevertheless, when the Republicans prepared to drive the Roosevelt administration out of power in 1936, newspapers reported that they too had assembled something like a brain trust, including Professor Thomas N. Carver of Harvard and Professor Edwin W. Kemmerer of Princeton, to advise the directors of the campaign. The following year when Republican managers began again to search for an explanation of their misfortunes and for an avenue to victory, they created a large council of advisers headed by Dr. Glenn Frank, who had recently been president of the University of Wisconsin — until the Progressives ousted him. It seemed, therefore, that it was not the professor as such but the style of his thought that excited praise or derision — according to circumstances and predilections. At any rate, wherever comprehensive knowledge and systematic thinking were regarded as useful, consultation with the possessors of brains was considered appropriate, and perhaps advantageous. Thought was elusive and troublesome and yet practitioners, high and low, apparently could not get along without it — or with it. In America it could scarcely be said of scholars as was said of Lavoisier when he was sent to the guillotine: "La Republique n'a pas besoin de savants."

Given the intimate and varied relations of professors in the academies, and of the students they trained, to the education of the nation from the primary school upward and to the conduct of practical affairs, inquirers into the nature and future of civilization in America had to ask what the professors were studying and teaching and thinking that had a bearing on American society in gross and in detail. Under what frames or schemes of social thought were they operating as teachers, advisers, and writers? Where did they stand in the conflict of ideas and interests, in the clash of tendencies and systems? Did they avoid issues or face them in the full light of their knowledge as courageous seers? Did they regard themselves as belonging to a privileged gild entitled to go its own way without reference to the fate of society? Did they favor particular interests or seek overarching hypotheses of values under which adjustments, reconciliations, and elisions might be made in theory and practice? To what extent was the appearance of schools and controversies among professors due to personal or institutional emulation in the competition for prestige? In what direction and in what manner were they prosecuting their researches in economics, political science, sociology, education, philosophy, and history? In what systematic and comprehensive treatises were they revealing their thought and the fruits of their investigations?

§

As befitted a country that esteemed itself eminently "practical," writers and teachers who dealt with economic matters stood first on the roll of popular consideration; and in books, papers, essays, journals, and proceedings the thinking of economists was fairly well revealed. Unlike members of the encyclopaedia group in the old regime of France, they did not have to write in a manner that required the public to distinguish between what they said and what they really thought. On the whole, so far as they were given to comprehensive schemes of theory, economists adhered rather closely to the classical heritage of laissez faire received from Adam Smith and Richard Ricardo, though in forms refined and polished by many hands in the intervening years. Despite the agitations of labor in town and country, the dislocating effects of inventions, the development of administered prices, the depletion of natural resources, recurring wars, and preparations for wars, no radical departures from accepted doctrine came to dominate the academies, considered collectively. Neither the optimism of the golden glow nor the afflictions of the business and social depression altered in any fundamental respect the perdurance of this general cast of thought in academic cogitations.

Indeed in 1931 right in the middle of the great disequilibrium, it was presented to the public by the president of the Chase National Bank in the form of a summary by Doctor

Benjamin Anderson, adviser of that institution. Taking for granted, without mention, his assumptions respecting the nature of man and the permanence, for practical purposes, of "the natural order," Anderson plunged into his thesis: "In general it is not the function of government under the capitalist system to produce or perform economic services. The actual direction of industry, the decision whether more wheat shall be planted and less corn, or more shoes shall be produced and less hats, is not made by the State, or by collective society, but is left to the choice of independent producers. These independent producers make their decisions with reference to the state of the market. The up-and-down movements of prices and wages determine whether more or less of a given thing shall be produced. . . . Under this system of free, private enterprise, with free movement of labor and capital from industry to industry, the tendency is for an automatic balance to be maintained and for goods and services to be supplied in right proportions. A social order is created, a social coöperation is worked out, largely unconscious and largely automatic under the play of the impersonal forces of market prices and wages. . . . The ability to understand the highly intricate economic life of today, the ability to see through it and to see the different parts in relation to one another, to coördinate wants and efforts, to distribute resources properly among conflicting claimants — this ability does not exist." Hence Anderson concluded that any effort to use economic theory effectively "in the actual regulation of economic life," in the way of social planning and control, "is an impossibility." In short, individuals, government, and society stood in the presence of an unconscious, largely automatic, self-adjusting system, akin to the mechanism of nature. Nothing constructive on a national scale could be done about it. It was too elemental.

Persistently as the classical doctrine hovered in the foreground or background of economic thought, it nevertheless encountered, even in academic groves, some neglect and dissent. No economist furbished it up in a grand re-statement that brought forth universal acclaim. Judging by the character of monographs and treatises turned out, there were several "schools" of economists at work and many economists were more interested in particular economic activities than in any comprehensive theory about their common nature or their overarching "laws." Rather than refine and recast syllogisms, scholars of this inclination preferred to study and describe particular economic institutions, such as banks, railways, corporations, public utilities, and trade unions, and for this reason were loosely called "institutionalists."

In some measure the tendency to institutionalism was due to discontent with classical theory, to a belief that the creed did not correspond to the facts in the case, that it assumed an economic man, a static order of society, and a "normal equilibrium" which did not exist anywhere, that it neglected change and development in society, that it minimized the influence of institutional loyalties on human conduct. To this extent, institutional economics acted as a dissolving force on economic orthodoxy and boded ill for the kind of thick-and-thin defense which capitalists were likely to expect in academies supported by endowments or taxes on property.

Whatever the explanation of their dissent or their proclivities, the institutionalists were by no means united on a platform of their own. Those who chose merely to study and describe a single institutional set-up, such as banking or transportation, could evade almost entirely the necessity of thought and the imputation of heterodoxy by sticking close to surface and reputable facts. Economists who did this were institutionalists in the strictest sense of the term. If, however, an economist went below the surface of reputable facts into underlying facts, for example those registered in law suits and legislative investigations, he encountered practices out of conformity with the canons of reputability and, by describing them or checking theory against them, was almost sure to collide with the advertised moral canons of the business community. If, perchance, an institutionalist thought persistently about the relation of any single branch of economic activity to the rest of society or considered the probable upshot of any special development, such as corporate concentration, he incurred the ethical hazard of committing himself to some theory or interpretation of all economy and its evolution.

So, to speak broadly, there were two schools of institutionalists: the strictly and narrowly descriptive who ventured no large interpretations; and the more thoughtful who accepted as their general guide either classical theory or some competing scheme of doctrine. A few institutionalists combined the function of description with that of interpretation, but this involved an occupational hazard perilous to academic calm. Apart from fine distinctions, what the institutionalists really did was to establish on a factual basis the integrated, national, and collective character of American economy without providing a corresponding theory for the guidance of practice.

With the institutionalists were sometimes bracketed the economists who devoted themselves to "quantitative analysis" and the preparation of graphs showing the fluctuations of production, prices, wages, and other elements of economy in time movement. Although the quantifiers stood on their own ground, the results of their researches, plotted in rises and declines, strengthened an institutionalist conviction that the normalcy or equilibrium of orthodox economics was somewhat mythical in nature. Coupled in spirit with such inquirers were economists who investigated and described what Americans were fond of calling "trends," that is, "lines of development" in selected institutions or practices. As early inquiries in geology, chemistry, biology, and ecology prepared the way for Darwin's synthesis, so the labors of the institutionalists, quantifiers, and trendists might be opening the road for a general reconstruction of covering theory.

Ranking high among the volumes and special studies produced by the institutional school was The Modern Corporation and Private Property, published in 1932, by Adolf Berle and Gardiner Means, both of whom later entered the service of the Federal Government. Their work was an elaborate description of corporate structures and operations. It showed that control over about thirty-eight per cent of all business wealth in the United States, apart from banking, was concentrated in the hands of two hundred immense corporations. After attempting to estimate, as far as the records would permit, the number of stockholders in these concerns, Berle and Means gave special consideration, on the basis of legal and other factual materials, to the managerial methods employed by the directors and heads of corporations.

The upshot was a demonstration that corporations were dominated, as a rule, by trustees who held only a small proportion of the stock, and that the multitude of nominal "owners" had little influence on the management of "their own property." Through loose charters of incorporation, secured in such states as Delaware, through the separation of "voting stock" from common stock, through voting trusts, and other legal devices, not mentioned in Adam Smith or Ricardo, a relatively small number of men, assisted or ruled by bankers, had a fairly free hand in managing the two hundred corporations, diverting surpluses, appropriating salaries to officers, and giving bonuses to members of the managerial personnel. In the light of this upshot the automatic distribution of wealth through the price mechanism did not seem to be quite perfect, unless the corporation trustees were to be regarded as automatons when they appropriated bonuses to their associates and themselves.

Having described the structure of corporate industry, Berle and Means compared it with the use and wont of property on which the assumptions of classical theory rested. The early manufacturer or business man owned real property, as distinguished from paper claims to property. He resided near his material possessions and generally carried direct responsibility in management. In those simple days the issue of paper was ordinarily for the purpose of extending operations, to acquire or construct real property, not merely to buy stock in other property, perhaps at a high price. That is, under the old system, moral responsibility generally went with ownership; under the new system, the multitudinous owners of corporations had little or no responsibility for management, labor, or anything else. Since highly profitable operations could be effected by merely combining or buying into existing corporations, entirely apart from any increase in plant or the production of wealth, a large section of business enterprise bore no relation to the function which justified its existence, even in classical theory, namely, the increase of real capital and the production of real wealth in the form of goods and services. This general picture of enterprise had been elaborated by Veblen long before; but not until Berle and Means published their treatise was the extent of the factitious element in business even dimly appreciated by those interested in such matters.

The study of the modern corporation was supplemented later by Liquid Claims to Wealth, by Adolf Berle and Victoria Pederson, published in 1934. This work, also factual and statistical, traced the historical development of the proportion which the paper expression of wealth bore to real wealth. In other words, here was a picture of a "trend." On the basis of elaborate evidence the authors showed that the proportion of liquid claims to real national wealth rose from about sixteen per cent in 1880 to around forty per cent in 1930, and that the jump between 1912 and 1930 had been almost equal to the rise from the foundation of America to the year 1880. In a brief term of years about one-sixth of the national wealth had shifted from the hands of responsible owners into the hands of corporate managerial or manipulating groups; another half a century, at the same rate, would see all real property blanketed by paper claims of one kind or another. In this development, Berle and Pederson found a "reorientation of life," of all moral relations connected with management, economy, responsibility, labor, thrift, and prudence. The direct ownership of real property accompanied by personal management had meant independence, liberty, and responsibility. Ownership through the possession of liquid claims — such as stocks, bonds, and bank deposits — meant dependence, inter-dependence, and a different kind of moral responsibility, if society itself was to endure.

In a minute study of price variations, made for the Department of Agriculture and published as a government document, Gardiner Means dealt with inflexible or managed prices and compared them with prices in areas where corporate control did not exist or had a slight effect on price variations — agriculture, for example. In part, Means declared, the inflexibility was due to monopoly elements, including control of patents. In part it came from the overhead costs and fixed charges of corporate structure and management. Whatever the source, stiff prices existed in large areas of economic enterprise, put a drag on rapid adjustments, and served as an economic drain on those areas where competitive flexibility prevailed, more or less. Here also was a picture of economic practice that did not correspond exactly with the configuration on which classical theory rested.

From the Brookings Institution in Washington, D. C., issued reports likewise descriptive in character, bearing such self-explanatory titles as America's Capacity to Produce, America's Capacity to Consume, and The Formation of Capital. These works, too, were institutional in approach and factual in supporting evidence. The first showed that even in the golden glow, in the year 1929, the productive plant of the United States was running at approximately eighty-one per cent of its capacity. Here was another statistical picture that did not precisely conform to the classical imagery, under which each enterpriser made the best and fullest use of his capital in the circumstances and the combined result of all operations was an almost peak output of national wealth.

The second Brookings study in institutional economics, dealing with America's capacity to consume, indicated that the American people were not fully supplied with the houses, consumers' goods, and services required for a high general standard of living. In other words, American business was not held down to a low level of capacity merely because the people had practically everything they needed; because the domestic market was saturated. Then what was the trouble? A statistical study of the distribution of income in the United States in 1929 indicated "that 0.1 per cent of the families at the top received practically as much as forty-two per cent of the families at the bottom of the scale." Although available figures did not permit perfect exactness by any means, the Brookings conclusions, if extensively discounted, showed a serious disparity in the buying power that went to the few and the buying power that went to the many.

If these conclusions did not invalidate the contention of classical economics that the distribution of wealth in capitalist economy roughly approximates deserts and justice, they did raise a question respecting the efficiency of that distribution, that is, its power to keep business enterprise producing at or near the capacity point. Mass production required a correlative mass buying power and in actual operation business enterprise did not seem to be furnishing it. This was another discrepancy between theory and practice and aroused some curiosity among those Americans whose reading was not confined to romances.

The third Brookings investigation, into the formation of capital, brought out still another discrepancy. According to classical theory, savings were necessary to the constant increase of capital and went into plant extensions which furnished employment and augmented the production of wealth, at least in the main and quite beneficently. Looking at the facts in the case, the Brookings Institution found that, between 1927 and 1929, the major portion of "surplus savings" went not into the construction of new wealth-producing plants but into refunding operations and into bidding up the prices of already existing liquid claims to wealth — stocks and bonds.

This also seemed to confirm earlier suspicions. About thirty years before the Brookings discovery, Veblen had concluded, on a factual basis less extensive, that a large share of capitalist operations had nothing whatever to do with the production of real wealth. In truth too, as Ida Tarbell's work on the Standard Oil Company indicated, a number of business men, not educated in the universities, had come to suspect the validity of the theory, taught by John Bates Clark, at Columbia University, that all economic activities, apart from the consumption of goods, were "productive" in character.

Somewhat in the vein of the Brookings inquiry into America's capacity to produce, although on different lines, was the study conducted by Harold Loeb and associates, including a number of engineers, which eventuated in the publication entitled The Chart of Plenty. The Brookings investigators took existing plant capacity as the area of their inquiry. Loeb and his associates extended the area to cover also natural resources and technological potentials in American economy. They sought to find out what and how much America could produce if all skills, machines, processes, and resources were brought into full and efficient operation. As a result of their researches they reached the conclusion that this full and efficient operation could provide every American family with goods and services to the annual value of approximately $5000. Although the Loeb philosophy and findings were sometimes confused with Technocracy, which made a popular furor about the time of the great economic crash, they stood on an independent footing.

Whether The Chart of Plenty really belonged in the domain of institutional economics was, however, a subject of dispute. In a strict sense it did not. It belonged rather in the sphere of engineering rationality. Dealing with what was technologically possible, it left more or less out of account what was sociologically possible. Not without some reason, therefore, did professional economists regard it as "utopian." At the same time there was significance for economic theory in the fact that managers of industries could produce twice as much wealth if they could get a free hand to operate at capacity speed.

Perhaps the best notable example of institutional economics in its most comprehensive form was Adolf Berle's memorandum on "Investigation of Business Organizations and Practices" prepared in the summer of 1938 for the federal committee engaged on the inquiry into monopolies, published in Plan Age for September of that year. In this document appeared the realism of Berle's approach to the subject, the meditative character of his analysis, and the constructive nature of his thought about policy. Early in this paper Berle warned the committee against taking for granted the easy assumptions of the marketplace — the folk lore of capitalism — such as the preconceptions that small business is necessarily competitive, that small business is necessarily humane, that the efficiency of a business bears a positive relation to size, that the highly praised productivity of industry does in fact meet the "legitimate claims" made against it by labor, consumers, and investors.

To this warning Berle added a caution against the common assumption that the relation of government to business is merely incidental to industrial processes. In a few pages as dispassionate as a telephone book, he cited illustrations: direct government subsidies, for instance, to aviation and the merchant marine; indirect subsidies — low mail rates to newspapers; government purchases; special privileges — patents, copyrights, and licenses; tariffs; protection against price fluctuations; collateral subsidies — to the automobile industry through highway construction; public relief to take care of industry's unemployed in unprofitable seasons; direct loans; credits and banking facilities; regulation of rates; privileges to organized labor.

Knowing very well that no investigation of such a complicated problem could get anywhere merely by heaping up miscellaneous facts, that general objectives should be set in the beginning, that every specific problem has intimate relations with culture in its wide ranges, Berle proposed that the federal committee test economic organization by the following criteria: "(*a*) Does it provide an adequate supply of goods as tested by the normal market? As tested by the apparent need? (*b*) Does it provide a maximum number of people with an opportunity to make a living under this process — a life under this process — conceived as conditions under which people can live, maintain families, expect to continue in the economic system, and end this side of the relief line or poorhouse? (*c*) Does it accomplish this process with due regard for the liberty and self-government of the individual?" The idea that an industry was to be judged by its dividends to stockholders and not also by the number of its unemployed workers on relief, Berle rejected as not pertinent to national policy. Taking the constructive line, he analyzed control by methods of incorporation, by competition, by capital financing, by taxation, by patent legislation, by regulation, by private monopoly, by quasi-public ownership, and by public ownership and public production. Devastating to the insulated and closed dogmatism of the communist and classical schools, Berle's memorandum brought the consideration of economics down to earth and related it to going practices, reasonable human expectations, and explicit possibilities.

§

While the classical economists, the institutionalists, the quantifiers, and the trendists, as a rule, kept within a frame of thought that implied no drastic modifications in forms and ownership of property, other schools of economic opinion contemplated alterations more or less fundamental. As a matter of course, the Marxians continued and expanded their exploration and critique along the lines of their presuppositions. The transformation of economy in Russia, Italy, and Germany by acts of state power and the collectivist sweep in general gave more point to their analysis and theory, and commanded more consideration beyond their own ranks. Yet, despite the voluminous nature of their output in the United States, it was on the whole either narrowly orthodox or quarrelsome. Many theoreticians battled for the position of dominance among the faithful, and none attained undisputed preëminence. Sidney Hook, professor of philosophy in New York University, made studies of Marxism that displayed a command of the materials, but he was attacked more bitterly by men who claimed to possess the true faith than by professors called "bourgeois" in the everyday canon.

After the downfall of Trotsky in Russia, the school of Marxian commentators was splintered in America and the adepts devoted more energy, if possible, to the denunciation of one another than to the application of their scheme of thought to the American scene. No Kautsky, Lenin, or Bukharin arose in the United States to a place of intellectual mastery, and directed the swirl of petty controversy to any objectives of significance in either theory or practice. The nearest approach to this consummation was to be found in the articles printed in the magazine Science and Society. After all, the dogmatism apparently indigenous to central and eastern Europe seemed to evoke slight sympathy and less intellectual respect in the somewhat loose-jointed society of the American continent. Difficulties on this score were increased by the fact that one branch of the faithful was supposed to receive instructions respecting the correct line from Moscow, whereas the successors of Ivan the Terrible and Peter the Great were more concerned with the exigencies of Russian politics at home than with the logical and epistemological exactitude of Marxism in the United States.

Another invasion of orthodox thought was made by a group known as agrarians, for whom Herbert Agar spoke with knowledge and special persuasiveness. This school of thought, with its chief center in the south, at Vanderbilt University, attacked capitalism and its ethics as severely as did the Marxists, but offered another exit from the dilemma. Capitalism, it insisted, led to centralization, socialism, and servitude. Democracy, liberty, and security required a wider distribution of property, the multiplication of petty owners and industries, decentralization, handicrafts, and community sufficiency.

A few of the agrarians seemed to find their utopia realized in the golden age of the Old South where no capitalists disturbed rural bliss and the weary were at rest in their mansions. However, a touch of realistic history, imparted by other agrarians of the Old South, took most of the bloom off the Red Rose. Well aware of the illusions in the idyllic picture, the dissident agrarians offered a compromise. They understood that railways, electric power, and utilities in general might be useful in their ideal society to come but a redistribution of this kind of wealth was scarcely possible. Parcelling out railway ties, rails, power houses, and transformers among the populace, as Huey Long had seemed to suggest, was, indeed, not feasible at all. Conceding the point, the "forward looking" agrarians proposed to combine public ownership of great utilities with the redistribution of land and manufacturing. In emerging from manors and magnolias, agrarianism thus assumed a configuration by no means strange to the practice of American politics; nor was it entirely out of line with the humanistic tradition in the United States.

Some support for the agrarian scheme of thought was furnished by Catholic economists who refused to accept the matter-of-fact presuppositions underlying capitalist and Marxian economics. Catholic thinkers had never ruled ethics out of account or treated ethics as incidental to the main chance. With marked tenacity, the boldest economists among them had clung to mediaeval teachings relative to the just price and the fair wage, and their pertinacity had been reinforced by the various encyclicals of the Pope on labor and economy. No doubt the generality of the papal language permitted a great variety of views among the faithful in practical applications, and many Catholic economists did not differ materially from the classical school as far as practical upshot was concerned. In fact, wherever any conflict approached a line-up between fascism and communism, they showed a tendency to accept capitalistic fascism, if with reluctance. In the main, however, the Catholic economists were inclined to approve the distributionism of the agrarian school. Leaders in their grouping, such as John A. Ryan, continued undaunted in their emphasis on the ethical basis of economic policy, on the rights of labor, and on a wider distribution of wealth as a necessity of justice and social welfare. Here and there they encountered strenuous opposition from colleagues and members of the hierarchy but, within the limits of essential doctrine touching faith and morals, they enjoyed their liberty of thought and exercised their freedom to explore practice and propose policy.

Apart from group excursions into economic thought were individual forays. By his Folklore of Capitalism, issued in 1937, Thurman W. Arnold, professor in the Yale Law School, gave a considerable jolt to the purveyors of current maxims in business and economics. Though received as a systematic treatise done in the grand manner, Arnold's volume really did not belong within that designation. It was rather a realistic and ingenious analysis of the sayings of the marketplace and the schools, which often had little relevance to practice and generally stood in the way of understanding and manipulating concrete situations. Its merit lay in the application of the scientific, or clinical, method to the maladjustments and distresses of going concerns. For example, Arnold called attention to the fact that the staff of an insane asylum did not devote time to classifying the ideas of the inmates, but employed their skill in trying to make the patients comfortable. Of course, this was both amusing and suggestive; at the same time it revealed the author's method. The illustration was an analogy and came dangerously near to the kind of folklore that he was subjecting to destructive analysis. At bottom the Folklore of Capitalism was diagnostic, rather than systematic or therapeutic, but in an age of easy assumptions it was effective in exploding many unreal maxims of the counting house, the corner store, and the cloister.

Other individuals, such as Paul Douglas, Stuart Chase, Mary Van Kleek, Walton Hamilton, Broadus Mitchell, James Bonbright, and Harry Pratt Fairchild, also challenged the presuppositions of the logical faith in economics and, having done so, considered things deemed possible as well as necessary. Yet their work was, in the main, exploratory and piece-meal rather than systematic and universal in range. In substance it was primarily institutional, but without the amoral disclaimers of that persuasion. When Miss Van Kleek surveyed the coal industry, for instance, she gave "the essential facts" of the industry, but did not stop there. From the survey she proceeded to a constructive proposal running counter to the philosophy of automatic beneficence. Realizing that a good logician could get out of a major premise all that had been put into it, Miss Van Kleek avoided preliminary commitments that prevented her from seeing the coal industry as disorganized and demoralized. She assumed that the business of the industry was to mine and distribute coal and, after inquiring into its actual state, advanced to an examination of the methods most likely to sustain the function for which the industry was supposed to exist. If not iconoclastic, this was at least critical, for orthodoxy had assumed that the coal industry must work about as well as possible "in the natural course" or under the "invisible hand" of Providence. In time the multiplication of such inquiries was bound to have an effect on the most adamant system of insulated thought.

§

A similar influence was to be exerted by the work and memory of Thorstein Veblen. As if symbolically, in 1929, the year of the great crack in business enterprise, Veblen died in a little cabin near Stanford University, long the scene of his labors and tribulations; but his work lived, and five years later Joseph Dorfman gave it additional vitality by publishing a comprehensive treatise on the life and setting of this singular figure in the realm of economic analysis and speculation. In all the history of American thought, few, if any, had been as well equipped as Veblen by acquaintance with foreign languages, by training in philosophy, by study of cultural anthropology, and by scientific detachment from the prestige of office, for dealing with economics in its social affiliations as a phase of culture, rather than as a hypothetical mechanism. As early as 1899 he examined the limits and probable consequences of the purely "scientific" or matter-of-fact treatment of economic activities. After pointing out the cultural values which capitalist society had inherited from early systems, he sought to discover in current tendencies the results that would flow from the preëminence of pecuniary considerations in American thought and practice, especially the effect of this preëminence upon the hitherto disciplined mass of machine workers. Although Ruskin and Carlyle in England had raised this problem near the middle of the nineteenth century, Veblen was the first American writer to treat it broadly in the language of academic scholarship.

Having called attention to the cultural context in which economic activities were carried on, Veblen discussed the epistemology of economic thought. He insisted that economic science of the most accepted and rigorous type took for granted, without suspicion or inquiry, subjective presuppositions respecting the nature and course of all things. By historical analysis, he related these unexamined "verities" to the intellectual and moral "axioms" of the handicraft and merchant economy which prevailed near the middle of the eighteenth century. In one essay after another Veblen brought under scrutiny such grand phrases as "the natural order," "the natural course," "the normal rule," "the beneficence of nature," "natural rights," and "the system of natural liberty." After he had finished his work of dissec-

tion, little was left of the delusion that the axioms of economic science were inescapable deductions drawn from the
observed phenomena of the twentieth-century marketplace.
Inherited thought and preliminary assumptions, Veblen
showed, had exerted a profound influence in shaping the
image of things supposed to exist in the world of practice —
the appearance of the reality.

With a philosophic groundwork firmly laid, Veblen made
an analysis of the theory of business enterprise, published
in 1904. A central point of economic orthodoxy had been
the contention that all economic activity except consumption was productive in nature, excluding, of course, mere
criminal undertakings penalized by the code. This, Veblen
maintained, was too simple for the facts in the case. The
interest of modern business enterprise was essentially pecuniary, as distinguished from the productive interest of the
craftsman, the manager, or the directing industrialist as
owner in a strict sense. Innumerable activities pertained
to the combination of existing concerns, the destruction of
competitors, the wrecking and reorganization of going enterprises. Such activities did not enlarge physical plant, increase production, or add to the output of wealth. Often
by closing competing works, business men actually reduced
output, enhanced prices, and destroyed capital goods. In
other words, a large number of business enterprisers were
not engaged in production at all, but were working in the
interstices between going industries, and their huge accumulations of riches flowed from interstitial operations rather
than from additions to national wealth or from personal
sacrifices.

Concerning the extent of subtractive and sabotaging activities as compared with the totality of genuinely productive
activities, Veblen was not dogmatic. Up to that time other
economists, if they considered interstitial activity at all, had
regarded it as practically negligible for economic science. But
Veblen emphasized it as a striking, persistent, and pervasive
characteristic of business enterprise. He did not live to

examine the multitude of illustrations produced by congressional investigations of foreign loans, banking, investment practices, security exchanges, the merchant marine, railroads, and naval construction after the great explosion of 1929, but years before his death he had divined the significance of such potentials in business enterprise for economy and social ethics.

In an analysis of business enterprise as practice, it was only a step to the consideration of competition as fact — competition which Richard T. Ely, John Bates Clark, and other economists had praised in the optimistic vein of Herbert Spencer, as the beneficent force that kept economy running at high speed. Veblen took the step. After a detailed examination of actual conduct under the head of competition, he discovered elements of cunning, dissimulation, and stratagem in business, such as prevailed in the jungle — in the materialist struggle for existence. Here again Veblen resorted to emphasis rather than to the measurement of exact proportions, but even a mere recognition of the facts seemed to the orthodox almost like a wanton riot in a Sunday school.

Other current maxims of the academicians Veblen subjected to observational tests. The automatic working and the beneficence of the price system were brought under scrutiny. Over against assumptions and theories, Veblen placed evidence of the restraining operations of the price system — the limitation as well as the promotion of production. As he saw it, the price system did not always assure the highest possible production of goods, but often checked and sabotaged production. As a kind of side remark, he pointed out that the country had never been in a state of high productive prosperity except in war periods and in times when business men were engaged in intense speculative activities, expanding credit and liquid claims to wealth, and that such periods were mere preliminaries to liquidating collapses. With economy so conceived, the business cycle as a phase of productive activity in itself took on the shadowy form of a myth. Capitalism, save for war and speculation, ran on a low level of production, not on the highest possible level. That finding was decidedly heterodox.

Holding that cultural values and institutional sentiments furnished an essential part of the very cement of society, in which economic activities were carried on, Veblen inquired into the effects of advertising, promotional psychology, the machine process, and competition in prestige upon real or sustaining morality and conventional morality. Here likewise his conclusions ran contrary to the theory that everything is good in the course of nature under the propulsion of the acquisitive instinct. If so, he inquired, what of the prospects?

With all the prescience he could command, Veblen sought to penetrate the future. After calculating probabilities as things stood in 1904, he thought it likely that business enterprise would become more and more entangled in the imperialist quest for foreign trade, markets, and raw materials, with wars and occasional prosperities as consequences. Out of the imperialist quest was likely to come a growing power of the State over business. With inherited moralities weakening under the machine process and the increasing dominance of pecuniary valuations, business might take flight to the military State and join it in restoring by force the loyalty, obedience, and subordination of labor which had been dissolved by the preceding emphasis on the motive of gain, the main chance, and the jungle law. Rejecting the "inevitability" of social democracy, while making occasional use of the Marxian analysis, Veblen thought in 1904 that the immediate future was more likely to comprise war, a growth of military force in society, the recrudescence of arbitrary discipline, the decline of laissez faire and civil liberties.

Although Veblen was widely regarded as a satirist, writing for the pleasure of the jest, instead of a truth-seeker in the correct line, the imputation was unjust. Occasionally his style seemed ironical, but it was the irony which was necessary to an accurate description of the difference between theory and practice. By the time Dorfman's life of Veblen appeared in 1934, a motif that once seemed derisive was discovered to be predictive rather than quizzical, and his method of intellectual procedure was more widely understood. At all events, a few younger economists found more substance and light in his economic science than, for instance, in J. Laurence Laughlin's dehumanized edition of John Stuart Mill's political economy.

Still, with the notable exception of Wesley Mitchell, most of the elders who had taken the place of the ancients continued to maintain an attitude of criticism or skepticism. When Dr. Alan R. Sweezy, a young instructor in Harvard University, proposed to take up the study of finance capital in Veblen's manner, he found that the Department of Economics believed Veblen "not worth studying," and in a short time this youthful preceptor of wayward inclination was dropped from the faculty by the authorities of the University. That may have been indicative — or merely an accident of academic readjustment.

§

As a result of the searching, inquiring, and thinking, coupled with the impact of events, the simple orthodoxy of the classical school seemed to be gradually losing its undisputed sovereignty in the academies and outside. To this fact there was impressive testimony. When, for instance, the editors of the Encyclopaedia of the Social Sciences, economists of unquestioned rank in the gild, came to planning their main article on Economics, published in 1931, they abandoned, if they ever entertained, the idea of covering the whole subject in a systematic and coherent manner within the scope of a single conspectus. Instead they opened with an introduction on the discipline of economics written by Professor E. R. A. Seligman, in which he stated that economics "has long been and will perhaps ever continue to be the battle ground of rationalizations for group and class interests. . . . The modern student regards these controversies not as dispassionate attempts to attain by logical means to eternal verities, but as the reflection in one field of changes in *Zeitgeist* and of shifts in the class structure of economic society." Having disposed of finality in this fashion, the editors then printed ten articles on economic thought: on the physiocrats, the classical school, marginal utility economics, mathematical economics, the Cambridge (England) school, the historical school, socialist economics, socio-ethical schools, romantic and universalist economics, and the institutional school.

Although a playful critic called economists "the astrologers of the machine age," the phrase was more amusing than just. Despite the conflicts of schools and all the dispersive forces, there were two or three signs of concentration on a higher level than that of scholastic contests in verbalism. Events, as well as thought, suggested revisions and new conclusions. Something like a free hand had been given to economic enterprisers during the beneficence of the golden glow and they had enjoyed the powerful patronage of government in the pursuit of their interests. Nevertheless, a cataclysm had shaken the capitalist system. On the assumption that minor modifications and the elimination of "abuses" would make the system run better, if not well, the Roosevelt administration, with much advice from economists compelled to grant concessions to a people distraught by the evident disequilibrium, made many experiments not contemplated by classical theory, without departing essentially from its presuppositions and predilections. All this was conducive to thought as well as hope and anger in academies and marketplaces, and economic discussion came to closer quarters with fundamentals in a freer spirit of inquiry.

Commenting on the state of economic thought in 1938, nine years after the great blizzard of 1929, Broadus Mitchell, professor of economics in Johns Hopkins University, declared in the Virginia Review: "The most significant thing in economic writing . . . is the increasingly important place occupied by collectivism of one sort or another. As recently as twenty years ago, in all but heretic quarters, the capitalist system was taken for granted. It rested upon private property, was motivated by private profit, functioned by means of prices competitively determined. . . . Capitalism is [now] on the defensive. Collectivism is no longer treated in footnotes, as a dangerous or engaging proposal, as a chance or minor variant, but occupies the text. Even in the meticulous descriptions of industry, major economic premises obtrude. Economic literature, for all the haste of its preparation and the fervor of its issuance, has reached a higher plane than it has occupied since the great days of Marx and Mill and George. Uneventful textual criticism, crossing of verbal swords, precious theory have given way to discussions in the large."

§

Perhaps even more tenaciously than in economics, institutionalists held the center of thought and research in what was called political science. The founders of the republic had been both theorists and practitioners and had united economic interests and corresponding policies in their operating philosophy. For a time in the middle period of American history realism had continued to mark the course of political thinking. But orthodox economics and the classes whose interests it fitted pushed government into a corner, if not entirely out of the domain, of social theory. Government was to do nothing — except define and protect property, which was something substantial, and perhaps to add protective tariffs, subsidies, and bounties. In the circumstances political science as a grand subject for thought and inquiry sank in the scale of esteem. After the destruction of the landed gentry in the South, from whose ranks had come such masters of political exposition as Madison, Jefferson, John Taylor, and Calhoun, no more great contributions to political thought came from that source. In the North, lawyers, as a rule, took charge of the subject and attention was focused on the outward trappings of government —

constitutions, forms of executive and legislative departments, statutes, administrative machinery, bureaus, offices, civil service, and similar externals of politics.

Though a profession devoted to the study of politics had arisen in the universities, interest in legal institutions and practices remained uppermost. In the main, the great contributions to politics, such as they were, assumed the garb of descriptions — accounts of the words and visible signs. No Veblen had appeared in that field to examine the very presuppositions on which adepts proceeded. The everlasting perdurance of "the American form of government" was generally taken for granted, and the probabilities of profound developments in government were neglected. Seldom were the historic forces of which government was an expression subjected to fine analyses. So hard-set was this mold of thought that even the battering effects of the world crisis failed to break entirely the sovereignty of formalism over the exploration of politics and the contemplation of political experience. No doubt it was safer for professors to stay within the sphere of symbolism, but the love of safety alone could not explain the supremacy of institutionalism in political science.

The ingrained dislike of English-speaking people for "grand theory," their distrust of it, an inveterate suspicion that it was a prime source of dangerous bigotry and tyranny, partly accounted for the tendency of American investigators to stick close to the description of particularities and to pragmatic tests. Besides there was an immense amount of work to be done in the realm of the matter-of-fact as legislatures enacted statutes by the thousands, courts handed down opinions by the cubic yard, and new boards, commissions, and other institutions were set up to deal with specific issues arising from day to day. So analysis, description, comparison, and criticism in detail proceeded apace, rendering immense services to practitioners and piling up knowledge in voluminous texts, treatises, reports, and monographs. Meanwhile political theorists, few in number, devoted their powers to surveys of the classics rather than to attempts to scale Parnassus themselves, not so much perhaps from lack of native ability as from qualms respecting the utility of the effort.

For all that, formalism did not pass undisputed. Nor did institutionalism escape criticism. Perhaps inevitably, the shocks of the time induced a consideration of fascism. At all events Charles E. Merriam, William Y. Elliott, Herbert Schneider, and Henry Spencer brought up for re-examination the politics of power, restored to the center of thought about the State the ambitions, passions, ferocities, and lusts of men. Machiavelli had taken note of these human qualifications for government. John Adams and Alexander Hamilton had given such uniformities their places in the scheme of things. But laissez faire economics, with its calculating man engaged in the peaceful pursuit of self-interest, had minimized or discarded the obvious experience of past politics. And the natural rights school, with its gratuitous assumption that man was "good by nature," or at least "decent," had pushed the Caesars and Napoleons of history out at the back door of political speculation. In democracies, politicians could hardly tell the voters that the people were irrational and loved evil; nor could they confess that they were themselves motivated by ambition and avarice. But the insurgency of Stalin, Hitler, and Mussolini in Europe, accompanied by more or less secret longings for "strong men" in the United States, suggested a re-exploration of power politics, based on ferocity and ambition, in which economic interests were bent to the ends of the dictator and his cohorts.

Other deep-seated conflicts affected the course of political thought. The temerity with which the Supreme Court struck down acts of Congress and asserted its "power to govern" invited a re-appraisal of the constitutional process itself. Interest in the matter was quickened by a revised edition of Charles Grove Haines' The American Doctrine of Judicial Supremacy, by Edward S. Corwin's The Twilight of the Supreme Court, and by Irving Brant's Storm over the Con-

stitution. These and other studies in the same field were
enlarged by numerous technical essays on the economic
theories and affiliations of Supreme Court judges in times
past. Having access to the Hamilton Fish papers, Sidney
Ratner, in an article in The Political Science Quarterly,
September, 1935, exploded the fiction that President Grant
had not "packed" the Supreme Court in connection with a
movement to secure a reversal of its decision in the Legal
Tender Cases in 1871. Works and essays dealing with former
justices, such as Taney, Miller, and Field, placed them in
their economic setting and disposed of the assumption that
the Constitution was a treatise in mathematical or symbolic
logic and that judges were mere adepts in ratiocination. Thus
the conception of the struggle for power broke into jurisprudence, much to the alarm of professional lawyers who
were sticklers for propriety in language, while quite practical
in matters of clients, retainers, and legal maneuvers.

Proceeding on lines already defined and piqued no doubt
by the successful use of symbols and mythology by fascism in
Europe, a few students of politics took up the psychological
aspects of human conduct in and under government — the
worship of power and the love of prostration. Appropriately
enough, at Chicago, Harold D. Lasswell inquired into the
psycho-pathology of political manipulations. Having a practical type of mind, he asked a pertinent, if impertinent,
question in politics: "Who Gets What?" At Yale University, Thurman W. Arnold, while teaching law, was impressed
by its ceremonials and myths and, after exploring the laby-
rinth, emerged with a volume entitled The Symbols of
Government. That Yale, which had given Chief Justice Taft
to public life, could later add Professor Arnold seemed strange
on the surface of things, but it happened that Arnold had
been a practicing lawyer and politician in the Far West before
mounting the rostrum in New Haven. In Wyoming the face
of jurisprudence had been less highly polished than in the
East.

A similar realism was introduced into political thought by

a small group occupied in examining the operating forces of government. As a result more was learned about back-stairs manipulations, to which Peter Odegard gave the name of Pressure Politics. From parliamentary halls, antechambers, and caucus rooms, E. P. Herring, of Harvard, carried the technique of inquiry into administrative offices where the galvanism of the lobby was persistent and effective, if less open to observation than in the legislative branches of government. Reaching out into the occupations, interests, and activities of the people, Arthur Holcombe, also of Harvard, sought the ultimate sources of political power in the United States. His economic analysis of party composition and tactics, The Political Parties of Today, published in 1924, Holcombe crowned by a supplementary volume, The New Party Politics, in which he showed the essentially middle-class character of the dominant strata in American life and suggested that tacticians and prognosticators had better reckon with this invincible fact.

The realistic sense displayed here and there in the exploration of domestic politics seemed to pause, however, at the gates of grand policy in world affairs, touching war and peace. Although armament expenditures in the United States steadily mounted until they rose above a billion dollars a year, students of government continued to neglect the role of the army and the navy in American society and in the formulation of public policies. Other countries, according to the common credo, might be militaristic, but never the United States.

Given this assumption, treatises on government and economics practically ignored military institutions as interests. Economists sometimes railed at war as if it were a kind of inexplicable madness that interfered with an otherwise almost perfect free market and price mechanism; academic works on government gave a few pages to the organization of the military and naval establishments; but the business of war, with its collateral military and naval interests, backed by the avarice of supply surveyors and the passions of men,

received relatively little attention, save in occasional pacifist pamphlets which were usually sentimental instead of
informative.

From the schools of warfare came no von Clausewitz to
reconsider the art and science. Though the loose and sentimental system of thought on sea power put forth by Admiral
Alfred T. Mahan at the turn of the century disintegrated
under analysis and the impacts of practice, no successor tried
to gather up the fragments and provide a more tenable
substitute. Nevertheless there were signs that the nature,
trappings, symbols, and interests of armed force were to be
carefully examined rather than taken for granted and celebrated. Beginnings were made in Silas B. McKinley's Democracy and Military Power, in Mauritz A. Hallgren's The
Tragic Fallacy, in the work of Stephen and Joan Rauschen-
bush based on the reports of the Nye munitions committee,
and in Alfred Vagts' History of Militarism. Such volumes
indicated a drift of inquiry and thought, a concern with
war as an institution, with military establishments as vested
interests, with the relations between the rise of military
power and the decline of civil society. The subject had
evoked trenchant thought among the founders of the republic
and it might again recover its rightful place in what was
called political science.

In the sphere of foreign affairs — aspects of domestic
economy and policy — academic inquiries ran mainly along
institutional lines. No one appeared to reaffirm Archibald
Coolidge's unquestioning faith in America as a World Power.
Indeed, devotion to the imperialism of Manifest Destiny was
diminishing, not mounting into a more holy zeal. Nor did
political literature show a notable recrudescence of isolationist
philosophy in the manner that had prevailed generally from
1789 to 1898. Edwin Borchard and W. P. Lage exposed the
inner nature of American neutrality from 1914 to 1917 and
made a plea for sturdy resistance to entanglements. But they
seemed to speak for a minority among professors and ideologues. Since 1917 the discussion of "foreign affairs" had

turned mainly around Woodrow Wilson's system of universal philanthropy. Societies had been established to promote it. Chairs had been founded in universities to advance it, under the protection, to be sure, of "scientific detachment."

Verily the exposition of foreign affairs became a kind of vested interest. Accepting at face value the thesis that world peace could be effected by governments, that the world image constructed by Woodrow Wilson was a truism, and that the going systems of economy would continue to go as in the past, writers on foreign relations were more inclined to recite than to reconsider. After all, as they were committed by faith to dogmas of internationalism, an application of the Socratic elenchus to their assumptions would have been profanation — and perhaps catastrophic to schools, lectureships, endowments, and other sources of supply and prestige. It was no accident, then, that Clark Foreman's The New Internationalism and Jerome Frank's Save America First — demands for a sound internal economy and for abstention from political entanglements abroad — came from men who had graduated from colleges to enjoy the privileges of freedom from academic constrictions.

§

Broader in scope than economics and politics, sociology had for its domain of thought and inquiry all human activities, institutions, and relations — family, church, community, economy, war, politics, and all other phases of civilization in statu quo and presumably in long-time development. But no American sociologist sought to grasp the scheme of things entire and to subdue the voluminous and intractable masses of fact to any comprehensive and coherent frame of thought. No single person or group of persons occupied the center of the stage as Lester Ward, William Graham Sumner, Franklin Giddings, Simon Patten, and Edward A. Ross had done in past years, and carried on in their style. No sociologist, aspiring to Newtonian simplicity, proclaimed a new formula such as "the consciousness of kind as the basis of society," which Giddings had put forward long before. Instead of presenting the subject as a unified discipline, R. M. MacIver devoted the article on Sociology for The Encyclopaedia of the Social Sciences to a history of the sociological schools, their characteristics, and their centers of interest, and showed that heavy emphasis had been laid in the United States upon "classifications and descriptions of particular social processes, such as assimilation, accommodation, adjustment." These were aspects of society especially considered by Charles Ellwood, Robert Park, and Ernest Burgess.

Something like a positive school controlled by a single conception emerged at the University of Chicago and was called by a biological name, "ecological," indicating that social patterns and differences were or might be determined by the influences of environment. But the majority of the sociologists, even those who conceded that they were working under some hypothesis respecting the nature of all things, confined their attention to classifying and describing particular phases or communities of society, urban and rural — habits, customs, institutions, and relationships in microcosm. Their work was well illustrated by Robert and Helen Lynd's two intensive studies of Muncie, Indiana, under the head of Middletown; by the surveys of Southern economy, culture, and regionalism carried out under Howard Odum and his associates at the University of North Carolina; and by the statistical studies of William F. Ogburn of the University of Chicago.

Such work was in sum and substance what MacIver called "an extensive and intensive mapping of the contemporary social scene," that is, essentially reportorial in the best sense of the word. It largely ignored historical perspective and the issues of prognosis. Disclaiming all assumptions except perhaps the assumption that such work was worth doing and that the notations of appearances corresponded with the realities, the institutional and folkway sociologists adhered tightly to "facts" and in so doing gave to the public an enlarged knowledge of American communities and behaviors, incidentally destroying many dream pictures in the process. Almost any student trained in the "techniques" of the school could pursue this kind of sociology; foundations provided generous grants of money to finance it; the results brought no basic disturbances to the five or six primary articles of the American credo.

Whenever a professor got far off this well-worn and well-oiled track, discarded the neutrality of the institutional school, and took up the ethical aspects of society, either directly or by intended implication, he was likely to run into severe criticism from his "scientific" colleagues and to be regarded as a kind of preacher, theologically inclined. By insisting upon the existence of ethical motives and the necessity of bringing ethical considerations into account in any comprehensive treatment of human society, Charles Ellwood and Charles Cooley drew upon their heads this imputation from some of their brethren who imagined that they themselves had harder heads. A worse fate befell Jerome Davis of The Divinity School of Yale University. Under the heading of Capitalism and Its Culture, he pointed out an intimate relationship between two aspects of civilization which other sociologists had been inclined to neglect, and documented the relationship by a wealth of citations, warmed to intense heat by a moral indignation presumably appropriate to a professor of sociology in a divinity school. Not long afterward, the connections of Professor Davis with the University were severed, "on other grounds," the authorities explained.

The process of intellectual catalysis encouraged by analytical research in the branches of social study was partly offset by the completion of The Encyclopaedia of the Social Sciences in 1935, under the editorship of E. R. A. Seligman and Alvin Johnson, with the counsel of representatives from all cognate professional associations. Designed to cover the whole "field," all schools of thought, and all fundamental presuppositions and methods, it was of necessity sociological in nature and the authors of its articles, however specialized in their own researches, were more or less affected by the requirements of system and comprehensiveness. Representing as a rule contemporary scholarship at its best, these articles rose above traditional naïveté and contributed to the elevation of social thought in many spheres.

Even so, just as economists shrank from correcting theory by the fruits of institutional research and from emulating Adam Smith, Ricardo, or Alfred Marshall, sociologists declined to grasp at the universal in the manner of Auguste Comte or Herbert Spencer. In the establishment of The Journal of Social Philosophy in 1935, awareness of the larger challenge seemed imminent but the display of awareness was not accompanied by great efforts on the part of American scholars to meet it by coming to grips with "the ultimate design of the universe." That commission was left to writers of European origins. Pitirim Sorokin undertook it and reported his observations, conclusions, and frame of social thought in four large volumes entitled Social and Cultural Dynamics. Although at the time Sorokin was professor of sociology at Harvard University, he had been born, reared, and educated in Tsarist Russia, had lived through the Bolshevik revolution, and had not reached the United States until 1923. He had experienced immense history and he brought to sociology the historical perspective so widely neglected by surveyors of contemporary scenes; but his thought was colored by his concrete experience and he dyed his treatise with strains of absolutism and mysticism out of harmony with the pragmatic thought, the democratic susceptibilities, and prevailing experiences of American scholars.

Another effort to overcome the American "deficiency" in breadth and depth of conception was the translation into English and the publication in New York City of Vilfredo Pareto's treatise on general sociology under the title of Science and Society. By emphasizing the role of the irrational in human affairs, Pareto, like Sorokin, gave a certain jolt

to fact-finders and compilers, but at the same time he suggested the imputation that he was also primarily a fact-finder
bolstering up his own preconceptions. Less heralded as
startling or epoch-making, but in truth more relevant to
realistic thought about all societies, including the American,
was the publication of another continental treatise in English, in 1935, namely, Karl Mannheim's Ideology and
Utopia, a work on the nature of social knowledge and a study
of the principal controlling conceptions under which the
writing up of social facts and thinking about them could
proceed. It asked in effect: Just what do you think you are
doing when you are collecting, classifying, and writing about
the behaviors and linguistic expressions of human beings in
society?

§

To educational thought the perpendicular and collateral
strokes of the economic depression brought troubled dreams.
In the evening of the golden glow all seemed serene and
secure. With utmost confidence many educators spoke of
"the science of education." The future of American institutions, of the sustaining environment, of the nourishing cultural heritage, could be taken for granted. If anything was
needed it was more of the same things — more school buildings, larger appropriations, and the multiplication of "research" projects.

Under the appearance of eternal prosperity, the function
of education was to prepare boys and girls for the professions,
trades, occupations, and crafts, which would provide unend-
ing and adequate demand for the human output of the
schools. By precise psychological and occupational measurements educators were supposed to discover the quantities of
whatever was needed for each of the multitudinous niches
into which graduates were to be fitted. Specialists presumably could also find out by research just the kind of courses,
methods, and instructional apparatus required to fit the several candidates for their several callings. Expert testers,

employing scientific "techniques" and "batteries" of blanks, questionnaires, and instrumentalities, could show with mathematical precision, it was thought, how far each of the millions of graduates would or could go in making a "success" in his or her pecuniary enterprise. All this was to be done without obliterating the notion of democratic opportunity and equalitarianism which had distinguished American education from, let us say, the stratified occupational therapy of old Prussian institutions of learning. In reality the matter was not quite so simple but, when boiled down, educational thought in the golden glow amounted to little more, and dissenters could be lightly brushed aside as "radicals" lacking in scientific and pedagogical discipline.

This dream of an educational science was interrupted by the crash of the economic depression, by the sharp curtailment of the employment for which the schools had been preparing their charges, by conflicts over New Deal legislation, by the breaking up of orthodoxy in many places, and by fascist upheavals and wars in Europe and Asia. Such events wrenched the business of education out of the groove and made the "science" of education appear far less scientifically sound. Teachers streamed out into the ranks of the unemployed. Schools by the thousands were closed. Bills were unpaid, even in the rich city of Chicago. Millions of graduates, correctly instructed and precisely tested according to the rigid canons of indubitable masters, could find no places in the scheme of things pecuniary. "Here we come, WPA!" was the cry of one graduating class. As the promoters of the New Deal made fierce attacks on "economic royalists" and pushed through Congress legislation different in purpose and upshot from the laws of the Full Dinner Pail or the New Freedom, and as the critics of the New Deal blasted away at such legislation and administration, calling it an emanation from Moscow, educators once safely ensconced in their solid science found the walls of their theory falling about their heads. They began to wonder whether their science was sufficient unto the day.

Commissions and individuals, equipped with knowledge and methods of inquiry, set to work zealously to take stock of education in the new situation and to find for it a philosophy and program more appropriate to the exigencies of the time. Through the stoutest ivory of the strongest towers swept reverberations from the marketplace and the forum, stirring active minds in the educational world to greater energy. Reports, volumes, essays, monographs, and learned papers began to jostle the old literature of education already mountainous in proportions.

In 1934 a Commission on the Social Studies, working under the auspices of the American Historical Association, completed a series of volumes, crowned by Conclusions and Recommendations, in which was set forth a collectivistic frame of reference for controlling the construction of curricula, methods, and expectations of education. In vital respects this report called for a reappraisal of the individualistic concepts on which "the science of education" had rested. Later the Educational Policies Commission of the National Education Association came to similar conclusions and, far from taking for granted the future of American democracy, asserted the obligation of public education to make positive contributions to strengthening, upholding, and developing that democracy, including the precious heritage of civil liberties, then so violently assailed by theory and practice. Indeed the persistent efforts of professional educators to think through the problems thrown upon them by actions and reactions in the secular world were spirited and courageous, displaying both vitality and comprehension.

On the upper level of education, called the "higher" learning for reasons not altogether conclusive, educational thought was apparently less agitated than on the lower level where teachers who managed to hold their positions came into direct contact with underfed children from the homes of the unemployed. Defaults in bonds curtailed incomes in college and university; great donations diminished in volume; graduates found fewer opportunities selling stocks and bonds or in the

professions. But honorary degrees and commencement orations brought continuous revelations of the fact that educational interest and thought on college campuses were substantially unchanged by the jars of the depression. The
tercentenary of Harvard University was conducted in the
spirit of the tradition and an effort to use it as a springboard
from which to launch a concentration of science and the
humanities upon the pressing problems of the contemporary
world died on the morrow of the hopeful day.

Only a few incidents whipped up the calm sea of educational thought in the "higher" ranges. In 1930 Abraham
Flexner brought out a comparative study of Universities,
American, English, German, in which he protested against
the invasion of learning by trivial, occupational, and pecuniary interests and found ideal contrasts abroad, especially in
Germany. The book made a temporary sensation, but the
charm of its constructive proposals was marred by the subsequent conduct of properly trained and conditioned professors
in Germany, after the advent of Hitler and his "Aryan"
learning. A few years later Norman Foerster assayed a similar
theme in The American State University, outlined a gloomy
picture of learning under the pressures of democratic politics,
and hinted at an escape through a new unity on a basis somewhat metaphysical. A still bigger discord was raised when
Robert Hutchins, president of Chicago University, issued his
reflections on the state of colleges and universities under a
title which Thorstein Veblen had made famous — The Higher
Learning in America.

On the one side President Hutchins' treatise was severely
critical. Without mercy he assailed the profusion, specialization, and "chaos" in the multitude of schools and courses
prevailing in the institutions of higher learning, and above
all the devotion to occupational and pecuniary interests. On
the constructive side, he proposed to introduce order and
simplicity by cleaning out a huge pile of courses in scientific
and humanistic studies, especially those directed to occupational and pecuniary ends, and substituting for them instruc-

tion in a few "principles." In substance he declared that "the heart of education will be, if education is rightly understood, the same at any time, in any place, under any political, social, or economic conditions," and the very center of the very heart should be metaphysics, that is, instruction in things highest by nature, first principles, and first causes.

As to upshot, if not specific intention, President Hutchins' scheme meant throwing overboard nearly everything that had been thought and done in the domain of the higher learning since the middle ages and returning to the apparent simplicities of the seven liberal arts adopted for Christendom — grammar, rhetoric, logic, arithmetic, geometry, astronomy, and music — with perhaps some alterations and condensations. This proposal, in effect, merely stopped a bit short of taking over the Roman Catholic view of the universe and the function of university learning — the truth, that is, our truth, is everywhere the same, good always, whatever change the years may bring.

In a critique, published in The Social Frontier, one of the prime leaders in the socialization of learning, John Dewey, replied to President Hutchins, by contrasting his proposed educational philosophy with that of Lancelot Hogben, the English author of The Retreat from Reason. "To Mr. Hutchins," Dewey explained, "the sciences represent in the main the unmitigated empiricism which is a great curse of modern life, while to Mr. Hogben the conceptions and methods which Mr. Hutchins takes to be the true and final definition of rationality are obscurantist and fatally reactionary, while their survival in economic theory and other branches of social 'science' is the source of the intellectual irrelevance of the latter to the fundamental problems of our present culture. Indeed, these disciplines are more than irrelevant and futile. They are literally terrible in their distraction of social intelligence and activity from genuine social problems and from the only methods by which these problems can be met."

Dewey might have added, had he been so inclined, a query

in respect of the great white hope contained in Hutchins' hypothesis : How did it happen that the higher learning of the liberal arts imposed on young minds in mediaeval Europe failed to bring order out of feudal chaos or to prevent the little western world, which ever imagines itself to be all civilization, from developing under God's providence into the modern world which seems so chaotic to believers who say they know and have "the" truth ?

Nevertheless President Hutchins' volume struck into an issue of thought which had long occupied the western mind — unity amid diversity, permanence amid change, order against liberty, peace against war, the true, the beautiful, and the good against the false, the ugly, and the evil. The issue had never been resolved; and skeptics, even while pursuing the quest, suspected that the human mind was not equal to the task of resolution. However that might be, a nation seeking to bend the multiplicity and conflicts of things to the uses of a good life did call for operating postulates, strong affirmations, and coördinating forces in education conceived as a preparation for heroic endeavors and achievements in practice. But if anything was known at all, a return to the middle ages, in which the seven liberal arts occupied the center of instruction, was as impossible as an escape from the pull of gravitation.

It might be that the work of framing the postulates, making the strong affirmations, and providing the coördinating forces would not fall to any single division of learning, and that leadership in the process of uniting the Emotional and the Intellectual would be taken by the scientists so cavalierly treated by President Hutchins and his school. Not, of course, by the simple adherents of Newton and Darwin, or the followers of the theological physicists, Jeans and Eddington, but, as Herbert J. Muller pointed out in The Southern Review for the summer of 1938, by "the scientists who on naturalistic grounds are bursting through the abstractions once identified with Reality, scrapping the absolutes that have tyrannized thought, pointing to an organic synthesis in which philosophy, art, and science may be reconciled again after some centuries of specialization in different kinds of 'knowledge' and dispute over different levels of 'truth.'"

When educational thought left the school room and invaded the world of practice it took the form of concern with what was loosely called adult education. Although the covering tradition ran far back into the days of the lyceum, this concern now turned particularly to a consideration of education in relation to the exigencies of social living. Vocational extension went on as before, to be sure, with perhaps less confidence as vocational opportunities diminished or at least failed to expand with the increase in the number of applicants. Yet interest was enlarged in matters of social adjustment and great public issues; and, in the application of adult education, forums of discussion sprang up over the country, in private and public buildings, under private and public auspices.

Underlying this movement was a conviction that if the major questions of the time could be examined and debated in the light of reason, in the relative quiet of auditoriums, the likelihood of resorting to the methods of violence would be diminished. Impressed by the opportunities and tensions of the political and economic scene, the United States Office of Education, under the direction of John W. Studebaker, formulated programs, aided in the organization of procedures and methods, and stimulated the growth of systematic discussion among adults from one end of the country to the other. If somewhat overlooked by those engaged in formal and higher instruction, thought in this division of educational interest was directed with increasing sophistication and zeal to the exploration of democracy, its operating methods, and its sustaining economy.

§

Called of old the crown of all learning, philosophy continued its quest for unity and order through the toss and pitch of "matter and spirit" and, in so doing, took somewhat

into account the events, experiences, and spirit of the midpassage. One historian disputed its right to the crown and
called it a mere phase of history but that had slight, if any,
effect upon adepts. They would insist upon standing outside
history, they thought, more or less emancipated from the
conditioning or determining influences of mundane, secular,
and economic interests and conflicts. Perhaps in fact the
philosopher, like other thinkers, was dominated by the social
frame of his own memory; still, when the idea was suggested,
it was not welcomed by universal acclaim, for it made the
philosopher a little lower than the angels.

As of old, there were still open to the philosopher the four
ways traced by Irwin Edman: "philosophy as logical faith,
as social criticism, as mystical insight, and as nature understood." These, at least, were the well-traveled highroads
and, while banks crashed, multitudes searched for work and
bread, and dictators threatened the "peace and order" of
the world, such as it was, most philosophers either re-explored
the ancient paths or sat and whittled away at fine points of
minor doctrine.

For the philosophers of logical faith there was little to do
except to restate historic maxims with new trimmings. They
asserted, that is, assumed, the existence of absolute truth and
the power of their minds to grasp it after attaining faith in
the assertion or presupposition. Karl Mannheim had maintained that social relationships influence the course of the
most abstract thought, that thinking does not develop in
accordance with imminent laws, pre-logic, inner dialectic, or
any other timeless or contentless process. But that meant
little or nothing to the possessors of logical faith. Their
chosen way was good enough for them. In fact if they left it,
they well knew that they might soon be sunk in the bog of
relativism or caught up in the drift of social action. The
main highway seemed more secure.

Philosophers of the Catholic persuasion were guided by
great masters of logical faith, especially the learned doctor,
Thomas Aquinas. Scarcely able to transcend the work of the

Church fathers, they were mainly content to expound and explain to new generations that which they had received from their predecessors, often with new illustrations more or less ingeniously picked and presented. Nor did things change much on the Protestant side. Josiah Royce had no successor to preach as effectively in the name of the absolute as he had done; and philosophers who accepted that faith seemed more inclined to polish and refine it than to restate it in language more penetrating, vital, and comprehensive. As for mystical insight, that belonged in the realm of personal experience. When expressed in terms of logic, facts, and "earthly discourse," the reports of mystical insight fell short of an independent philosophy. Experiments in telepathy, mind reading, and supersensory perception, although they created an excitement similar to that raised by spirit-rappings in the Millerite age, disclosed little or no knowledge that was not more easily ascertained by direct observation.

There remained the two other ways: social criticism and the understanding of nature, which certainly crossed at many points, if they did not entirely blend. Philosophers of these directions kept on making the pragmatic assertion: Words, declarations, syllogisms have no meaning for us apart from the things done under them by the professors, expounders, and true believers. How can an idea be true if one cannot find it as a tangible in reality or express it in life and conduct? What is the use of proclaiming a theory to be absolutely true when practices contradict it every day? These questions, although certainly pertinent, did not materially disturb the possessors of logical faith; nor did this line of inquiry itself lead to "constructive formulations." Just where it would lead no one seemed able to say and there was no tribunal for passing unequivocal judgment upon its merits. If regular attendance at church services was a test of the popular concern, then a majority was on the side of the skeptics. Yet in a pinch a majority might be found in favor of the proposition that words uttered on Sunday were truer than things done on the other six days.

Although it was not always openly admitted, the philosophy of social criticism involved an interpretation of "nature" and indeed of all history, which Hegel sought to rationalize as revealing the ultimate design of the universe. It was doubtless a sign of the times that John Dewey, called the Dean of the American Philosophers by naturalists, sometimes accused of being an "atheist" by clergymen, became increasingly interested in the social implications of thought and in efforts to construct a social system more in harmony with conceptions of justice, truth, and beauty. From the academic chair he stepped out into the sphere of hazardous actions, seeking to apply the formulas of his thought. At another seat of learning Sidney Hook tried to bring the critique of Karl Marx to bear on the consideration of truth and action, theory and practice — philosophy in its largest reaches. Other philosophers, T. V. Smith, of Chicago, and William E. Hocking, of Harvard, for example, also ventured away from the cloister to test words uttered, "syntactical sentences," in the forum where practitioners strove, not always successfully, to combine virtue and the main chance.

In the realm of the concrete, strange things happened to philosophers. Amid the dust of the forum and the marketplace, where programs were drawn up and action taken, were often associated philosophic thinkers who differed diametrically in the calmer atmosphere of academies. For example, at opposite poles in metaphysical fundamentals stood John Dewey, the naturalist, and John A. Ryan, indomitable defender of the logical faith. Yet in matters of social procedure they had more in common than in dispute. If Morris Cohen, who held mediaeval philosophy in deep respect, found Dewey's pragmatism incomplete, perchance wholly unsatisfactory, he could join Dewey in any bitter struggle for the maintenance of civil liberties.

Upon occasion, as a cynic had remarked, it might be the duty of the philosopher, as of the historian or economist, to make the worse cause appear the better; yet as the golden glow paled to shadows, many of those leaders among American philosophers who commanded national consideration chose no such course. Criticizing the metaphysical aristocracy for aloofness, even when agreeing with its assumptions and syllogisms, they went into the highways and byways where men and women were battling for bread, struggling to hold families intact, and striving to employ the engines of organization and government in the interest of social security. After all, neither the founder of the logical faith nor the inventor of naturalism had ignored common clay and common purpose. And perhaps the best that philosophers could do was to accept the basic human values of civilization which had been asserted against sheer force and empty speculation in ages past, and reassert them amid the encircling menaces of tyranny and intolerance in their own times.

§

All thought about economics, politics, sociology, education, and philosophy, indeed all theory and practice in government and business, in entertainment, letters, the arts, and sciences, were in fact but phases of history, were enmeshed in history as actuality. The golden glow, the dissolutions, and the New Deal, however construed in terms of advancing or declining civilization, were outcomes of history and forerunners of destiny to come. And since this is true, out of the study of history, near and distant, was to flow such fundamental understanding of American society and its fortunes among the nations as human intelligence and knowledge could supply to prognosis and provision, in shaping the fleeting present and the oncoming future. If any facts known to the human mind were irreducible, this fact was certainly among them. What, then, were historians in the academies and beyond the campuses doing with it?

Committed by their craft to the study of the past, historians were not ostensibly so concerned with thought about contemporary affairs as were the professors of economics, politics, or sociology, and could, if they wished, keep on their way unperturbed by the events which impinged so sharply upon their colleagues. For a long time they had operated on the assumption that they could write history in a "scientific" manner and describe the past "as it actually had been," somewhat as the chemist correctly pictures by exact formulas the reactions in his test tube, and they had confined their attention mainly to political and military events. It was not their business, according to the maxims of the gild, to serve any practical needs of a society feverishly hunting solutions for its pressing problems.

This style of research and composition, called Historism, had been derived mainly from German scholasticism of the nineteenth century, itself largely an outcome of the inhibitions placed upon German historians by their bureaucratic status and by their rivalry for advancement, that is, competition in the mass of accumulated data, the multiplicity of footnotes and illustrations, the weight of their volumes. Impressive scholarship of that kind continued to control historical writing in the United States. Documentary research and indefatigable industry, coupled with extreme caution about the open admission of controlling conceptions, were its principal characteristics. What Alfred Cohn looked for in straight scientific thought, namely, the attainment of the simple generalization of a Newton or a Faraday or a Darwin, was not set as the goal of labors by historians of the scientific school. On the contrary they were inclined to regard as queer any member of the gild, such as Henry Adams, who sought to arrive at brief formulas in historical studies. Like minor workers in natural science, they restricted their activities principally to the collection and analysis of records and the meticulous piecing together of "facts" regarded as well authenticated. When true to form, they crowded their work with details, avoided colorful phrases, and aimed at a severity of style appropriate to a treatise on physics or chemistry, all in unquestioning faith, apparently, that such patterns of words faithfully described the past actuality which they were supposed to know.

Working more or less in this style, under such a theory of their function, historians continued to produce solid and scholarly volumes of high quality in matters of exactness and documentation. Shrinking from the mammoth enterprises requiring ten or fifteen volumes in the tradition of Gibbon, Mommsen, and Bancroft, they confined their attention to special periods or to particular phases and personalities. Charles McLean Andrews went forward with his meticulous survey of the colonial period in America; Tyler Dennett reconstructed the historic figure of John Hay; Douglas Southall Freeman completed a microscopic biography of Robert E. Lee; Allan Nevins reworked the life of Grover Cleveland and wrote a massive biography of Hamilton Fish; Samuel Flagg Bemis illuminated dark corners of American diplomacy in its historical development; John D. Hicks, after painstaking researches and journeys to and fro over the continent, portrayed The Populist Revolt in an urbane manner which Mark Hanna and Joseph Choate in 1896 might have called revolutionary; Henrietta Larson revamped the history of Jay Cooke, the financier of the civil war, on the basis of materials that had eluded the older biographers; George Clinton, Andrew Jackson, and Andrew Johnson were revived again in new configurations. These and other historical works done in the style of the craft displayed both vitality and critical energy which showed no signs of weariness or relaxation.

Nevertheless historians did not pursue their peaceful course without meeting groundswells of considerable proportions. Their main thesis that they really could describe history as it actually had been was denied by some members of the gild. Their claim to Olympian impartiality was subjected to inquiry and drastic revision. Since facts do not select and order themselves on the printed page, the historian, critics insisted, selects his own facts and arranges them according to some scheme of values and, in choosing the linguistic forms, sees them from some angle of social vision. In the spirit of this criticism, the president of the American Historical Association declared in 1933, the great year of the banking crisis and New Deal inauguration, that written history is not a science or an art, but contemporary thought about the past, instructed and delimited by the records and documents of history as actuality — "record and knowledge authenticated by criticism and ordered with the help of the scientific method."

On another flank James Harvey Robinson created a commotion by asserting that it was one of the prime functions of historiography to throw light upon "our present quandaries" by tracing the rise and development of the circumstances from which they sprang. Historical research and construction done in this spirit, with due respect for the authenticity of documents and for scientific exactitude in respect of details, was bound, in the nature of things, to give a different appearance to the past and the present. Although when expressed without adornment, this idea seemed heretical to keepers of orthodoxy, what it actually suggested was that historians do consciously what they had been doing more or less unconsciously.

Likewise disturbing to professors of political and military history was the widening of historical inquiries to include in the stream of history other aspects — business, the arts, medicine, literature, science, manners, customs, and commonplace ways of life in all ranks of society. Arthur M. Schlesinger and Dixon Ryan Fox brought near to the conclusion their editing of their twelve-volume coöperative series, A History of American Life. Albert Deutsch, in his history of The Mentally Ill in America, covered a long-neglected phase of barbarism and humanism in theory and practice. Richard H. Shryock, in The Development of Modern Medicine, related medicine to its social setting, and dealt with the reciprocal influences of the relationships. Applying a similar method, Vernon Parrington brought literature into the Main Currents in American Thought, demonstrating the shallowness of any criticism merely concerned with style and form and at the same time putting secular history in a new perspective.

More alarming to gild orthodoxy was the increasing emphasis on the economic interpretation of history, especially as the origin of this type of empirical realism was falsely ascribed to Karl Marx in spite of his disclaimers. Cautiously applied, with a sense of its limitations, the economic interpretation merely meant the persistent association of ideas and personalities in historical writing with the relevant economic interests in which they were entangled in history as actuality. An excellent example of this style was afforded by J. Franklin Jameson's The American Revolution Considered as a Social Movement, published in 1926. Since Jameson was in fact the beloved dean of the Historical Association, it was clear that the economic "taint" had gone rather deeply into the ranks of the fraternity. Dealing with a narrower field, Western Lands and the American Revolution, Thomas P. Abernethy showed the intimate affiliation of politics and land speculation in the heroic days of winning and establishing independence. In the extreme form employed by communist writers, the economic interpretation became materialist determinism, and history was written merely "from the class angle," but this type of historiography gained few if any adherents in the academies.

Either as mild reasonableness or closed dogma, the economic interpretation played havoc with the pleasing conceptions of history entertained by patriotic societies and bar associations and supplied fuel for contemporary politics and economics. Accordingly at the fiftieth anniversary of the American Historical Association, it received a severe drubbing at the hands of the professor chosen to review past achievements and present troubles.

While adepts were debating the theory of history writing, individual historians were illustrating the intellectual dilemma in works of many grades. How, for instance, should the civil struggle between Americans at the middle of the nineteenth century be viewed as human experiences? That struggle had been described in various terms: correct Whiggery, abolitionist idealism, planters' philosophy, Southern Democracy, the Republican conception of cause and effect, and judicious mixtures of the several assumptions, with emphasis somewhere. Now two professors, Francis B. Simkins and James W. Patton, found fundamental support for the Southern cause among the Women of the Confederacy. Remembering or discovering that a yeomanry, as well as the planters' caste, had existed in the South, other historians interpreted the civil conflict in terms of a Southern class struggle, in part at least, as the American revolution had been interpreted by J. Franklin Jameson. Into this reverie and assertion, William Burghart DuBois injected a Negro's opinion of the conflict, selecting his facts from facts which other versions had missed or discarded, making his own emphasis, and demonstrating that Negroes had played a larger role in the great drama than white historians had assigned to them. And a group of new writers on history, among whom Louis Hacker was a prominent representative, sought to remind readers of history that working people, white and black, agricultural and industrial, had been involved in that social upheaval so sweeping and revolutionary in character. What then was "the whole truth" of this immense social war conceived precisely "as it had been"?

Certainly all this writing from various "angles" influenced historical thought in general and in particular. Its effects were clearly traceable, for example, in J. G. Randall's The Civil War and Reconstruction — a work by a Northern historian which was warmly commended, for its treatment of the civil conflict, by a Southern historian, B. B. Kendrick. After referring at the outset to the narrow and partisan character of traditional writing on that vexatious subject, Randall declared that "on many a scholarly front the boundary of research has been extended; what is more significant is that there have come upon the historical world a fresh interpretative power, a new insight, a greater resourcefulness, a growing appreciation of human factors, an understanding of social and economic forces, and a sharpened sophistication in facing time-worn assumptions, which have given to historical writing a new tone and a new orientation."

When the geography of ideas was taken into account, it was perhaps just to say that the most fertile and penetrating historical writing of the midpassage was produced by Southern investigators, such as F. L. Owsley, B. B. Kendrick, A. M. Arnett, D. D. Wallace, Rupert Vance, and C. Vann Woodward, to make a selection. In some respects, Southerners were well fitted by experience and temper for writing history at a time when industrial civilization was suffering from pangs of disorder and twinges of conscience. In spite of the railroads, cotton mills, and blast furnaces in the South, the region remained essentially agrarian in economy and sentiments.

By 1933 the earlier generation of Southern historians who felt impelled to write romantically on the Old South, or to paint the Reconstruction blacker than it may have been on the whole, had passed away or done their work. The time for more critical thought was at hand. From the beginning Southern thinkers had refused to accept at face value the capitalist system and its maxims of virtue in the fashion of their Northern colleagues. They had been in opposition — not proletarian but agrarian. They could not swallow, without gagging at least, many aphorisms so palatable above the Mason and Dixon line, and they brought to the selection and arrangement of facts, called historiography, a frame of reference marked by many local peculiarities. Of this generalization innumerable illustrations were provided; for instance, in Wallace's History of South Carolina, in Woodward's Tom Watson, Agrarian Rebel, and in the long line of articles and reviews published in the Virginia Quarterly, The Southern Review, and other magazines of the region. The solid mentality of the solid South was dissolving "like mists before the morning sun," as Henry W. Grady might have put the case.

While reports on human experience from various angles of experience were coming into the thought of history, woman's experience through the ages received more critical attention and consideration. Largely composed and taught by men, written history had mainly represented the ambitions of men — of warriors, politicians, lords of creation, labor leaders, planters, and proletarians. If women appeared at all in the lectures and pages, they did so in identical or subsidiary capacities or as abstractions such as "women in industry" or as persons but newly introduced to society through the triumph of the suffrage movement. But studies on other than conventional lines indicated that the history of men alone was partial history; that men and women had shared human experiences throughout the past; that women had always been at or near the center of private and public affairs where history was made; that women also had distinctions and contributions to record. Thus the superficial notion that women had been a passive sex in history, counting for nothing in the molding of their own lives and in the molding of the common life, uneducated until they got the chance to attend modern colleges, was supplanted by a larger and more accurate view. Out of nothing, could something leap into being?

However useful the notion had been as a weapon of feminist agitation for enlarged civil and political advantages, its inadequacy was now shown in numerous and striking forms of historical writing. One instance illustrates the point: Dr. Kate C. Hurd-Mead's History of Women in Medicine — the work of a physician trained at Johns Hopkins, a linguist, a scholar accustomed to the precisions of research, and a researcher over a period of more than thirty years not only in the great libraries of the western world but out in the byways of the world where primitive medicine is still the rule. Writing on women in medicine called for writing on medicine itself, and writing on medicine required descriptions of social settings for the art of healing.

Historical documents were of course essential instruments for developing the knowledge required for realistic thought. Recognizing this requirement, interested women organized a movement having for its purpose to establish a World

Center for Women's Archives in New York City and began
the systematic collection, listing, and calendaring of letters,
journals, programs, speeches, and other materials bearing on
the activities and thought of women. They had not gone
far when they came to the conclusion that the vaunted
"equal education" in colleges and universities was little
more than coeducation in men's thought of their own history. To the growing concern with history as the great
all-human experience the records of women's interests and
activities could not fail to add substance and essentials.

If to persons busy at polite letters or practical affairs, the
controversies and ferments among historians seemed like
battles of kites and crows, such was not the case. Whatever
the primary nature of other divisions of thought, such as
economics, politics, or ethics, they were all phases of general
history and enclosed in that enveloping medium. Every interpretation of economic conflicts and trends at the same
time made an interpretation of history and rested on assumptions relative to the nature of history as actuality or
positive human experience. Every formulation of public
policy, domestic or foreign, was also an interpretation of
history, that is, expressed calculations respecting things
probable, possible, and necessary within the heritage from
the past, within the borders of history ever in the process
of becoming. Historical writing had been employed by
Catholics and Protestants in their long struggle for possession of the human mind in the West. Voltaire had made
it a dynamic force for the French Revolution. Under the
guise of romanticism, history had served the reaction. Other
illustrations were abundant. If historians working in the
scientific spirit, seeking emancipation from the tyranny of
old assumptions, persisted in the effort to bring all schemes
of selection into some kind of articulation and stronger consensus, and could perform this function in historiography,
even to a limited extent, then all divisions of contemporary
thought and all formulations of public policy were bound to
receive a higher and wider illumination.

CHAPTER XVII

Toward a Reconsideration of Democracy

ALL the major events and tendencies of the midpassage — the economic crisis, political conflicts arising out of national efforts to grapple with it, the multiplication of public functions and responsibilities, increased centralization in economy and government, the expansion of military and naval establishments, the rise of dictators and the spread of wars abroad, official declarations of foreign policies involving participation in the quarrels of Europe, tumult in the labor movement at home, outbursts of the vigilante spirit, degrading tendencies in commercialized entertainment, growing dissidence in literature, standardization and conservatism of the press, popular affirmations in the arts, the forces of science and invention, and the forms of social thought — all bore upon the fortunes of democracy and at every turn called for a reconsideration of its nature, its perduring power, its ability to cope with the complexities of a disjointed yet great society. In consequence, popular institutions long taken for granted were reëxamined and analyses once lightly dismissed were seriously reviewed as Americans

920

became more conscious of democracy — of the contrasts opposing it and bidding for supreme favor everywhere.

From the close of the civil war to the end of the world war, democracy, or "the American way," had been loosely, though by no means universally, accepted as a fact and seldom probed to the bottom in journals and forums of public opinion. That it might pass, as other systems of government had passed, and within the time of living men and women, was generally deemed so improbable as to be unworthy of grave thought and discourse. Henry Adams and Brooks Adams might spend laborious days tracing the degradation of the democratic dogma but for the main body of the people nothing remained save the hymning of "further progress in democracy." Philosophic doubts were entertained and expressed by many politicians; but such doubts, if noticed, were taken to be the curious vagaries of nervous persons rather than sober reasoning and warning. Admittedly there were blemishes on the bright escutcheon; but education and the invincible spread of enlightenment would overcome them, gradually.

However, after 1929, in the midst of turbulence and shocks, the theory and practice of democracy confronted unequivocal denunciation abroad and wide-open questioning at home. An upheaval was due and it arrived. Individuals and groups that had never been associated with popular movements called democratic in the progressive era and the age of normalcy suddenly blossomed out as the "true custodians of democracy," as its defenders to the last trench. Individuals and groups that had set themselves down as democratic all along began to reinterpret their political philosophy in terms of the issues defined by centralization in capitalism and by its obvious inadequacies over a long period of years, with no promise of permanent security for individuals or groups in sight. For this conflict George S. Counts of the Teachers' College at Columbia University drew up in 1938 an impressive balance sheet of assets and liabilities in The Prospects of American Democracy, laid down a program for constructive action, and issued a call for a concert of the popular powers in America. Within the framework of an agrarian philosophy, Herbert Agar reinforced Counts' plea, by telling the story of American democracy in The Pursuit of Happiness.

In one sector of the celebration directed by the "true custodians of democracy" were leaders of bar associations, apologetic columnists of conservative newspapers, representatives of publishers, big industrialists, financiers, officers of the American Legion and other professional patriotic societies, and ideologues at large. These exponents of the democratic creed commonly identified it with the philosophy of "let us alone" and appointed themselves as its protectors against the "dictatorship" of the Roosevelt administration. With kindred vehemence Roosevelt and his supporters nominated themselves as true guardians of the democratic faith against "economic royalists." If words meant anything, both factions were strong upholders of democracy. Syntactical unanimity was almost perfect. It seemed no longer a question of representative government against democracy, as in the early days of the republic, but a matter of the best means for sustaining the democracy that now existed and was to be praised to the end of the world. If to the broad public this appeared to be in accord with the settled custom of the country, to Americans familiar with its background the situation was an interesting and significant novelty.

For at no time, at no place, in solemn convention assembled, through no chosen agents, had the American people officially proclaimed the United States to be a democracy. The Constitution did not contain the word or any word lending countenance to it, except possibly the mention of "we, the people," in the preamble. Nor, indeed, did the Constitution even proclaim a republic. It did guarantee a republican form of government in the states, but as John Adams wrote to Mercy Warren, during their heated controversy over political aims, nobody knew just what that meant. As a matter of fact, when the Constitution was framed no respectable person called himself or herself a democrat. The very word then had low connotations, though it was sometimes mentioned with detachment; and the connotations became distinctly horrible to Respectability after the outbreak of the reign of terror in France. Though denounced as a Jacobin by Federalists, Jefferson did not call his party "democratic," and was chary about mentioning the term even in private correspondence. As was said long afterward, the founders of the republic in general, whether Federalist or Republican, feared democracy more than they feared original sin. Not until Andrew Jackson had retired from the presidency did his followers completely discard the old name "Republican" and officially call themselves "Democrats." After that date references to democracy usually meant "the Democracy," that is, Jackson's party which, strange to relate, soon passed largely under the control of slave owners.

The Whigs and their successors, the Republicans, whatever their popular inclinations, could hardly style themselves democrats, or the United States a democracy, after Jackson's partisans seized the title and identified democracy with their peculiar organization. Moreover one strong wing of the Whig-Republican combination was just as much opposed to everything that savored of democracy as any slaveholder or as any good Federalist of the Hamilton school had been in the latter days of the eighteenth century. If a "sound Republican" had been asked to characterize the United States between 1865 and the end of the century, he would doubtless have called it "a representative republic." Democracy he would have identified with direct government, the initiative, the referendum, popular election of Senators, majority rule, and disrespect for the Supreme Court. As the battle over "more democracy" intensified in the early years of the twentieth century, conservative Republicans grew still more suspicious of democracy. If they mentioned it with any favor, they were quick to make a distinction between "the true democracy" which they espoused and "the false democracy" which "demagogues" were trying to promote.

Not until the United States entered the world war was the conception of the nation as a democracy given something that looked like official sanction and general approval, if often in the form of lip-service only. Whatever may have been the real reason for opening the war on the German government, President Wilson declared it to be a war for democracy, to make the world safe for democracy as against autocratic power. Wilson was, it is true, a Democratic president, but in the fury of the conflict his war cry was little disputed in public if not whole-heartedly accepted in private by conservatives who cheered his war. At last the United States was somewhat officially and generally proclaimed to be in fact a democracy, engaged in a conflict to save democracy from the force of authoritarian States. Even the most strenuous opponents of the initiative, referendum, popular election of Senators, woman suffrage, and other features of "more democracy" were found sanctioning Wilson's official ideology. The word once so hated and feared, so long reprobated, so reluctantly accepted in the United States, became for the hour the sign and symbol of American unity and government, for which the people were to pay, fight, and suffer. Could George Washington, John Adams, Thomas Jefferson, and James Madison have witnessed the scene and heard the chorus they certainly would have been surprised to find their representative republic universally and vociferously hailed as a democracy.

After the war was over objections became more articulate and doubts were entertained. In its manual for the instruction of young men in the art and science of military tactics, the War Department repudiated the doctrine proclaimed by President Wilson, namely, that the United States was a democracy. It did more than reject. It assailed democracy as a form of mobocracy leading to attacks upon property and to communistic heresies — a true-blue Federalist-Whig view of the peril, now put forth by the military. While the United States army derided the idea of democracy for which it had just been ostensibly fighting, communists also attacked democracy and condemned it root and branch as a mere "bourgeois dictatorship" for the oppression of the proletariat. The communist version was also approved by fascists. Mussolini called democracy a "mask for capitalism" and "rotten" besides, ready for burial. So for different reasons, official directors of the United States army, communists, and fascists agreed on one proposition: democracy is a menace or a farce. What is more: neither President Harding nor President Coolidge nor President Hoover resorted to any official action designed to offset the criticisms or to refurbish the symbol under which Wilson's war had been fought.

It took the great economic depression, the domestic conflict, the rise of Hitler, and the consolidation of fascist forces abroad, to arouse what appeared to be a fierce affection for democracy and to produce a tumult of praise for the idea and its institutional embodiments. Another Democratic President, Franklin D. Roosevelt, who liked especially to remember his predecessor, Andrew Jackson, in official addresses formally and solemnly identified the United States with democracy and suggested a second union of all the faithful against the autocracies of the earth. His opponents likewise seized upon democracy as the device under which to wage war at home on the Roosevelt "dictatorship."

Yet few if any of the contemporary disputants took pains to define the term, democracy, in any comprehensive manner. From the view of the White House anything done by the administration was for the purpose of safeguarding and perfecting democracy. In the eyes of the Liberty League or the National Manufacturers Association or Alfred M. Landon, nearly everything done by the Roosevelt administration, except its call for larger and larger armaments, violated the canons of democracy and savored of fascist or authoritarian ambitions. In an age of confusion, defeatism, myths, and symbols, this verbal tempest seemed appropriate. Moreover, besides being effective party politics, it was "safe," in that it raised no fundamental questions.

Any exploration of the reality beneath the term democracy would have led below equal suffrage, popular elections, public education, majority rule, "let us alone," and freedom of the press into the real basis of American civilization, into the forms and distribution of property which conditioned, and to some extent determined, the rise and growth of any democracy that existed. It would have meant a re-reading or, perhaps more correctly stated, a first reading of the papers and letters left by the founders who established American institutions, and also a re-examination of the Declaration of Independence. And such an intellectual labor would have been ruinous to the patois of the new debate or at least to the glibness with which its idioms were put into circulation.

§

Unlike the classical economists who later dominated academic thinking, the leaders in public affairs who drafted the Constitution of the United States and the first state constitutions regarded government and economics as things intimately associated, not as separable and separated. They did not assume that property is something definite, an independent invariable, fixed by nature, and having no relation to the forms and functions of government or to the structures and operations of political parties. Nor were they subject to the illusion that government is a mere matter of popular will — the counting of heads equal and alike, whether of a class or the whole population. On the contrary they recognized that the form of every government, whether tyranny, monarchy, aristocracy, or democracy, is closely connected with the forms and distribution of wealth. They knew that all fundamental actions of governments reflect and affect diverse interests in society and that such interests appear inexorably in every complex and civilized society. Hamilton and his school deliberately sought to attach powerful interests to the Federal Government. Jefferson clung tenaciously to the proposition that freehold agriculture bore a vital relation to the independence of spirit essential to popular rule. All these concepts John Marshall understood and employed in policy and action. Within the schemes of early republican thought, wealth and its distribution were central to law and administration.

Speaking later, after the industrial revolution was well under way in the United States and mechanics and artisans were demanding and winning equal suffrage, Daniel Webster grasped the unity of economics and politics as firmly as Hamilton and Jefferson had done long before. He went still further and made economics the determining force in shaping the forms and processes of government. "The idea is as old as political science itself," Webster observed, ". . . It seems to me to be plain that, in the absence of military force, political power naturally and necessarily goes into the hands which hold the property. In my judgment, therefore, a republican form of government rests, not more on political constitutions, than on those laws which regulate the descent and transmission of property. . . . It would be monstrous to give even the name of government to any association in which the rights of property should not be competently secured. The disastrous revolutions which the world has witnessed, those political thunderstorms and earthquakes which have overthrown the pillars of society from their very deepest foundations, have been revolutions *against property*" [Webster's italics]. In sum and substance, this was saying that property is the true basis of political power, and that political revolutions spring from conflicts over property. If this was not thorough-going determinism, it would be difficult to characterize it.

Calling attention concretely to the American scene, Webster declared that the frame and form of government were "fixed" by economic realities. "Our New England ancestors," he said, "brought hither no great capitals from Europe; and, if they had, there was nothing productive in which they could have been invested. They left behind them the whole feudal policy of the other continent. . . . They came to a new country. There were as yet no lands yielding rent, and no tenants rendering service. The whole soil was unreclaimed from barbarism. They were themselves, either from their original condition, or from the necessity of their common interest, nearly on a general level in respect to property. Their situation demanded a parcelling out and division of the lands, and it may be fairly said that this necessary act *fixed the future frame and form of their government* [Webster's italics]. The character of their political institutions was *determined* [our italics] by the fundamental laws respecting property. . . . The consequence of all these causes has been a great subdivision of the soil and a great equality of condition; the true basis, most certainly, of popular government." So Webster, differing from Jefferson in party politics, agreed with him in making a wide distribution of landed property the foundation and hope of popular government in America.

Webster likewise agreed with Jefferson in holding that concentrated property and political democracy are incompatible and point in the direction of a revolution of some kind. "The freest government," continued Webster, "if it could exist would not be long acceptable, if the tendency of the laws were to create a rapid accumulation of property in few hands and to render the great mass of the population dependent and penniless. . . . Universal suffrage, for example, could not long exist in a community where there was great inequality of property. . . . In the nature of things those who have not property, and see their neighbors possess much more than they think them to need, cannot be favorable to laws made for the protection of property. When this class becomes numerous, it grows clamorous. It looks on property as its prey and plunder, and is naturally ready, at all times, for violence and revolution. It would seem, then, to be the part of political wisdom to found government on property; and to establish such distribution of property, by the laws which regulate its transmission and alienation, as to interest the great majority of society in the protection of the government.

This is, I imagine, the true theory and the actual practice of our republican institutions."

Here Webster departed from economic determinism and spoke of "political wisdom," in other words, of that enlightened statesmanship which refuses to be a mere reflection of economic interests, and by act of will "establishes" a "distribution of property" calculated to maintain the economic basis of popular institutions. Yet in emphasizing the possibilities of such positive policy, Webster insisted that it be directed to appropriate economic ends.

§

Given this realistic combination of politics and economics, what upshot may be expected in case there is a serious maldistribution of property? One answer to this question was made by John Adams, Alexander Hamilton, and James Madison; namely, prevent the majority from attaining actual power by establishing an "independent" Executive, Senate, and Judiciary — agencies that do not bend to election returns but firmly defend the rights of property against democratic, or leveling, tendencies. This was, indeed, the kind of government which the majority of the men in the constitutional convention of 1787 intended to establish, although none was exactly satisfied with the Constitution as finally drafted.

While popular mythology had to some extent obscured this original conception of the negative aspects of the Constitution, it had never been lost to the sight of informed practitioners on either side, or of the more acute thinkers among academicians. John W. Burgess long taught the doctrine from his chair in Columbia University. Woodrow Wilson, as an academician, before he saw his star of political destiny, upheld it, especially in his opposition to popular election of United States Senators and his defense of judicial independence. This conception of constitutional checks on democracy appeared continuously in debates over the popular election of Senators, over the initiative and referendum, over "assaults on the judiciary," and over efforts of radicals and progressives to block the confirmation of conservatives nominated for the Supreme Court. Those concerned with the instant need of things, as distinguished from the arm-chair philosophers, still understood, if they did not always praise openly, the conception of the Constitution as a barrier in the way of the majority of the people who have no property.

Nowhere was the doctrine stated with more force and precision than by the President of Yale University, A. T. Hadley, in 1907. Writing of the position of property owners, he said that "the sum of the conditions which affect their standing for the long future and not for the immediate present is far stronger in the United States [than elsewhere]. The general status of the property-owner under the law cannot be changed by the action of the legislature, or the executive, or the people of a state voting at the polls, or all three put together. It cannot be changed without either a consensus of opinion among the judges, which should lead them to retrace their old views, or an amendment of the Constitution of the United States by the slow and cumbersome machinery provided for that purpose, or, last — and I hope most improbable — a revolution.

"When it is said, as it commonly is, that the fundamental division of powers in the modern State is into legislative, executive, and judicial, the student of American institutions may fairly note an exception. The fundamental division of powers in the Constitution of the United States is between voters on the one hand and property owners on the other. The forces of democracy on one side, divided between the executive and the legislature, are set over against the forces of property on the other side, with the judiciary as arbiter between them; the Constitution itself not only forbidding the legislature and executive to trench upon the rights of property, but compelling the judiciary to define and uphold those rights in a manner provided by the Constitution itself.

"This theory of American politics has not often been stated. But it has been universally acted upon. One reason why it has not been more frequently stated is that it has been acted upon so universally that no American of earlier generations ever thought it necessary to state it. It has had the most fundamental and far-reaching effects upon the policy of the country. To mention but one thing among many, it has allowed the experiment of universal suffrage to be tried under conditions essentially different from those which led to its ruin in Athens and Rome. The voter was omnipotent — within a limited area. He could make what laws he pleased, as long as those laws did not trench upon property right. He could elect what officers he pleased, as long as those office-holders did not try to do certain duties confided by the Constitution to the property holders."

Here was the negative philosophy of Hamilton, Adams, and Madison as conceived and set forth at the beginning of the twentieth century by an eminent university president. Its historicity and nuances were evident. It was accurate in that it showed how Hamilton, Adams, and Madison wished to block by checks and balances the encroachment of the propertyless majority upon the rights of the rich and well-born. It was correct in so far as it stated that democracy had been tried under peculiar conditions, namely, under a Constitution which, in a line of judicial decisions, had been interpreted to mean that political democracy could not alter in any fundamental way the distribution and accumulation of property. To what extent, however, the framers of the Constitution intended to rely upon the judiciary, as barrier or arbiter, as contrasted with the Senate and the Executive, was a matter of historical doubt.

Perhaps in 1907, when President Hadley wrote his essay, popular election of presidential electors, established long before, and the growing demand for popular election of Senators led him to lay undue emphasis upon the last bulwark — the judiciary. Moreover, in emphasizing negation, he lost sight of the fact that the framers of the Constitution also intended the Federal Government to act strongly upon property, in the interests of commerce and manufacturing as against agriculture, to the detriment, it was charged, of agriculture. Yet the central thesis was true: There is an opposition between the voters at large and property owners and the very form of government serves as a moderating check on the hasty exercise of majority rule under the theory of democracy.

A similar antithesis between "our representative republic" and democracy was made by President Nicholas Murray Butler of Columbia University, in an address on Why Should We Change Our Form of Government? delivered before the Commercial Club of St. Louis in 1911. Although the address was directed especially against the initiative, referendum, and recall, or direct democracy, it reviewed the larger aspects of the American system. The makers of the Constitution, said President Butler, "built a representative republic." He called democracy an antithesis to this conception, and referred to Aristotle "who first told us how a democracy as well as a tyranny may become a despotism." He quoted John C. Calhoun: "The government of the uncontrolled numerical majority is but the absolute and despotic form of popular government, just as the uncontrolled will of one man is monarchy."

Then President Butler drew his conclusion: "If democracy is not to become a tyranny, it must recognize and build upon those constitutional limitations and guaranties that are so precious to the individual citizen and that protect him in his life, his liberty, and his property." These limitations and guaranties are contained in the American Constitution; but their sanction transcends law; it partakes of natural law; these fundamental guaranties "are beyond the legitimate reach of any majority because they are established in the fundamental laws of human nature upon which all government and civilization and progress rest. Sweep them away, if you will; a majority may have that power, but with the power does not go the right. If they are swept away, all government and all liberty go with them, and anarchy, in which might alone makes right and power alone gives place, will rise upon their ruins."

According to this view of things, the Constitution of the United States incorporates "the fundamental laws of human nature" and the judiciary enforces these laws. "The judges," President Butler consistently argued, "are primarily the servants not of the people, but of the law. It is their duty to interpret the law as it is, and to hold the law-making bodies to their constitutional limitations, not to express their own personal opinions on matters of public policy."

The antithesis to this system, President Butler made "a socialistic democracy." He did not repudiate democracy entirely; for the time had passed in American history when that could be done with Federalist brusqueness by any person with political ambitions. On the contrary he made his principles "the principles of true democracy," thus distinguishing between his kind, which is "true," and the other kind, which is "false." "It may be, perhaps," he conceded, "that under the institutions of a socialistic democracy mankind would be happier, opportunity more free, property more equally distributed, and the satisfaction of man's wants more easily accomplished than now. All these things may be; but if a socialistic democracy is to be substituted for a representative republic, please do not overlook the fact that it can only be so substituted by revolution" — a revolution in our political beliefs, accustomed forms of political action, our ambitions, and aspirations.

In short American history and political philosophy were identified by President Butler with the Federalist interpretation of that history and political philosophy: the Constitution embodies the laws of human nature; the judges guard the laws and say what they are; this is "our" form of government; the antithesis is false democracy — a socialistic democracy — which seeks to make "opportunity more free, property more equally distributed, and the satisfaction of man's wants more easily accomplished than now" — a false democracy opposed to "principles of true democracy and representative government."

§

Early thinkers and writers in the domain of politics nevertheless expressed doubts respecting the perpetuity of the system of checks and balances as safeguards against the movement of events. In their conceptions of the problem, doubts took two forms. Gouverneur Morris and John Adams, for example, feared plutocracy about as much as they did democracy. In opposing the plan of the Constitution which placed no property qualifications on voters and office holders, Morris declared his principal objection: "It threatens this country with an Aristocracy. The Aristocracy will grow out of the House of Representatives. Give the votes to people who have no property, and they will sell them to the rich who will be able to buy them. We should not confine our attention to the present moment. The time is not distant when this country will abound with mechanics and manufacturers [industrial workers], who will receive their bread from their employers. . . . The man who does not give his vote freely is not represented. It is the man who dictates the vote [who is represented]."

On similar grounds, John Adams likewise sought safeguards against the dangers of a plutocracy rising in America. "In every society where property exists," he warned his contemporaries, "there will ever be a struggle between the rich and poor. . . . There is a constant effort and energy in the minds of the former to increase the advantages they possess over the latter, and to augment their wealth and influence at their expense. . . . As the former have most address and capacity, they gain more and more continually, until they become exorbitantly rich and the others miserably poor." This, Adams continued, is the source of parties, tumults, and war; the masses look for a leader and protector; here is "the history of that progress of passions and feeling which has produced every simple monarchy in the world; and if nature and its feelings have their course without reflection, they will produce a simple monarchy forever." A constitution, a powerful executive, and an independent judiciary might hold the balance, but Adams was not certain of the outcome. He despised the speculative plunderers who gathered around Hamilton's system; he feared the predatory poor who rallied around Jefferson; he fell between two stools and was driven from the White House a disappointed and bitter man.

In developing his conception of the problem presented by the antithesis between the possessors of property and the propertyless, Madison shaded his emphasis according to time and circumstances. Speaking in 1787 behind the closed doors of the convention he said frankly: "Viewing the subject in its merits alone, the freeholders of the country would be the safest depositories of Republican liberty. In future times a great majority of the people will not only be without landed, but any other sort of property. These will either combine under the influence of their common situation; in which case [if the authority be in their hands by the rule of suffrage — (crossed out)] the rights of property and the public liberty will not be secure in their hands; or, which is more probable, they will become the tools of opulence and ambition, in which case there will be equal danger on another side. . . . The greatest part [of the representatives in the British Commons] are chosen by the cities and boroughs, in many of which the qualification of suffrage is as low as it is in any one of the United States, and it was in the boroughs and cities rather than the counties that bribery most prevailed and the influence of the Crown on elections was more dangerously exerted." Here was the positive fear, expressed by Gouverneur Morris and John Adams, that American society would in time be composed mainly of the propertyless and that opulence, through bribery and intrigue, would marshal indigent voters behind a dictatorship dangerous to the middle class.

However, these passages did not contain all of Madison's system of thought. Shortly after he entered the first Congress

under the Constitution, he associated himself with Jefferson's
party, which was appealing to the masses against "the rich
and well born." Later in life, when the passions of the political conflict had diminished and Madison had contemplated
anew the central problem of government, he set forth a
modified scheme of politics. In his final program, Madison
stated that his speech in the convention, as quoted above,
did not convey his "more full and matured view of the
subject."

This matured view, however, presented the old problem in
all its original force. The antithesis between the concentration of wealth and political equality was still recognized and
stress was laid upon it. The inexorable increase in the population, including those without property, was taken as the
basis of his thought about the problem. Writing in 1829-30,
Madison predicted that the population of the United States
would probably be ninety-six millions in seventy-five years,
that is in 1905, and one hundred and ninety-two millions in
a hundred years, that is by 1930. Directing his attention
especially to the members of the Virginia constitutional convention, he warned them that "as we are to prepare a system
of government for a period which it is hoped will be a long
one, we must look to the prospective changes in the condition and composition of the society on which it is to act."

A great density of population, Madison was sure, lay
ahead and an increased mass of laborers. Not only this.
"It is a lot of humanity, that of this surplus [of people beyond
those having an immediate interest in the soil] a large proportion is necessarily reduced by a competition for employment
to wages which afford them the bare necessaries of life. The
proportion being without property, or the hope of acquiring
it, cannot be expected to sympathize sufficiently with its
rights to be safe depositories of power over them. What is to
be done with this unfavored class of the community?"

Madison pondered his own query. "If it be, on one hand,
unsafe to admit them to a full share of political power, it
must be recollected, on the other, that it cannot be expedient

to rest a republican government on a portion of the society having a numerical and physical force excluded from, and liable to be turned against it, and which would lead to a standing military force, dangerous to all parties and to liberty itself. This view of the subject makes it proper to embrace in the partnership of power every description of citizens having a sufficient stake in the public order and the stable administration of the laws, and particularly the house-keepers and heads of families, most of whom 'having given hostages to fortune,' will have given them to their country also." Thus Madison's latest solution of the contradiction was to grant the suffrage to "housekeepers and heads of families," that is, freeholders, and to "those who, although not possessed of a share of the soil, are deeply interested in other species of property," that is, to merchants and capitalists not owning land.

Only so far was Madison prepared to go. "It would be happy," he conceded, "if a state of society could be found or framed in which an equal voice in making the laws might be allowed to every individual bound to obey them." But this theory of happiness required "limitations and modifications." The conflict remained : the suffrage must be restricted in some degree.

The future opened before the seer. The majority will be without landed or other property. There will be "a dependence of an increasing number on the wealth of a few." It will spring from the relations between landlords and tenants, between "wealthy capitalists and indigent laborers . . . from the connection between the great capitalists in manufactures and commerce, and the numbers employed by them. Nor will accumulations of capital for a certain time be precluded by our laws of descent and distribution." Still, Madison mused, in the future this tendency to concentration "may be diminished and the permanency defeated by the equalizing tendencies of the laws." Of this no one could speak with certainty : "How far this view of the subject will be affected by the republican laws of descent and distribution, in equalizing the property of the citizens . . . cannot be inferred from any direct and adequate experiment."

Nevertheless the challenge will press upon American society in times to come. "To effect these changes, intellectual, moral, and social, the institutions and laws of the country must be adapted; and it will require for the task all the wisdom of the wisest patriots." Into the nature of the legislation adapting the institutions of the country to this economic conjuncture — legislation touching the descent, distribution, and equalization of property — Madison did not venture. The problem he stated. The economic conflict he described. The political implications he frankly faced. The solution of the contradiction, if there was to be one, he left to coming generations. Hesitant in dealing with remedies, Madison was certainly prescient in foreshadowing the crisis likely to be at hand a hundred years later, in 1930. The population was not as large as he had predicted, but the concentration and indigence he had foretold certainly called for "all the wisdom of the wisest patriots."

Like Madison, his neighbor and successor in the White House, Jefferson scanned the long future in America, even while he dealt with the instant need of things. He accepted the dictum that politics and economics are inseparable and based his hopes for popular government on a wide distribution of freehold farms. Primogeniture was to be abolished; a diffusion of estates was to be facilitated; and the people were to be educated to know their rights and obligations. There were perils to democracy in commerce, manufacturing, and banking, which work for the concentration of wealth and "paper" claims to wealth; the distant future was uncertain and doom might lie ahead. The outlook for popular government was only good, Jefferson wrote to Madison, "as long as we remain virtuous; and I think we shall be so, as long as agriculture is our principal object, which will be the case while there remain vacant lands in any part of America." Beyond that was darkness. "When we get piled upon one another in large cities, as in Europe, we shall become corrupt as in Europe, and go to eating one another as they do there." While Madison hoped that "wise" statesmanship might do something effective in this crisis, Jefferson was pessimistic and saw no certain exit from the dilemma.

On the other hand, Webster's prediction respecting the outcome of the contradiction between accumulated wealth and democratic equality was positive. The element of military force, he recognized, was always present or imminent. "Numbers, nevertheless, constitute, ordinarily, the most important consideration, unless indeed there be *military force* [his italics] in the hands of the few, by which they can control the many." In case there is a "rapid accumulation of property in few hands," the great mass of the population is "dependent and penniless," and universal suffrage exists, then "popular power must break in upon the rights of property, or else the influence of property must limit and control the exercise of popular power. . . . The holders of estates would be obliged in such case, either in some way to restrain the right of suffrage, or else such right of suffrage would ere long divide the property."

There was the lesson of a Caesar. "Let it never be forgotten," Webster admonished his auditors, "that it was the popular magistrates, elevated to office where the bad outnumbered the good, where those who had no stake in the Commonwealth, by clamor, and noise, and numbers, drowned the voice of those who had, that laid the neck of Rome at the foot of her conqueror." The Senate sought to declare Caesar a public enemy. "To this decree the popular tribunes, the sworn protectors of the people, interposed their negative; and thus opened the high road of Italy, and the gates of Rome herself, to the approach of her conqueror." The application was obvious. If in such circumstances Rome was overcome by Caesar, America might, in similar circumstances, encounter the same fate. This message Webster bequeathed to posterity.

Far more systematic than the thought of either Madison or Jefferson was the political science of a contemporary, John

Taylor, of Virginia, who may be called the philosopher of agrarianism, although now almost forgotten. Like his Virginia friends, he believed freehold agriculture to be the only secure basis for popular government. Before Webster, he recognized the antithesis between the concentration of wealth and the diffusion of political power. But his solution of the contradiction differed from their replication. It did not rely vaguely on the hope of future wisdom in statecraft; it did not display the pessimism of Jefferson; nor did it present the choice between general confiscation and a military dictatorship implicit in Webster's speculations on the future.

Taylor's system made a distinction between "legal, factitious or fraudulent property" and "substantial, real or honest property" — between "that species of private property founded only in law, such as is gained by privilege, hierarchy, paper [public debts and bank money, for instance], charter [corporations], and sinecure; and that founded in nature, arising from industry, arts, and sciences." Taylor insisted that there was danger in uniting "these two opposite moral beings in a defensive war" against confiscatory measures.

The economic conflict, so evident in politics, was not, according to Taylor, a struggle between the propertied and the propertyless; it was essentially a conflict between "privileged, stipendiary, or factitious property" and property "founded in nature, arising from industry, arts, and sciences." Holders of the latter, he urged, should dispossess the former, thus breaking up the concentration effected through liquid claims to wealth, and bringing about the wide diffusion of wealth so essential to popular government.

This drastic action, Taylor contended, was justified by history. "All societies," he wrote, "have exercised the right of abolishing privileged, stipendiary, or factitious property, whenever they have become detrimental to them; nor have kings, churches, or aristocracies ever hesitated to do the same thing, for the same reason. The king of England joined the people and judges, in abolishing the tenures and perpetuities

of the nobles; the king and nobles united in abolishing the
property of the popish clergy; the consistory of Rome suppressed the order of Jesuits and disposed of its property;
and several of these states [in the American union] have
abolished entails, tithes, and hierarchial establishments.
What stronger ground can be occupied by any species of law-
begotten wealth than by these?"

Taylor's remedy, therefore, was to sweep away property
rights founded on paper, corporation bank notes, protective
tariffs, and "factitious" claims to wealth, and preserve property founded on nature, industry, sciences, and arts. By
uniting with holders of the former kind of property in defense
of all property, holders of the latter would make a fatal error,
and jeopardize their own position.

§

Running through the years beside the cold and fatalistic
analysis of the relations between economies and forms of
government, between the nature and distribution of wealth
on the one side and the institutions of politics on the other,
was a broad stream of thought which furnished the dynamic
of what may be called, with fair precision, humanistic democracy. This thought was concerned with the resolution of
contradictions by democratic methods in the interest of
human welfare and social stability. Its sources lay far back
in western history, in the Christian tradition and the older
humanism of the Greeks.

In colonial times it was represented by such thinkers and
spokesmen as John Wise and John Woolman. Its widest and
deepest formulation in the revolutionary period was made by
Thomas Paine, especially in his Rights of Man and Agrarian
Justice, wherein he set forth the principles of a leveling
democracy in terms economic and political. Within Paine's
scheme of thought, laid down in the Rights of Man — the
counterblast to Edmund Burke's plea for the status quo in
England — came a wide distribution of landed property, old

age pensions, free and universal education, subsidies for
maternal care, workshops for the employment of the casual
poor, a "plan of progressive tax" operating to extirpate the
unjust and unnatural law of primogeniture and the vicious
influence of the aristocratical system, and international
agreements for the reduction of armaments and promotion
of peace. War, he said, "serves to keep up deceitful expectations, which prevent people from looking into the defects and
abuses of government. It is the *lo here!* and the *lo there!* that
amuses and cheats the multitude."

For a time humanistic democracy showed a tendency to
rally around Thomas Jefferson, to whom Federalists applied
the epithet of "atheist" as well as "Jacobin," but it never
collected completely under the banner of his party. The
truth seems to be that Jefferson himself was more an agent
of popular forces than a creator and was prodded into leadership and action by spontaneous and wide-spread outbursts of
democratic fervor among "the plain people." After the slave-
owning planters got possession of the party machinery, a
left-wing, loyal to the humanistic tradition, split off, especially in the North, and men calling themselves "Democratic" denounced the humanists as communists, anarchists,
and feminists.

Then it was that a host of men and women not whole-
heartedly committed to either party undertook to make
America conscious of human values, alive to the dangers of a
purely acquisitive economy, and willing to carry out programs of reform ranging from hard money to free schools,
from agrarianism to utopian socialism. The names of this
host would fill a bulky volume but in a selection from the
long list of orators, lecturers, writers, organizers, and political
leaders may be cited Horace Greeley, Charles A. Dana,
Wendell Phillips, Dorothea Dix, Ralph Waldo Emerson,
William Lloyd Garrison, Elizabeth Cady Stanton, Hinton
Rowan Helper, George Henry Evans, Lydia Maria Child,
Susan B. Anthony, Andrew Johnson, and William H. Sylvis
— all powerful personalities. Year after year they discussed

with their countrymen the problem of realizing the democratic ideal in the rearrangement of human affairs, institutions, and economic practices.

When the pall of the slavery conflict settled over other
issues, leaders of humanistic democracy concentrated, for the
time being, on abolition as the supreme task of the hour. A
combination of Whigs and Democrats was formed and to this
combination was given, in full recognition of its appeal, the
title of Jefferson's old party, namely, Republican. Humanistic sentiments then gathered around Abraham Lincoln,
whose expressed opinions were in harmony with the "democratic" as distinguished from the "aristocratic" tradition.

In democratic spirit Lincoln was Jeffersonian. "The principles of Jefferson," he said, "are the definitions and axioms
of free society." To the agrarians and their affiliated labor
reformers, the Republican party promised a distribution of
the public domain in the form of free homesteads for free
families. To industrial workers, then engaged in desperate
efforts at unionism involving strikes disagreeable to the
public, Lincoln, in a speech at Hartford, Connecticut, in
March, 1860, extended his sympathies; he "thanked God
that we have a system of labor where there can be a strike.
Whatever the pressure, there is a point where the workman
may stop." At Cincinnati, he exclaimed at a mass meeting:
"I agree with you, Mr. Chairman, that the working men are
the basis of all governments, for the plain reason that they
are the more numerous." When Lincoln wavered on the
question of slavery it was the democratic humanists who
prodded him, as humanists had prodded Jefferson, brought
pressure on him, and rallied popular support for emancipation — women taking a leading part in this form of pressure
politics, especially the feminists, with their strong emphasis
on general equality.

After the civil conflict, amid the upswing of industrialism
in economy, with its shadowing philosophy of Darwinism
and tooth-and-claw laissez faire, exponents of humanistic
democracy turned from the slavery issue to the consideration

of the social problems raised by the ruthless advance of capitalism. The ink was scarcely dry on the Proclamation of Emancipation when Elizabeth Cady Stanton challenged the common assumption that "the new birth of freedom" had closed American history, raised the broad question of labor in industrial society, and started to make, year after year, long journeys up and down the land discussing the issue from the lecture platforms, indefatigably, until near the close of her long life in 1902.

In the year 1868 she sounded the keynote of her humanistic philosophy : "A knowledge of the history of the past teaches us that the law governing human affairs is change, progress, development in the world of thought as well as action. . . . A healthy discontent is the first step of progress. . . . In the long battle we have fought in this country for the emancipation and enfranchisement of the African race, the principles of slavery and freedom have been so fully described that it does not require much discrimination to see that the condition of the laboring classes at the North differs little from that of the colored race under the old system of the plantations of the South. I ask those in the full enjoyment of all the blessings that wealth can give to look around you in the filthy lanes and byways of our cities, at the surging multitudes, ragged, starving, packed in dingy cellars and garrets where no ray of sunshine or hope can penetrate, no touch of light or love to cheer their lives. Look in the factories and workshops where young and old work side by side with tireless machines from morn to night through all the days, the weeks, the months, the years that make up the long sum of life, impelled by that inexorable necessity that knows no law — toil or starvation. . . .

"Under all forms of government about seven-tenths of the human family are doomed to incessant toil, living in different degrees of poverty, from the man who hopes for nothing but daily bread for himself and family to the one who aims at education and accumulation. . . . Self-preservation was considered the first law of nature prior to all duties to neighbors, society, government. This principle is, however, theoretically and practically reversed in civilization. The individual, it is now said, must be sacrificed to society, the one to the good of the whole. The higher idea, it seems to me, is that the interests of the individual and society lie in the same direction, that the highest good of the individual is the highest good of society. . . . Those who believe that poverty is a part of the divine plan will consider their duty done in the manifestation of sympathy and charity. But for those who believe that it is the result of human ignorance and selfishness and can be remedied, a widely different course of action must be pursued. To the last class I belong."

Three years after Elizabeth Cady Stanton sounded her tocsin, Wendell Phillips went over to the labor reform movement and at a labor convention in Worcester, Massachusetts, presented a set of resolutions approving "the overthrow of the whole profit-making system, . . . the abolition of privileged classes," and the same public aid "to coöperative efforts that has hitherto been given to railroads and other enterprises." In his address to the convention, Phillips advanced to what he believed to be the central concern of the republic and uttered formulas that were to ring through the coming years: "The land [the landed aristocracy] of England has ruled it for six hundred years. The corporations of America mean to rule it in the same way and, unless some power more radical than that of ordinary politics is found, will rule it inevitably. I confess that the only fear I have in regard to republican institutions is whether, in our day, any adequate remedy will be found for this incoming flood of the power of incorporated wealth. . . . The great cities are the arsenals of great wealth, where wealth manages everything in its own way."

At this very moment, far out in California, Henry George was turning over in his mind the problem that troubled Stanton and Phillips and the other thinkers of their direction. In 1879 he offered to mankind his solution in Progress and

Poverty and profoundly moved the humanists of the world by his vigor and logic. The next great upsurge of humanistic democracy was well under way. A forceful leader of the Knights of Labor, Terence V. Powderly, while adhering to the party of Lincoln and revolutionary emancipation of the Negroes, carried on an agitation for the abolition of the wages system and the substitution of coöperative production. The militant spokesman of industrial workers and agrarians, John P. Altgeld, "the forgotten eagle," became governor of a major state, Illinois. Socialistic and populistic parties entered the arena and all the "lunatic fringes," as their censors characterized them, were fused into the democratic movement led by William Jennings Bryan in 1896. Blocked in the campaign of that year and depressed by the *lo here! lo there!* of the Spanish-American war and by the headlong plunge into imperialism, the old democratic currents emerged soon afterward and sapped away at the foundations of conservatism.

In the "progressive era," the ferment of humanistic democracy continued to work everywhere in the country — as expressed by innumerable personalities, notably by Robert M. La Follette, Theodore Roosevelt, Jane Addams, Oswald Garrison Villard, Graham Taylor, Florence Kelley, Harriot Stanton Blatch, Eugene V. Debs, John R. Commons, Julia Lathrop, Edith Abbott, Grace Abbott, Louis Post, Judson King, James Weldon Johnson, Hamlin Garland, and William S. U'Ren, selections from the huge who's who in "reform." By 1912 the popular movement had become so strong that it split, not the Democratic party, but the Republican party with its heritage from Lincoln and revolutionary emancipation. In the upheaval, the Progressive party was formed and Theodore Roosevelt was chosen as its candidate for the presidency. This spokesman of progressive democracy had been educated by events, he confessed, and took the position that the Republican party had been founded in the days of Lincoln as "the radical progressive party."

In the political dissolution, provoked by the revolt within

the Republican ranks, Woodrow Wilson, who, as professor, had hitherto not ventured far beyond Edmund Burke and Richard Ricardo in his political and economic thought, modified most of his philosophy and, as a politician, made a direct bid for the votes of "progressives." Aided by the dissension among the Republicans, Wilson won the presidency but soon afterward came the world war and its attendant holocaust, followed by the interlude of normalcy and the golden glow.

§

During the entire interlude the tide of humanistic democracy still beat upon the strongholds of the mighty and kept Congress in turmoil, until the detonations of the depression shook apart the fabric of complacency. Out of that convulsion emerged Franklin D. Roosevelt, who, also educated by events, finally combined in his thinking the severe economic analysis of the Hamilton-Webster tradition with the humanistic democracy of the parallel tradition. Whatever his merits or demerits as statesman or administrator, he eventually gave expression to the two most powerful tendencies in American history. In his second inaugural he took cognizance of the fundamental conflict of Western civilization, the antithesis between the ideal and the real — the conflict that perplexed philosophy, science, art, and letters, as well as every other interest of mankind; and having accepted this conflict as a challenge, President Roosevelt expressed the conviction that it was the function of statesmanship to bring the real into closer conformity to the ideal — the conception of humanistic democracy.

And the major measures of the Roosevelt regime, however open to criticism in details or in execution, looked in the direction of strengthening the economic foundations of democracy — salvaging agriculture, fortifying the bargaining power of industrial workers, minimum wages, social insurance, old age pensions, employment for the idle, security of livelihood and home, protection against the hazards of economic defeat. In presenting to Congress, on April 29, 1938, his message on the problem of so-called monopoly, a central issue of American political economy, President Roosevelt described factually the growing concentration of economic and financial power. He quoted Daniel Webster's dictum that free government is incompatible with a rapid accumulation of property in a few hands, thus bringing together, in a single state paper, the economic analysis and the affirmation of humanistic democracy.

It was well within the circle of factual description to say that in his numerous discourses Franklin D. Roosevelt discussed the basic human and economic problems of American society with a courage and range displayed by no predecessor in his office; that he thrust their challenges into spheres hitherto indifferent or hostile; that he set in swift circulation, through the use of the radio, ideas once confined to groups more or less esoteric; that he both reflected and stirred the thought of the nation to the uttermost borders of the land. And in doing this he carried on the tradition of humanistic democracy which from colonial times had been a powerful dynamic in the whole movement of American civilization and culture — economic, political, literary, scientific, and artistic.

After all the criticisms brought against him, justly and unjustly, had been weighed and assayed, that much remained written in the record and implanted in the accumulating heritage of thought and aspiration. Moreover the popular response to his appeal, which gave him forty-six of the forty-eight states in the election of 1936, bore witness to a profound moral and intellectual disturbance such as had characterized great epochs of the past. Even the relative failure of his effort to eliminate conservative Democrats in the congressional campaign of 1938 did not mean a material decline in the influence of his thought upon the broad masses of the people.

Important as was the role of directors and counselors in the development of American civilization, however, the destiny of coming years turned upon the fortunes of no single personality or group of personalities, of no political parties, for they were all passing particulars in the great movements of history, manifesting in thought and action forces that had long been at work in American society and were working for the future. As the speeches of candidates and the platforms of the parties demonstrated in the campaign of 1936, American democracy was engaged in bending the strength of talents, skills, natural resources, and property to humanistic purposes publicly declared and in process of realization however tedious and painful the procedure. Critical leaders of this democracy had no illusions about the peril of sheer force and cruelty, exalting the irrational, despising justice and mercy — despite noble professions on all sides. That terror, they well knew, had haunted the framers of the Constitution and had been condemned by George Washington when he rejected the suggestion of a dictatorship for himself as a crown of the American revolution; returning his sword, in sign of his fidelity, to the civilian Congress which had entrusted it to him, he surrendered, as he said, "with satisfaction the appointment I accepted with diffidence," to take up in time of peace the burdens of civilian public service. Aware that Caesar's empire of blood, if it came, would perish, as did even the colossal monument of Ozymandias the mighty with the sneer of cold command upon his lips, and fortified by a long and tenacious tradition, the humanistic wing of American democracy sought to provide the economic and cultural foundations indispensable to a free society, by rational methods of examination, discussion, legislation, administration, and coöperation, employing the sciences, letters, and arts in efforts to fulfill the promises of its heritage and aspirations.

INDEX

Abbott, Grace, 946.
Abernethy, Thomas P., 915.
Adamic, Louis, 594, 682, 722 f.
Adams, Brooks, 921.
Adams, Charles Francis, 166, 168.
Adams, Henry, 912, 921.
Adams, James Truslow, 659.
Adams, John, 376, 893, 922, 924, 929, 930.
Adams, John Quincy, 632, 783.
Adams, Maude, 642.
Addams, Jane, 568, 799, 946.
Adkins case, 283. *See also* District of Columbia.
Adler, Mortimer, 611.
Administration reorganization bill, suggested, 347; defeated, 377.
Advertising, by radio, 644, 645, 646, 647 f., 650; Veblen's theory of, 888. *See also* Finance capitalism.
Agar, Herbert, 881, 922.
Agrarians, economic theory of, 881 ff. *See also* Taylor, John; agriculture; etc.
Agricultural Adjustment Act, 1933, 145, 215 f., 226 ff., 249, 251, 265, 307, 319, 450, 466, 544; Supreme Court invalidates, 229, 268 ff., 272, 278, 343, 358, 361; strengthened, 1935, 267; successors to, 271, 344; of 1938, 377.
Agricultural Adjustment Administration, 229 f.
Agricultural Marketing Act, 1929, 40 f., 65, 228.
Agriculture, decline of exports, 18; collapse of, 28; unrest, 29; McNary-Haugen bill, 30; in campaign of 1928, 36; Agricultural Marketing Act, 40; in the depression, 65; and the Philippines, 84; Democratic promises in 1932, 131, 140, 145; Agricultural Adjustment Act of 1933, 226; administration of, 230; financing of, 242; Act declared unconstitutional, 268; Soil Conservation Act, 271; Republican promises in 1936, 307; Farm Tenant Act, 344; Agricultural Adjustment Act of 1938, 377; and Reciprocal Trade Act, 474; Committee on Tenancy, 544; extent of tenancy, 545;

farm debts, 546; farm labor, 548; Tenant Union, 548; proposed alterations in tenure, 549; farmer-labor combinations, 550; failure of Homestead Act, 552; labor on the land and civilization, 574.
Agrobiology, 831 f.
Air Transport Act of 1936, 297.
Alabama, Supreme Court upholds state insurance, 360 f.
Alabama Power Company, Supreme Court upholds U. S. contract with, 273.
Alaska, 238, 241.
Albania, on U. S. foreign policy, 484.
Alcoholic beverage tax, federal, 219.
Aldrich, Nelson, 373.
Alexander Hamilton, The Greatest American, Vandenberg, cited, 302.
Allegheny stock, "cut-in" selling of, 169 f.
Allen, Frederick Lewis, 16.
Allen, Hervey, 673.
Allen, Robert S., 732.
Alsberg, Henry, 778.
Altgeld, John P., 799, 946.
Amalgamated Clothing Workers, 510, 534 f.
American Artists Congress, 802.
American Association for the Advancement of Science, 850.
American Bankers Association, 156, 261.
American Bar Association, 571.
American Branch Factories Abroad, cited, 82 f.
American Brown Boveri Electric Corporation, 52.
American Car and Foundry Company, 146.
American Civil Liberties Union, 571.
American Civilization school of foreign policy, 452 ff., 457, 468, 475. *See also* Neutrality Act.
American Doctrine of Judicial Supremacy, The, Haines, cited, 893.
American Engineering Council, 841.
American Federation of Labor, 64, 119, 308, 373, 395, 519 f., 535; and depression, 105 f., 115, 265, 515; and labor-movement crisis, 513 ff.; increasing

951

653 ff.; 1926–35, 659 f., 661 ff.; 1936–38, 660 f., 661 ff.; humorous, 684 ff.; proletarian, 686 ff., 689 f.; on the American scene, 691 ff., 695 ff., 699 ff., 703 f., 704 ff.; on futility, 707 ff.; imaginative compared with newspaper and magazine, 743 f. *See also* Novels; Short stories; Poetry; Biographies; Literary criticism; Columnists; Reporting.
Writers' Congress, N. Y. C., 1937, 720 f.
Writers Project, of F. A. P., 788 f.
Wynn, Ed, 630.

Yale Review, The, cited, 556, 741.
Yale University, Workshop in drama, 642 f.; Institute of Human Relations, 824; social thought at, 894, 899.
Yeaman, Elizabeth, 614.
You Can't Do That, Seldes, cited, 567 f.
Young, Owen D., 103 f., 371.
Young, Stark, 677.
Yountz, Philip N., 763.

Zimmermann, Erich, 450.
Zugsmith, Leane, 666.